THE GENTLE ANARCHISTS

THE GENTLE ANARCHISTS

*A Study of the leaders of the Sarvodaya Movement
for Non-violent Revolution in India*

GEOFFREY OSTERGAARD

AND

MELVILLE CURRELL

CLARENDON PRESS OXFORD
1971

Oxford University Press, Ely House, London W.1

GLASGOW NEW YORK TORONTO MELBOURNE WELLINGTON
CAPE TOWN SALISBURY IBADAN NAIROBI DAR ES SALAAM LUSAKA ADDIS ABABA
BOMBAY CALCUTTA MADRAS KARACHI LAHORE DACCA
KUALA LUMPUR SINGAPORE HONG KONG TOKYO

PRINTED IN GREAT BRITAIN BY
BUTLER AND TANNER LTD
FROME AND LONDON

PREFACE

THIS book attempts to make a detailed and systematic examination of the social characteristics, organization, and opinions of the leaders of the Sarvodaya movement in India. It thus constitutes a case study of a social movement in a developing country. However, the study was undertaken with the primary object of contributing to knowledge and understanding of the Gandhian approach to non-violence.

Like many others of my generation, my interest in non-violence was first aroused by participation in the Campaign for Nuclear Disarmament, and, particularly, by the acts of mass civil disobedience initiated by the Committee of 100. Reflection on the use and results of non-violent action in the cause of nuclear disarmament led, naturally, to a desire to study more closely the ideas and activities of those who have followed Gandhi in accepting non-violence as the central tenet of their philosophy of political action, rather than simply used non-violent action as an expedient, if unconventional, political technique.

The opportunity to pursue such a study was provided when I was seconded to Osmania University, Hyderabad, 1962-5, as visiting professor of political science, under the scheme of Commonwealth Educational Cooperation. The initial field research on which the study is largely based was undertaken in the summer of 1965. My thanks are due to the British Council for facilitating this research during the concluding period of my tour of secondment. Completion of the study was made possible by the generous award of a Small Grant in the Social Sciences from the Nuffield Foundation, which enabled me to visit India again in the autumn of 1969. To the University of Birmingham I am obliged for its readiness to allow me leave of absence and study leave, and for research grants to meet the costs of analysing the survey data.

Like all studies of this kind, the present book is the product of the co-operative efforts of many individuals besides the two whose names appear on the title page. Among the colleagues who have answered the authors' queries we must mention: Colin Harbury, David Morris, M. G. Kanbur, Charles Madge, Neil Thomas, and

Stuart Wabe. Mrs J. E. Taylor kindly undertook the statistical calculations in Appendix Two, and Miss Marjorie Davies, Secretary of the Political Science Department, shouldered the main burden of typing. To Ken Newton and Bob Hinings the authors are especially indebted for careful reading and critical comments on the first draft of the study. The second draft was read with equal care and profit to its authors by Professor W. H. Morris-Jones of the Institute of Commonwealth Studies, Dr Dennis Dalton of the School of Oriental and African Studies, Mr Devi Prasad of the War Resisters' International, and Mr Donald Groom of the National Peace Council, to all of whom grateful thanks are due.

Among friends and colleagues in India who have assisted the study in various ways are Radhakrishna, Secretary of the Gandhi Peace Foundation, Dr T. K. Oommen of the Delhi School of Social Work, and several members of the Gandhian Institute of Studies, Varanasi, especially B. N. Juyal, Nageshwar Prasad, B. B. Chatterjee, and S. S. Iyer. To Professor Sugata Dasgupta, Joint Director of the Institute, thanks are due for his help and encouragement from the first formulation of the study to its completion.

Although they have contributed to whatever merits the study may have, none of those mentioned above bears any responsibility for the faults that, alas, remain. This also applies, if not in quite the same sense, to those without whose co-operation the study could not have started: the Sarvodaya workers themselves, who completed the questionnaire, responded so readily to requests for interviews, and showed many practical kindnesses to me in my quest for a deeper understanding of Gandhian non-violence. Their contribution, as anonymous co-authors, will be evident in the many quotations from the completed questionnaires used throughout the book.

Dr Currell and I trust that, despite its faults, the Sarvodaya workers will permit us to dedicate this book to them and to the cause they seek to serve. From distant Birmingham, we salute them with the *mantra* of Vinobaji: Jai Jagat! Victory to the World!

3 February 1970   GEOFFREY OSTERGAARD

CONTENTS

LIST OF TABLES

CHAPTER ONE
THE SETTING

I. THE SARVODAYA MOVEMENT: ITS ORIGINS AND DEVELOPMENT

THE Sarvodaya movement in India represents an attempt to apply to the task of social reconstruction the ideas originally developed by Mahatma Gandhi. These ideas themselves may be seen as a manifestation of a wider movement for the revitalization and transformation of Indian values, norms, and institutions which began in the early nineteenth century. The first stirrings of this wider movement, for which the introduction of modern education by the British rulers in India provided the catalyst, took the form of a cultural renaissance centred on an aspiration to fulfil the universalism of the *Upanishads*. The chief pioneer of 'The Indian Renaissance' was Ram Mohan Roy, the founder of the Brahmo Samaj, a movement of reformed and militant Hinduism.[1] In the teachings of Roy and his successors, such as Ranade, Gokhale, Vivekananda, and Aurobindo, we find an attempt to reconstitute the ancient values of Hinduism, to purge Hinduism of its outmoded accretions, and to restore the key concept of dharma (the law of right conduct). The rebirth of learning awakened in the urban, educated élite new aspirations, which in the late nineteenth century found a constructive outlet in the promotion of legal and institutional changes. The founding of the Indian National Congress in 1885 was one product of the movement for reform. Then, in the wake of renaissance and reform, came the movement for more far-reaching changes: social reconstruction. Among the earliest expressions of attempts at social reconstruction were the projects of Rabindranath Tagore in his zamindari in East Bengal and of Maharaja Sayajirao Gaekwad in Baroda.[2] Unlike the movements of renaissance and reform, which were largely products of the urban élite, social reconstruction was mainly rurally oriented.

---

[1] See D. Mackenzie Brown, *The White Umbrella: Indian Political Thought from Manu to Gandhi*, 1953, Ch. VII, and its sequel, *Indian Political Thought from Ranade to Bhave*, 1961.

[2] cf. Sugata Dasgupta, *A Great Society of Small Communities*, 1968, p. 3.

Focused at first on the reconstruction of specific rural communities, it awaited the arrival of Gandhi to transform it into a national movement for total social reconstruction. This transformation Gandhi achieved through the exercise of his philosophy of action, satyagraha.

In the West Gandhi's place in the modern Indian tradition beginning with Ram Mohan Roy is often ill understood. He is widely regarded primarily as a nationalist politician whose main objective was to win independence for India by the use of the novel technique of non-violent resistance. But Gandhi was as much concerned with social and moral as with political change. His was an integral philosophy, based on the twin principles of Truth and Non-violence, which carried implications far beyond those concerned with the ousting of the British Raj. For Gandhi, political independence was only the first, if necessary first, step towards a radical reconstruction of the whole social order. Swaraj (self-government) meant for him a stage in the attempt to establish Ram Raj, the Kingdom of God, or what his followers, using a word he had coined earlier, now term 'the Sarvodaya society', that is, a society committed to the raising or welfare of all.[1] Swaraj and Sarvodaya were thus for Gandhi interwoven objectives. And the method of struggle used so successfully against the British was for him never merely a technique of political action. 'Non-violent resistance' is, in fact, a feeble translation of 'satyagraha', the import of which is better conveyed by its literal meaning: 'holding fast to Truth'—provided one realizes that for Gandhi 'Truth is God'—the ultimate reality—and 'God is Love', so that Truth and Non-violence are seen as but two sides of a single coin.

Both in the West and in India 'satyagraha' is now widely used to denote many kinds of agitation and protest, but, in the sense intended by Gandhi, it is not a negative concept. Non-violence or ahimsa (non-injury) was for Gandhi essentially a positive force. If it included resistance to moral and political evil, its more important aspect was the constructive one. Gandhi above all was an exponent of *constructive* non-violence, and it was for this reason

[1] The term 'Sarvodaya' was first used by Gandhi as the title of his translation into Gujarati of Ruskin's *Unto This Last*. 'I believe', Gandhi wrote later in his autobiography, 'that I discovered some of my deepest convictions reflected in this great book of Ruskin, and that is why it so captured me and made me transform my life.'—M. K. Gandhi, *Sarvodaya*, 1954, p. 3.

that he developed and placed so much emphasis on what he called his Constructive Programme.

The Constructive Programme is central to the understanding of 'Gandhism'. It was a programme that Gandhi developed piecemeal, beginning with Khadi (hand-spun, hand-woven cloth) in 1922, proceeding to Hindu-Muslim communal unity in 1925, to prohibition in 1930, to the abolition of untouchability in 1932, to the promotion of village industries in 1935, and so on. From one narrow perspective the programme of constructive activities initiated by Gandhi may be seen as a means by which the Indian National Congress sought to build up support among the masses. In addition, these activities provided a training ground for independence fighters and a necessary outlet for their energies at times when a halt had to be called to direct confrontation with the British Raj. The shrewd Gandhi no doubt appreciated this role of the constructive programme in the independence movement, but the programme for him—whatever it may have been for the politicians in the movement—was never simply a matter of expediency. On the contrary, it was for him the heart of the matter. In 1931 he wrote: 'My work of social reform was in no way less than or subordinate to political work. The fact is that when I saw that to a certain extent my social work would be impossible without the help of political work, I took to the latter and only to the extent that it helped the former. I must therefore confess that the work of social reform or self-purification of this nature is a hundred times dearer to me than what is called purely political work.'[1] This view he held to the end. Speaking of the programme in 1944, he said to his followers: 'Through it you can make the villagers feel self-reliant, self-sufficient and free so that they can stand up for their rights. If you make a real success of the constructive programme, you will win Swaraj for India without civil disobedience.'[2] And in the very last year of his life—the year of independence, but for Gandhi a year not of rejoicing but of sadness and heartsearching—he confessed: 'In placing civil disobedience before constructive work I was wrong . . . I feared that I should estrange co-workers and so carried on with imperfect Ahimsa.'[3]

In 1941 Gandhi published the pamphlet *The Constructive*

[1] *Young India*, 6 Aug. 1931, p. 203.
[2] Pyarelal, *Mahatma Gandhi: The Last Phase*, vol. i, 1956, p. 44.
[3] ibid., p. 314.

Programme: its meaning and place,[1] listing eighteen items of social work. These were: the building of communal unity; the removal of untouchability; the introduction of prohibition; the development of khadi; the promotion of other village industries; improvement in village sanitation; adoption of new or basic (craft-centred) education; the introduction of universal adult education; the amelioration of the condition of women and securing them equality of status and opportunity; education in health and hygiene; assisting the preservation and development of provincial languages; adoption of Hindustani as the national language; working to secure economic equality; organizing the kisans (peasants), protecting their rights, and helping them to lead a happy and non-violent life; organizing industrial labour on the basis of truth and non-violence; looking after the welfare of the adivasis (tribal peoples); giving adequate care to lepers; and, finally, working with students to improve their mental, moral, and physical equipment. These items were not listed in order of importance, nor was the list exhaustive. The constructive worker was invited to add to the list any item, provided it was consistent with the principle of non-violence. Gandhi himself, however, did attach particular importance to the attainment of economic equality, which he regarded as 'the master key to non-violent Independence'.[2]

Gandhi had no doubt that constructive work would be as necessary for sustaining independence as it had been for attaining it. He had intended to re-write the Constructive Programme pamphlet to show how the programme could be used to realize the full content of independence in terms of the masses; but his assassination on 30 January 1948 prevented this. Since his death, the Congress Governments have actively espoused many items in the original programme, while, at the same time, pursuing certain policies, such as developing heavy industries and building up the military forces, which are contrary to Gandhian ideals. Since Congress can and does lay claim to be inspired by Gandhian ideals, it is important to understand clearly the relation between constructive work and politics, as seen by Gandhi himself in his last years.

Immediately after independence there was a strong feeling among certain constructive workers that Congress was ignoring the Programme. These workers therefore suggested that they should

[1] Navajivan, Ahmedabad. The revised edition used here was published in 1945.   [2] ibid., p. 20.

form a separate organization which would seek to place workers in the governments, both Central and State, so that political power could be used to further the goal of a non-violent social order. Gandhi opposed the idea, arguing that the moment non-violence assumed political power it contradicted itself and became contaminated. The role of the constructive workers, he suggested, was to guide political power and to mould the politics of the country without taking power themselves. 'Politics have today', he said, 'become corrupt. Anybody who goes into them is contaminated. Let us keep out of them altogether. Our influence will grow thereby. The greater our inner purity, the greater shall be our hold on the people, without any effort on our part.'[1] Gandhi did, however, admit the need to re-organize the constructive work activities. To carry out the various items of the programme, he had inspired the creation of a number of specific associations, such as the All India Spinners' Association; the All India Village Industries Association; the Harijan Sevak Sangh—the body devoted to the uplift of the 'untouchables' whom Gandhi had re-named Harijans, or children of God; the Hindustani Talimi Sangh—the body devoted to the furtherance of Basic Education; and several others. To make these bodies more effective, he proposed that, instead of functioning independently of each other, they should combine in one umbrella-type organization. More significantly, in the last proposal he made, the document known as his Last Will and Testament, written on the day preceding his assassination, he proposed that Congress should disband as a political party and flower again in the form of what he called a Lok Sevak Sangh or Association of Servants of the People. 'Congress in its present shape and form, i.e. as propaganda vehicle and parliamentary machine', he wrote, 'has outlived its use. India has still to attain social, moral and economic independence in terms of its seven hundred thousand villages as distinguished from its cities and towns.'[2]

As we know, this proposal was rejected by Congress—on the ground that its dissolution would create a political vacuum, leading to anarchy and ruin for the country.[3] But at a conference of constructive workers held in March 1948 the decisions were taken to form a loosely structured fellowship of Lok Sevaks (Servants of

---

[1] Pyarelal, op. cit. ii. 664.   [2] ibid. ii, Appendix 8.
[3] See Shankarrao Deo, 'Congress and Constructive Workers', *Harijan*, 20 & 27 Feb. 1949.

the People), known as the Sarvodaya Samaj, and to pursue the idea of uniting the Gandhian constructive associations. Out of the latter decision emerged in the following year a new organization, the Akhil Bharat Sarva Seva Sangh, the All India Association for the Service of All. Subsequently, four national Gandhian associations[1] merged with the new body, but the others, for various reasons, preferred to retain their separate identities. Among these were the Harijan Sevak Sangh and the Kasturba Memorial Trust, a foundation established in 1944 in memory of Gandhi's wife and devoted to the general welfare of poor and needy women and children in the rural areas of India. Another important foundation, the Gandhi Smarak Nidhi (Gandhi National Memorial Trust), established in 1948 in memory of Gandhi himself, with an original endowment of some £8 million raised by public donations, also continues as an independent organization.

The contemporary Sarvodaya movement is the direct descendant of the Constructive Programme and of the institutions and persons involved in it. In its widest sense, the movement embraces all those who hold themselves committed to the Gandhian social philosophy, and would include many politicians in both the Congress and other political parties. It is useful, however, to distinguish different types of 'Gandhism' in post-independence India. The first type, which we shall call 'political Gandhism', is expressed by those who have sought to realize at least some of the Gandhian goals by orthodox political action. To the extent that they have been successful, this type finds institutional expression in a number of official organizations and policies, such as the Khadi and Village Industries Commission and the programmes of Community Development and Panchayati Raj (local self-government). These organizations and policies constitute what we shall refer to as 'official Gandhism', a sub-type of 'political Gandhism', which is a broader concept, since it embraces politicians in parties other than the Congress, especially the Socialist parties. The second main type, which we shall call 'institutional Gandhism', finds expression in a number of independent and voluntary organizations concerned with promoting particular aspects of the Constructive Programme. Included in this category would be those associations

---

[1] The Spinners' Association, the Village Industries Association, the Basic Education Association, and Go Seva Sangh—the association devoted to animal welfare, especially 'cow protection'.

noted above which did not combine with Sarva Seva Sangh. The most important of these is the Gandhi Smarak Nidhi, which has a more general programme than the others, and its off-shoot, the Gandhi Peace Foundation, a body set up in 1958, which includes among its objectives the establishment of an international centre of study and research in the principles of Non-violence.[1]

The third and final type we shall call 'revolutionary Gandhism'. This has its organizational base in Sarva Seva Sangh, but it is distinguished from the other types by its avowed revolutionary (albeit non-violent) spirit and objectives. In their general approach to the problems of social reconstruction and political action, those associated with Sarva Seva Sangh come closest of all to carrying on Gandhi's work along the lines envisaged in the last years of his life. This third type is revolutionary in another sense: it is creative Gandhism, a movement of thought and action conceived in the spirit of Gandhi which has developed new insights into the potentialities of non-violence. Gandhi himself was well aware of the danger that his followers might develop into a sect after his death. 'There is no such thing', he once said, 'as "Gandhism" and I do not want to leave any sect after me.'[2] It would be an exaggeration to say that Gandhi has escaped the fate he feared. But, to the extent that this is so, the main credit must go to the acknowledged leader and inspirer of Sarva Seva Sangh, Vinoba Bhave, who, characteristically enough—like Gandhi before him in relation to Congress after 1934—is not even a member of the organization. It was Vinoba, Gandhi's 'spiritual heir', who discovered the talisman needed to give new impetus and shape to the Gandhian constructive movement. This was the first land-gift, made on 18 April 1951 at Pochampalli, which marked the beginning of the campaign for Bhoodan.

The 'revolutionary Gandhians' constitute the vanguard of the wider Sarvodaya movement,[3] and exhibit in their approach and organization certain features which are rare, if not unique, and

[1] For an account of the Gandhi Smarak Nidhi see T. K. Mahadevan, *Gandhi National Memorial Trust, an Introduction*, 1965.

[2] This statement is used as an epigraph by *Gandhi Marg*, the quarterly journal of Gandhian thought, published by the Gandhi Peace Foundation, New Delhi.

[3] It would be wrong to give the impression that the three types of Gandhism are sharply separable in the field of action. They represent tendencies rather than clear-cut distinctions; there is considerable overlap between all three; and to some extent the three approaches are complementary as well as, on occasions,

which, therefore, are of special interest to students of social movements. The study that follows is concerned with this third type of Gandhism, and in the subsequent pages the term 'Sarvodaya movement' should, unless otherwise indicated, be construed in the narrower sense of the movement centred upon Vinoba Bhave and the Sarva Seva Sangh.

Vinoba's general approach to Gandhism is evident in his Christmas address to the World Pacifist Meeting held at Sevagram in 1949, before he had emerged as a prominent public figure.[1] 'Ahimsa', he said, 'is not merely non-participation in destructive activities; it principally manifests itself in constructive activities— services which lead to the upward growth of man. People say that the Goddess of ahimsa has no weapons; I say that is wrong. The Goddess of ahimsa has very powerful weapons at her command. They are the weapons of Love and therefore creative and not destructive.' But he proceeded to warn his listeners: 'The light of ahimsa cannot be spread by the external and formal mechanism of organizations. . . . I keep on telling myself in the words of St Francis: "Do not get entangled in organizations." ' Some people, he continued, feel that we are forgetting Gandhi. The truth is that we remember him too much: our first thought is always what did Bapu (Father) do or say in such a situation? This sheds darkness not light. We must 'begin to think for ourselves about ahimsa and have courage to make new experiments on our own account'.

Two years later this creative approach led to Bhoodan and, with it, the revitalization of the Gandhian movement.[2] Bhoodan, the

competitive. The overlap is particularly noticeable between political and institutional Gandhism in respect of both their leading personnel and their programmes. Congress politicians, for example, constitute the largest proportion of the trustees of the Gandhi Smarak Nidhi; and movement between the unofficial Gandhian institutions and Government welfare agencies is easy and not uncommon. Because of its rule that members shall not belong to any political party or accept office in any Government agency, Sarva Seva Sangh remains largely free from such trafficking.

[1] *Harijan*, 8 Jan. 1950.

[2] This does not mean that the constructive movement was inactive in the period from Gandhi's assassination to the launching of Bhoodan. In this period Sarva Seva Sangh sought to develop the concept of Sarvodaya planning in the context of the national debate which resulted in the First Five-Year Plan. Constructive workers were also involved in relief work among refugees from Pakistan, and in small-scale experiments in Gandhian living, such as Vinoba's attempt to develop his ashram as a moneyless economy. None of these activities attracted the kind of publicity that Bhoodan rapidly won for itself.

campaign to persuade landowners to donate voluntarily a proportion of their lands for redistribution to the landless labourers who
constitute the poorest fifth of India's rural population, could be
seen as a new addition to the items listed in Gandhi's Constructive Programme. But, in the eyes of its promoters, it rapidly became much more than this: it came to be seen as the vital lever by
which revolutionary social change on Gandhian lines might be
effected. Intuitively, Vinoba sensed that, in India as in other
Asian countries, the peasants held the key to social revolution.
Critics might condemn Bhoodan as organized charity and as involving no more than the redistribution of poverty, but Vinoba
saw it otherwise. Describing the aim of the campaign, he said: 'In
a just and equitable order of society, land must belong to all.
That is why we do not beg for gifts but demand a share to which
the poor are rightly entitled. The main objective is to propagate
the right thought by which social and economic maladjustments
can be corrected without serious conflicts.'[1]

Although the campaign came to be widely known as the Bhoodan movement, it gradually became evident that Bhoodan itself
was only a symbol of something greater: the first step in arousing
the conscience of the people, the beginning of a mass revaluation
of values which was designed to lead ultimately to the establishment of a new social order based on Sarvodaya ideals. This was
underlined by Vinoba's willingness, on occasions, to accept land
donations from those owning a few acres or less—the equivalent
of the widow's mite. In his eyes there are no 'have-nots'; 'attachment may lurk even in a loin-cloth';[2] and the movement is a
movement of giving and sharing in which every individual can
and should participate. 'My aim', he explained, 'is to bring about
a three-fold revolution. Firstly, I want to change people's hearts.
Secondly, I want to create a change in their lives. Thirdly, I want
to change the social structure. . . . We do not aim at doing mere
acts of kindness but at creating a Kingdom of Kindness.'[3]

The campaign for Bhoodan, conducted by padayatra (pilgrimage on foot) from village to village, spread rapidly throughout the
country. As the initial target figures were exceeded, enthusiasm
mounted, and, with millenary optimism, the objective of 50 million

[1] Quoted in *India 1964*, Government of India, New Delhi, 1964, p. 224.
[2] *Harijan*, 29 Nov. 1952.
[3] *Bhoodan*, 18 Apr. 1956.

acres was set to be reached by the end of 1957.[1] In the event
that year, heralded in the movement as the Year of the Land
Revolution, ended with a total of some 4·2 million acres donated.
But by that time the campaign had already widened into Gramdan
(gift of the village), and the movement was calling not for donations of a proportion of every landowner's land but for the complete surrender of property rights in land in favour of the village
community. From the first, Gramdan had been implicit in the
Bhoodan concept; but the differences between the two are significant. Bhoodan involved donations from individuals: Gramdan
involves community action. Under Bhoodan individual ownership
of land was retained: under Gramdan it is abolished and ownership
vested in the village community. And, thirdly, whereas under
Bhoodan the beneficiary was an individual or a group of individuals, under Gramdan the beneficiary is the whole village
community. In short, the substitution of Gramdan for Bhoodan
represented a move from a basically individualist to a basically
socialist programme.

The patently revolutionary character of Gramdan made it more
difficult to promote. Although Congress and other political parties
were persuaded to endorse Gramdan as a desirable method of
land reform, in practice it elicited less enthusiasm and support
from such quarters than had Bhoodan. Nevertheless, in the wake
of Vinoba's march, village after village declared for Gramdan. By
the end of 1956 the number of Gramdans had reached 1,935, and
by March 1964 it was 6,807. (See Table 1.) Their distribution
throughout the country, however, was much less even than in the
case of Bhoodan, and the villages concerned were generally small,
very poor—even by Indian standards—and concentrated in low-
caste and tribal areas, such as the Koraput District of Orissa. By the
early 1960s the pace of the movement had slackened considerably.

In this situation, a new approach was developed in the form of
Sulabh (simplified) Gramdan. This concept will be explained
later. It suffices to note here that it represents a concession to the
principles of private ownership, and that its effects are decidedly
less egalitarian than Gramdan in its original form. From the movement's point of view, however, its adoption has more than justi-

---

[1] The target represented Vinoba's estimate that about one-sixth of the total
acreage of cultivable land could meet the needs of the landless labourers, if only
the landowners would recognize their obligations to the landless.

TABLE I

The distribution of Bhoodan, Gramdan, and Sarvodaya workers by States

	CENSUS DATA			BHOODAN						GRAMDAN				SARVODAYA WORKERS	
State or Union Territory	Population (1961 Census) (thousands)	No. of districts	No. of villages	Land gifts (acres)	Land distributed (acres)	Uncultivable land: gift cancelled (acres)	Land still to be distributed (acres)	No. of donors	No. of donees	No. of 'villages' declared as Gramdan: (March 1964)	(October 1969)	No. of blocks declared as Blockdan: (October 1969)	No. of districts declared as Districtdan: (October 1969)	No. of Lok Sevaks (March 1964)	No. of Shanti Sainiks (May 1964)
Andhra Pradesh	36,983	20	27,084	241,952	103,051	86,385	52,216	16,627	22,733	651	4,231	14	1	335	346
Assam	12,209	19	27,702	11,935	265	—	11,670	7,344	N.A.	966	1,648	1	—	622	237
Bihar	46,455	17	67,665	2,127,453	351,443	1,364,637	411,372	297,200	224,850	121	60,065	574	15	1,560	3,027
Gujarat	20,633	17	18,584	103,530	50,924	—	52,606	18,337	10,270	164	1,040	3	—	348	78
Jammu and Kashmir	3,561	9	6,559	211	5	—	206	N.A.	N.A.	—	1	—	—	—	—
Kerala	16,904	9	1,573	26,293	5,774	7,999	12,520	N.A.	N.A.	559	418	—	—	508	24
Madhya Pradesh	32,372	43	70,414	405,786	173,062	56,477	176,246	58,375	47,445	191	7,925	39	5	620	213
Madras (Tamilnad)	33,687	13	14,124	51,330	16,394	3,316	34,936	21,809	11,153	254	14,604	143	4	307	60
Maharashtra	39,554	26	35,851	105,094	70,950	—	30,828	19,953	15,199	790	4,000	17	—	450	1,301
Mysore	23,586	20	26,377	15,864	2,123	—	13,741	5,017	941	58	1,156	4	—	190	97
Orissa	17,549	13	46,466	185,782	96,464	—	89,318	84,856	42,614	2,425	12,622	70	1	401	217
Punjab (and Haryana)	20,307	20	21,269	14,739	3,601	3,380	7,758	N.A.	N.A.	6	3,986	17	—	430	214
Rajasthan	20,156	26	32,241	432,368	84,781	122,489	225,598	8,391	13,158	234	1,736	1	—	460	347
Uttar Pradesh	73,746	54	112,624	435,458	210,991	201,653	23,733	38,206	73,318	56	25,729	147	5	2,018	1,601
West Bengal	34,926	16	38,454	12,960	3,868	8,426	636	N.A.	N.A.	347	748	—	—	330	194
Delhi	2,658	1	276	300	180	120	—	N.A.	N.A.	—	—	—	—	27	151
Himachal Pradesh	1,351	6	10,438	5,240	2,531	—	2,709	N.A.	N.A.	4	**	**	—	6	7
Others	3,433	3	11,252	—	—	—	—	N.A.	N.A.	—	74	—	—	—	—
Total: All-India	439,072	322	566,878	4,176,815	1,175,838	1,854,882	1,146,095	575,885	461,681	6,807	140,020	1,030	31	8,621	8,114

SOURCES: Figures for population, number of districts, and number of villages: India 1964, Government of India, 1964.
The Bhoodan statistics are derived from Appendix 6 of Report on Activities, May–September 1960, Sarva Seva Sangh, Varanasi, 1969 (in Hindi). The figures have been rounded to the nearest whole number. It should be noted that the figures for land distributed, uncultivable land, and land still to be distributed do not always add up accurately to the number of acres of land donated.
The Gramdan statistics for March 1964 and the figures for Lok Sevaks and Shanti Sainiks were supplied by Sarva Seva Sangh in April 1965. The remaining statistics for Gramdan, Blockdan, and Districtdan are those presented to the 18th Sarvodaya Sammelan, 25 October 1969. See People's Action, 3, 11 November 1969, p. 31.

NOTES: *Gramdan villages do not necessarily coincide with 'revenue' villages as counted in census returns. This applies particularly to figures in the 1964 column, which relate mainly to Gramdan in its original (pre-Sulabh) form.
**Included in the figures for Punjab and Haryana.
N.A. = Not Available.

fied itself. In the autumn of 1965 the movement launched a toofan
(whirlwind) campaign for Sulabh Gramdan that, within the space
of four years, multiplied by the factor of sixteen the number of
Gramdans. By October 1969 the movement could claim that
140,020 villages—approximately one-quarter of the total number
of villages in India—had declared for Gramdan. But perhaps the
most significant aspect of this recent campaign is not the number
of Gramdan declarations achieved but the fact that, for the first
time, villages in large contiguous areas are joining the movement.
Gramdans are no longer separate islands in a sea of non-Gramdan
villages. Just as Bhoodan had paved the way for Gramdan, so
Gramdan has paved the way for Blockdan—a 'block' being a
unit for planning and administration in the Government's Community Development Programme, and consisting of about one
hundred villages. By October 1969 there were 1,030 Blockdans.
Blockdan, in its turn, is paving the way for Districtdan—a district
being one of the main administrative areas into which the country
is divided. By October 1969 the movement was able to declare 30
of India's 330 districts as meeting its definition of Districtdan. The
rapid ascent from Gramdan through Blockdan to Districtdan inevitably raised the prospect of Statedan in at least one of the seven-
teen states of the Indian Union. Concentrating its main efforts in
Bihar, the movement set itself the objective of achieving Bihardan
by the end of the Gandhi Centenary Year. In the event, it did not
completely succeed in reaching this objective, twelve blocks remaining undeclared in October 1969. But with 98 per cent of the
587 blocks in Bihar within the movement's fold, there was some
justification for regarding Bihardan as virtually achieved.

While villagization of land in the form of Sulabh Gramdan is
the most striking plank in the movement's programme, it is by
no means the only one. Vinoba's fertile imagination has widened
the concept of dan (gift) and created other forms of it. These
include: Shramdan (gift of labour), Sampattidan (gift of money,
income, or wealth), Buddhidan (dedication of one's mental
abilities to the realization of Sarvodaya ideals), and Jeevandan
(dedication of one's life to the cause). In addition, in 1957 Vinoba
initiated the Shanti Sena (Peace Army), open to all those who
pledge themselves to work for Truth and Non-violence. This army
numbered some 8,000 in 1964, and four years later enrolments
had reached the figure of 12,000. The Shanti Sena and its related

organizations—the Shanti Sevak Dal, confined to peace work within a member's own village, and the Tarun Shanti Sena, the youth corps—are intended to function primarily as a non-violent police force, but since the Sino-Indian border war of 1962 the Shanti Sena has made a special effort to do constructive work in the border areas. The development of khadi and other village industries also remains a central part of the movement's programme, so that the programme of action is now a three-fold one, which emphasizes Gramdan, Khadi, and Shanti Sena.

Some indication of the size of the movement may be gauged from the number of workers involved in it. Because of the extremely loose structure of the movement, and the overlap with institutional Gandhism, no accurate estimate is possible. In 1964, however, Sarva Seva Sangh quoted the figure of 8,621 Lok Sevaks (Servants of the People) who had signed a pledge to serve humanity without recognizing differences of caste, class, and creed, and to remain free from association with any kind of party and power politics. Not all of these would be active and full-time workers, and some of the latter would have conscientious objections to taking the pledge. Perhaps a figure of 5,000 would be a fair estimate of the real activists in 1965, with 20,000 others capable of mobilization for short periods or part-time activity.

The figures so far quoted provide some measure of the degree of practical success of the movement. But without interpretation and analysis the published statistics of the movement may be misleading. Well over half a million landowners contributed to Bhoodan, and their donations have benefited rather less than half a million peasants who formerly owned little or no land. This was no small achievement, but a large class of landless labourers still remains. Moreover, it must be noted that the 4·2 million acres of Bhoodan land included 1·85 million which were uncultivable or legally disputed. Further, of the remainder only just over half had, by 1969, actually been distributed. Distribution proved to be beset with many difficulties, not all the fault of the movement, which the Bhoodan workers found impossible to surmount.[1]

The Gramdan figures, too, may be misleading if they are taken

---

[1] Distribution of the remaining Bhoodan land has now virtually ceased. Under the Sulabh Gramdan concept, a landowner's Bhoodan donation counts towards the proportion which he undertakes to provide for cultivation by the landless of the village.

to imply that observable revolutionary changes have taken place
in the villages concerned. The typical Gramdan village is far from
being the Indian equivalent of an Israeli kibbutz. The aggregate
figure of 140,020 relates to villages which, according to the movement's records, have *declared* for Gramdan. The overwhelming
majority of these represent 'declarations of intent' which have not
yet (in early 1970) been followed by action. In only a few thousand
has the title to the land actually been transferred to the village
council and the village officially registered as a Gramdan village.
In the great majority of villages nothing much has happened after
the declaration, and they remain potential rather than actual
centres of revolutionary change. In 1965 perhaps in no more than
500 Gramdan villages could an observer have seen obvious signs
of development and social reconstruction; and five years later that
number had not noticeably increased, certainly not in proportion
to the increase in the number of declarations. The movement
lacks the resources, both of finance and of trained personnel, to
follow up its propaganda work effectively.

The over-all picture of Gramdan in India is clearly very different
from the picture one would obtain by generalizing the situation
that can be found in the relatively small number of villages where
development and reconstruction are taking place. The gap between
the ideal and reality remains vast. Nevertheless, it would be unfair
to judge the movement, as some critics have done, as a fraud and
a hoax. Given its resources, the host of difficulties encountered,
and the social context in which it operates, it is remarkable that
the movement has achieved so much in so relatively short a time.
Its achievements so far, it is true, have been mainly at the propaganda level; but it is no small achievement to have persuaded a
majority of landowners in one-quarter of India's villages to agree
to the idea of villagization of land. Nor, in any assessment of the
movement, should its contribution to changing the climate of
opinion in the country at large be overlooked. The Bhoodan
campaign focused public attention on the land question in a
spectacular fashion, and contributed in no small measure to sustaining or smoothing the way for the Indian Government's land
reforms, notably the abolition of absentee landlordism, the imposition of ceilings on land holdings, and the encouragement of
co-operative farming.

More generally, by presenting a vision of a new social order in terms that can be easily understood by the illiterate masses, the movement has helped to undermine the moral foundations of the old social order. As the movement has grown, it has developed a fairly well rounded, though still incomplete, theory of non-violent social revolution, applicable to Indian conditions, which enables its adherents to make critical observations at many points on public policy. Speaking what Morris-Jones has called 'the language of saintly politics', in contrast to both the 'traditional' and the 'modern' languages,[1] the Sarvodaya movement constitutes in large measure the repository of the Indian conscience. As such, it has provided widely accepted standards by which the people at large can judge politicians and their performances.

Perhaps the fairest summary comment to make in 1970 is that the movement has some substantial achievements to its credit, but that it has not yet fulfilled the expectations it has aroused. No more than a few bricks have been laid in the foundations of a non-violent social order. And only a rash observer would confidently predict that the building which eventually arises in the new India will conform, even approximately, to the canons of Sarvodaya social architecture. For the movement the next few years are likely to prove crucial. Much of the initial public interest in the Bhoodan campaign stemmed from the fact that it appeared to offer a possible non-violent alternative to a Communist-directed revolution. In the politically confused, crisis-ridden situation that India finds herself in as she enters the 1970s, the forces of Communism appear stronger than they have been at any time since 1951. Bitterly divided among themselves though these forces are, they have gained substantial ground in recent years, especially among the poor and landless peasants of West Bengal, Kerala, Andhra Pradesh, and Tamilnad. The forcible seizure of land and the temporary establishment of a 'red base' in the Naxalbari district of West Bengal in 1967 has inspired similar attempts elsewhere to promote a Mao-ist type of revolution. The recent breakthrough in Indian farming has brought greater prosperity to the upper strata of the peasantry, but it has also created new social tensions which nurture the 'Naxalite' movement. In this situation, the Sarvoday-ites find themselves faced with the need to demonstrate with some urgency that a non-violent social revolution through Gramdan is

[1] W. H. Morris-Jones, 'India's Political Idioms', in C. H. Philips (ed.), *Politics and Society in India*, 1963.

indeed a realizable concept. Constituting as they do the vanguard of non-violent revolutionary forces throughout the world, their success or failure is likely to have a significance extending far beyond India.

II. TYPES OF SOCIAL MOVEMENT

Having attempted to place the Sarvodaya movement in its historical setting, we may now consider its sociological setting. The question to be discussed here is: What kind of social movement is it?

Social movements may, of course, be classified in various ways. Perhaps the most popular distinction is between 'reformist' movements which use peaceful and constitutional means to achieve their objectives, and 'revolutionary' movements which use violent and unconstitutional means. The Sarvodaya movement, with its commitment to non-violence and peaceful, loving persuasion, is clearly not revolutionary in this sense. However, the terms 'reformist' and 'revolutionary' may also be used in a more sophisticated sense to distinguish different attitudes to social values. A movement may then be described as 'reformist' when it seeks only the modification of existing values, or changes which will implement such values more effectively than at present. In contrast, a movement may be described as 'revolutionary' when it challenges accepted values and seeks to replace them with other values. These other values need not be novel: they may be ancient values which have been displaced in the existing society. In this special case, a movement may be both revolutionary and reactionary, seeking a return to ancient values.

It is in the second sense of 'revolutionary' that the Sarvodaya movement is often described by its participants as a revolutionary movement. As we shall see when we discuss its goals, the movement also has reactionary aspects: some, though not all, of the values it espouses are rooted in the traditional Indian culture. At this point, however, we wish to draw attention to some implications of the 'reformist-revolutionary' disjunction. Whether a movement is reformist or revolutionary in the popular sense (which focuses on the means employed) will affect the way it is seen by the society of which it is a part. And how it is seen will be a critical determinant of the type and tactics of the opposition with which it is confronted, the circumstances under which it may recruit members, and the degree to which it may operate openly, using legitimate channels.

Judged in terms of its ultimate goals, the Sarvodaya movement is clearly and avowedly a revolutionary movement in the second sense, challenging some of the fundamental values of Indian society, particularly those concerned with ownership of property, the caste system, and the modern (Western-type) political process. At the same time, it shares some of the characteristics associated with reformist movements, especially the attribute of legitimacy. Despite its revolutionary aims, it is permitted to operate openly, it is not denied access to the established channels of communication, recruitment of members is not inhibited in any way by official actions, and its programme receives the passive, and on occasions the active, support of the governing authorities.

The somewhat paradoxical characteristic of being a *legitimate* revolutionary movement is probably the resultant of several factors. One, of course, is its association with Gandhi, 'the Father of the Indian Nation', a national symbol of still considerable efficacy. Closely related to this, is the movement's commitment to the principle of Non-violence. While this commitment does not preclude the movement from adopting tactics directly challenging the existing power-holders in Indian society, it does inhibit the power-holders themselves from defining the movement as an overt threat to the established order. This inhibition has been aided by Vinoba's interpretation of Non-violence. As we shall see, Vinoba, by and large, has *not* sanctioned attempts to achieve the movement's objectives by the use of non-violent resistance on the lines made familiar in Gandhi's satyagraha campaigns. This eschewal of 'negative' satyagraha (except in limited situations) has enabled the movement to avoid a direct struggle with the existing power-holders. It should, in any case, be noted that, despite the potentially revolutionary character of satyagraha, this political 'technique' enjoys a large measure of legitimacy in India because of its association with Gandhi and the struggle for independence. The few occasions on which the movement or, rather, local elements in it, have adopted the technique of non-violent resistance have not, therefore, seriously endangered its legitimacy. Whether a mass satyagraha campaign on the lines suggested by some of the militants in the movement, would do so is another matter; the issue has never been put to the test.

A further factor contributing to the movement's legitimacy is its concentration on its immediate programme of land reform, the promotion of Khadi and village industries, and the development of the Shanti Sena. This immediate programme is consistent with the existing value system and may be seen as supplementary or complementary to the programme of the Congress governments.

Another factor endowing the movement with legitimacy is its 'nativistic' character. The movement presents itself, and is interpreted by others, as an essentially indigenous movement, pursuing 'the Indian road to socialism' and seeking to preserve and to rehabilitate peculiarly Indian values that have been lost or are in danger of subversion as the result of the process of 'modernization'. The values the movement seeks to affirm are those associated with rural life and the (idealized) village community of ancient India.

As a fifth factor in this context we should note also the religious character of the movement. The movement's ideology, as we shall see, attaches great importance to religious values. Its leadership is largely in the hands of religious men whose convictions are consistent with the universalistic values of Hinduism. The movement's emphasis on universalistic religious values makes it difficult for opponents to attack it without, at the same time, appearing to question these values.

The factors which have contributed to making the movement legitimate and respectable help to account for whatever success it may be thought to have achieved. At the same time, these very factors may also help to account for its lack of success. The movement, in other words, has had to pay a price for its respectability. The price includes a failure to fashion for itself a distinctive public image. It is seen by some as an offshoot of the Congress party and, as such, becomes associated with the failures of that party to realize Congress policies. Its apparent unwillingness to challenge directly the existing power-holders and the Government has led it to adopt what even some of its own supporters see as compromising stands on important issues, such as the Sino-Indian and Indo-Pakistan conflicts. Further, while its universalistic appeal encourages wide support, such an appeal is inevitably shallow: the movement, so far, has failed to elicit the enthusiasm of any important segment of society. Although its immediate programme of Bhoodan and Gramdan has been especially directed towards improving the position of a substantial and depressed element in

Indian society—the landless labourers—it has not, by and large, succeeded in presenting itself as the spokesman for this class. Again, while the emphasis of the movement on nativistic and religious values has contributed to its support among the more traditional elements of Indian society, it has militated against attracting sustained support from the intellectual strata most sympathetic towards modern and secular values.

Distinguishing reformist from revolutionary movements in both the senses used above is not the only way of classifying movements. Based on the degree to which the internal interaction of members, the maintenance of membership, and the conception of what constitutes success are oriented about the predominance of one aspect of a movement, Turner and Killian classify social movements into three fundamental types.[1] The first, the value-oriented movement, is one in which to a large degree the support of the members is derived from a conviction of the worth of the movement's manifest programme, and in which, also to a large degree, the key decisions governing the movement's course from within are directed towards promoting that programme. The second, the power-oriented movement, is one that leaves its value objectives flexible or undefined, and which is primarily devoted to dominating the larger group or society of which it is a part. The third is the participation-oriented movement; that is, one in which the major characteristics of the movement centre on the satisfaction that members gain from the mere fact of participation in the movement itself. However, Turner and Killian emphasize that these are 'ideal types' in the Weberian sense of intellectual constructs to be used for analysing actual movements. No particular movement will be a pure instance of any one type, and all movements possess in varying degrees features of all three ideal types.

Although, as we shall show, the Sarvodaya movement does not see itself as power-oriented, it is so in some degree, in the sense that it has a deliberately formulated strategy for gaining its objectives. However, it is distinguished from most other movements in that this strategy does not involve an attempt to gain power in the usual sense. It does not seek to capture power positions for its members so that they may dominate society and implement the movement's objectives. On the contrary, its value objectives are defined in such a way as to preclude this. The movement's strategy

[1] R. H. Turner and L. M. Killian, *Collective Behavior*, 1957, Part Four.

demands, rather, that the people, individually and collectively, should themselves generate the power to realize Sarvodaya values. The workers organized in the Sarvodaya movement are simply the catalytic agents of the process.

The Sarvodaya movement is also participation-oriented in that its members derive satisfaction from belonging to it and working for it. Although the material rewards it offers are small and even negative, for many members, at least, participation is seen as contributing to their own personal and spiritual salvation. Even if the movement fails to achieve its programmatic objectives, participation for such members may well be deemed worth while. As apostles of Truth, Love, and Compassion, they are armed against failure and are convinced that they will never be proved false prophets. They believe that the law of love in human relationships is not one that is subject to repeal: it is a law that remains operative whatever men may do, and it is a law unaffected by the results of human action.

The Sarvodaya movement thus has both power-oriented and participation-oriented aspects. But, to date at least, these remain subordinate to the value-oriented aspect. As a primarily value-oriented movement, however, it does exhibit a distinctive feature. The ideology and programmes of such movements usually point in one of two directions: either towards changing social institutions or towards changing individuals directly. A movement pointing in the first direction generally develops a strategy preoccupied with gaining power over the institutions of society; a movement pointing in the second tends to emphasize the satisfactions to be derived from participation, and it gains much of its strength from the sense of personal satisfaction which follows a member's act of conversion. The Sarvodaya movement, however, is distinctive in that it points in *both* directions at the same time. In theory at least, a balance is maintained between individual and institutional change. The two are seen as equally necessary, and it is believed that individual change will inevitably produce institutional change. The Sarvodaya society is to be realized by converting individuals, wholly or partly, in such a way that the conversion proceeds simultaneously to lead to desired institutional changes. The ultimate objective is the new man in the new society.

Using essentially Parsonian concepts of social action, Smelser has developed a theory in which two types of social movement—

the norm-oriented and the value-oriented—are distinguished as the most complex of a series of 'collective behaviour'.[1] Values are more general components of social action than norms. They state in general terms the desirable ends which serve as a guide to human endeavour. Norms, in contrast, specify certain regulatory principles which are necessary if values are to be realized. A norm-oriented movement is then defined as an attempt to restore, protect, modify, or create norms in the name of a generalized (norm-oriented) belief. People subscribing to such beliefs may demand a law or a regulatory agency to control behaviour. Political pressure groups of all kinds are typical norm-oriented movements.

The value-oriented movement[2] Smelser defines as a collective attempt to restore, protect, modify, or create values in the name of a generalized (value-oriented) belief. Such beliefs involve a basic reconstitution of self and society, and a preoccupation with the highest moral bases of social life. The regeneration of values, suggests Smelser, is the identifying characteristic of a value-oriented belief. Its adherents envisage a new world and not merely an improvement of individuals or a reform of institutions, even though the latter are aspects of regeneration. Such beliefs contain a vision of future harmony and stability which is in direct contrast with the decay and instability of the present. A value-oriented movement is necessarily more complex than a norm-oriented movement, since it involves a reconstitution of values *as well as* a redefinition of norms.

Norm-oriented movements are usually reformist in the popular sense, while value-oriented movements are often, but not always, revolutionary. Typical examples of the value-oriented movement are messianic religious movements, utopian socialist movements, and revolutionary political movements, such as Fascism and Communism. In terms of this classification, Sarvodaya, as we shall see, is clearly a value-oriented movement.

III.   THE FOCUS OF THE STUDY

The initial success of the campaign for Bhoodan in the early 1950s attracted considerable attention not only in India but also in other

---

[1] N. Smelser, *Theory of Collective Behaviour*, 1962.
[2] Not to be confused with Turner and Killian's type of the same name.

countries. Observers, not surprisingly, were struck by the spectacle of an attempt to solve one of India's major social problems—the plight of the landless labourers—by the seemingly impossible technique of persuading landowners, in a 'land-hungry' peasant economy, to give a portion of their lands for redistribution to the landless. Popular accounts were published, in England and elsewhere, focused on the personality and techniques of India's newly discovered 'saint', relating the progress of his 'mission' and the details of his 'march' throughout the length and breadth of India.[1] At the outset less attention was paid to the social and political philosophy of which Bhoodan and Gramdan were practical expressions. Now that popular interest in the movement has receded, partly no doubt because it failed to achieve its short-term objective of abolishing landlessness, students have turned to a more detailed and sometimes highly critical examination of its philosophy.[2] But there remain many aspects of the movement which have not been studied, particularly those that interest social scientists most. No published study, for example, is available on the social and economic impact of Bhoodan.[3] The situation in respect of Gramdan is somewhat better. In recent years several case studies of Gramdan villages have been published, and others are in process of completion.[4] But these empirical studies are still too few in number

[1] See Hallam Tennyson, *Saint on the March*, 1956; R. P. Masani, *The Five Gifts*, 1957; Lanza del Vasto, *Gandhi to Vinoba: The New Pilgrimage*, 1956; B. R. Misra, *V. for Vinoba*, 1956; Suresh Ram, *Vinoba and His Mission*, 1st edn., 1954, 3rd edn., 1962. For a scholarly account see J. Bondurant & M. W. Fisher, *Indian Approaches to a Socialist Society*, India Press Digests, Monograph Series No. 2, 1956.

[2] For sympathetic expositions see Vishwanath Tandon, *The Social and Political Philosophy of Sarvodaya after Gandhiji*, 1965; and Vasant Nargolkar, *The Creed of Saint Vinoba*, 1963. For critical analyses see Usha Mehta, *Social and Political Thought of Sarvodaya*, 1963; and, especially, the works of Adi Doctor: *Anarchist Thought in India*, 1964, and *Sarvodaya, a Political and Economic Study*, 1967.

[3] One unpublished study has been privately circulated: *An Evaluation of the Working of the Bhoodan Movement*, a pilot study of six Gujarat villages conducted by the Agricultural Economics Section of the Department of Economics, the University of Bombay, no date but *c.* 1957. In its conclusion the report underlines the 'marked gap between the intentions of the Bhoodan Movement and its performance'.

[4] For an account of Gramdans in Orissa see A. W. Sahasrabudhe, *Report on Koraput Gramdans*, 1960. On Gramdans in Kerala see Sachidinand, *Sarvodaya in a Communist State*, 1961. On Gramdans in Bihar see P. N. Mukherji, 'Report on Gramdans in Bihar', unpublished, Gandhian Institute of Studies, Varanasi, 1964, and the same author's 'Gramdan in village Berain', *Human Organization*,

and too limited in scope to permit a comprehensive evaluation of the impact of Gramdan on village India. The present study makes no attempt to fill this gap. Instead, it deals with one important aspect of the movement which, so far, has not been studied at all: the people most actively involved in it. The kinds of question it seeks to answer are: What sort of people are the disciples of 'the Saint on the March'? What are their social origins and background? What was their religious upbringing and what are their present religious views? Where do they stand in politics and what do they think of their country's political parties in relation to the movement? How committed are they to the values of Sarvodaya? Where do they stand on certain policy issues that confront the movement? In short, who are the revolutionary Gandhians?

In the literature on the movement there is no systematic information which would help us to answer such questions. We know, of course, the names and perhaps something of the background of a score or so of the more prominant leaders, but beyond that, next to nothing. As students of social movements we cannot be satisfied with such information. Nor are the questions we have posed irrelevant for the movement itself. As R. P. Masani has pointed out,

for this kind of revolution in the minds of the people, leaders from all ranks, especially from the masses, should come forward to further the movement throughout the country. Leaders such as Shankarrao Deo, Dada Dharmadhikari, Jayaprakash Narayan, Nabkrushna Chaudhuri, Suresh Ramabhai, Dhirendranath Mazumdar, Vallabhswami, Ravi Shankar Maharaj, and A. K. Karanbhai have dedicated their lives to the cause. But they come from the ranks of the élite. It would be interesting

25 (Spring 1966), pp. 33–41. On people's perceptions of Gramdan see B. B. Chatterjee et al., Gramdan and People, 1969. The forthcoming study by S. S. Iyer et al., Gramdan and Development, Gandhian Institute of Studies, Varanasi, deals with selected Gramdans in Bihar and Tamilnad. The most systematic analysis to date by an independent scholar is that of T. K. Oommen, which compares a sample of Gramdan with a sample of non-Gramdan villages in Rajasthan: 'Charismatic Movements and Social Change: An Analysis of Bhoodan-Gramdan Movement in India', unpublished Ph.D. thesis, the University of Poona, 1967. See also the same author's: 'Problems of Gramdan', Economic Weekly, 26 June 1965; 'Myth and reality in India's communitarian villages', Journal of Commonwealth Political Studies, IV, 2 (1966); 'Non-violent approach to land reform', Zeitschrift für Ausländische Landwirtschaft, Heidelberg (Jan. 1970); and 'Charisma, social structure and social change', Comparative Studies in Society and History, X, 1 (Oct. 1967).
TGA—C

to know how many capable leaders have sprung from the masses. For a mass movement aiming at the total revolution of society, it is not enough that, inspired for a while by Vinobaji, or stirred by popular and trusted leaders like Jayaprakash during their visits, villagers should sing hallelujahs, offer land at the altar of Bhoodan, pulsate with new life, but lapse into inaction after their leaders' backs are turned.[1]

In an effort to answer the kinds of question posed above, a survey was made of the leading activists in the movement. With the consent and co-operation of the Secretary of Sarva Seva Sangh and the assistance of the Gandhian Institute of Studies, a postal questionnaire was sent to the leaders of the movement. The questionnaire sought biographical information about the respondent, asked for his views about the goals and programme of the movement, and, in addition, his reaction to a list of statements involving issues of policy within the movement.[2] For the purpose of the enquiry, 'leaders' were defined as those occupying at the date of the survey—April 1965—the following offices in Sarva Seva Sangh: members, whether elected or invited, of the Prabandh Samiti (Executive Committee); nominated members of the Sangh; secretaries of State Sarvodaya Mandals (Circles); District Representatives; and District Convenors—a total of 479 individuals. Such an operational definition of 'leader' excludes at least some persons who would be regarded within the movement itself as leaders, but who, like Vinoba, occupy no office in Sarva Seva Sangh. The survey thus constituted an attempt to take a census of the office holders, although, since replies were received from only 228, our data relate to this self-selected sample of the whole group. We are satisfied, however, that this sample is reasonably representative of the whole.[3]

The bulk of our study consists of an analysis of the social characteristics and opinions of the leaders, so defined. We must emphasize that we are dealing with a population of office-holders, not the larger group of 'Sarvodaya workers'.[4] Our study does not purport

---

[1] Masani, op. cit., pp. 176–7.

[2] The English version of the questionnaire is reproduced in Appendix One.

[3] See Response to the Questionnaire, Appendix Two.

[4] An attempt was made to collect similar information from activists who were not office holders, but the 75 respondents were not representative of their group. From inspection of their completed questionnaires, it appears that none of the 'individual activists' was typical of the 'grass roots' activists in the Gramdan villages. Until recent years almost all Sarvodaya workers were drawn from the élite. Many of them might succeed in identifying with the rural masses but very

to be a study of the movement as such, but of the movement's leaders and of the movement as seen through the eyes of these leaders. This last point also warrants emphasis. We shall have occasion, for example, to discuss the goals of the movement and its achievements. But we shall be dealing with *perceived* goals and *perceived* achievements. How these perceptions relate to reality, what purposes the movement 'really' serves, and what it has actually achieved, are beyond our scope.

Our study is essentially a descriptive analysis: the primary objective was not to test the utility of concepts or the relevance of models about social movements. Our object was the more modest one of establishing, as far as possible, 'the facts' about a little known but interesting group. Facts in themselves, we appreciate, have little significance, and the facts presented in studies of this kind reflect to a large extent the preconceptions and theories (conscious or unconscious) of the authors. The facts that we present are no exception, and our sympathy with the aspirations of the Sarvodaya movement for non-violent revolution will be apparent. We trust, however, that scholarly concern for truth and Sarvodaya commitment to Truth are not inconsistent, and that we have not ignored or disguised unpalatable facts.

While the study is essentially descriptive, some attempt has been made to interpret our factual findings in the light of models and theories, and to relate them, where possible, to relevant comparative material. In addition, certain specific narrow-range hypotheses (for example, that level of leadership is associated with social status) have been examined and tested. The end result, however, does not add up to a complete sociological study of either the Sarvodaya movement or its leaders. We are conscious that our study raises more questions than it answers. But in social research, as in all other fields of knowledge, understanding begins with the posing of questions. Whether we have asked or raised the right questions we must leave the reader to judge.

---

few were of the masses. The situation is now changing. Increasingly, workers are being recruited from the Gramdan villages themselves, men who are often Harijans or tribal people. Such activists may often be illiterate or barely literate, and none was represented in the group.

CHAPTER TWO

THE IDEOLOGY OF SARVODAYA

THE first step towards understanding a social movement is to answer the questions suggested by common sense: What does the movement seek to achieve? What are its aims, its goals and its programme? How do its members propose to achieve their objectives? And, more fundamentally, with what reasons do they justify their endeavours? Such questions all relate to a movement's ideology: 'the entire complex of ideas, theories, doctrines, values, and strategic and tactical principles that is characteristic of the movement'.[1]

In this chapter we shall not attempt to summarize or to analyse critically all aspects of Sarvodaya ideology, accounts of which are available elsewhere.[2] The intellectual 'foundations' of the ideology rest on interpretations of Hindu metaphysics and ethics. While knowledge of these foundations is essential for a full understanding of Sarvodaya, all we shall attempt to provide here is a general description of the content of the social and political doctrines of the movement and of its programme necessary for an appreciation of the main sections of our study. This description will be based largely on authoritative statements of prominent leaders, such as Gandhi, Vinoba, and Jayaprakash Narayan, resolutions of Sarva Seva Sangh, publications of the movement, and information supplied by respondents in answers to questions about the goals and programme of the movement.

---

[1] R. Heberle, *Social Movements*, 1951, p. 23. Heberle's definition leaves open the important question of the truth of the constituent ideas. It differs from the Marxian usage of the term, in which 'ideology' is contrasted with 'scientific knowledge' and seen as the product of 'false consciousness', a set of selected and distorted ideas in defence of an existing social system. See H. M. Johnson, 'Ideology', *International Encyclopaedia of the Social Sciences*.

[2] See V. Tandon, *The Social and Political Philosophy of Sarvodaya after Gandhiji*, 1965; and A. Doctor, *Anarchist Thought in India*, 1964. Of the many studies of Gandhi's thought, see especially: G. Dhawan, *The Political Philosophy of Mahatma Gandhi*, 3rd edn., 1957; J. Bondurant, *Conquest of Violence*, 1958; I. Rothermund, *The Philosophy of Restraint*, 1963; N. K. Bose, *Studies in Gandhism*, 3rd edn., 1962.

I. SOME GENERAL CHARACTERISTICS OF SARVODAYA IDEOLOGY

However, before outlining the content of Sarvodaya doctrines some preliminary observations about the character of the ideology may be helpful. As noted in the previous chapter, the original source of inspiration of Sarvodaya ideas was Gandhi. Without Gandhi India would undoubtedly, sooner or later, have achieved political independence, but without Gandhi there would have been no Sarvodaya movement. At the same time, Gandhi was a man of action, not a social and political theorist.[1] His ideas were formulated largely on the basis of his own experience and as a result of reflection on that experience. Although he wrote voluminously, on no occasion did he attempt a systematic exposition of his philosophy. Not surprisingly, when others have made the attempt, the result reveals certain gaps, incoherencies, and ambiguities in the philosophy. Gandhi himself was aware of inconsistencies, but dismissed them lightly: as a humble seeker after Truth, he made no claim to being perfectly consistent, recognized that all known truth was relative, and advised his followers to accept his later statement on any particular point as representing his more considered but still unfinalized judgement. This attitude remains characteristic of current Sarvodaya doctrine. It is a developing doctrine, still largely expressed in the form of the intuitions of those actively engaged in what Gandhi called 'experiments with Truth'; it is far from being complete, if, indeed, it can ever be thought capable of completion; and it is an experimental doctrine which reveals itself only in and through action.

From this, one important implication follows for Gandhi's position in relation to current Sarvodaya ideology. The texts of the founding father are worthy of respect, but they are not sacred: his successors stand on his shoulders and may well see further than he did. Gandhi's central principles remain unchallenged, but the application of those principles in action is a matter of continual adaptation in the light of changing conditions, fresh experience, and new insights.

---

[1] In traditional Hindu terms, Gandhi was a karmayogi, seeking self-realization (or God) primarily by the Way of Disinterested Action rather than by the Ways of Knowledge, of Contemplation, or of Devotion—the four ways distinguished in the *Bhagavad Gita*.

Related to this observation is the undoubted fact that Gandhi's successors, notably Vinoba, have developed the revolutionary implications of the founder's ideas. Gandhi never disguised the fact that his ideas were revolutionary, but while attention was focused on the struggle for political independence, it was easy for others, including many in Congress, to play down their revolutionary character. The ambiguity of some of Gandhi's social concepts, such as 'trusteeship', and his approach as a 'practical idealist' made it easier to do this.[1] His ideal society was a condition of enlightened anarchy,[2] but he spent little time describing this vision, and was much more concerned with suggesting practical courses of action. His Constructive Programme could easily be interpreted as a programme of social reform, a list of norm-oriented rather than value-oriented beliefs and proposals, in Smelser's terminology. In fact, this is not how Gandhi himself saw the Programme, and, more clearly, it is not how his successors in Sarva Seva Sangh see it. Bhoodan might appear at first sight as an additional item in a norm-oriented programme, but its latent revolutionary implications soon became manifest, especially with the flowering of Bhoodan into Gramdan. In the hands of Vinoba, the revolutionary —some would say 'utopian'—aspects of Gandhi's thought have been emphasized, and the doctrine has now become an explicit and avowed gospel of revolution, a call for the total reconstruction not only of Indian but of all human society.[3]

[1] On the ambiguity of the 'trusteeship' concept, and its role in gaining and holding support for the independence movement of groups with apparently diverse interests, see P. J. Rolnick, 'Charity, trusteeship, and social change in India', World Politics, XIV, 3 (1962).

[2] Gandhi's ideal society was one in which social life had become so perfect as to be self-regulated. 'In such a state every one is his own ruler. He rules himself in such a manner that he is never a hindrance to his neighbour. In the ideal state, therefore, there is no political power because there is no State.' Young India, 2 July 1931; quoted in Dhawan, op. cit., p. 282.

[3] Three examples of Vinoba's emphasis on the revolutionary aspects of Gandhi's ideas may be cited. The concept of trusteeship has been given its most radical, socialist interpretation. See Rolnick, op. cit. The ideal of enlightened anarchy has become more pronounced. See Doctor, op. cit., Ch. IV. And Gandhi's views on caste have been interpreted to imply the abolition of caste. Gandhi himself on occasions defended the traditional varna system in its ideal form, while pressing for the abolition of 'untouchability'. Vinoba, however, has stated categorically: 'The ugly distinctions of caste have no place any more . . . there is no support for caste distinctions in our religion.'—Bhoodan, 11 July 1956. The new education, he argues, will help all to be twice-born, and in a Sarvodaya society every individual will have to learn to combine in himself the

Our final general observation on Sarvodaya ideology is more difficult to state precisely. It concerns the relation of the ideology to traditional elements in Indian culture. We have already noted that Sarvodaya can be presented as an indigenous creed, the specifically *Indian* approach to socialism, and that it seeks the rehabilitation of what it regards as distinctive Indian values.[1] And yet a major theme of Doctor's recent critique of the ideology is that it has no basis in ancient Indian political thought.[2] The substance of this judgement relates to the Sarvodaya ideal of a stateless society. Doctor agrees that passing references to an ideal stateless society are to be found in Vedic, Buddhist, and Jaina literature, but these, he argues, represent no more than allusions to a mythical 'golden age' contrasted with man's present sinful lot. Hindu political theories, in fact, start from an assumption of the inherently wicked nature of man, and paint a Hobbesian picture of the strong preying on the weak—'like fishes in shallow water'— until men see the wisdom of placing themselves under the protection of a king. Kingship, tempered and moderated by dharma, was regarded as both natural and necessary if social chaos was to be avoided.

Doctor is undoubtedly correct in his main contention that a philosophy of anarchism is absent in ancient Indian political thought. Certainly, in the *Arthashastra* tradition of Kautilya, 'the Indian Machiavelli', there is no basis for such a political philosophy. But Doctor's argument misses a central point about Sarvodaya ideology: that it represents, in part at least, an attempt to reconstitute another tradition of ancient Indian thought, particularly religious thought. Like Vivekananda before him, and like his contemporary, Aurobindo, Gandhi did not use the *Arthashastra*

---

ideal qualities of the Brahmin, the Kshatriya, the Vaishya, and the Sudra. For a note on the usages of 'caste', and for a description of the four varnas, see p. 75 below. The revolutionizing of 'Gandhism' is one reason why some Gandhians have found it impossible to follow Vinoba. For a conservative criticism of Bhoodan by a Gandhian see Maganbhai Desai, 'Whither Bhudan?', *Gandhi Marg*, 2 Feb. 1958. 'Conservative Gandhism' has since found its political outlet in the Swatantra Party, founded by the eminent Gandhian, C. Rajagopalachari.

[1] Bashan suggests that the chief inspiration of modern Indian political thought probably derives from Europe and America. He notes, however, that 'The Sarvodaya movement . . . is more solidly based on ancient norms, but even this owes something to outside sources, and its influence is far less than that of the major political parties.'—A. L. Bashan, 'Indian society and the legacy of the past', *Australian Journal of Politics and History*, XII, 2 (1966).

[2] Doctor, op. cit., Ch. II.

tradition or refer to those passages in the *Santi Parva* which describe the 'logic of the fishes', but, instead, he drew upon those sections of the *Upanishads* and the *Bhagavad Gita* which suggest the divine nature of man. Among the key concepts that Gandhi drew and reinterpreted from the ancient traditions were those of satya, ahimsa, karmayoga, and varnasramdharma.[1] Of these, perhaps the most important *for his anarchism* was the second. The anarchism of Sarvodaya is, in fact, arrived at largely, if not wholly, by spelling out the social and political implications of Gandhi's re-interpretation of the principle of Non-violence. Once this is appreciated, the indigenous roots of this part of the doctrine stand revealed. The apparent paradox of an emphasis on Non-violence combined with the absence of a philosophy of anarchism in ancient Indian political thought is explained by the fact that, until Gandhi, ahimsa was seen simply as an ethical principle for the self-realization of the *individual*. Ahimsa was not a principle to be applied in politics and in the organization of social life. It was Gandhi's great contribution to make it a principle of *social* ethics and to insist on its application, as far as possible, to all social relations.

In doing so, Gandhi undoubtedly rejected the assumption of the inherent wickedness of man that we find in the *Arthashastra* tradition. This rejection, however, was not based on a simple-minded assertion of the contrary: that man is naturally good. 'Every one of us', said Gandhi, 'is a mixture of good and evil.'[2] But he believed most firmly that all men have a potentiality for goodness, that 'no soul is beyond redemption', and that the nature of man is not static but dynamic. Like Godwin, he did not think that men were perfect or could ever be made so, but he did believe that they were *perfectible*. Indeed, he seems to have posited an inevitable evolutionary process by which men, as they gained increasing insight into spiritual Truth, would become progressively less violent.

The central value of Non-violence provides the main link between Sarvodaya ideology and traditional Hindu culture. But related to it are other traditional values of a less ultimate kind,

---

[1] *Satya*, truth; *ahimsa*, non-injury; *karmayoga*, the doctrine of self-realization through disinterested action; *varnasramdharma*, the law of right conduct relating to the four-fold division of Hindu society and the four stages of life.

[2] *Harijan*, 10 June 1939, p. 158.

notably those of village life, the joint family, and decisions by consensus. At the same time, there is a clear rejection of certain ancient values, particularly those associated with the traditional caste system. The short answer to the question whether current Sarvodaya ideology is traditional or modern is that it is neither: it is a synthesis of both, with Non-violence providing the criterion for the acceptance or rejection of either traditional or modern values. More accurately, the disjunction between 'traditional' and 'modern' may be misleading. As the Rudolphs point out, of Gandhi,

It would be difficult to place him with either the new or old society, although his symbolism was traditional. His ideology and tactics stressed non-violence, asceticism, compromise, and consensualism, themes that are as susceptible to a fatalistic and other-worldly interpretation as to an activist and this-worldly one. Whether one or another of interpretations is valid depends upon the meaning with which they are infused and the purposes to which they are put. In fact, Gandhi harnessed them to the requirements and purposes of a modern mass movement whose goals were national independence, coherence, and self-esteem.[1]

In Gandhi's writings we find a reasonably balanced blending of traditional and modern symbolism. In Vinoba's speeches the blending may appear less balanced, perhaps because he usually addresses village audiences. But the appearance is probably deceptive. As Bondurant and Fisher observe, he communicates his philosophy in Hindu scriptural terms, using old phrases, familiar aphorisms, and mythical allusions from the body of Sanskritic culture, but the traditional concepts have all undergone a change, as they have been adapted to the contemporary scene, and as influenced by the rationalist-humanist traditions of the West.[2] Like Gandhi, Vinoba displays a remarkable ingenuity in investing traditional concepts with new, modern meanings. Further, as if to compensate for Vinoba's use of the traditional idiom, Jayaprakash Narayan's writings are couched largely in the modern idiom: he 'translates' the language of Sarvodaya into the language most readily appreciated by the educated élites. Whether the purposes to which Sarvodaya's reinterpreted traditional concepts are

[1] R. I. and S. H. Rudolph, The Modernity of Tradition, 1967, p. 11. See also J. Bondurant, 'Traditional polity and the dynamics of change in India', Human Organization, 22, 1 (1963), and J. Bondurant and M. Fisher, 'Ethics in action', Australian Journal of Politics and History, XII, 2 (1966).
[2] J. Bondurant & M. W. Fisher, Indian Approaches to a Socialist Society, 1956, p. 43.

put are modern is another question: that depends on one's judgement of what constitutes 'modernity'. If 'modernity' means 'Westernization', then, of course, the purposes of Sarvodaya are not modern; but that is precisely the issue in dispute.

II. SARVODAYA: INDIAN ANARCHISM[1]

For students familiar with Western social and political thought Sarvodaya ideology may be conceptualized in various ways. It might be seen, for example, as one of the Indian variants of populism, with perceptible resemblances to nineteenth-century Russian populism.[2] Or it might be seen as an Indian expression of 'communitarian socialism', of which Owenism provides a familiar example.[3] However, we have chosen to conceptualize it as an Indian version of anarchism. To do so may appear to invite misunderstanding, since the Sarvodayites themselves do not use the anarchist label. In India, as in the West, anarchism is popularly associated with violence, and like Tolstoy, the greatest Western exponent of non-violent anarchism, the Sarvodayites prefer a label which bears no traces of dynamite. However, if we examine the content of Sarvodaya social and political doctrine, it clearly emerges as a species of the anarchist genus.[4] We propose, therefore, to present a summary account of Sarvodaya doctrine in terms of a comparison and contrast with the mainstream of classical Western anarchism from Bakunin through Kropotkin to Malatesta.[5]

---

[1] This section draws extensively on G. Ostergaard, 'Indian anarchism', *Anarchy*, 42 (1964).

[2] See F. Venturi, *Roots of Revolution*, 1960, and G. Ionescu & E. Gellner (eds.), *Populism*, 1969.

[3] See J. F. C. Harrison, *Robert Owen and the Owenites in Britain and America*, 1969.

[4] Woodcock defines anarchism as a 'a system of social thought, aiming at fundamental changes in the structure of society, and particularly—for this is the common element uniting all its forms—at the replacement of the authoritarian state by some form of non-governmental co-operation between free individuals.' —G. Woodcock, *Anarchism*, 1963, p. 11.

[5] This procedure inevitably involves a judgement about what constitutes the mainstream of Western anarchism. This protean doctrine encompasses thinkers as diverse as Godwin, Stirner, Proudhon, Tucker, and Tolstoy, as well as those mentioned above. Of these, Tolstoy, who is not in our judgement in the mainstream, comes closest to Sarvodaya anarchism, particularly in respect of his belief in the existence of 'the law of love' and his preferred mode of action. And, of course, there is a direct link between Tolstoy and Gandhi. 'Next to the late Rajachandra (a Jain reformer), Tolstoy', wrote Gandhi, 'is one of the three

The extent of the common ground between Sarvodaya and mainstream Western anarchism is considerable. Both see the modern state, with its claim to a monopoly of the legal instruments of coercion, as a great obstacle to a free, co-operative social order in which men will really practise *self*-government. Echoing the familiar anarchist critique of what now passes as self-government, Vinoba asks: 'If I am under some other person's command, where is my self-government? Self-government means ruling your own self. It is one mark of swaraj not to allow any outside power in the world to exercise control over oneself. And the second mark of swaraj is not to exercise power over any other. These two things together make swaraj—no submission and no exploitation.'[1] For both the anarchist and the Sarvodayite the duty of the individual to obey his own conscience is the supreme norm, taking precedence over the state's claim to political obedience. Neither envisages a society without some restraints on the individual, but both demand that the restraints necessary to maintain an ordered society be submitted to voluntarily. Both emphasize the factor of moral authority in maintaining social control and cohesion, and believe that, given the appropriate social institutions, it could entirely replace political and legal authority.

In their conceptions of the necessary conditions for the realization and maintenance of a society of free, self-governing individuals, again there is close agreement. First and foremost is the abrogation of the institution of private property in the means of production. As in the family, so in society, property is to be held in common, each contributing according to his capacity and each receiving according to his needs. For the Sarvodayites in contemporary India this implies pooling of the ownership of village lands through Gramdan, and, for those outside the villages, a full acceptance of Gandhi's principle of trusteeship—the idea that any private property one may possess, including one's talents, is held on behalf of, and is to be used in the service of, society. With the abrogation of private property goes, it is believed, the abrogation of the inequalities it engenders. Both Sarvodayites and anarchists envisage a society in which individuals are at the same time free *and* equal. Absolute equality, of course, is not feasible, but, as

moderns who have exerted the greatest spiritual influence on my life, the third being Ruskin.'—*Young India*, III, p. 843; quoted in Dhawan, op. cit., pp. 33–4.
[1] Vinoba Bhave, *Democratic Values*, 1962, pp. 13–14.

Vinoba puts it, the inequality that may be permitted will be no more than that which exists between the five fingers of one's hand. The important point stressed by both Sarvodayites and anarchists is the need to recognize the equal value, moral, social, and economic, of the various kinds of work performed by different individuals. Echoing Kropotkin's plea for integrated work and Tolstoy's insistence on 'Bread Labour', Gandhi and Vinoba call for the abolition of the distinction between mental and manual labour and for the recognition of the dignity of work done with the hands. Part at least of the Sarvodaya emphasis on the charkha (spinning-wheel) stems from its symbolization of the kind of productive work that all men and women should rightly be expected to perform.

A further important condition of a free society, stressed by Sarvodayites and anarchists alike, is decentralization: social power must be widely dispersed if tyranny and exploitation are to be avoided. For nineteenth-century anarchist-communists this condition could be achieved if the local commune were regarded as the basic unit of social organization. Enjoying complete autonomy with regard to its internal affairs, it would be linked on a federal basis with other communes at the regional, national, and supra-national levels for the administration of business involving relations with other communes. For the Sarvodayites the village would be the basic unit. Each village would constitute a miniature republic and be linked with other villages, as Gandhi put it, not in a pyramidal fashion 'with the apex sustained by the bottom'. Rather the structure will be

an oceanic circle whose centre will be the individual always ready to perish for the village, the latter ready to perish for the circle of villages, till at last the whole becomes one life composed of individuals, never aggressive in their arrogance but ever humble, sharing the majesty of the oceanic circle of which they are integral units. Therefore, the outermost circumference will not wield power to crush the inner circle but will give strength to all within and derive its strength from it.[1]

Such a decentralized polity implies a decentralized economy. Large-scale industry and its concentration in vast megapolitan centres is to be avoided or reduced to the absolute minimum. Industries are to be brought to the villages, so that it will be pos-

[1] M. K. Gandhi, *Sarvodaya*, 1954, pp. 70–1.

THE IDEOLOGY OF SARVODAYA

sible for a village, or group of villages, to constitute an agro-
industrial community practically self-sufficient in respect of the
basic needs of its inhabitants. The present generation of Sarvodayites, like most nineteenth-century anarchists, do not see economic
decentralization as an attempt to put back the clock. Less am-
biguously than Gandhi, Vinoba does not reject modern technology
as such. On the contrary, like Kropotkin, he welcomes it as a
means of avoiding drudgery and increasing production: he insists
only that technology should be humanized and applied for the
welfare of all instead of being used to bolster a system of social
exploitation.

In working for their goals, the Sarvodayites join with the
classical anarchists in condemning orthodox political action. No
good service can be rendered by the state. 'My voice', says Vinoba,
'is raised in opposition to good government. Bad government has
been condemned long ago by Vyasa in the Mahabharata. People
know very well that bad government should not be allowed, and
everywhere protest against it. But what seems to me to be wrong
is that we should allow ourselves to be governed at all, even by a
good government.'[1] Those who seek political power, even for
beneficent ends, will inevitably be corrupted. The seat of power,
argues Vinoba, casts a magic spell over those who occupy it. 'If
instead of those at present occupying it, we were to occupy it, we
would do things very similar to what they are doing. The seat of
power is such. Whoever sits on it becomes narrow in outlook.'[2]

Parliamentary democracy stands condemned for several reasons.
Despite the institution of popular elections, it does not really
result in state policy being guided by public opinion. It involves
also the principle of majority rule which in practice may mean the
tyranny of the majority over the minority, not the welfare of all.
For the Sarvodayites, decisions consistent with the latter can be
reached only by adherence to the principle of unanimity which compels the search for a consensus. Again, parliamentary democracy
involves political parties which are divisive forces, and seek power
by hook or by crook, by vilification of their opponents, and by
bribes and threats. 'Difference of views is a healthy sign', says
Vinoba, 'and I regard it as necessary and inevitable. But when
parties are formed on the basis of different views, they are less

[1] Vinoba, op. cit., pp. 12–13.
[2] Quoted in Doctor, op. cit., pp. 57–8.

concerned with ideology than with organization, discipline and propaganda. The party is an instrument for attaining political power. And power predominates while ideas become mere convenient trade-marks used for power and political rivalry.'[1]

In place of orthodox political action, the Sarvodayites, like the anarchists, advocate direct action by the people themselves. The politics of the power-state, Raj-niti, must be replaced by the politics of the people, Lok-niti. The former involves conflict and competition, the jostling and struggling of élites, the conciliation and containing of sectional interests, the exercise of pressures, the striking of bargains, and playing the well-worn party game. Lok-niti, in contrast, involves an attempt to make the people aware of their own inner strength and encourage them to solve problems for themselves. Explaining the distinction, Vinoba points out: 'It is just this strengthening of society that is the object of the Bhoodan movement. It is therefore a political movement, but one that is opposed to current political methods. Our aim is to build up a new kind of politics, and in order to do so we keep ourselves aloof from the old kind.'[2]

It was this 'new kind of politics' which attracted to the movement in 1952 the outstanding leader of the Indian socialists, Jayaprakash Narayan. In his essay *From Socialism to Sarvodaya* Jayaprakash explained the reasons that led him to take this step.

I decided to withdraw from party-and-power politics not because of disgust or sense of any personal frustration, but because it became clear to me that politics could not deliver the goods, the goods being the same old goals of equality, freedom, brotherhood, peace. . . . The politics of Sarvodaya can have no party and no concern with power. Rather its aim will be to see that all centres of power are abolished. The more this new politics grows the more the old politics shrinks. A real withering away of the state![3]

The strategy of 'the new politics' is based on the belief that 'revolutions are never achieved by power or party politics'.[4] The Sarvodaya revolution, like the anarchist revolution, can be made only from below, not from above. The Sarvodaya workers do not constitute a revolutionary party appealing to the people for support

---

[1] Quoted in Suresh Ram, *Vinoba and His Mission*, 3rd edn., 1962, p. 385.
[2] Vinoba, op. cit., p. 56.
[3] Jayaprakash Narayan, *Socialism, Sarvodaya and Democracy*, 1964, p. 156 & pp. 170–1.   [4] Vinoba, op. cit., p. 86.

and promising to usher in the millennium. They exist only to give help and advice: the people themselves must take the initiative and work out their own salvation.

If, thus, Sarvodaya shares much common ground with classical anarchism of the West, there are nevertheless important areas of disagreement. For an understanding of the movement the contrasts are perhaps even more illuminating.

The most obvious difference is the Sarvodaya attitude to religion. Of the great anarchist thinkers discussed by Eltzbacher[1] and Woodcock, only one, Leo Tolstoy, based his anarchism on religious foundations.[2] Many, perhaps the majority, of Western anarchists have followed Bakunin in coupling God and the State, and rejecting both for the same reason: their denial of the sovereignty of the individual. In the West, atheism and anarchism appear as natural bedfellows, the twin off-spring of Protestantism when taken to its logical conclusion. Sarvodaya anarchism, however, is fundamentally religious. An unshakable faith in God and an insistence on the primacy of spirit constitute the core of the philosophy of most, though, as we shall see, not all Sarvodayites. However, it is important to note the catholicity of their religious opinions. Gandhi and Vinoba are Hindus, but they claim no special status for the Hindu religion: all religions are merely different ways of finding God. Moreover, according to Gandhi, even the sincere atheist may qualify as a religious man. If the atheist subscribes to a 'belief in the ordered moral government of the universe',[3] then, despite his denial of God, he has the essence of religion in him. As if to make it easier for those who boggle at metaphysics, Gandhi reversed the familiar equation and asserted 'Truth is God'—adding that this was the most perfect definition of God so far as human speech could go.[4]

Clearly for the Sarvodayites the importance of religion lies in its buttressing of the belief in an objective moral order. Belief in God they see as ruling out ethical relativism; and moral injunctions, therefore, take on the character of absolutes. This ethical absolutism provides a further contrast with most Western anarchists who,

---

[1] P. Eltzbacher, *Anarchism*, 1960.

[2] There was, however, a strong anarchist strain in the thought of the seventeenth-century religious sect, the Diggers. See Woodcock, op. cit., p. 42. And, more generally, Christianity has influenced the ideas which have given force to anarchism in the West.

[3] *Harijan*, 10 Feb. 1940.   [4] Dhawan, op. cit., p. 42.

like Godwin and Kropotkin, have attempted to provide rational and naturalistic foundations for their ethical codes. The consequences of this different approach to ethics are vividly apparent in respect of the central moral principle of Sarvodaya, Non-violence. For the Sarvodayites, Non-violence is not something one argues for or against: it is something one either accepts or rejects. It is not, most certainly, a matter for utilitarian consideration. In this connection, we may note Gandhi's distinction between passive resistance and satyagraha. The former is a technique which may be, and often has been, used by those who do not rule out the use of violence in certain circumstances. Its use may be dictated by the fact that the resisters have no other equally effective means of resistance at their disposal. This kind of Non-violence Gandhi regarded as the Non-violence of the weak. Satyagraha, in contrast, is the Non-violence of the strong, adopted because it is felt to be the only morally right course of action: it would be used even when the resisters had superior physical force on their side. Relatively few Western anarchists even now, despite the sorry history of the use of violence by some anarchists in the past, would be prepared to accept Non-violence as an absolute moral injunction—although many might be prepared to admit the futility of 'offensive' as distinct from 'defensive' violence. Even most pacifist anarchists would argue that they can see no circumstances in which the use of violence would be justified. This is very different in theory, if not in practice, from accepting Non-violence as a categorical imperative. The latter, though not the former, involves a willingness to suspend the rational mode of thinking in terms of cause and consequence, the mode which now dominates the Western mind.

To complicate the matter still further, the Sarvodayites combine an absolute commitment to Non-violence with a flexibility which, on occasions, even to Western sympathisers, appears to be outrageously inconsistent. In part, this flexibility stems from Gandhi's insistence that absolute truth cannot be known to the as yet unfulfilled human mind. A human being, however good, can arrive only at relative truth. Since Non-violence is deemed to be *the* way to Truth, it follows that no human being can ever achieve perfect Non-violence: a person is always more or less non-violent; the ideal is achieved only in death. Combined with the premise of an evolutionary tendency towards Non-violence which is unevenly distributed among mankind, this leads to the conclusion that non-violent resistance, in the Gandhian sense, is not always possible as a practical collective policy. It was not possible, for example, so many Sarvodayites believed, in the Sino-Indian border war of 1962 because the Indian people, for all Gandhi's and Vinoba's efforts, were not strong enough to adopt ahimsa. And, since genuine ahimsa is a doctrine of the strong, and even violence is preferable to Non-violence adopted for cowardly reasons[1], armed resistance was justifiable, although of course the Sarvodayites themselves could not participate in it.

This kind of reasoning leads to a further difference between Sarvodaya and mainstream Western anarchism. The latter is predicated on the assumption not only that it is possible for men to live an ordered existence without the state but that it is possible for them to do so *now*. In its extreme form, this assumption finds expression in the Bakuninite theory of spontaneous revolution, according to which the masses, inspired by the heroic endeavours of dedicated revolutionaries, would shortly rise to throw off, once and for all, the artificial chains of the state. Today some Western anarchists are prepared to countenance 'gradualism', but usually only *faute de mieux*, in the absence of a 'revolutionary situation'. The Sarvodayites, however, are convinced 'gradualists': they see the anarchist goal in much the same way as Godwin did, as something to be reached only after men have become more perfect than they are now. This position, known in the West as 'philosophic anarchism', partly explains the apparent inconsistencies of Sarvodayites towards the institution of government.[2] Until all men, or at least a large proportion of them, are fit for non-governmental society, government, as a matter of fact, will continue to exist.

[1] Gandhi frequently insisted that violent resistance was preferable to cowardice. 'My creed of non-violence is an extremely active force. It has no room for cowardice or even weakness. There is hope for a violent man to be some day non-violent, but there is none for a coward. I have therefore said more than once in these pages that if we do not know how to defend ourselves, our women and our places of worship by the force of suffering, i.e. non-violence, we must, if we are men, be at least able to defend all these by fighting.'—*Young India*, 16 June 1927, p. 196.

[2] Krimerman and Perry argue that the disagreement between immediatist and gradualist anarchists is not merely factual: are men now ready for complete anarchy or not? The gradualist proceeds 'to act on the assumption that one can decide for another which goals he is qualified to seek'; and this is 'to govern'. Consequently, 'the gradualist position lends itself to the perpetuation of authority.'—L. I. Krimerman & L. Perry, *Patterns of Anarchy*, 1966, p. 556.

In this situation, it seems reasonable to accept the best government of which society is presently capable. For Sarvodayites this means at least a democratic government, with all its faults. Vinoba's gradualism is apparent in his visualization of three distinct stages of political development: first, a free (i.e. independent) central government; second, the decentralized self-governing state; and third, pure anarchy, or freedom from all government.[1] With political independence, India entered the first stage; and with the introduction of Panchayati Raj (local self-government) institutions, it is proceeding into the second stage. Sarvodaya political proposals, including the furtherance of partyless democracy, are conceived as contributing to the development of this second stage.

Elaborating the Sarvodaya theory of government, Vinoba writes:

We have before us three different theories of government. The first is that the state will ultimately wither away and be transformed into a stateless system; but in order to bring that about, we must in the present exercise the maximum of power. Those who accept this theory are totalitarians in the first stage and anarchists in the final stage. The second theory is that some form of government has always existed in the past, exists now, and will continue to exist in the future; a society without a government is a sheer impossibility. . . . There may be a certain amount of decentralization, but all important matters must be under the Centre. . . . The third is our own theory. We too believe in a stateless society as our ultimate goal. We recognize that in the preliminary stages a certain measure of government is necessary, but we do not agree that it will continue to be necessary at a later stage. Neither do we agree that totalitarian dictatorship is necessary to ensure progress towards a stateless society. On the contrary we propose to proceed by decentralizing administration and authority. In the final stage there would be no coercion but a purely moral authority. The establishment of such a self-directing society calls for a net-work of self-sufficient units. Production, distribution, defence, education—everything should be localized. The centre should have the least possible authority.[2]

In the Sarvodaya view, therefore, the stateless society will develop to the extent that the people become more self-reliant and create new self-governing institutions. There is thus to be no direct frontal attack on the state, but a progression from free central government through the decentralized self-governing state to the condition of pure anarchy. This view is different from that of

[1] Doctor, op. cit., p. 65.   [2] Vinoba, op. cit., pp. 29–30.

THE IDEOLOGY OF SARVODAYA

both classical anarchism and Marxism. Like the Marxists and unlike the anarchists, the Sarvodayites believe that the state will—under certain conditions—wither away rather than be abolished; but like the anarchists and unlike the Marxists, they believe that action must be taken *now* to dispense with the institution of ultimate and organized violence.

At a deeper level, however, the suggestion of stages of development disappears in the Sarvodaya theory of social action. This is a consequence of the Gandhian rejection of the means-end dichotomy which underlies most Western patterns of thought. For the Gandhian, means and end are part of a continuous process, and are morally indistinguishable. Put in another way, means are never merely instrumental: they are always end-creating. What is regarded as the objective is conceptually only a starting-point: the end can never be predicted and must necessarily be left open. All that is certain is that from immoral or even amoral 'means', no moral 'end' can result.[1] Applying this philosophy of action to the point under discussion—the ultimate goal of a stateless society—the fusion of means and end implies that there is no transition period, or, what amounts to the same thing, every period is one of transition. With Truth and Non-violence as both the means and the end, the Gandhian acts *now* according to these principles, as far as he is able, and thereby achieves the goal he is striving for. For him, as for Bernstein and Sorel, 'The movement is everything; the final goal is nothing.' The Sarvodaya 'utopia', one might say, is not something to be realized in the distant future: it is something men begin to achieve here and now. The important thing is not to 'arrive' at utopia: it is to make a serious attempt to travel in that direction. And this can be done only by men behaving *now* in the way they want people in utopia to behave: truthfully, lovingly, compassionately. Such a utopia, one might suggest, is not really a goal at all: it is a convenient way of thinking about, ordering, systematizing, and concretizing one's values, a guide not to the future but to *present* activity.

Commitment to such a philosophy of action helps to account for yet a further difference between Sarvodaya and Western anarchism.

---

[1] For an illuminating discussion of Gandhi's views on the means-end question, and its importance for social theory, see Bondurant, op. cit., Ch. VI. See also R. N. Iyer in G. Ramachandran & T. K. Mahadevan, *Gandhi, his Relevance for Our Times*, 1964.

It would be incorrect to say that Western anarchists have shown no interest in constructive activity. There have been persistent attempts to develop anarchist co-operatives and communities, while the anarcho-syndicalists believed that in building their trade unions the workers were constructing the social organization of the new society. But, in the main, Western anarchism has been content to echo Bakunin's famous dictum: 'Destruction is itself a form of creation!' In historical retrospect, classical anarchism—including syndicalism, now that the unions have proved broken reeds in the revolutionaries' hands—appears essentially as a movement of protest: a protest against the whole social and political structure of modern industrial society. The Sarvodayites, in contrast, have never been content with mere protest. With their emphasis on the Constructive Programme, 'Be ye also do-ers of the word!' has always been their text.

One particular item in Gandhi's Constructive Programme, prohibition, points to another difference between Sarvodaya and Western anarchism: the former's severely ascetic character. Western anarchism has its intellectual roots in the puritan tradition and has always had its 'simple lifers'. Indeed, from one perspective, all anarchism may be seen as a plea for the radical simplification of life—a plea symbolized in a bureaucratic world by the passionate slogan: 'Incinerate the documents!' But the asceticism of Indian anarchism extends far beyond anything found in the West. The loin-clad figure, carrying all his worldly possessions in a small bundle and without a penny in his purse, is the Indian ideal. The ascetic, puritanical character of Sarvodaya anarchism is manifest in the ethical principles enunciated by Gandhi as necessary for self-realization. Besides Satya and Ahimsa, these include: Brahmacharya, which involves not merely celibacy or sexual restraint but complete control over the senses; Aswad, or tastelessness, which implies looking upon food and drink as a kind of medicine, to be taken only in the limited quantities necessary to maintain the body; Aparigraha, or non-possession; Asteya, or non-stealing, which is related to non-possession, since it involves refraining from taking anything of which we have no real need, not merely that which does not belong to us; Fearlessness; Removal of Untouchability; Bread Labour; Religious Tolerance; and Swadeshi, literally 'belonging to one's own country', but defined by Gandhi as 'that spirit in us which restricts us to the use and service of our immediate surroundings to the exclusion of the more remote'.[1] The free and easy bohemian relations that tend to characterize anarchist circles in the West, and especially an emphasis on sexual freedom, find no echoes in Indian anarchism.

Finally, in their strategies of revolution there are significant differences between Sarvodaya and mainstream Western anarchism.[2] The Sarvodayites see the revolution as in essence a revaluation of values. The first step in the revolution is to convert individuals, if possible on a mass scale, to the new point of view by appealing to both their intellect and their emotions. The new values chosen for emphasis are those which have a direct bearing on some major social problem, such as the plight of the landless labourers, so that their acceptance and practice are likely to lead to radical social change. As with Tolstoy, the revolution takes place as a result of individuals beginning here and now to live the values of the new society, the process others have called the 'one-man revolution'.[3] Since the new values are difficult to practise, a phased programme is contrived, so that ordinary men are able to advance by relatively easy steps towards the new society. Gradually, through co-operative effort, the people proceed to create new institutions and new forms of social life. The theory is a theory of social change, and not merely, like Moral Rearmament, for example, a plea for individual regeneration. It does involve changing the social structure in a radical fashion. If the Sarvodayites appear to place greater emphasis on transforming individuals than on changing the social structure, it is because they insist that it is individuals who start the process of revolution, and because they believe that the desired social structure can be achieved and maintained only by individuals who are adequately developed morally. They recognize, however, that if the new thought does not meet a favourable situation it remains confined to a narrow circle: it spreads to the masses only if the times are propitious. In seeking the conversion of individuals to the new values, the Sarvodayites direct their appeal to all men and women, without discrimination by sex, caste, creed, or class.

In comparison with classical anarchism (and, of course, with Marxism), it is the absence of any appeal to class which most

---

[1] Quoted in Dhawan, op. cit., p. 93. See also Tandon, op. cit., Chs. III–V.
[2] See Jayaprakash Narayan, op. cit., pp. 165–70, and Tandon, op. cit., Ch. V.
[3] See Ammon Hennacy, *The Autobiography of a Catholic Anarchist*, 1954.

distinguishes the Sarvodaya strategy of revolution. In the West anarchism as an organized social movement developed in part on the basis of a critique of the Marxist strategy of revolution. From a narrow perspective, the anarchism of Bakunin, Kropotkin, and the syndicalists may be seen as a form of deviation from Marxism. Classical anarchism has much in common with Marxism, especially in its analysis of capitalist society. Anarchists, other than the syndicalists, have not assigned to the industrial proletariat the central role assigned to it by (Western) Marxists, but they have always directed their revolutionary appeal primarily to the oppressed and the dispossessed. They have not expected to enlist the oppressors, the powerful, and the privileged in the cause of revolution.

The Sarvodaya rejection of class appeal and any form of class struggle rests on the explicit belief that the 'real' interests of any individual, or groups of individuals, are never in conflict with those of the rest of mankind.[1] In this respect (as well as in others) Sarvodaya anarchism is more akin to the so-called 'utopian social-ism' of the British Owenite co-operative movement. Sarvodaya, like Owenism, sees itself as essentially a universalistic movement. In its activities it finds itself concerned to improve the lot of par-ticular social groups—especially 'the low, the lost, the last, and the least'—but, in principle, it espouses no interest less than that of the whole of mankind. Put in another way, Sarvodaya sees itself as the true philosophy for all mankind, and 'the Sarvodaya society' will be achieved as and when all men begin to practise this philosophy

---

[1] 'Sarvodaya means that the good of all resides in the good of one. That there could be interests of one person, which are against the interests of another, is inconceivable. Similarly, there could be no interests of any one community, class or country which would be against the interests of any other community, class or country. The idea of opposition of interests is itself wrong.'—Vinoba Bhave, *Revolutionary Sarvodaya*, 1964, p. 2. The logical status of this belief in 'the natural harmony of interests' is that of a presupposition. It is not disproved by pointing to patent conflicts of *social* interests, since these are held to be rooted in what Godwin called 'positive institutions', such as private property, which can and should be changed. Western thought of the pluralist school makes a contrary presupposition. But any notion of 'the natural *dis*harmony of interests' is, despite appearances, no more empirical than its opposite. For the Sarvodaya presupposition this much may be said: it may encourage men not to accept conflict as inevitable (a socially conservative stance), but to search for the causes and conditions of conflict as a prelude to removing them. In the atmosphere of what Sorokin called 'our Sensate culture' many people today find it difficult to accept the Sarvodaya belief. See P. A. Sorokin, *The Ways and Power of Love*, 1954, pp. 47-8.

in their daily lives. The success of its non-violent revolution is to be measured by the extent to which Sarvodaya ceases to be a separate movement and liquidates itself in such a way that 'movement' and 'society' are no longer distinguishable.

III. THE LEADERS' PERCEPTIONS OF THE MOVEMENT'S GOALS

In outlining the content of Sarvodaya ideology, comparing and contrasting it with Western anarchism, we have drawn principally on literary sources. However, from our survey we have additional information about the movement's ideology. From answers to the open-ended question: 'How would you describe briefly the goal or purpose of the Sarvodaya Movement?' we can determine how the leaders themselves perceive the goals of the movement.

Inspection of the answers confirms our judgement that, in Smelser's terminology, Sarvodaya is a value- rather than a norm-oriented movement. The answers abound with statements of generalized value-oriented beliefs. Norm-oriented beliefs also occurred, but only the occasional respondent answered the question wholly in norm-oriented terms. As an example of this rare type of response, we may quote the reply of a nominated member of the Sangh: 'Sarvodaya means wearing of Khadi. Use only articles produced by village industries. Service of the cow and use of its milk and other milk products.'

A full savouring of the responses may be obtained from the following answers, which are quoted verbatim. A District Representative:

To solve the land problem on the basis of Truth and Non-violence. To change the social, economical and moral values in India and in the world through non-violent means.

A Secretary of a State Sarvodaya Mandal:

Equal chance for all, especially to the last should be given. As far as the land question is concerned, land should be made the common property of the village concerned and in possession of the tiller until he or his progeny is so. Above all the caste system should be eradicated. To me, this should be the chief aim and purpose of the movement because in India nothing, however divine it may be, will flourish until and unless the caste system dies.

A member of the Prabandh Samiti:

The Sarvodaya movement is the courier of a Bhoodan-based and village industry-centred non-violent revolution. I personally feel that all programmes aimed at the weaker sections also lead toward realization of Sarvodaya. That political power (Raja-niti) should be subservient to people's power (Loka-niti), that elections should be held on the basis of unanimity and common consensus, that State funds should mostly be spent for the good of the weaker sections, and that suitable legislation should be enacted for the purpose enumerated above—all these measures would lead in the direction of Sarvodaya.

A Representative:

The movement represents the model of a stateless, exploitation-free, decentralized social order. It strives to work in the direction of location of 'village republics'. Gramdan represents the medium of bringing about 'Gramswarajya' (village self-government). Like the U.S.S.R., the Sarvodaya movement seeks to build up a U.S.V.R. (Union of Sarvodaya Village Republics of India). Sarvodaya also seeks to achieve democratic socialism which will end exploitation and promote kinship among individuals and thus achieve national unity as well. Thus it aims at abolishing all sorts of sectarian feelings, abolishing all sorts of exploitation, changing the social values and reconstruction of the economy.

A District Convenor:

The object of the Sarvodaya movement is to create a stateless and classless society, through non-violent means, in which there will be no exploitation by man and man, and where there will be no classes of rich and have-nots. In which every individual will have freedom of expression and adopt any profession, and of residing anywhere he likes. Where there will not be any kind of hatred among the different religious peoples on the basis of religion; and where all people of different religions respect their own religions as well as pay equal respect towards the other religions. Where every person will work according to his capacity and voluntarily give the rest of his income for the welfare of the others.

A Convenor:

The goal of the Sarvodaya movement is as follows: 1. International: one world without war, disarmament. 2. National: economic equality and political democracy. 3. Economic: abolition of private property. 4. Political: partyless decentralized democracy. 5. Social: classless society; inter-caste marriage. 6. Cultural: culture of man; art for life. 7. Education: all round development. 8. Personality: science and self-knowledge.

A Samiti member:

The goal of the Sarvodaya movement is to change the heart of man, in order to enable him to be uplifted, lessening the selfishness in him to the lowest degree.

A Convenor:

1. That God's spirit resides in all beings and that man has to dedicate his entire being to the service of God, by serving human beings.
2. Social ownership of all means of production—land, factories, etc.
3. Familial organization in all productive organizations.

It will be seen that, although these answers have much in common, there are differences of emphasis. With this in mind, the answers were coded as falling within one or more of the following six categories, according to whether or not mention was made of a particular kind of value: political, economic, social, moral and religious, non-violence, and universal. Since the question was open-ended, it was assumed that respondents would mention those kinds of value which they personally regarded as the more important value-goals of the movement.

There is, of course, an element of artificiality in distinguishing our six kinds of value. Political, economic, and social values, in particular, are not easily distinguishable. To illustrate our coding procedure, we may therefore consider each kind of value in turn, quoting examples of the main recurring phrases which we classified as political, economic, etc.

1. *Political*

This category includes answers which emphasize the role of the village as the basic unit of a new decentralized stateless social order. Typical phrases include: 'no state power', 'no military', 'stateless society', 'partyless democracy', 'Gramswarajya', 'freedom from state coercion', 'replacement of Raj-niti by Lok-niti', 'unanimity and consensus' in elections.

2. *Economic*

Answers in this category emphasize the solution of the land

problem through Gramdan, the development of village industries, agro-industrial communities, the provision for all of basic economic needs such as food, clothing, shelter, and employment, and the application of the Gandhian concept of trusteeship to property. Typical phrases used include: 'rejuvenating the countryside by having Gramdans in all villages', 'spread of Khadi and village industries', 'trusteeship of privately owned properties', 'abolition of poverty', 'provision of basic necessities of life for everyone', 'removing unemployment', 'equal opportunities of prosperity', and 'economic equality'.

3 Social

In this category are included answers emphasizing the abolition of caste and class differences, the establishment of social equality, and the ending of exploitation of man by man. Among the phrases used are: 'classless society', 'eradication of the caste system', 'removal of all forms of exploitation', 'equal opportunities for all', 'all property belongs to God, so we are all brothers and have equal claims to land and other properties', 'equalitarian society', and 'a familistic pattern of society, divided into communities with face to face relationships'.

4. Moral and religious

This category includes those answers which stress the moral development of individuals, the spread of the values of truth, love, and compassion, and religious values. Phrases used include: 'spiritual advancement in line with the growth of science for the harmonious development of human growth', 'to promote spirituality and direct the human mind on right lines', 'to raise humanity to a self-less status, i.e. towards godliness in all aspects of life', 'living for others as well as for oneself', 'to change the heart of man', 'removal of religious sectarianism', 'full development of each individual personality', and 'liberating man from all bindings to attain the spiritual prosperous life through the scientific progress'.

5. Non-violence

Answers coded in this category were those which explicitly mentioned the movement's commitment to the principle of Non-violence. Typical phrases used include: 'non-violent revolution', 'through non-violent means', 'on the basis of non-violence', 'a non-violent society', and 'by love and non-violence'.

6. *Universal*

Coded in this category were all answers which indicated that the goals of the movement are not restricted to India but have a universal or world-wide significance. Among the phrases used are: 'a world commonwealth of free peoples', 'creation of a world family', 'universal peace and brotherhood with an understanding of co-existence, non-interference, and mutual toleration', 'a world social order', 'the well-being of all beginning from a single person up to the vast universe', 'to change the social, economical and moral values in India and in the world', 'setting an example for the world at large', 'to make the world rural-minded', and 'a non-violent social order . . . beginning from the village as the basic unit till the world community at large'.

The following table presents the distribution of the leaders' answers between the six types of value-goal. It will be noted that

TABLE 2:1

Types of value-goal mentioned by Sarvodaya leaders

	%
Social	62
Economic	39
Political	33
Moral and religious	33
Non-violence	32
Universal	21
(N = 228)	

most respondents mentioned more than one type of goal. In interpreting the table it should be borne in mind that the non-inclusion of an answer in any particular category does *not* imply that the respondent did not believe in that kind of value. It may be safely assumed, for example, that *all* respondents valued Non-violence. Nevertheless, when given the opportunity, only one-third of them saw fit to mention this value explicitly. From this it may be inferred only that some respondents valued Non-violence more highly than others.

The interest of the table centres on the frequency of mention by the leaders of the various types of value-goal. The most popular 'choice' of social values is not really surprising. These values are not exclusive to Sarvodaya, but are widely shared by socialists and Communists. Our finding helps to confirm, if such a confirmation is necessary, that Sarvodaya is a form of socialism and is supported as such by a majority of the leaders. Certain values in the economic category are also not exclusive to Sarvodaya, but some of them, such as the development of village industries, are. We might reasonably expect, therefore, that economic values would be less frequently mentioned than the social. The political values are, in the Indian context, largely exclusive to Sarvodaya, although there is some support in Congress and elsewhere for partyless democracy at the local level. This may account for the relative lack of emphasis on political values. But it is also possible, indeed likely, that not all the leaders whole-heartedly subscribe to Sarvodaya political values, which, in any case, have been made more explicit only in recent years. Some of these values, notably the anarchist value of a stateless society, are most readily open to the charge of being 'utopian'.

The relatively low ranking of moral and religious values compared with social values may suggest that most leaders do not 'balance' individual and social change in the way we have stated above that the strategy of the movement demands. In other words, the leaders are more interested in social than in individual change. Nevertheless, 'balanced' or not, the emphasis on individual moral and religious regeneration is still marked.

In the Indian context, Non-violence is widely regarded as a distinctively Gandhian value. It is perhaps somewhat surprising that only 32 per cent mentioned it explicitly. It is possible, however, that in this case it was taken so much for granted that the majority felt no necessity to mention it. Smelser has argued, 'Because of the hostile component in the beliefs of all value-oriented movements, the *potential* for violence is always present in such movements.'[1] Common sense would suggest that any such potential is minimal in the case of the Sarvodaya movement. But, if it does exist, it may be that it is stronger among those who did not explicitly mention Non-violence as a value.

Finally, the proportion mentioning universal values is relatively small, but, in the absence of comparable data on other social and political movements, the fact that one in five of the leaders referred

---

[1] N. Smelser, *Theory of Collective Behaviour*, 1962, p. 319.

to them is worthy of comment. The movement, of course, has always focused on the situation in India, and its universal implications have been stressed only in recent years. A notable symbolic step in this direction was the dropping in 1963 of the words Akhil Bharat (All India) in the title of Sarva Seva Sangh. Socialists and Communists also espouse universal values, but we doubt whether a survey of leaders of most contemporary Socialist and Communist parties would reveal such a high proportion of them explicitly mentioning universal values in statements of their parties' goals. To our knowledge, there is no Socialist or Communist leader who regularly concludes his speeches with a slogan comparable to the mantra used by Vinoba: Jai Jagat! (Victory to the World!) The frequency of the mention of universal values is also worth pointing out to those who uncritically assume that the espousal of the localistic ideal of village republics is inconsistent with a universalistic outlook.

IV. THE PROGRAMME OF THE MOVEMENT

The programme of a movement may be defined as a statement of the more or less definite procedures it advocates for getting its values expressed in social organization.[1] The Sarvodaya movement's current programme focuses on three well-defined procedures: the establishment of Gramdan, the development of Khadi (by which, in this context, may be understood all village industries as well as the production of hand-spun, hand-woven cloth), and the building up of the Shanti Sena. At the Sarvodaya Sammelan (annual conference) held at Raipur in December 1963 these three items were linked together and labelled 'The Triple Programme'. And the call went out from the conference for a vigorous nation-wide drive to implement this integrated programme. However, there are several other items which may be regarded as part of the movement's programme. These include: the development of Gandhian Basic Education; the full implementation of prohibition; the promotion of animal welfare, particularly 'cow service'; and other items of Gandhi's original Constructive Programme. In addition, individual Sarvodaya

[1] cf. R. H. Turner & L. M. Killian, *Collective Behavior*, 1957, p. 332. In Smelser's terminology, programmes are norms designed to realize more general values.

workers, or groups of them, may promote items which they regard as particularly important, such as nature cure and a 'shrinking currency'—the latter being the 'fad' of one notable zealot.[1] The only qualification for the inclusion of such additional items is that they should be consistent with Sarvodaya values. However, Vinoba is noted for his single-mindedness, and he has frequently called on the workers to concentrate their efforts on the items of The Triple Programme. These items, therefore, must be regarded as of special significance and require extended discussion.

Gramdan

In its Bhoodan campaign the movement asked landowners to donate one-sixth of their land for redistribution to landless labourers. The concept of Gramdan grew naturally out of Bhoodan as a consequence, so to speak, of 'over-subscription' by the land-owners of a village. The first village to 'over-subscribe' to such an extent as to change Bhoodan into Gramdan was Mangroth in Uttar Pradesh. In May 1952, when the event occurred, Mangroth had a population of 585, consisting of 105 families of various castes, of whom 65 owned land while 40 were landless. The largest land-owner, the head man of the village, was Diwan Shatrughana Singh. His decision to donate all his land in Bhoodan inspired the other landowners in the village, excepting one small-holder (but includ-ing the second largest landowner, who lived in another village), to do likewise. The land so given was vested in the village community, and subsequently redistributed among the villagers in amounts which varied with each family's capacity and need. Diwan Singh, who had given 100 acres, received back 40 acres and joined with 32 Harijan families in forming a co-operative farm. The remaining 71 families preferred to continue farming as separate units.

Mangroth's example set the pattern for other villages, but in the early years of the new campaign there was no clear definition of what constituted a Gramdan village. Ideally, it was a village in which all the landowners had agreed to pool the ownership of their lands in a village, vesting them in the village community in such a way that the villagers as a whole—the landless as well as the former landowners—became the collective proprietor. In the Koraput District of Orissa, among the tribal villages, this ideal was often realized, although landowners living outside a village frequently

---

[1] Appa Patwardhan, *A Plea for Shrinking Currency*, 1963.

refused to participate. In other areas, the proportions of both land given and owners participating varied considerably.

Following a conference between representatives of the movement and representatives of the Union Government and Congress, and other party leaders, at Yelwal in Mysore State in 1957, the Planning Commission set up a working group to review the legal, organizational, and administrative issues arising from Gramdan. From the deliberations of the group emerged a draft Gramdan Bill which, if adopted, would provide a legal framework for the constitution and management of Gramdan villages.[1] The provisions of the Bill clarified the concept of Gramdan. Among the suggested provisions were the following:

(i) Any person holding land directly under Government and any tenant enjoying permanent rights might join Gramdan. In either case the person joining must donate his entire land. A landless person living in the village might also join by making a declaration of his desire to participate in the Gramdan community.

(ii) A village could be declared Gramdan if it met the following conditions: (a) Gramdan declarations must be confirmed in respect of 50 per cent of the total land held under private ownership in the village; (b) not less than 80 per cent of the total number of persons owning land and residing in the village must join; and (c) not less than 80 per cent of the adults living in the village must also join. (iii) For the purpose of Gramdan, a village might be defined more broadly than the concept of the 'revenue village', the familiar administrative unit. Thus, a hamlet (tola or para) of a revenue village could be treated as a unit and regarded as a Gramdan village if it met the above conditions.

(iv) The land donated in Gramdan should be vested in the Gram Sabha, a corporate body representing the village community and consisting of all adult residents and persons owning land in the village. Villagers not joining in Gramdan would retain all their rights in their land, but would, nevertheless, be entitled to participate fully in the deliberations and the management of village land and properties as members of the Gram Sabha.

(v) The lands vested in the Gram Sabha might be cultivated directly by the Sabha itself or might be allotted to the residents, including both donors and the landless, either singly or jointly, on such terms as the Sabha might determine. Where individual allotments were made, the allottees were not to have heritable or transferable interests in the

[1] *Gramdan Movement*, Planning Commission, 1964, pp. 9–11. See under India, Government of, in Bibliography.

land, so that periodical redistribution of lands on an equitable basis
would not be impeded.

(vi) In addition to managing the lands vested in it, the Gram Sabha
would undertake development functions, as well as the administrative
functions normally performed by village panchayats (councils) in the
area.

(vii) In the management of lands and village affairs the decisions of the
Gram Sabha should, as far as possible, be based on unanimity or near-
unanimity.

A draft Bill incorporating the suggestions of the working group
was forwarded to all State Governments for adoption. Nine State
Legislatures subsequently passed a Gramdan Bill or amended
existing Bhoodan Acts to incorporate the suggestions.[1] Such
legislation usually contains provision for the verification of Gramdans by the State Government. Verification, however, has proved
a lengthy and complicated procedure. Most of the villages included
in the movement's statistics of Gramdan declarations have not yet
been verified. By January 1965, for example, only 120 of the then
960 Gramdans in Assam had been verified and listed in the State
Government's Gazette.[2]

One of the major problems of the concept of Gramdan outlined
above centred upon the question of the redistribution of the village
land. The intention was to achieve equality or equity as far as
possible. But it soon became apparent that, in many villages,
although participants were prepared to surrender ownership of
their entire holdings and also to part with possession of a portion
of their holdings, they were reluctant to accept that degree of
equality which the redistribution of the entire land would have
involved. Consequently, in practice, equalitarian redistribution
was rare. It also became apparent that the owners of larger holdings were reluctant to participate. Since the success of the move-

---

[1] The States of Bihar, Madras, Maharashtra, and Orissa have Gramdan Acts;
Andhra, Assam, Gujarat, Rajasthan, and West Bengal have amended their
original Bhoodan Acts.

[2] Sarva Seva Sangh, *Notes on Agenda for the meeting of the National Advisory
Committee for collaboration with Akhil Bharat Sarva Seva Sangh to be held at
New Delhi, 22nd January 1965.* Of the 8,160 villages that have joined Gramdan
in the Purnea District of Bihar, only 33, by early 1969, had been formally
declared under the Gramdan Act. Another 88 villages had been confirmed by
the authorities, but their formal declaration was pending.—*Sarva Seva Sangh
Monthly News Letter*, 3, 3 (Mar. 1969), p. 9.

THE IDEOLOGY OF SARVODAYA

ment depended on allaying the fears of such owners and on persuading them that the movement was not aimed at their true interest, a modified concept of Gramdan was developed in 1963 to meet the realities of the situation. This concept, known as simplified or Sulabh Gramdan, makes a distinction between 'ownership' and 'possession'. It was felt that a person joining Gramdan might be prepared to surrender ownership of his entire land in a village, even if he would not give up possession of the entire area.

To clarify the concept of Sulabh Gramdan a new model Bill has been prepared which contains the following provisions.

(i) For the purpose of Gramdan, ownership is distinguished from possession. Any owner of land may donate all his land, subject to the condition that he shall not continue to possess more than nineteen-twentieths of it, the actual land making up this proportion being specified by him. In computing the nineteen-twentieths, any land donated by him earlier by way of Bhoodan would be included. In joining Gramdan the owner surrenders ownership of the entire area and also possession of one-twentieth of the land, this proportion being used for redistribution to the landless in the village.

(ii) Any owner of land who makes a donation will also undertake to join the Gramdan community of the village, and to make a periodic contribution of one-fortieth of his produce to the community.

(iii) Any person who does not own land may also join by making a declaration to that effect, and also agreeing to make a periodical contribution to the Gram Sabha of one-thirtieth of his income.

(iv) Every Gramdan declaration has to be verified by a prescribed authority.

(v) A village may be declared Gramdan if it meets the following conditions: (a) 51 per cent of the total extent of lands owned by the resident private owners in the village has been donated in Gramdan and the declarations confirmed; (b) the number of persons whose declarations have been confirmed is not less than 75 per cent of those owning land and residing in the village; and (c) the number of adult residents in respect of whom declarations have been confirmed is not less than 75 per cent of the adults residing in the village.

(vi) In respect of the nineteen-twentieths of the land retained in his possession, the donor—known as a Gramdan kisan—enjoys permanent, heritable rights. His right of transfer, however, is restricted to any other person who has joined the Gramdan. He may also mortgage his interest in favour of the Government or any other public institution as security for any money borrowed by him. Prior approval of the Gram Sabha of such transfers is not necessary, but he must inform the Sabha of them. Transfer of land to a person who has not joined the Gramdan is not permitted.

(vii) In respect of the pooled land (i.e. the one-twentieth area), the Gram Sabha may allot land to any individual or group of landless persons residing in the village for individual or joint cultivation, as the allottees may voluntarily agree upon. The rights of allottees in the land allotted to them are broadly the same as those of a Gramdan kisan, except that an allottee must obtain the prior approval of the Gram Sabha before making any transfer.

It will be seen that Sulabh Gramdan is much less radical than the original concept of Gramdan. It is less egalitarian and it also involves significant concessions to the principles of private property. All land donated in Gramdan is formally vested in the village community, but up to nineteen-twentieths of it remains in the possession of the donors, who can pass it on to their heirs. On the other hand, Sulabh Gramdan does prevent village land passing out of the control of the village: the principle of villagization of land is safeguarded.

Sulabh Gramdan is now the official policy of the movement, and since 1963 all declarations of Gramdan have been of this form. In justification of the new concept, it can be said that it does appear to be succeeding in one of its objects: allaying the fears of the larger landowners. More of such landowners are joining the movement, and Gramdan villages are no longer confined, as they broadly were under the old concept, to the small, very poor, and predominantly low-caste or tribal villages. The development of the Sulabh Gramdan concept may also be seen as an application of Vinoba's 'gentle, gentler, gentlest' approach to non-violent revolution, which will be discussed in Chapter Six.

The success of the toofan campaign for Sulabh Gramdan launched in 1965 has generated the additional concepts of Blockdan, Districtdan, and Statedan. Blockdan is defined as a block in which 85 per cent of the revenue villages or 75 per cent of the population (excluding that of the towns) have decided to join in Gramdan. Districtdan is a district in which all blocks have met the condition of Blockdan; and Statedan is a State in which all districts are Districtdans. The realization of these newer concepts amounts to more than a simple increase in the number of Gramdans. It opens a new, more global perspective on the problem of rural reconstruction and development.

Gramdan, however, remains the basic concept. Considered as a process, it involves three stages: (i) *prapti*, in which the people are persuaded to join Gramdan and, voluntarily, to transfer the ownership of their land to the village council; (ii) *pushti*, in which the village implements the primary conditions of Gramdan, such as the redistribution of the one-twentieth part of donated land among the landless (the verification of gifts and the legal transfer of titles take place at this stage); and (iii) *nirman*, the stage in which, through the Gram Sabha, resources are mobilized and a programme of reconstruction and development of the village begins.[1] In the great majority of Gramdans only the first stage has yet been reached, and there are relatively few villages in which nirman is well advanced. As we shall see, one of the tactical issues in the movement is the extent to which the movement's limited resources should be devoted to propagating the Gramdan idea, as opposed to developing existing Gramdan villages.[2]

Khadi

Khadi, the second item in The Triple Programme, was the best known item in Gandhi's Constructive Programme. Gandhi saw the spinning wheel as the key to India's moral and economic regeneration, and also as a symbol of the struggle for independence. Khadi production, he believed, provided the most widely available means to solve the problem of rural unemployment and under-employment. From 1921, when Congress took up its promotion, Khadi became, in the words of Nehru, 'the livery of freedom', and around it developed the complex symbolism of a new social order, dedicated to plain living and high thinking, free from inequities and inequalities, and emphasizing the Tolstoyan precept of Bread Labour.

To the disgust of many Western economists, the Indian Government since independence have taken steps to further this Gandhian 'fad'. The First Five-Year Plan launched in 1951 recommended the establishment of a special all-India body to organize programmes for the production and development of Khadi and other village industries, such as oil-pressing, hand-pounding of paddy, hand-made paper, and bee-keeping. Accordingly, the Union Government in 1953 set up the Khadi and Village Industries Board (now Commission) which executes its programmes through

[1] Dasgupta, op. cit., pp. 16–18.　　　　[2] See Chapter Six.

other bodies: State Khadi and Village Industries Boards, registered non-official institutions, and co-operative societies. As a result of the various measures taken, which include subsidies on both production and sales, there has been a substantial increase in the output of Khadi: in the period 1955–61, for example, the quantity produced more than doubled.[1]

Among the Gandhian institutions which merged with Sarva Seva Sangh was the All-India Spinners' Association. Sarva Seva Sangh, therefore, retains a direct interest in the promotion of Khadi, quite apart from its inclusion in the movement's programme. Many of the movement's workers are heavily involved in Khadi activities, and the various official, semi-official, and private Khadi organizations have been and remain an important source of recruitment of Sarvodaya workers. Sarva Seva Sangh, however, has not been very impressed by the Government's efforts to promote Khadi. It has criticized the Government for not doing more, for continuing to permit the expansion of mill-cloth production, and, more particularly, for introducing the spirit of commercialism into the industry. By 'commercialism' is meant the production of Khadi for the market rather than, as Gandhi envisaged, as part of a programme of village self-sufficiency.

In response to criticism, and after protracted negotiations, the Khadi Commission agreed in 1964 to revise the basis of the Government's subsidy to the industry. Instead of taking the form of a rebate on the price charged to the customer, the subsidy henceforth was to be made through the introduction of free weaving. By the Government's paying the cost of the weaving, roughly equal to the former rebate to customers, the price of Khadi in the shops would not be much affected, but it was hoped that the new form of subsidy would give a fillip to Khadi work by providing an additional incentive to villagers to use Khadi, and especially by encouraging more villagers to grow and spin their own cotton.

Five years later, it is perhaps too early to judge the results of this attempt to reorientate the Khadi industry towards the village economy rather than towards the commercial market. But the general impression is that the initial results have proved dis-

[1] In 1955–6, 28·9 million square yards valued at Rs. 55·4 million were produced; in 1960–1 the corresponding figures were 64·7 million and Rs. 142·2 million.—*The Khadi Industry*, Ministry of Information, 1962, p. 24. See under India, Government of, in Bibliography.

appointing. Khadi production continues to account for only a tiny fraction of India's production of cloth, and large stocks of Khadi remain unsold.[1] The long-term prospects of the industry do not appear at all bright, and there is evidence to suggest that, even in Gramdan villages, it is proving difficult to resuscitate the industry.

Shanti Sena

The third plank in The Triple Programme is the development of the Shanti Sena or Peace Army. The idea of such an army originated with Gandhi, but he was not able to give it practical form. In May 1950 a conference of constructive workers, meeting at Wardha and presided over by Vinoba, decided to start three units; but, again, nothing came of the plan.[2] It was not until the Bhoodan campaign had almost reached the zenith of its first enthusiastic phase in 1957 that Vinoba finally succeeded in launching it during his padayatra in Kerala. Since then it has grown in strength, and in 1964, according to the movement's records, had a membership of 8,114. By 1969 the membership was in the region of 12,000. Enrolment increased considerably in the period following the Sino-Indian border war of 1962, but the primary purpose of the Army was conceived to be broader than helping to work for peace between nations. Its objectives have been defined as: (i) to prevent any outbreak of violence in the country; (ii) if violence nevertheless does break out, to bring it under control by non-violent methods; and (iii) to create in India such an atmosphere of non-violent strength that war may be outlawed from the international field and the spirit of co-operation strengthened.[3] So

[1] According to figures quoted in Shankarlal Banker, 'Re-orientation of khadi in retrospect', *Sarvodaya*, XVII, 10 & 11 (Apr. & May 1968), khadi *sales* declined from Rs. 211·2 million in 1964–5 to Rs 196·7 m. in 1965–6. In the same period, *production* of khadi rose from 64·8 million metres to 72·3 m. Stocks of yarn at the beginning of 1965–6 were valued at Rs. 29·8 million but rose to Rs.44·1 m. towards the end of the year. Stocks of khadi cloth likewise rose in the same period from Rs. 85·6 million to Rs. 129·3 m. The number of spinners on the traditional charkha rose from 1,279,000 in 1964–5 to 1,568,000 in 1965–6, but owing to slackening demand for their product many were faced with unemployment. Khadi cloth remains more expensive than mill-made cloth. In recent speeches Vinoba has stated that the extra expenditure on the purchase of khadi should be regarded as a sacred dan, indeed the highest dan.—*Sarvodaya*, XVII, 10, p. 442.

[2] *Harijan*, 6 May 1950.

[3] Akhil Bharat Shanti Sena Mandal, *The Indian Shanti Sena*, brochure, n.d. See also Bhave, Vinoba, *Shanti Sena*, 1961, and Narayan Desai, *A Hand Book for Shanti Sainiks*, 1963.

far, its activities have been mainly concerned with preventing and helping to quell communal riots and violence in India, although it has also initiated constructive work in the Northern border areas through the establishment of Peace Centres in NEFA (North East Frontier Agency), Assam, North Bengal, North Bihar, Uttarakhand, Himachel Pradesh, and North Punjab. Vinoba is the Peace Army's Supreme Commander, but in this role he has never issued a command to his 'troops'.[1]

The leaders' perceptions of the movement's programme

Having described the content of the movement's programme, we shall conclude this chapter by considering the leaders' perceptions of it. Our information on this point derives from answers to the question: 'To which three aspects of the Movement's programme do you attach greatest importance today?'

From what we have said earlier, we might expect Gramdan to loom largest in the leaders' perceptions. This expectation is reinforced by a rough analysis of the kinds of work the leaders had been mainly engaged in since joining the movement. 24 per cent had been chiefly concerned with Bhoodan and Gramdan; 16 per cent with Khadi; 10 per cent with office work; 4 per cent with Basic Education; 1 per cent with welfare work among Harijans; 19 per cent were classified as part-time workers; and the remaining 26 per cent had been engaged in various other Gandhian activities, including Shanti Sena.[2] The predominance of Bhoodan-Gramdan activities is evident, and it is probable that most respondents had been involved in these activities, in one way or another, for shorter or longer periods of time during part of their career in the movement.

The following table presents our findings about the relative importance attached by the leaders to the items in The Triple Programme.

From section (a) of the table we can derive some measure of the extent to which the leaders accepted, at the time of the enquiry, the call for concentration on the items of The Triple Programme. It will be seen that only just over half mentioned all three, and

[1] The Shanti Sena Mandal, however, has issued a few commands, directing Shanti Sainiks to certain areas.

[2] N = 203. Usable information was not supplied by nearly 11% of the respondents.

that one in twenty failed to mention either Gramdan, Khadi, or Shanti Sena. Clearly, in the eighteen months following the Raipur conference the movement had not succeeded in persuading a large proportion of the leaders to concentrate on The Triple Programme as such. From section (b) we can derive some measure of the relative importance attached by the leaders to the individual items of The Triple Programme. In this context, it should be noted that Khadi includes other village industries, although these were rarely mentioned except in conjunction with Khadi proper. The expectation that Gramdan would be seen as the most important item by

TABLE 2:2

The Sarvodaya leaders' perceptions of items in The Triple Programme

Proportion of leaders mentioning:

		%
(a)	All three items of The Triple Programme	53
	One or two items only	42
	No item (other items only)	5
(b)	Gramdan	86
	Khadi (including other village industries)	67
	Shanti Sena	74
	(N = 218)	

the great majority of leaders was fulfilled. More surprising is the finding that Shanti Sena was a more popular 'choice' than Khadi. As noted earlier, Khadi was *the* central item in Gandhi's Constructive Programme, whereas Shanti Sena is a fairly recent development and has made nothing like the same impact as Khadi on the consciousness of the Indian public. From the relatively low ranking of Khadi in the perceptions of the Sarvodaya leaders we may reasonably infer that some of them have doubts and reservations about this item of the movement's programme. As we shall see in Chapter Six, this inference is supported by answers to another question.

CHAPTER THREE

SOCIAL FOUNDATIONS AND SOURCES OF RECRUITMENT

THE universalistic character of Sarvodaya ideology—its claim to be the true philosophy for all mankind—may be taken as a useful starting-point for the analysis of the social foundations of the movement. However, we cannot accept this claim simply at its face value: many movements attempt to legitimize their actions and institutions in terms of their particular reading of 'the general interest'. To probe in any depth the movement's universalistic claim is difficult. Empirically (which is not the same as the 'objectively' of certain Marxists) this can be done only by observing what the movement actually does or seeks to do—whose 'interests' it serves and promotes.

This *cui bono?* approach is the one which, in a limited way, we shall adopt. On the assumption that social movements may be the vehicles for the expression of the interests (material and ideal) of particular social groups, and on the further assumption that men are apt to seek their own interests, indications of the character of a movement may be derived from an analysis of its participants— its leadership, its membership, and its clientele.

From this perspective, we may begin by trying to establish whether the composition of the Sarvodaya leadership reflects the universalistic character of the movement's ideology, or, in more specific terms, how far the movement has been successful in recruiting from all existing social groups. According to the movement's own implied criteria of success, the 'ideal' expectation would be that the movement mirrors in microcosm the society of which it is a part. Discrepancies between the 'ideal' and the 'actual' may then have both considerable theoretical interest for our understanding of the movement and practical value for members sincerely trying to implement universalistic goals.

Members of a national society may be grouped in a variety of ways, only some of which are prima facie likely to be relevant to the study of social movements. The variables which provide the bases of the social groups or categories that we shall consider may be classified into five main types: (i) demographic, such as age, sex, and regional origin; (ii) stratification variables, such as caste, class, and status; (iii) environmental, such as type of family structure and type of childhood environment; (iv) religious; and (v) political. Under each of these headings we shall consider a set of variables which will enable us to describe in some detail the social characteristics of Sarvodaya leaders. For example, under the general heading of stratification variables, we shall indicate, among other things, the caste composition of the leadership. These data may be used to confirm or to reject generalizations which have been made about the movement, such as that the majority of leaders are Brahmins. But our analysis may also proceed beyond the purely descriptive level in an attempt to determine how 'representative' the leaders are of the larger society. To do this we need to consider not only that, say, n per cent of the leaders are Brahmins, but also, by a comparison with the distribution of Brahmins in society at large, whether that n per cent indicates that Brahmins are disproportionately represented in the leadership. The over- or under-representation of a particular social group raises interesting questions. Is the disparity sufficient to suggest the presence of a bias for or against the recruitment of members of the group to leadership positions? In other words, has the movement a special appeal for that group? Are there certain factors operating as hidden forces of selection favouring or impeding one group rather than others? Unfortunately, data about the distribution of variables in Indian society at large are not always available or sufficiently precise to enable us to make valid comparisons. In such cases, we are limited to the recital of bare descriptive facts whose 'meaning' may become apparent only in the light of further research.

Comparisons between the Sarvodaya leaders and the general population are not the only kinds of comparison worth making. If such comparison reveals that certain groups are significantly over-represented in the leadership, we may, indeed, conclude that it has a special appeal for those groups, or that forces of selection favour them; but we cannot conclude that the factors involved are 'internal' to the movement. It may be that 'external' factors are at work and that the Sarvodaya movement merely exemplifies a general situation found in all or some other social movements. For example, if Brahmins are over-represented in the Sarvodaya leadership, they may be over-represented to the same or similar degree in all social movements in India. In this case, we should look for possible explanations in the structure and culture of the national society, rather than in the structure and culture of the Sarvodaya movement. Unfortunately, comparative data on other Indian social movements are rarer than data on the national society. But where available or known to us, reference will be made to them. Likewise, we shall occasionally refer to non-Indian social movements where we consider that the Sarvodaya movement exemplifies propositions applicable to social movements as such. The utility of such cross-national comparisons, however, may be limited. Apart from anthropological studies of millenarian movements among 'primitive' peoples, most research on social movements has been centred on those in advanced industrial societies. It is possible that at least some of the concepts and categories employed in analysing Western social movements may not be very helpful in the context of developing countries.

I. DEMOGRAPHIC CHARACTERISTICS

Sex composition of the Sarvodaya leadership

We begin our social analysis by considering the simple variable of sex, and ask: How well are women, as distinct from men, represented in the movement's leadership? One of the achievements of Gandhi was that he successfully promoted the participation of women in Indian public life. He judged the issue of women's emancipation so important that, as we have seen, he included it as an item in his Constructive Programme. Men, he wrote, 'have considered themselves to be lords and masters of women instead of considering them as their friends and co-workers. . . . It is up to Congressmen to see that they enable them to realize their full status and play their part as equals of men.'[1] Since independence some women have in fact occupied the highest positions in Indian public life, including the premiership of the Union Government. But, at the same time, the vast majority of Indian women have continued to experience an inferior status, symbolized in its extreme form by the still not uncommon practice of purdah (seclusion of women).

From personal observation, we would judge that within the

[1] M. K. Gandhi, *Constructive Programme*, 2nd ed., 1945, pp. 17–18.

Sarvodaya movement the Gandhian ideal is practised as well as preached: women do appear to be accepted as equal co-workers with men, although there may be a tendency for them to concentrate on particular forms of social work, such as the uplift of women and children, for which women might be thought to be better suited. Despite its acceptance of the principle of equality, however, the Sarvodaya movement, like most other non-sex-oriented movements in India and elsewhere, remains predominantly a movement of the male sex. Females, of course, constitute roughly half the population,[1] but of the 479 office-holders of Sarva Seva Sangh included in our survey only 16 (or 3·3 per cent) were women. This figure is comparable to the number of women elected to the first Lok Sabha (House of the People), 1952: 19 out of 499 members, or 3·8 per cent.[2] Comparisons may also be made with Kochanek's finding that, of the 639 members of the All-India Congress Committee, 1956, women constituted only 4 per cent,[3] and with the Communist Party of India's estimate that, out of a total party membership of 16,000 in 1943, 5 per cent were women.[4]

Marital status of the leadership

While women are heavily under-represented in the movement's leadership, in terms of marital status the leadership more closely mirrors the general population of India. In 1961, of Indian males aged twenty years and over, 79 per cent were married, 7 per cent were widowed, less than 1 per cent were divorced, and 13 per cent were single.[5] The corresponding figures for male leaders were: 79 per cent married, 10 per cent widowed, less than 1 per cent divorced, and 10 per cent single. These figures suggest that there is no bias in recruitment to the movement's leadership favouring the single male. Further, the relatively high proportion of married and widowed men is worthy of comment. One aspect of the popular image of the Sarvodayite is that he shares something of the saintly qualities of Vinoba who, in early adolescence, consciously chose

---

[1] In 1961, according to the Census, the ratio of females per 1,000 males was 941.—*India, 1964*, Ministry of Information, 1964, p. 16. [See under 'India, Govt of,' in Bibliography.]

[2] T. K. Unnithan, *Gandhi in Free India*, 1965, p. 149.

[3] S. A. Kochanek, *The Congress Party of India*, 1968, p. 366.

[4] G. D. Overstreet and M. Windmiller, *Communism in India*, 1959, p. 358.

[5] *India, 1964*, p. 17. These figures omit those whose age and marital status are unknown.

the life of a brahmacharya (celibate). Sexual continence, of course, as Gandhi observed, is not incompatible with the married state, and it may be that many of the married office-holders are dedicated to this Gandhian ideal in some form. The figures, however, suggest that, in so far as marriage is thought in India to be incompatible with 'saintliness', the Sarvodaya leaders are not so far removed from ordinary men as the popular image would lead us to suppose. As with many popular images, it is the extraordinary qualities of a minority which are frequently taken to represent the norm.

The marital status of the Sarvodaya leaders is also of interest in the light of a comparison that may be made between the movement and Indian political parties. Referring to the social changes in the growth of parties and interest groups in India, Weiner has observed:

There is some reason to argue that political groups in India assume some of the functions which family and caste groups performed, especially for the large number of displaced intellectuals in India's urban centers. The intensity of devotion of members of political groups, the absence of continuous and ready communication with outside groups, the importance of the group and factional leaders to their members, the development of a *Weltanschauung* in many political parties which provides a new orientation toward life, all indicate the enormous needs which political groups fulfill for so many of their members. . . . It is also interesting to note how few Indians have several group identifications. . . . Party workers in India generally come from urban areas where traditional values have been disrupted and where the traditional social structure for many Indians has been breaking down. Young party workers have often broken from the tight-knit organization of their village, their caste, and even their joint family. Many party workers, for example, are bachelors whose bachelorhood represents a break from the joint family. The party thus provides both an alternative set of values and an alternative social structure. There are few outside loyalties to temper the intensity of party membership. . . .[1]

Considering Sarva Seva Sangh as a political group (albeit of a non-conventional type), Weiner's points may be held to be relevant to the movement. We shall have occasion later to present some data about the group affiliations and social psychological background of the Sarvodaya leaders. Here it suffices to note that Weiner's hypothesis that 'many party workers are bachelors' does *not* seem to be

[1] M. Weiner in R. L. Park and I. Tinker (eds.), *Leadership and Political Institutions in India*, 1959, p. 35.

true of Sarvodaya leaders. As we have seen, only 10 per cent of male office-holders in our sample are bachelors. For this minority, however, Weiner's other remarks about the latent social functions of the parties may apply.

Age distribution of Sarvodaya leaders

Age is another demographic variable in terms of which we may compare Sarvodaya leaders with the general Indian population. Few, if any, social movements, it may be averred, accurately reflect the age structure of the general adult population. Some are specifically oriented to younger or older age groups; others, with more general aims, such as political parties, might be expected to approximate more closely to the age distribution of the adult population—although it is a fair generalization that most social and political movements in Western societies, with some obvious exceptions, are drawn disproportionately from the older age groups. It is in movements with general aims (i.e. aims not oriented towards particular age groups) that age distribution may be a significant index of the state of the movement. In the British Co-operative Movement, for example, a movement which in some ways seeks to be as universal as the Sarvodaya movement, there is evidence of an increasing tendency for leaders to be drawn from the more elderly age groups.[1] A 'gerontological revolution' of the kind that appears to be taking place in the British Co-operative Movement, as far as its lay members are concerned, hardly suggests a dynamic movement. The tendency may be seen as one aspect of the institutionalization of a movement, presaging its slow atrophy. When radical movements fail to achieve their goals, they tend to adapt to the situation in a number of different ways. Given time, they usually accommodate to the world as it is and become more moderate or less radical. In this case, 'moving with the times', they might be expected to recruit from the younger age groups in the population. Movements which retain their original objectives or are slow to change them, however, might be expected to keep the old original members but to recruit few new young members. It could be argued that this is what is happening in the British Co-operative Movement. However, this model of the institutionalization of social movements has to be used with care. While a preponderance of elderly members may be taken as an indicator

[1] G. N. Ostergaard and A. H. Halsey, *Power in Co-operatives*, 1965, p. 88.

of institutionalization, continued recruitment of younger new
members is not *necessarily* a sign that the movement is adapting to
the world and becoming more moderate.

As far as the Sarvodaya movement is concerned, the leaders are
drawn not too unevenly from all adult age groups. More than half
of them (55 per cent) are under 50 years, and one-quarter are aged
sixty years and over. The movement is clearly not one led *mainly*
by old men. Nevertheless, since the Indian population is heavily
skewed towards the younger age groups, 'the gerontological factor'
is at work in the selection of leaders. The following table compares

TABLE 3:1

Age distribution of Sarvodaya leaders compared with Indian popula-
tion, members of the House of the People, 1952, members of the
All-India Congress Committee, 1956, and Congress M.P.s, 1960

| | Age group in years | | | | | | | | |
	20–9	30–9	40–9	50–9	60–9	70+	Not known	%	N
Indian population*	33	25	18	12	7	4	<1	100	223M
Sarvodaya leaders	4	22	29	20	20	5	—	100	208
House of the People, 1952**	5	22	29	27	8	—	9	100	499
All-India Congress Committee, 1956***	5·4	24·7	34·6	23·2	9·3	2·7	‡	100	590
Congress M.P.s, 1962****	0·6	11·7	29·2	30·1	26·1	2·3	—	100	357

*Sources. *Census of India, 1961. **W. H. Morris-Jones, Parliament in India, 1957,*
p. 115. ***S. A. Kochanek, *The Congress Party of India,* 1968, p. 362.
****ibid., p. 395. ‡ Age not known, 49.*

the age distribution of Sarvodaya leaders with that of the male
population of India as a whole and with that of members of other
political groups.

From the table it is evident that the two youngest age groups,
the ones in which members are likely to bear the greatest family
responsibilities, are heavily under-represented and the older age
groups correspondingly over-represented in the Sarvodaya leadership. But it will also be observed that the age distribution of
Sarvodaya leaders is remarkably similar to that of members of the
House of the People in 1952, and of members of the All-India

Congress Committee in 1956, especially in the age groups under 50 years. Compared with Congress M.P.s in 1962, Sarvodaya leaders tend to be more representative of all the age groups. Compared with the leadership of the Communist Party of India, however, Sarvodaya leaders are distinctly older: at the First Congress of the C.P.I. almost 70 per cent of the delegates were under 35 years of age.[1]

Age on joining the movement

While age appears to be one of the factors affecting the selection of leaders in the movement, the bias in favour of the older age groups does not mean that the movement recruits disproportionately from the older age groups. On the contrary, the reverse is the case. Although our data in this respect must be treated with caution, since information is available about only 158 of the 228 leaders in our sample, it would appear that nearly three out of every four leaders joined the movement before their thirtieth year. In greater detail, 22 per cent joined when they were between 12 and 19 years, 52 per cent joined in their twenties, a further 18 per cent in their thirties, and only 8 per cent when they were aged 40 years and over.

Date of joining the movement

The discrepancy between the two distributions just mentioned— age at the time of the survey and age on joining the movement—is readily explained by the hypothesis that in the Sarvodaya movement, as in most other social movements, length of service is a factor affecting selection for leadership positions. A member of a movement normally has to serve a period of 'apprenticeship', during which he demonstrates his loyalty and adherence to the movement's ideals and becomes known to other members, before he will be considered eligible for a leadership position. Exceptions to this rule are usually people who have achieved a leadership position in another movement before joining, of whom the best example in the Sarvodaya movement is the former socialist leader, Jayaprakash Narayan.

Although, again, our data are not complete, it is clear that most Sarvodaya leaders have experienced a fairly lengthy period of service in the movement, if by 'movement' here we understand not

[1] Overstreet and Windmiller, op. cit., p. 358.

merely that led by Vinoba but also the movement in all its aspects
—political as well as constructive—led by Gandhi until his
assassination. In the case of 11 per cent of the respondents, it was
not possible to pin-point the year in which they joined the movement, although all of these had joined before 1951. But at least
29 per cent reported twenty-five or more years of service, 5 per
cent indicating that they had joined in 1920 or earlier. At least a
further 27 per cent had joined in the 1940s. Particular interest, however, attaches to those who have joined since 1951, the year in which
Vinoba launched the Bhoodan campaign. 33 per cent of the leaders
appear to have joined in this period, of whom 22 per cent (i.e. two-
thirds) had joined in the years 1951-6 inclusive, during which the
Bhoodan campaign reached its zenith and the movement was
receiving wide-spread publicity in India.[1]

From these figures two conclusions emerge. One is that a substantial minority of the present leaders was drawn into the movement during the early 'enthusiastic' phase of Bhoodan. The other is
that the Bhoodan-Gramdan movement of 'revolutionary Gandhism'
is a direct successor or continuation of the earlier Gandhian movement in terms of its leading personnel.

The second of these conclusions is further confirmed by answers
to the question whether respondents had been active in the Independence Movement. Only 15 per cent of the leaders reported that
they had not been active, while another 11 per cent stated that
they were too young at the time to have participated. Thus, nearly
three out of every four of the leaders reported activity in the
Independence Movement; and, moreover, one in five reported that
they had been imprisoned for such activity.[2]

---

[1] The figure of 33% may be compared, roughly, with the figure of 7·5% of
members of the All-India Congress Committee who joined Congress *after independence* (1947).—Kochanek, *The Congress Party of India*, p. 362. The low
figure for the A.I.C.C. is explained by Kochanek as a consequence of older
Congressmen's normally attempting to retain any position of power as long as
possible.

[2] The proportion of Sarvodaya leaders imprisoned for activity in the independence movement may be compared with the proportion of former prisoners
among the delegates attending the First Congress of the Communist Party in
India: almost three-quarters.—Overstreet and Windmiller, op. cit., p. 358. Of
224 Congress M.P.s in the second Lok Sabha, 52·7% had spent a period in jail.
—Kochanek, *The Congress Party of India*, p. 397, Table XV—12. However, the
Sarvodaya proportion may be an under-estimate: information on this point was
not specifically asked for but was volunteered.

The regional origin of Sarvodaya leaders

As the last of our demographic variables, we may consider regional origin. Sarva Seva Sangh is an all-India body with organizations in about two-thirds of the country's 330 or so districts. All the states of the Union, with the exception of the small state of Nagaland, have felt the impact of the campaigns for Bhoodan and Gramdan. But the campaigns have been notably more successful in some states than in others, partly as the result of the policy of concentrating the campaigns in particular states. Thus, the second most populous state, Bihar, provided just over half the total acreage of land donated in Bhoodan.[1] When Bhoodan flowered into Gramdan, Orissa emerged as the leading Sarvodaya state, and by March 1964 more than one-third of the then total number of Gramdan villages were situated in this state. Bihar, at this stage, lagged far behind. Subsequently, as the result of the toofan (whirlwind) campaign for Sulabh Gramdan launched in Bihar in the summer of 1965, Bihar again came to the fore. By October 1969 Bihar had over two-fifths of all Gramdan villages in India, and together the two states of Bihar and Orissa accounted for more than half the total number of Gramdans. Measured in terms of its practical achievements in Bhoodan and Gramdan, it is evident, therefore, that the movement is unevenly concentrated throughout the country. Variations in the degree of penetration between states may be largely explained as the product of variations in the strength of the movement's organization, the presence of outstanding leaders, and of decisions to concentrate campaigning efforts in particular areas where a favourable response might be expected.

Given the uneven penetration of the movement, the possibility arises that this unevenness may be associated with regional diversities and that the composition of the leadership will reflect these diversities. Perhaps the most important single diversity of this kind is that between North and South India, which, in recent years, has manifested itself in agitation over the adoption of Hindi as the official language, although the diversity is not confined to linguistic and cultural matters. In pursuing this line of analysis we shall consider the four states of Andhra, Mysore, Madras, and Kerala as constituting the South Region, and the rest as belonging to the North. The four southern states embrace approximately

[1] See Table 1, Chapter One.

25 per cent of the Indian population. In terms of the movement's penetration as measured by Bhoodan and Gramdan, the South lags behind the North. Less than 9 per cent of the total acreage given in Bhoodan was located in the four southern states, and in October 1969 these states accounted for about 14 per cent of all Gramdan villages.[1] However, the difference between North and South is less marked with respect to the proportions of Lok Sevaks registered in the two regions. Of the movement's 8,621 Lok Sevaks in 1964, 15·5 per cent were in the four southern states. As far as the leaders are concerned, the difference is further reduced. According to their reported place of birth, 19 per cent of the respondent office-holders were of southern origin, 2 per cent were born in the territory of what is now Pakistan, 1 per cent were of Western origin, and the remaining 78 per cent came from the northern states. These figures suggest that the present Sarvodaya leaders are broadly representative of the Indian population in terms of their regional origin. The slight over-representation of Northerners in the leadership is probably due to the stronger organization of the movement in the two most populous northern states, Uttar Pradesh and Bihar. The Sarvodaya leadership is certainly more representative in this respect than the leadership of the Communist Party of India, 53 per cent of whose delegates at the Fourth Congress of 1956 were drawn from the South.[2]

Although the movement is a genuinely all-India one, for particular campaigns, such as the campaign for Bhoodan in Bihar, 1952-4, and the more recent campaign for Gramdan in the same state, 1965-9, workers may be drawn from all or many states. But normally a worker will be occupied in his own area. And for this purpose 'his own area' means the state in which he was born and where the language spoken will almost certainly be his mother tongue.

The vast majority of office-holders do in fact work in the same state in which they were born. Apart from West Bengal, where the movement is weak and where three respondents born in Pakistan territory now work, Uttar Pradesh is the only state where there is more than a slight 'discrepancy' between a respondent's 'work-

---

[1] Only about 12 % of India's villages are located in the four southern states, but it should be noted that many Gramdan villages, especially in Andhra, are Harijan hamlets attached to 'revenue villages'.

[2] Overstreet and Windmiller, op. cit., p. 359.

state' and his 'birth-state'. And this discrepancy may be simply explained by the fact that the headquarters of Sarva Seva Sangh was, at the time of our enquiry, situated at Varanasi (Benares or Kashi) in Uttar Pradesh.

The close correspondence between place of birth and place of work of the Sarvodaya leaders may also be simply explained. According to demographic studies, geographic mobility is slight in India, the vast majority of people living within the *district* of their birth. In 1931, according to the census figures of that year, only 3·59 per cent of the population lived outside their native *province* or *state*; and Kingsley Davis has argued that even this low figure probably exaggerates the extent of migration.[1]

The point about correspondence between 'birth-state' and 'work-state', however, is of some general interest, because what may be termed 'localization' of leadership in the movement may have consequences parallel to those that are now becoming evident in Indian national politics: to the extent that 'localization' militates against the production of all-India leaders, it may make it more difficult in the future for the movement to find an acceptable national leader. 'Localization' of leadership, however, is consistent with the ideology of Sarvodaya, which emphasizes decentralization, and also with its long-term objective of dispensing with the very concept of leadership.

II. SOCIAL STRATIFICATION CHARACTERISTICS

Like all known national societies, Indian society possesses a system or systems of social stratification. In its most general sense, the concept of 'social stratification' refers to the fact that members of a society are observed to be socially unequal in one or more respects, and that the inequalities are patterned in such a way that the members may be divided into groups, each of which may be regarded as higher or lower than another. Historically, the most influential tradition of social thought employing this concept is the Marxian, which argues that the most fundamental source of stratification in societies is the differential power that men have with respect to ownership of the means of production; all other dimensions of stratification, such as political power, income, and

[1] Kingsley Davis, *The Population of India and Pakistan*, 1951, pp. 107 ff.

prestige are to be seen as ultimately derivative from the fundamental relationship. Another influential tradition of thought is the
Weberian, which distinguishes analytically three dimensions of
stratification based on economic power (position in relation to the
market), status (social prestige), and political power ('parties'): the
extent to which these three dimensions are correlated and the
causal relations between them are matters for empirical determination in any particular historical context. Both the Marxian and the
Weberian concepts of stratification involve the notion that members of a society are divided into groups (classes and/or statuses)
which are to some extent 'open': an individual will be born in a
particular group, but the possibility remains that he may achieve
in the course of his lifetime membership of another, higher or
lower, group. In this respect both are inapplicable to the special
system of social stratification found in traditional Hindu society,
which divides men into 'closed' groups or castes from which, in
theory, there is no possibility of escape in a single lifetime.[1] The
social standing of an individual is wholly ascribed at birth and
cannot be affected by any subsequent achievement on his part,
although, depending on his deeds, he may in a *later* life be reborn
into a higher or lower caste.

Much research into Western social and political movements has
employed the concept of social stratification, and there is abundant
evidence to support the general contention that in contemporary
Western societies 'most major social movements are movements of
social classes, or of certain parts of classes, or of combinations of
classes or parts of classes.'[2] *A priori* there is no reason to believe
that this contention does not apply to social movements in contemporary India, and the remainder of this section, therefore, will
be devoted to analysing the composition of the Sarvodaya leadership in terms of a set of variables related to caste, class, and status.
A set of variables will be employed, since no single or simple
variable is by itself sufficient to categorize the leaders into meaningful social groups. Each variable may be regarded as a measure
of ranking the leaders into a separate system of social stratification,
although, as we shall see, certain of the variables are significantly
interrelated. The set of variables which we shall use comprises the

---

[1] 'In theory' because in practice caste groups have been able to rise in the
varna hierarchy by changing their customs, rituals, ideologies, and ways of life
in the direction of a high caste: the process known as Sanskritization.

[2] R. Heberle, *Social Movements*, 1951, p. 150.

following: the reported 'caste' or varna of the respondent's father; the father's occupation and his ownership of land; the respondent's ownership of property; the declared income of the respondent; the respondent's occupation before joining the movement; the level of education attained by him; and, finally, his self-rated class (or status) position. Since our objective is to determine the degree to which the Sarvodaya leadership is representative of Indian (adult) society, the main significance of our findings lies in comparisons between the distributions for the leaders and the distributions for the general population. The data on the latter, when available, are often sketchy and not always reliable, but the differences are usually obvious enough to warrant broad tentative conclusions.

Caste origin[1]

As is well known, the ancient teachers of India distinguished four main classes of people in Hindu society: Brahmins, Kshatriyas,

[1] The term 'caste' has several different referents: caste as varna; caste categories which are aggregates of persons, usually in the same linguistic region, usually with the same traditional occupation, and sometimes with the same caste name; and caste as jati.—L. Reissman in N. Smelser (ed.) *Sociology*, 1967, p. 245. Bendix's succinct explanation of the social distinctions used in the text is:

According to the classical formula the system was divided into four groups, or varnas (originally meaning color): the Brahmins (priests), the Kshatriyas (warriors), the Vaisyas (merchants), and the Sudras (laborers). The first three are the so-called twice-born castes, which are entitled to wear the sacred thread. Every male child who belongs to a twice-born caste undergoes an elaborate ceremony of initiation, in the course of which the right to wear the sacred thread is conferred upon him. Sudras, on the other hand, are not entitled to wear the sacred thread and therefore are 'once-born'. Below the Sudras rank the untouchables, who are barred from entry into temples and who may not be served by any member of a twice-born caste. Untouchables are believed to defile others by mere touch or in some cases by their presence at a distance. The four varnas and the untouchables are divided into a vast number of sub-castes (jati). Today these broad categories may perhaps be regarded as a nation-wide standard, which has a clear-cut meaning only at the top and the bottom of the hierarchy. Although disputes over rank are rife throughout the hierarchy, the classical division retains its importance, in part because the conflicting claims are made in terms of that division and because presumed historical antecedents are cited in order to justify the ranking of a caste in one of the four categories. Since there is a bewildering variety of ritual practice, one can say only that among the twice-born castes rank appears to vary according to strict adherence to endogamy, child-marriage, the chastity of widows, cremation of the dead, sacrifices to ancestors, the vegetarian and non-alcoholic diet, and correct conduct in relation to Sudras and untouchables. Among the lower castes rank also depends upon the rank of the Brahmins who are still, or no longer, ready to render services to the caste in question and also upon which other castes are willing or unwilling to accept water from that caste.—R. Bendix, *Max Weber*, 1962, p. 143 n.

Vaishyas, and Sudras. The Brahmins were those dedicated to the service of Brahman, i.e. Truth, and to the preservation and enrichment of the society's cultural and spiritual heritage. They included priests, teachers, sages, and philosophers. The Kshatriyas were those entrusted with the functions of maintaining law and order, external defence, and also administration. They included, therefore, not only the warriors but also the rulers and their administrative officers. The Vaishyas were those responsible for the production and distribution of material wealth and included all those engaged in business and trade. The Sudras constituted the service class and included manual labourers and domestic servants. Besides these four varnas, there were the 'untouchables', who fell outside ancient Hindu society. This class, re-named by Gandhi the Harijans, included the primitive aboriginals or tribal peoples (adivasis), and those engaged in the most menial and, by Hindu standards, the most 'unclean' jobs, such as scavenging and cobbling.

To each of the four main classes was attached a set of rights and obligations, the fulfilment of which constituted an individual's dharma (duty). The varna system was also related to the concepts of karma (the doctrine of existence conditioned by the sum of good and evil actions) and of the transmigrations of souls—concepts which served to legitimize the system and also to justify the ranking of the classes in a descending order of status. Thus, the Sudra, if he conscientiously fulfilled his dharma, could hope to be reborn as a Vaishya, or a Kshatriya, or a Brahmin, and so eventually to attain the ultimate objective of moksha (self-realization and enlightenment). In theory, however, the status attached to these various classes was essentially a spiritual or religious one which might be quite unrelated to socio-economic status. A poor Brahmin might thus be higher in the status scale than a powerful ruler or a wealthy businessman. And, in fact, in India there is a persisting tradition which accords the highest place of honour to the sage who has cast aside all attachments to property and material position and who leads a life of dedicated self-sacrifice for the good of humanity. We should also note that within the varna system a special status is attached to the first three varnas. These are the high castes whose members belong to the important Hindu category of 'the twice-born' who alone are entitled to wear the sacred thread.

In terms of their reported position in the varna system (or what in a caste system amounts to the same thing, the position in it of their fathers), the outstanding fact about the Sarvodaya leaders is that the vast majority belong to the twice-born varnas. Of the respondent office-holders only 10 per cent do not come within this category, and this figure includes, besides the Sudras and scheduled castes, the few Christians and the odd Sikh and Muslim.[1] Despite the movement's programme of Bhoodan, which may be thought of as oriented especially towards the low castes and Harijans, these are significantly under-represented in the leadership. Precisely how much under-represented it is impossible to say in the absence of accurate figures for the proportion of 'once-born' in the total population. But an approximate measure may be obtained from the fact that the Scheduled Castes and Tribes recognized under the Indian Constitution comprise some 21 per cent of the total population, Muslims constitute a further 11 per cent,[2] and Sudras form over half the population of India.[3]

Of the three twice-born varnas, the Brahmins constitute the largest single group of leaders. In our sample of respondents, 38 per cent reported that their fathers were Brahmins, 26 per cent were Kshatriyas, and 26 per cent were Vaishyas. The over-representation of the twice-born, who are estimated to constitute about 20 per cent of the total population,[4] is thus of the order of 70 per cent. The Brahmins appear to be the varna most heavily over-represented. According to census data, Brahmins form a small and diminishing minority among the Hindus of India: 7·14 per cent in 1891 falling to 6·37 per cent in 1931, the date of the last census in which statistics on caste were compiled on an all-India basis.[5]

Although Brahmins are heavily over-represented in the Sarvodaya leadership, it will be seen that they still constitute a minority: the common assertion that 'most of the leaders are Brahmins' is thus an exaggeration. The over-representation of Brahmins, it

---

[1] It includes also 5 Kyasthas and 3 Nairs, two castes which have special relationships with Brahmins. The number of members of low castes appears also to be small in the CPI leadership. At its First Congress only three untouchables were present among the delegates.—Overstreet and Windmiller, op. cit., p. 358.

[2] *India 1964*, p. 114 & p. 18.

[3] S. A. Kochanek, 'The relation between social background and attitudes of Indian legislators', *Journal of Commonwealth Political Studies*, VI, 1 (Mar. 1968) p. 35.

[4] ibid.

[5] Kingsley Davis, op. cit., p. 168.

SOCIAL FOUNDATIONS AND

should also be noted, is in line with the general proposition, derived from stratification theory, and confirmed in studies of other social movements: that leaders of social movements tend to be drawn disproportionately from the higher status groups.[1] Given this expectation, perhaps a more interesting question is whether Brahmins are over-represented in the Sarvodaya movement in comparison, not with the general population, but with other Indian social and political movements. The scarcity of empirical research on other movements prevents a definitive answer to this question. However, two studies of trade-union leadership *in Bombay*, made in 1958 and 1960, reported even higher proportions of Brahmins. In the first study, 29 out of 45 (60 per cent) trade union leaders were found to be Brahmins; and in the second study 28 out of 64 (44 per cent).[2] A similar predominance of Brahmins also prevails among the top leadership in national politics. In an analysis of the origins of members of the Union Council of Ministers, in 1956, North reported that nearly 50 per cent were Brahmins.[3] Of the 224 Congress members of the second Parliament, Kochanek reported that 18·3 per cent were Brahmins.[4] However, it is unlikely that this picture is repeated at the state level. Crouch, in fact, reporting on the trade-union studies, observes that of the 25 Ministers and Deputy Ministers in the Maharashtrian Government in 1964, only one appeared to be a Brahmin. Over-all, it seems likely that, so far as political parties, including Congress, are concerned, Brahmins constitute a diminishing proportion of political leaders as a consequence of the rise in influence of other caste groups. If this is in fact the case, it may be that the Sarvodaya movement provides for Brahmins a surrogate political organization in which their traditionally high status continues to manifest itself in over-representation at the leadership level.

---

[1] This is a major theme in R. Michels, *Political Parties*, 1915.
[2] H. Crouch, *Trade Unions and Politics in India*, 1966, p. 30.
[3] R. C. North in Park and Tinker, op. cit., p. 114.
[4] Kochanek, 'The relation between social background and attitudes of Indian legislators', op. cit., p. 36. Other caste groups, Kochanek reported, were distributed as follows: Kshatriya 11·2%; Vaishya 10·7%; Kyastha 2·7%; Sudra 9·8%; Harijan 17%; Tribal 7·1%; Non-Hindu 7·1%; Caste rejector 9·4%; and Unknown 6·2%. The representation of Harijans and Tribals, roughly proportionate to their popular strength, is explained by the provision of reserved seats and their strong support for Congress.

Occupational class origin

The traditional varna system was, as we have noted, a system of stratification based in theory on broad occupational categories. Today, however, with increased mobility and the increasingly economic values of modern society, there is no longer a very close association between an individual's varna and his occupation, except that only Brahmins can be priests. The trading sub-castes (jati) are still largely Vaishya, but all four classes include large numbers of cultivators. It is necessary, therefore, to consider separately the stratification of leaders in terms of their actual occupations—the most frequently-used index of modern economic class systems.

We may begin by looking at the occupational class origins of Sarvodaya leaders, using information furnished by the respondents about the occupations and landholdings of their fathers.

The data supplied on the occupations of fathers were not always sufficiently precise to enable us to determine accurately their class. This applies particularly to answers couched in such general terms as 'Businessman' and 'Government Servant', although as these terms are used in India they would usually connote middle-class status. Another broad category, 'Professional', which includes doctors, lawyers, and teachers, carries a more definite connotation of middle-class status. The category 'Private Service' is a distinctively Indian one, used in contrast to 'Government Service'. It implies employment by private individuals or firms in a subordinate capacity, and will be taken here to involve less than middle-class status, as, of course, does the 'Artisan' category. The remaining categories employed are 'Priest' and 'Agriculturalist'. The former, since it includes only Brahmins, may be safely regarded as middle-class. With respect to the latter—the most important general category in the Indian context—we were able to make sub-divisions which correspond to reasonably well defined rural social classes.

Our data reveal that rather less than half the respondents' fathers were engaged in non-agriculturalist occupations. This proportion (46 per cent) was made up as follows: Business 16 per cent, Government Service 12 per cent, Professional 12 per cent, Priest 1 per cent, Private Service 3 per cent, and Artisan 2 per cent. It will be observed that the proportions in what we have considered middle-class occupations heavily outweigh the others.

The 54 per cent of fathers who were agriculturalists might be taken as reflecting the rural orientation of the movement. However, since agriculturalists constitute about 70 per cent of the total working force of India as a whole,[1] it is clear that the Sarvodaya leadership is drawn disproportionately from the non-agriculturalist occupational classes. This characteristic it shares with the Congress parliamentary leadership, since, according to Kochanek,[2] 43 per cent of the fathers of Congress M.Ps in 1960 were agriculturalists and a further 8 per cent were Rajas or zamindars. It is probably less non-agriculturalist than the leadership of the CPI, 22 per cent of whose delegates at the First Congress of 1943 were described as peasants, landlords, and petty landlords, and of whose estimated total party membership 36 per cent were peasants.[3]

But perhaps the most significant findings emerge when we consider the sub-divisions within the Agriculturalist category. The 54 per cent is made up as follows: Absentee Landlords 6 per cent; Owner Cultivators 44 per cent; Tenant Cultivators 3 per cent; and Landless Labourers 1 per cent.[4] What these figures signify about the occupational class origin of the leaders may be judged from the table below, which compares the Agriculturalist fathers of Sarvodaya leaders with the distribution of Indian Agriculturalists according to the 1951 Census.

From the table opposite it is evident that the Sarvodaya leaders of Agriculturalist class origin are drawn disproportionately from the two upper rural classes, the absentee landlords and the owner cultivators. What is most notable is the smallness of the group with fathers who were landless labourers—a category which has been the special concern of the movement in its Bhoodan and Gramdan campaigns. Sarvodaya may be (among other things) a movement *for* landless labourers, but, so far as the leadership is concerned, it is evidently not a movement *of* landless labourers.

In sum, taking our data as a whole, the occupational class origin of Sarvodaya leaders is heavily biased in the direction of the middle

---

[1] *Census of India 1961*, Final Population Totals, p. 433.

[2] Kochanek, *The Congress Party of India*, p. 337. The figures are derived from Table XIII—2. Kochanek's sample of Congress M.P.s excludes ministers, those born before 1891 or after 1930, and those whose age was unknown. The remaining father's occupation categories were: Business 17%; Government Service 18%; Professional 12%; Public Work 1%; Unknown 1%.

[3] Overstreet and Windmiller, op. cit., pp. 357–8.

[4] All the three landless labourers in our sample were of the Kshatriya varna.

(including upper) of both rural and urban classes. Assuming tenant cultivators, landless labourers, private servants, and artisans to be non-middle-class, 91 per cent of Sarvodaya leaders had

TABLE 3:2

Agriculturalist fathers of Sarvodaya leaders compared with Indian agriculturalists

	Non-cultivating owners (absentee landlords) %	Owner cultivators %	Tenant cultivators %	Cultivating labourers (landless labourers)[1] %	%
Indian agriculturalists	2·1	67·2	12·7	18·0	100
Agriculturalist fathers of Sarvodaya leaders	11·1	81·5	5·5	1·9	100

Source. Figures for Indian agriculturalists derived from census data in D. Thorner, *Land and Labour in India*, 1962, p. 131. It should be noted that Thorner is highly critical of the 1951 Census categories. He argues that the number of non-cultivating owners is understated, the number of owner cultivators is greatly inflated, and the number of cultivating labourers is 'substantially understated'.—ibid., pp. 146–9.

middle-class fathers—a proportion similar to that of fathers who belonged to the twice-born varnas.

Analysis of the reported amount of *cultivable* land owned by the respondents' fathers confirms this conclusion. The proportion (65 per cent) owning such land was in fact higher than the proportion reported as having mainly Agriculturalist occupations (54 per

[1] The cultivating labourers of the census may not be exactly equivalent to our landless labourers, since the former includes some who owned small areas of land and thus were not strictly landless. However, the term 'landless labourer' is used in India and in the movement to include such people, since the amount of land owned is insufficient to provide an independent livelihood. Authorities do not always agree on the proportion of labourers in India's agricultural classes. One standard text states that in 1951 21% of the total agricultural population were labourers, half of whom were landless.—M. B. Nanavati & J. J. Anjaria *India's Rural Problems*, 5th edn, 1960, pp. 35–48. It should be added that there are wide variations in the incidence of agricultural labourers between states. To illustrate: in 1961 29% of agriculturalists in Andhra Pradesh were labourers, compared with 4% in Assam. Figures for some other states were: Bihar 23%; Uttar Pradesh 11%; West Bengal 15%; Kerala 17%; Mysore 16%; and Madras 18%.—*Census of India 1961*, p. 436.

cent). In terms of the size of their holdings, the 65 per cent is made up as follows: 15 per cent owned 5 acres or less; 28 per cent owned between 6 and 20 acres; 15 per cent owned between 21 and 100 acres; and 7 per cent were comparatively large landowners with holdings of more than 100 acres. The significance of these figures may be judged in the light of the estimate that the mean size of holdings in India in 1951 was 7·5 acres, nearly three-fifths of the holdings being 5 acres or less, and only slightly over one-fifth being 10 acres or more.[1] The direction of the bias towards larger-than-average holdings is underlined by the fact that the 22 per cent of fathers owning more than 20 acres belonged to the 8·2 per cent of the Indian agricultural population who owned 41 per cent of the total agricultural land, and that the 7 per cent of fathers owning more than 100 acres belonged to the tiny group (0·4 per cent) of the agricultural population who owned 6·7 per cent of the land.[2]

Occupational class of Sarvodaya leaders

The preceding analysis of the occupations of their fathers is concerned with the class *origin* of the leaders. A person's class origin is likely to be an important determinant of his present class position, but, of course, mobility both upward and downward is possible in a class, as distinct from a caste, hierarchy. Turning now to the present class position of the leaders, we shall begin with an analysis of their occupations before they joined the movement.

Unfortunately, our data in this respect are distinctly patchy. Respondents were asked to list the jobs they had done since leaving school and college before and after joining the movement, but the replies were not always very specific. From the information supplied, however, we estimate that nearly one-quarter (23 per cent) of the leaders had had no previous job experience, and that, after leaving school or college, service in the movement had been their only occupation. Of a further 19 per cent it was impossible to determine more than that they had served in the movement (in the widest sense) since before 1951. Many of these, probably, had joined the movement, under Gandhi, straight from school or college. For these two groups the possibility arises that service in the movement presented itself as an alternative to unemployment,

---

[1] Nanavati and Anjaria, op. cit., pp. 76–84.
[2] Figures derived from Table 11, 'Land ownership in rural India', in R. Braibanti and J. J. Spengler (eds.), *Administration and Economic Development in India*, 1963, p. 299.

since some of them had been unemployed prior to joining. But it would be rash to presume that unemployment was an impelling factor in their joining. This may have been true of some, but it seems more likely that most of them joined out of a desire for

TABLE 3:3

Comparison of occupations of fathers with occupations of leaders prior to joining[1]

Occupation	Fathers	%	Leaders	%
Absentee landlord	6	5	3	2·5
Owner cultivator	55	46	18	15
Tenant cultivator*	1	<1	1	<1
Landless labourer*	3	2·5	1	<1
Business	26	22	22	18
Government Service	12	10	17	14
Professional	12	10	46	38
Priest	1	<1	0	0
Private Service*	3	2·5	10	8
Artisan*	1	<1	2	2
N	120	100	120	100

*For the purposes of analysis, these occupations have been regarded as 'Lower-Class'. All other occupations have been deemed 'Middle-Class'.

[1] The distribution of the leaders' occupations may also be compared with the distributions relating to members of the All-India Congress Committee, 1956, and Congress M.P.s, 1962.

Occupation	A.I.C.C. %	Congress M.P.s. %
Agriculturalist	21	27
Professional	56	42
Business	12	8
Public work	6	17
Service	1	4
Other	4	2
N	344*	341*

Source. Kochanek, *The Congress Party of India,* p. 358 (Table XIV—6) and p. 380 (Table XV —4).
Note. *Data unknown in respect of 295 A.I.C.C. members and 16 Congress M.P.s.

service when they were in a position to obtain satisfactory employment elsewhere.

Of the remaining 58 per cent we have information about 120 leaders which permits us to compare their occupations prior to joining with the occupations of their fathers. Table 3 : 3 above presents the comparison in terms of the occupational categories previously employed.

The group of 120 leaders is not perfectly representative of our total sample of respondents, sons of Businessmen being somewhat over-represented. But the divergences between the group and our total sample are not large enough to distort certain broad conclusions. It will be seen that, whereas approximately 54 per cent of the fathers were Agriculturalists, only about 19 per cent of the leaders had been employed in agricultural occupations. The two categories where divergences between fathers and leaders are greatest are Owner Cultivator and Professional. Whereas 46 per cent of the fathers were Owner Cultivators, only 15 per cent of the leaders were. On the other hand, 38 per cent of the leaders had been employed in the Professions compared with 10 per cent of the fathers.[1] This suggests that pressure on land, leading to a reduction of employment opportunities in agriculture, *may* have been a factor inducing sons of Owner Cultivators to find employment outside agriculture. Since these sons had found such employment, we cannot conclude that lack of employment opportunities was a factor inducing them to join the movement. It may, however, have been the case that some of them found their non-agriculturalist occupations unsatisfying, and, as a consequence, were attracted to join a rurally oriented social movement.

These observations, it must be emphasized, are conjectures whose truth or falsity could be confirmed only by further research. It should be noted in any case that the tabulated comparisons veil considerable movement between occupational categories on the part of the sons. The majority of leaders were *not* employed in the

---

[1] Kochanek's comparison of father's occupation with occupation of Congress M.P.s (ibid., p. 389) shows a similar pattern of divergences. Thus, whereas 43% of fathers were agriculturalists, only 24% of Congress M.P.s were; and whereas 12% of fathers were professionals, 30% of Congress M.P.s so described their occupations. Kochanek comments: 'In a country where role is supposed to be ascriptive, it comes as something of a surprise to discover that there has been a higher degree of occupational mobility than in many highly developed countries. In short, Congress Members of Parliament have not followed in their fathers' footsteps.'

same occupation as their father: only 39 of the 120 (32·5 per cent) had been so employed. And sons of Owner Cultivators were not remarkable in this respect, since nearly 30 per cent of this group had followed the same occupation as their fathers.

Table 3:3 also enables us to compare fathers and sons in terms of broad occupational class, middle and lower. Whereas 93 per cent of the fathers may be considered to have enjoyed middle-class occupational status, 88 per cent of the sons did so. Downward social mobility, therefore, has been experienced by a small proportion of the leaders. But it is doubtful whether this proportion is large enough to be considered significant, statistically or otherwise. In detail, 9 leaders, of whom 6 were sons of Owner Cultivators and 3 were sons of Businessmen, had moved down socially, while 3 leaders, 2 the sons of fathers in Private Service and one the son of an Artisan, had moved upward.

Ownership of property

Another important determinant of class, in the Marxian theory the crucial determinant, is ownership of property. With respect to this variable we have information which enables us to draw conclusions about the property class position of most of the respondent leaders. Our data derive from answers to the questions: 'Do you own or share in the ownership of any immovable property? If "yes", what is the present approximate value of your own property, or your own share of the property?' Since it was not possible to make an independent check of the answers, the information supplied cannot be accepted without reserve, although we have no reason for doubting the veracity of respondents. The need for caution is underlined by the fact that the questions were not answered by 17 per cent of the respondents. Some of these may have ignored the questions because they had no property; but it is also likely that the relatively high rate of non-response was due to the feeling that these were 'sensitive' questions. Since we shall ignore the non-respondents in the analysis that follows, it may well be that the extent of property ownership by the leaders is under-estimated up to the extent of 12 per cent.

Of the 189 leaders who answered the questions, 32 per cent stated that they owned no immovable property. The replies of the remainder distinguished between residential, landed, and 'other' immovable property, such as investments. 47 per cent of the 189 leaders reported owning residential property, 51 per cent landed, and 13 per cent 'other' kinds of property. A further 6 per cent stated that they owned property but gave no details. (The percentages do not add up to 100, since some owned more than one kind of property.) The figure of 51 per cent owning landed property may be compared with the 65 per cent of fathers with landholdings, previously noted. Even allowing for the possibility that non-respondents to this question owned land, the difference between the two figures suggests that the leaders are less rooted in the landholding class than were their fathers.[1] For this, as we shall see, there may be a simple explanation: some of the leaders who owned land have donated all of it in Bhoodan or Gramdan.

No direct comparison with fathers is possible in terms of acreage of cultivable land owned. Instead we have the respondents' own estimates of the value of their landed property. Of the 94 who owned land and provided estimates of its value, 42 per cent estimated that their land (or share of it) was worth Rs. 5,000/- or less; 24 per cent estimated its value in the range Rs. 5,001–10,000/-; 17 per cent in the range Rs. 10,001–20,000/-; and the remaining 16 per cent valued it in excess of Rs. 20,000/-. At the then prevailing land prices in India, which of course vary considerably according to region and type of land, these figures suggest that most of the landholdings of the leaders are comparatively small-scale.[2]

Income classes

In the popular conception of social class, level of income is an important element, and it is indeed true that in most societies stratification by class is related to income level, although in the Marxian meaning of 'class' *source* rather than level is the primary

---

[1] They would also appear to be less rooted in the landholding class than Congress M.P.s. In Kochanek's sample only 29% of Congress M.P.s in 1960 are reported as having no landholding.—Kochanek, *The Congress Party of India*, p. 337. (Figure derived from Table XIII—3.) No hard data are available on the extent of property ownership among the Indian population as a whole, but a sample survey of *rural* households undertaken in 1962 estimated that approximately one-third of them owned no land and that one-thirteenth did not own their own home.—*All-India Rural Household Survey*, Vol. II: *Income Investment and Saving*, 1965, Table 25, pp. 114–15.

[2] The landholdings of Sarvodaya leaders are probably smaller, on the average, than those of Congress M.P.s. Of the 144 Congress M.P.s with landholdings, in Kochanek's sample, 75 owned holdings of 21 acres or more.—ibid.

factor. In order to analyse the Sarvodaya leaders in terms of income classes, respondents were asked: 'What is the approximate present monthly income of your household *from all sources*, including wife's and dependents' earnings, if any, rents, investments etc.?' As with the questions on property ownership, it was not possible to check the answers; and, again, the question proved 'sensitive'—nearly 15 per cent of the leaders not replying. The data provided must therefore be treated with reserve. In the Indian context, there is the additional difficulty that some element of real personal income may not be received in monetary form. For example, the peasant growing most of his own food is unlikely to regard its market value as part of his income. The income of agriculturalists may therefore be under-stated. This probably applies to some of our respondents. Further, some of the leaders, particularly those living in ashrams (communities), may enjoy a hidden income in the forms of subsidized board and lodging and enjoyment of communal amenities. The answers to our question must therefore be interpreted as expressing *cash* income only.

Two measures of income levels may be derived from our data: monthly household income and monthly *per capita* income—the latter derived from the former by simply dividing the stated household income by the number of those dependent on it. With regard to the first measure, we distinguished for purposes of analysis six income groups between which the respondent leaders were distributed as set out in Table 3:4(a) below.

It will be seen that nearly one-quarter of the leaders reported a monthly household income of Rs. 100/- or less, and that over one-half reported an income of Rs. 200/- or less. At the other end of the scale, slightly more than one-tenth reported an income of over Rs. 500/- per month.

It is difficult to compare Sarvodaya leaders with the Indian population as a whole, since the reliability of the available statistics of household incomes in India is open to doubt. Two different surveys of rural households conducted in recent years have produced significantly different income distributions. (See (b) and (c) in Table 3:4.) It would appear, however, that the incomes of Sarvodaya leaders generally are higher than those of rural households, and roughly similar to those of urban households, according to the 1959 survey. The statistics relating to middle-class families

SOCIAL FOUNDATIONS AND

in the four major cities may, perhaps, be more reliable than those derived from All-India surveys. If we compare the Sarvodaya leaders with these families, it will be seen that the proportion of leaders in the lowest income group is substantially greater than the

TABLE 3:4

Income of Sarvodaya leaders compared with Indian population, Poona voters, and middle-class families in four Indian cities

	Monthly household income in Rupees:							
	0–100	101–200	201–300	301–400	401–500	Over 500	Total %	N
(a) Sarvodaya leaders, 1965	23	32	18	10	6	11	100	194
(b) All-India households, 1959								
Urban	30	27	17	11	6	9	100	1,293
Rural	62	24	8·5	2	1·5	2	100	1,818
(c) All-India households, 1962								
Rural only	44	31	10	6	9		100	8,527
(d) Sample of voters in Poona, 1962	55	27	12	2	2	2	100	1,215
(e) Middle-class families, 1958–9, in:								
Bombay	1·4	26·8	27·5	26.4		18	100	N.A.
Calcutta	4·4	30·4	22·5	21·4		21·2	100	N.A.
Delhi	2·4	32·2	25·2	24·7		15·6	100	N.A.
Madras	11·9	38	21·2	18·4		10·5	100	N.A.

Sources.

(b) *A First All-India Survey of Rural Incomes, Assets, and Expenditure.* Monthly Public Opinion Survey, Indian Institute of Public Opinion, New Delhi, Vol. V, Nos. 9–11, 1959, p. 2.
(c) *All-India Rural Household Survey*, National Council of Applied Economic Research, New Delhi, 1966. Vol. III: *Basic Tables with Notes.* Adapted from Table 1, pp. 4–5.
(d) V. M. Sirsikar, *Political Behaviour in India*, 1965. Adapted from Table 5, p. 162.
(e) *India 1964* [India, Government of], 1964. Adapted from Table 65, p. 152.

comparable proportion in each of the four cities. At the other end of the scale, the proportion in the highest income group (over Rs. 500/– per month) is less than the comparable proportion in three of the cities, and is approximately equal to the proportion in Madras. We may fairly conclude, therefore, that the household incomes of Sarvodaya leaders are generally lower than those of middle-class families in the four major cities of India.

Comparison of the leaders with a representative sample of the Poona electorate (Table 3:4(d)) enables us to give a more graphic description of their income status. Well over half the Poona voters, compared with less than one-quarter of the Sarvodaya leaders, reported monthly incomes of Rs. 100/– or less; while, at the other end of the scale, only 1 per cent of Poona voters, compared with 11 per cent of leaders, reported an income of over Rs. 500/–. Sirsikar, the source of the Poona statistics, describes the lowest income group as 'the poor'; those in the Rs. 100–200/– range as 'lower middle class'; and those with incomes in excess of Rs. 400/– as 'higher middle class'. Using this terminology, we may conclude that most Sarvodaya leaders enjoy a higher income than the average Poona voter, and that, compared with Poona voters, the Sarvodaya group contains less than half as many 'poor', about the same proportion of 'lower middle class', twice as many 'middle class', and four to five times as many 'higher middle class'.

By using the measure of *per capita* monthly income, we can make a broad comparison between the leaders and the Indian population as a whole. In 1962–3 the *per capita* income in India was estimated to be Rs. 339/– per annum, or approximately Rs. 28/– per month. Our data show that 41 per cent of the leaders reported a monthly *per capita* income of Rs. 30/– or less. We may conclude, therefore, that about two-fifths of our respondents (and their dependants) enjoyed a *per capita* income *below or not much more than* that of the average Indian.

In brief, it seems reasonable to conclude from our analysis that most of the Sarvodaya leaders enjoy a cash income which is no better than that of the urban lower middle class, and that a considerable minority has an income approximating to that of the poor. All Sarvodaya leaders are not the 'saints' dedicated to 'holy poverty' of the popular image, but enough of them are sufficiently near to being so, as far as income is concerned, to justify the image.

Educational class

The standard of formal education that a person attains is likely to be related to his class origin. This is so even in societies where 'equality of opportunity' prevails, since such equality may be largely formal, and social conditions and attitudes rooted in the class structure may militate against actual equality. In India even formal equality of opportunity is still largely an ideal, and, compared with the situation in advanced industrial countries, class factors are more obvious determinants of educational attainment. From this perspective, a person's educational attainment may be seen as a dependent variable—dependent, that is, to some extent on his class origin. From another perspective, however, educational attainment may be treated as an independent variable. When a person has attained a certain standard of education, the achievement constitutes a kind of intangible 'property', which in its turn is likely to determine his class and status. If, for example, by some good fortune a child of low-class parents attains a standard of education normally achieved only by children of high-class parents, then the low-class child is likely himself to enjoy a higher position in the class and status hierarchies than his parents. In advanced industrial societies there is some evidence that educational attainment is becoming one of the more important kinds of 'property' a person may possess and a principal determinant of his class and status. It is necessary, therefore, to consider standard of education along with our other criteria of class and status.

Unlike questions about property and income, questions about educational attainment are not particularly sensitive, and all but two of our respondents answered the relevant question. However, it should be pointed out that the nature of the enquiry from which we derive our data about the education of the leaders may affect our findings to an indeterminate extent. Although we have reasons for believing that, in certain important respects, our sample of respondent leaders is representative of the whole leadership, it is plausible to suggest that in this particular respect it may not be fully representative. Returns of postal questionnaires are likely to be biased in the direction of the more highly educated, who are more conversant with them and find them easier to complete. In our own enquiry we know that, although the questionnaire was printed in both Hindi and English, respondents who replied in Hindi (or some other Indian language) were less highly educated than those who replied in English.[1] It may therefore be that, compared with respondents, the non-respondents were less familiar

[1] Slightly over half (52%) of our respondents replied wholly or partly in an Indian language.

with English and less highly educated. If this is in fact the case, our findings are likely to exaggerate the educational attainment of the Sarvodaya leaders as a whole.

Bearing in mind this reservation about our data, the reader may consider our findings, which were as follows. 24 per cent (including 1 per cent with no formal education) had been educated up to the level of Primary School only; a further 30 per cent had been to High School; another 12 per cent had achieved the Intermediate level; 15 per cent were University graduates with a first degree; and a further 19 per cent were graduates with two degrees, the second usually postgraduate, such as M.A.

Even allowing for the probable bias of our sample, it is clear from these figures that Sarvodaya leaders are heavily recruited from India's educated élite. In 1961 the literacy rate in India was only 24 per cent, the male and female rates being 34·4 per cent and 12·9 per cent respectively.[1] Simply by completing the questionnaire our respondents indicated that their educational attainments were superior to those of the vast majority of their fellow countrymen. Some measure of how highly educated the leaders are, compared with the general population, may be gathered from the fact that in 1951 only 0·3 per cent of the population aged 25 years and over had reached what UNESCO statisticians refer to as the third level of education, which includes universities, teachers' training colleges, and higher professional schools.[2] A manpower study carried out by the Indian Planning Commission in 1955 on 'educated persons' defined such persons as those of general matriculation standard and above. In rural India 0·5 per cent of the population were estimated to be in this category; in urban India the comparable figure was 4·7 per cent. The total number of 'educated persons' in all India was estimated to be 4·7 million, of whom 4 million were men. Of these men, 68 per cent had been educated up to matriculation standard, and 16 per cent to graduate standard or above.[3] Since 34 per cent of all our respondents were graduates, these figures indicate that the leaders are drawn disproportionately from the more highly educated of the small class of 'educated persons'.

[1] *India 1964*, p. 66.
[2] UNESCO, *Statistical Yearbook, 1964*, p. 67.
[3] *Educated Persons in India*, Manpower Studies, Planning Commission, 1955, p. 2. [See under 'India, Govt. of', in Bibliography.]

This conclusion will surprise no one familiar with India's political parties and movements. As in other developing countries, the political élite draws heavily on the educated élite. Of Congress M.P.s in the second Lok Sabha in 1960, 64 per cent were graduates.[1] In the first Lok Sabha, 1952–7, it was estimated that over half the members had university degrees, and that only 15 per cent had received no education above the Primary School level. In the state legislative assemblies, the proportion in the latter category is higher, perhaps one-third falling within it.[2] The proportion of graduates among the Sarvodaya leaders is roughly similar to the proportion among the members of the Madras Legislative Assembly in 1953, 29 per cent of whom were reported as holding degrees or diplomas.[3] Of the delegates to the First Congress of the Communist Party of India, almost half were college graduates.[4]

On examining the educational record of the 74 graduates among our respondents, we find that 73 per cent graduated in Arts subjects (including Social Science); 12 per cent in Science; a further 4 per cent had a degree in Arts and also one in Science; 8 per cent graduated in Professional subjects, such as engineering, medicine, and law; and 3 per cent had a degree in Agriculture. From the available comparative data, *relating to the year 1957*, this distribution suggests that the graduate leaders may be more heavily recruited from those with Arts than those with Science degrees. In 1957, of all Indian students in higher education, 62 per cent were studying Arts subjects and 26 per cent Science subjects. The proportion of graduate leaders in the Professional and Agriculture categories, however, are broadly in line with the proportions of students in these fields: 10 per cent and 1 per cent respectively.[5]

Our data also enable us to judge whether the graduate leaders are recruited disproportionately from certain Indian universities, the point here being that some universities may be notable centres of political radicalism of the kind likely to appeal to potential

[1] Kochanek, *The Congress Party of India*, p. 339. Figure derived from Table XIII—5. Of 213 A.I.C.C. members, 1956, who supplied Kochanek with educational information, 65% were post-graduates, and a further 32% had some college education.—ibid., p. 366.

[2] N. D. Palmer and I. Tinker in Park and Tinker, op. cit., p. 119.

[3] W. H. Morris-Jones, *Parliament in India*, 1957, p. 125.

[4] Overstreet and Windmiller, op. cit., p. 358.

[5] UNESCO, *Basic Facts and Figures, 1960*, 1961, re-calculated from Table 8, p. 58.

recruits to the movement. In fact, no university or group of universities was an outstanding source of graduates among the leaders. The following table compares the distribution of graduate Sarvodaya leaders with the distribution of students registered at selected Indian universities in 1952–3.

The comparison is very rough and rests on questionable assumptions, but it does suggest the possibility that four universities, Allahabad, Benares, Lucknow, and Agra, may have provided

TABLE 3:5

The universities of Sarvodaya graduate leaders

University	Sarvodaya Graduate leaders %	Students at Indian universities, 1952–3 %
Agra	7	3·7
Alighar	3	1·1
Allahabad	7	1·5
Benares	7	2·1
Bombay	8	7·7
Calcutta	4	16·9
Delhi	1	2·4
Madras	11	12·4
Lucknow	6	1·8
Other Indian universities	42	50·4
Non-Indian universities	3	—
N	100% 71	100% 398,718

Source: For students at Indian universities, *Yearbook of the Universities of the Commonwealth*, 1955. [See under Assoc. of Univs. in Bibliography.]

a rather disproportionate number of Sarvodaya leaders, while one university, Calcutta, may have provided disproportionately few. The position of Calcutta University in this respect is in line with the fact that the movement is—and has been since Gandhi's day—notably weak in West Bengal.

Only three of the Indian-born Sarvodaya graduates had received part of their university education in the West: one was a Ph.D. of Ohio State University, one an M.A. of Iowa State University, and the third possessed a diploma in education of London University.

Two other leaders, one born in England and the other in the U.S.A., were graduates of Cambridge, and of Yale and Chicago, respectively.

Finally, in addition to the question about standard of education reached, respondents were asked whether or not they possessed technical or professional qualifications (other than degrees). These qualifications were classified into two broad types: 'Gandhian', such as a qualification in Khadi or village industries; and 'non-Gandhian', such as a teacher's training certificate. 69 per cent of the leaders possessed no such qualification, while 20 per cent had a 'non-Gandhian' and 12 per cent a 'Gandhian' qualification (1 per cent possessing both types).

Self-rated class of Sarvodaya leaders

The stratification variables that we have so far considered are all objective in character. That is to say, we have classified the leaders into various caste, class, and status groups by using criteria which are in some sense independent of the respondents, although the information was supplied by them and not independently verified. It is also possible, however, to stratify a given population into classes by using criteria derived from the respondents' own views about their position in the social hierarchy. We are then employing the concept of subjective class (or self-rated class or status). This concept assumes that the respondent sees the social order as a stratified one in which it is meaningful to think of any given status as either lower or higher than another, and that his social experience enables him to locate his position in the hierarchy.

Of course, the fact that an individual may rate himself as belonging to a particular class does not imply that he regards the existing system of social stratification as legitimate. He may well subscribe to an ideology which posits a 'classless society' as the ideal. All that the act of self-rating implies is that he recognizes the *existing* social order as a stratified one, not that he wishes to perpetuate it. The fact, then, that Sarvodaya leaders think of themselves as belonging to various social classes does not mean that they are being inconsistent and do not believe in the movement's stated goal of a classless society.

Without a definition of the term 'class', our respondents were asked: 'If you *had to* place yourself in one of the following social classes, which one would you say you belonged to? Upper, Middle,

Lower Middle, Working Class, or Peasant?' The first four categories may be assumed to relate to the respondents' feelings of
social status, although, as we shall see, such feelings are also
related to their class or economic position, particularly as measured
by the occupational class of their fathers. 'Peasant' is much more a
class (economic) than a status (prestige) category, and, by itself,
indicates no clear social status, since 'peasant' includes landless
labourers as well as wealthy landowning agriculturalists. It was
included because it was believed that the rural orientation of the
movement would lead some respondents to express a sense of
identity with the peasants, even though their social origins might
not be peasant in character.

For 23 per cent of the 218 who answered this question the
Peasant category appeared the best single choice. However, a
further 8 per cent combined this choice with a choice of another
category.[1] Thus we can say that nearly one-third of the leaders
rated themselves as Peasants of one kind or another.

The distribution of the 77 per cent of respondents who did not
tick only the Peasant category was as follows: Upper 1 per cent;
Middle 33 per cent; Lower Middle 31 per cent; and Working
Class 12 per cent.

It is not possible to compare these figures with those for other
populations in India. Taken as they stand, perhaps the most striking conclusion that emerges is that 65 per cent of all Sarvodaya
leaders think of themselves as belonging to the Upper, Middle, or
Lower Middle Classes. In the light of what we have already said
about their objective social characteristics, this proportion suggests
that the leaders as a whole have a realistic appreciation of their
position in the social hierarchy. Possible determinants of the
leaders' choices of self-rated classes will be discussed later.

Relationships between caste, class, and status among Sarvodaya leaders

So far we have analysed the composition of the Sarvodaya leadership in terms of a set of separate stratification variables. We have
proceeded as though each variable provided us with a criterion for
dividing the respondents into distinct stratification systems: a
varna system, an occupational class system, an educational class
system, and so on. In theory, it is possible that each stratification

---

[1] 18 respondents combined Peasant with another category: 6 with Middle
Class; 3 with Lower Middle Class; 8 with Working Class; and one with more
than one other category.

TABLE 3:6

Contingencies of caste, class, and status characteristics among Sarvodaya leaders

		Brahmin	Kshatriya	Vaishya	Middle	Lower	Rs. < 30/-	Rs. > 30/-	Graduate	Non-graduate	Yes	No	Middle	Lower middle	Working	Peasant	Non-peasant
CASTE (Varna)	Brahmin				(a) 0·10		(b) **0·05**		(c) 0·30		(d) 0·30		(e) 0·10			(f) 0·10	
	Kshatriya																
	Vaishya																
FATHER'S OCCUPATIONAL CLASS	Middle	(a) 80	51	53			(g) **0·01**		(h) 0·10		(i) 0·80		(j) **0·01**			(k) 0·20	
	Lower	3	8	4													
INCOME (per capita monthly)	Rs. < 30/-	(b) 27	27	13	(g) 65	11			(i) **0·001**		(m) **0·05**		(n) 0·20			(o) **0·01**	
	Rs. > 30/-	47	23	32	106	4											
EDUCATIONAL LEVEL	Graduate	(c) 33	15	20	(h) 70	3	(l) 13	50			(p) **0·05**		(q) 0·10			(r) **0·02**	
	Non-graduate	52	44	38	131	16	62	63									
PROPERTY OWNER	Yes	(d) 47	38	28	(i) 117	9	(m) 55	60	(p) 37	89			(s) 0·30			(t) 0·80	
	No	25	13	19	54	**5**	13	33	28	33							
SELF-RATED CLASS (i)	Middle	(e) 33	13	27	(j) 70	2	(n) 18	46	(q) 32	42	(s) 43	18					
	Lower middle	24	20	12	58	8	26	36	22	44	40	18					
	Working	7	9	6	20	6	9	10	5	21	11	10					
SELF-RATED CLASS (ii)	Peasant	(f) 28	22	10	(k) 63	3	(o) 31	22	(r) 15	52	(t) 41	18					
	Non-peasant	55	36	43	133	15	44	87	57	92	84	41					

EXPLANATION OF TABLE

The figures in the cells to the left of the main diagonal comprise a set of sub-tables giving the distribution of the respondent Sarvodaya leaders between major stratification variables. Thus, e.g., the sub-table setting Father's Occupational Class against Caste [cell (a)] shows that 80 Brahmin leaders were children of middle-class fathers, 3 Brahmins were children of lower-class fathers, etc. Each sub-table has been subjected to a chi-square test. The conventional figure of 0·05 or less has been adopted as indicative of a statistically significant association. The figures in the cells to the right of the main diagonal give the level of significance found in testing the corresponding sub-table, bold-type figures indicating that the association is statistically significant, i.e. 0·05 or less. Thus the distribution in the sub-table, Father's class against Caste, is *not* statistically system is in fact distinct. It is conceivable that a society might be composed of individuals who are radically unequal as measured by all the relevant criteria, but that the inequalities are randomly distributed. In such a society an individual who occupied a low position in one stratification system would have an equal chance, with all other individuals, of occupying a high position in another stratification system. For example, a Sudra would have an equal chance with a Brahmin of belonging to the high-income class. Such a society would not be 'classless' in the usually accepted sense of that term, where 'classless' connotes the absence of social inequalities, a socially homogeneous population. But it would be classless in another sense: one could not predict from knowledge of a person's position in any single social hierarchy what his position would be in other social hierarchies.

In the real world, social systems approximating to the model of a classless society in the second sense are as rare as classless societies in the usual sense. The pyramids of class and status are not separate but overlapping. Thus, an individual of high-class origin is more likely than one of low-class origin to have a high income, to rate himself as high-class, and so on. We may safely assume that this is broadly true of Indian society at large. But is it

---

significant. Lower-case letters in brackets at the top of the cells provide means of identifying sub-tables referred to in the text.

Chi-squares and degrees of freedom for the sub-tables are:

χ^2, d.f.: (a) 4·92, 2; (b) 6·79, 2; (c) 2·82, 2; (d) 2·53, 2; (e) 8·59, 4; (f) 5·25, 2; (g) 7·12, 1; (h) 2·84, 1; (i) o·10, 1; (j) 9·64, 2; (k) 1·85, 1; (l) 14·66, 1; (m) 5·15, 1; (n) 3·69, 2; (o) 9·69, 1; (p) 4·96, 1; (q) 5·07, 2; (r) 5·24, 1; (s) 2·47, 2; (t) o·10, 1.

NOTES

Caste: only leaders belonging to the three 'twice-born' varnas have been included.

Father's Occupational Class: The following occupational categories have been assumed to be 'middle-class': Absentee Landlord, Owner-cultivator, Business, Government Service, Professional, and Priest. The remaining occupational categories used, Tenant-cultivator, Landless Labourer, Private Service, and Artisan, have been assumed to be 'lower-class'.

Property Owner: This variable refers to the respondents' reported ownership of *any* form of property, whatever its estimated value.

Self-rated Class (i): Sub-tables relating to this variable *exclude* those respondents who rated themselves as Peasants, unless they also indicated another of the classes listed. 'Middle' includes those who rated themselves as 'upper-class'.

Self-rated Class (ii): The Peasant category includes all respondents who rated themselves as Peasants, including those who also indicated another class. The Non-Peasant category includes all those who indicated a class other than Peasant.

also true of the population we are dealing with, 'the society of Sarvodaya leaders'? We have seen that this 'society' is not classless in the usual sense; but is it classless in the other sense? Put in another way, if we know one class characteristic of any leader, can we predict, within limits, what his other class characteristics are likely to be?

Table 3:6 presents the data we require to answer this question. In the form of a matrix, it provides information concerning twenty relationships between caste, class, and status variables among the Sarvodaya leaders. As far as the variables used are involved, if 'the society of Sarvodaya leaders' were in fact classless, we should expect none of the twenty relationships to be associated in a significant way. On the other hand, if all the relationships were significant and in the expected direction, consistent with stratification theory, then we could conclude that the leaders formed a perfect class society, i.e. the higher (or lower) any leader was in one social hierarchy, the higher (or lower) he would be in all the other social hierarchies.

As it turns out, the real world is more complex than any model of it. Our 'society of leaders' is neither perfectly classless nor perfectly class-ridden, but a bit of both; and also with some unexpected features. This conclusion may be verified by inspection of the following list of statements describing the twenty relationships. Eight relationships reveal associations which are statistically significant at the widely-used conventional level of significance (0·05).[1] The remaining twelve are not statistically significant, but ten of them may be significant in another sense; the distribution figures, when expressed in percentages, hint at the possibility that there *may* be an association which *might* be statistically significant if our sample of leaders were larger and we are able to make more refined distinctions. Particularly when hints of possible associations appear in several relationships, and all point in one direction, it would be absurd to ignore them on the ground that, taken separately, the associations are not statistically significant at a conventional level of significance.[2] For convenience, we present statements about the statistically significant relationships first.

[1] For an explanation of our use of the term 'statistically significant' see Chapter Eight, pp. 314–15 below.

[2] cf. J. K. Skipper, A. L. Guenther and G. Nass, 'The sacredness of 0·05: a note concerning the uses of statistical levels of significance in social science', *The American Sociologist*, 2, 1 (Feb. 1967).

Statistically significant relationships (at the 0·05 level)

1. *Caste and Income* (cells (b) in Table 3:6). Among the twice-born varnas, there is a significant association between caste and *per capita* income. But the relationship is non-linear; it is *not* true that the higher the caste, the more likely are its members to enjoy a *per capita* monthly income of Rs. 30/– or more. Brahmin leaders are only slightly better off than the twice-born as a whole, while the Kshatriyas are significantly poorer and the Vaishyas significantly richer.

2. *Father's Occupational Class and Income* (g). There is a highly significant association between father's occupational class (middle or lower) and respondents' *per capita* income. Sons of middle-class fathers are more likely than sons of lower-class fathers to enjoy a *per capita* monthly income of Rs. 30/– or more.

3. *Father's Occupational Class and Self-rated Class (other than Peasant)* (j). There is a highly significant association between father's occupational class and respondents' rating of their own class (middle, lower middle, or working). The relationship is linear: the higher the respondent's self-rated class, the more likely is he to be the son of a middle-class father.

4. *Income and Educational Attainment* (l). There is a highly significant association between *per capita* income and educational attainment (graduate or non-graduate). Graduate leaders are more likely than non-graduates to enjoy a monthly *per capita* income of Rs. 30/– or more.

5. *Income and Ownership of Property* (m). There is a significant association between income and property ownership (ownership of any immovable property or non-ownership). But the relationship is the *reverse* of what might be expected from stratification theory: leaders who own property are *less* likely than non-owners to enjoy a monthly *per capita* income of Rs. 30/– or more.

6. *Income and Self-rated Class (Peasant or Non-Peasant)* (o). There is a highly significant association between income and respondents' rating of their own class as peasant or other than peasant. Self-rated peasants are *less* likely than non-peasants to enjoy a *per capita* monthly income of Rs. 30/– or more.

7. *Educational attainment and Ownership of Property* (p). There is a significant association between educational attainment and ownership of property. But the relationship is the *reverse* of what might be expected from stratification theory: owners of any immovable property are *less* likely than non-owners to be graduates.

8. *Educational Attainment and Self-rated Class (Peasant or Non-Peasant)* (r). There is a highly significant association between educational attainment and respondents' rating of their own class as peasant or other than peasant. Self-rated peasants are *less* likely than non-peasants to be graduates.

Relationships which are not statistically significant (at the 0·05 level)

9. *Caste and Father's Occupational Class* (a). Although the association is not statistically significant, the distribution suggests that Kshatriya leaders are rather *less* likely than Brahmins or Vaishyas to be sons of middle-class fathers.

10. *Caste and Educational Attainment* (c). Although the association is not statistically significant, the distribution suggests that Brahmin leaders are *more* likely, and Kshatriya leaders *less* likely, to be graduates.

11. *Caste and Ownership of Property* (d). Although the association is not statistically significant, the distribution suggests that Kshatriya leaders are *more* likely, and Vaishya leaders *less* likely, to own immovable property.

12. *Caste and Self-rated Class (other than Peasant)* (e). While the association is not statistically significant, the distribution suggests that Kshatriya leaders are *less* likely than either Brahmins or Vaishyas (particularly the latter) to rate themselves as middle-class. There *appear* to be linear relationships between self-rated class and membership of the Brahmin and Kshatriya castes: the higher a leader's self-rated class, the *more* likely is he to be a Brahmin, while the *less* likely is he to be a Kshatriya.

13. *Caste and Self-rated Class (Peasant or Non-Peasant)* (f). While the association is not statistically significant, the distribution suggests that Vaishya leaders are *less* likely, and Kshatriya leaders *more* likely, to rate their class as peasant.

14. *Father's Occupational Class and Educational Attainment* (h). The association is not statistically significant, but the distribution

suggests that sons of lower-class fathers are less likely than sons of middle-class fathers to be graduates.

15. *Father's Occupational Class and Ownership of Property* (i). There is very clearly no association between the father's occupational class and the leaders' ownership of property.

16. *Father's Occupational Class and Self-rated Class* (*Peasant or Non-Peasant*) (k). While the association is not statistically significant, the distribution suggests that sons of middle-class fathers are *more* likely than sons of lower-class fathers to rate themselves as belonging to the peasant class.

17. *Income and Self-rated Class* (*other than Peasant*) (n). While the association is not statistically significant, the distribution suggests that there may be a linear relationship between self-rated class (middle, lower middle, or working) and income: the higher the self-rated class of a leader, the more likely is he to enjoy a monthly *per capital* income of Rs. 30/– or more.

18. *Educational Attainment and Self-rated Class* (*other than Peasant*) (q). While the association is not statistically significant, the distribution suggests that there may be a linear relationship between self-rated class (middle, lower middle, or working) and educational attainment: the higher the self-rated class of a leader, the more likely is he to be a graduate.

19. *Ownership of Property and Self-rated Class* (*other than Peasant*) (s). Although the association is not statistically significant, the distribution suggests that there may be a linear relationship between self-rated class (middle, lower middle, or working) and ownership of property: the higher a leader's self-rated class, the more likely is he to own property.

20. *Ownership of Property and Self-rated Class* (*Peasant or Non-Peasant*) (t). There is very clearly no association between a leader's ownership of property and his self-rating as a peasant or non-peasant.

Comments on the relationships

Several of the listed relationships call for special comment. The absence of any association between father's occupational class and respondents' ownership of property (statement 15 above) is remarkable: in other societies, including the Indian national society, one would expect to find a positive association. So, too, is the absence of any association between ownership of property and a leader's self-rating as a peasant (20), although it should be noted that 'property' here means 'any immovable property of whatever value' and not merely land. One might have expected that those leaders who identified with the peasants would be more likely to own property. But, of course, in the Sarvodaya movement the possession of private property is not an esteemed value: quite the opposite. The ownership of property certainly does seem to be a somewhat peculiar attribute in the 'society of Sarvodaya leaders'. It will have been noted, in addition, that owners of property are less likely to enjoy the higher *per capita* monthly incomes (5) and less likely to be graduates (7), with the odd implication—by ordinary standards—that property ownership is a predictor of *low* income status and *low* educational attainment. The statistically significant association between identification with the peasant class and low income is less peculiar. The majority of non-peasants, as we have seen, identified with the middle and lower middle classes, and so it is not surprising that they are more likely to enjoy higher incomes. However, there remains something of a puzzle even here, since there is the suggestion of a positive association (not statistically significant) between identification with the peasants and being the son of a middle-class father.

All the remaining relationships calling for special comment (i.e. those not consistent with stratification theory) involve the leaders who are Kshatriyas. Kshatriya Sarvodaya leaders enjoy a *per capita* monthly income lower than that of the other twice-born leaders (1); it is also possible that they are less likely to be of middle-class origin (9), less likely to be graduates (10), and less likely to rate themselves as middle-class (12). On the other hand, they are more likely to own property (11) and more likely to identify with the peasants (13): both attributes which in the 'society of Sarvodaya leaders', at least, are associated with low income status. No explanation immediately presents itself of the special position of Kshatriya Sarvodaya leaders: it remains a puzzle which might merit further research.

Identification with the Upper Class category

At this point we may conveniently return to the concept of self-rated class. Particular interest attaches to three classes (or statuses) selected by minorities of the leaders: upper, peasant, and working. (Those who identified with the middle and lower middle classes are less interesting, since on most of the indices of caste, class, and status we should expect the majority of leaders to identify with these two classes.)

The leaders who rated themselves as upper-class may be dealt with biographically, since only three respondents are involved. Two were top leaders (members of the Prabandh Samiti) and one was a District Representative. Of the former, one was the son of a money-lender and zamindar who owned about 2,000 acres of land. A post-graduate who had studied law, he served in the army until 1942, when he retired from the service in order to look after the zamindari. He had given 2,200 acres in Bhoodan plus one-tenth of his income from other sources, and at the time of the survey owned no property. In his case, clearly no 'false consciousness' was present in rating himself as upper-class. The second top leader was the son of an owner cultivator possessing a relatively large estate of 300 acres. Prior to joining the movement, he himself had been an owner cultivator. He reported having given 100 of his 500 acres in Bhoodan. Despite belonging to the class of rich peasants, he had been educated up to Primary School level only. The Representative who rated himself as upper-class had been educated up to High School standard, and afterwards had studied Sanskrit, Hindi, and Accountancy. His father was a priest but owned no land. For sixteen years this respondent had been the sub-editor and later editor of an Indian daily newspaper. He reported the *per capita* monthly income of his household at the time of the survey as Rs. 100/-.

Identification with the Peasant Class category

In discussing the inter-relationships of class, we have already indicated some attributes of those who identified with the peasants. They were less likely than non-peasants to be graduates and to enjoy high income. It is also possible that peasant identifiers were more likely to be sons of middle-class fathers, and to be Brahmins and Kshatriyas rather than Vaishyas. None of these attributes helps us to explain why they should identify with the peasants. The absence of an association between peasant identification and property ownership was also puzzling. However, other data which are available prove more illuminating. Although not statistically significant, there does appear to be an association between owner-ship of *land* (as distinct from other forms of property) and choice of peasant status: leaders who owned land appeared to be more likely than non-landowners to rate themselves as peasants. There is a much stronger association between choice of peasant status and *father's* ownership of land. While 65 per cent of all the leaders' fathers owned land, 95 per cent of the peasants' fathers did so. Self-rated peasants were also more likely than others to be the sons of agriculturalists: while 54 per cent of the leaders fell into this category, 75 per cent of the peasant identifiers did so. As a final point in this explanation, 91 per cent of self-rated peasants were brought up in a village, compared with 68 per cent of all the leaders.[1] These facts may not account for every leader who rated his own class as peasant. Some may have deliberately identified with the peasants, despite their lack of peasant background, as a symbol of their identification with a peasant-oriented movement; but the majority of peasant identifiers had one or more other good grounds for their choice.

Identification with the Working Class category

Accounting for the 12 per cent of the leaders who rated themselves as working-class presents little difficulty. The strongest factor in their choice appears to have been that more than three out of four of them were not the sons of middle-class fathers. Although the associations were not statistically significant, it is also possible that they were less likely to own property, to be graduates, to enjoy high income, and to be Brahmins. Examination of the data in more detail further suggests that Working Class identifiers were less likely to be sons of fathers who owned land, less likely to own land themselves, more likely to have been the sons of tenant cultivators than of owner cultivators, more likely to have been educated up to Primary School level only, and more likely to be either Kshatriyas or 'once-born'. Interestingly enough, however, they were as likely as other leaders to have been brought up in a village.

---

[1] See Section III below

Status consistency among Sarvodaya leaders

To conclude our analysis of the caste, class, and status characteristics of the leaders, we shall now consider what has been termed
'a non-vertical dimension of social status'.[1] The concept to be
employed here is that of status consistency (or crystallization or
congruence). This concept is largely self-explanatory, and has been
implicit in our discussion above of the relationships between the
class characteristics of the leaders. Status consistency refers to the
extent to which an individual's rank positions in given social
hierarchies are at a comparable level.[2] The concept assumes importance as the basis of the general hypothesis that status inconsistency creates for the individuals concerned a number of social
and psychological problems, in particular uncertainty, frustration,
and stress, which in turn provide motivations for social action (or
inaction). Recent research has suggested at least six different
responses to status inconsistency: enhanced mobility striving,
withdrawal into social isolation, psychosomatic symptoms of stress,
political liberalism, preference for and attempts to change the social
order, and prejudice.[3]

In the light of what has been shown above about the class characteristics of the Sarvodaya leaders, it seems likely that the
majority of them could be classified as status inconsistents. Nine
out of ten are of high caste and of high occupational class origin;
three out of four have been educated to High School standard or
above; and two out of three own immovable property and rate
themselves as upper-, middle-, or lower-middle-class. So far, these
facts suggest a high level of status consistency rather than status
inconsistency. The inconsistency arises in connection with the
leaders' positions in the income class hierarchy. Less than one in
two enjoy a monthly household income of Rs. 200/– or more, a
level of income enjoyed by the majority of middle-class families in
the cities of Bombay, Delhi, and Calcutta; and two out of five
enjoy a *per capita* household income below or not much more than
that of the average Indian.[4]

[1] G. E. Lenski, 'Status crystallization: a non-vertical dimension of social
status', *American Sociological Review*, 19 (Aug. 1954).
[2] G. Rush, 'Status consistency and right-wing extremism', *A.S.R.* 32 (Feb.
1967), p. 86.
[3] J. A. Geschwender, 'Continuities in theories of status consistency and
cognitive dissonance', *Social Forces*, 46 (Dec. 1967), p. 161.
[4] See p. 88 above.

But, of course, of all the social hierarchies mentioned, the income hierarchy is the one in which an individual, especially an individual who otherwise enjoys a relatively high status, can most easily improve his ranking by his own efforts. If, measured by income, many of the Sarvodaya leaders are poor, it is because they have deliberately chosen to be so by joining a movement in which material rewards are not highly valued. In other words, it seems likely that many of the Sarvodaya status inconsistents are 'spurious' or 'voluntary' inconsistents. It would certainly be rash to assume that their status inconsistency was a cause rather than a consequence of their participation in the movement. This is not to deny that at least some of the leaders may experience frustration as a result of their low income status: choosers of 'holy poverty' are less likely to experience frustration than those who are thrust into it; but voluntary choice may not dissolve all frustration, and what remains may provide motivation for action within the movement; for example, action designed to secure Sarvodaya workers a better and more assured income.

These considerations do not necessarily render the concept of status inconsistency useless for our analysis. We shall employ it, however, within the context of the movement itself. Although our measures of status are societal, applicable to Indian national society, we shall confine our attention to 'the society of Sarvodaya leaders'. Knowing how the leaders are distributed between the various levels of the several social hierarchies, we shall adopt definitions of high and low status which seem appropriate to 'the society of leaders', even though they might not be the most appropriate definitions for the national society.[1]

Using our measure of status consistency on five dimensions of status, we were able to classify all but 13 per cent of our 228

---

[1] The following procedure was used to determine whether or not an individual leader was status consistent. Five dimensions of status were considered. On the first, father's caste, twice-born castes, including Kyasthas, were defined as high, all others low; on the second, father's occupational class, tenant cultivators, landless labourers, private servants, and artisans were defined as low, all others as high; on the third, educational attainment, no formal education and primary school only were defined as low, all others as high; on the fourth, respondent's reported monthly household income, groups of Rs. 100/- and below were defined as low, all others as high; and on the fifth, respondent's self-rated class, upper, middle, and lower middle classes, with or without peasant identification, were defined as high; working class and 'working class and peasant' were defined as low; and peasant by itself was defined as either high or low.

leaders. Ignoring the unclassifiable, we found that 45 per cent of the leaders were status consistents and 55 per cent status inconsistents. All but one of the former were *high* status consistents. The status inconsistents were distributed as shown in the following table.

TABLE 3:7

Status inconsistents among Sarvodaya leaders

(a)		(b)	
Low on:	%	*Low on:*	%
Education	46	Education only	25
Income	39	Income only	25
Self-rated Class	23	Self-rated Class only	8
Father's Occupational Class	17	Father's Occupational Class only	7
Father's Caste	12	Father's Caste only	7
N	110		79

The percentages in section (a) of the table do not add up to 100, since, as section (b) shows, 31 leaders were low in more than one status hierarchy, most of them in two hierarchies, but eight in three or four.

Consideration of associations between Sarvodaya status inconsistency and other variables, such as attitudes to issues within the movement, will be taken up in Chapter Eight below.

III. ENVIRONMENTAL AND FAMILY CHARACTERISTICS

The broad conclusion which emerged from our discussion in the previous section of the caste, class, and status characteristics of Sarvodaya leaders is that most of them are drawn from, and still see themselves as belonging to, the higher social strata of Indian society. For the Marxist this conclusion would constitute the most important single fact about the movement. On the assumption (or hypothesis) that all social movements can be explained in terms of the struggle between classes, the Marxist would seek to interpret all other aspects of the movement as, in some way, derivative from the class situation of its members and clientele. Without prejudging the validity of the Marxian hypothesis, there are, however, kinds of factors other than direct class factors which appear relevant to answering the question what sort of people join particular social movements. Among these other factors are what we may call early

environmental and family characteristics. Under this heading we
shall include: whether a person's childhood was spent in an urban
or a rural setting; and the type of family he was brought up in.

Childhood environment: rural versus urban

One of the significant divisions of modern societies is that between
the rural and the urban. Until fairly recent times all human societies have been predominantly rural in character. It is only since the
Industrial Revolution that predominantly urbanized societies have
emerged; and one index of an 'advanced society' is often thought
to be the degree to which it has undergone 'the Urban Revolution'.
As is well known, this revolution has only recently got under way
in India, although of course cities have been a feature of Indian
civilization since ancient times. Urbanization is proceeding apace
in contemporary India, but at a rate which is not very much faster
than the rate of population growth. Thus the balance between the
rural and the urban sectors remains fairly static, and India today
is still a society in which about four out of every five of its people
live in villages.[1]

For Gandhi the 'real India' was the India of the villages. This
was so not merely in the demographic sense but even more in the
sense that village life was the ideal to be cherished and preserved.
'I regard the growth of cities', he once wrote, 'as an evil thing,
unfortunate for mankind and the world, unfortunate for England
and certainly unfortunate for India. The British have exploited
India through its cities. The latter have exploited the villages. The
blood of the villages is the cement with which the edifice of the
cities is built. I want the blood that is today inflating the arteries
of the cities to run once again in the blood vessels of the villages.'[2]

This attitude to the village was central to Gandhi's social philosophy. It is linked with his opposition to industrialism and with

---

[1] The proportion of rural to total population in 1961 was 82·03%, compared
with 82·71% in 1951, 88·01% in 1931, and 89·16% in 1901.—*The Gazeteer of
India*, Vol. 1, Ministry of Information, 1965, p. 525. [See 'India, Govt. of', in
Bibliography.] In censuses prior to 1961 all places with a population of 5,000
and more, and in some special cases even places with less than 5,000, were
defined as towns. In the 1961 census a town was defined as a place which
satisfied the following conditions: a population of more than 5,000; a density
of not less than about 400 per sq. km.; and not less than 75% of the adult male
population engaged in non-agricultural activities.

[2] *Harijan*, 23 Apr. 1946, p. 198. Quoted in M. K. Gandhi, *Village Swaraj*,
1963, p. 25.

his plea for radical decentralization of social and political life. And both are linked, more ultimately, to the fundamental principle of ahimsa. One of the essential conditions of a non-violent society, Gandhi in effect argued, is that it should consist of a network of more or less self-sufficient 'village republics', since the concentration of power in large urban industrial centres inevitably leads to exploitation and social conflict. Gandhi's espousal of village life may have derived, in part at least, from an over-idealized conception of the role that villages have played in the development and perpetuation of traditional Indian civilization, although it should be added that Gandhi had few illusions about the typical Indian villages of his own day: 'dung-heaps', as he once described them.[1]

Gandhi's followers in the Sarvodaya movement have continued to emphasize the crucial role of the village. In their schemes of social reconstruction the village remains the basic unit of social organization, even though some of them are prepared to admit that self-sufficiency should be sought in a *group* of villages rather than in each single village. The value attached to the village is clearly evident in the movement's programme for land reform: 'villagization' rather than 'nationalization' of land is the aim.

Given this perspective, it is plausible to suggest the hypothesis that one factor which attracts people to join the movement is its evident concern for village values, a factor which in turn may be related to their early life experience. To have spent one's childhood in a village may be an important determinant of whether or not one accepts an ideology emphasizing the values of village life and culture.

Our data about the Sarvodaya leaders enable us to estimate the proportion with a rural as distinct from an urban upbringing. Respondents were asked to state whether, up to the age of fifteen years, they had spent most of their life in a village, a small town (up to 25,000 population), or a large town or city. Since precise definitions of these three categories were not supplied, our findings are not strictly comparable with census data in which towns are defined, broadly speaking, as places with populations of 5,000 and more. It should also be noted that an Indian might describe as a 'village' what in the West would be regarded as a small town, although large villages are comparatively few and three-fifths of all

[1] *Harijan*, 10 Nov. 1946.

Indian villages in 1961 had under 500 inhabitants. With these qualifications, our findings are as follows: 68 per cent of the leaders reported that all or the greater part of their early life was spent in a village; 16 per cent were brought up in a small town; and a further 16 per cent in a large town or city.

These figures suggest that the majority of the leaders enjoyed the kind of rural upbringing experienced by four-fifths of their countrymen. In terms of the rural–urban division, the leaders are broadly representative in this respect of Indian society, although there is clearly a distinct bias in favour of recruitment of leaders of urban origin. If we assume that people brought up in a village are more likely than others to cherish village values, our findings may be interpreted as consistent with the hypothesis suggested above. They do not, of course, confirm the hypothesis, since we have no direct information about the part played by early environment in the recruitment process. Nor are there any reliable data which would enable us to compare Sarvodaya leaders with leaders of other social and political movements in India. It is commonly alleged that leaders of Indian political parties and movements are disproportionately drawn from the ranks of urban intellectuals.[1] If this is in fact the case, it seems likely to be less true of the Sarvodaya movement. By origin, at least, most of its leaders are *not* urban intellectuals and they do not live or work in urban centres, even though they belong to the educated élite.

Childhood environment: joint versus nuclear family

If a childhood spent in a village may be considered a possibly significant factor in shaping attitudes conducive to recruitment to the Sarvodaya movement, so may the type of family a person is brought up in. In advanced industrial societies the typical family is of the nuclear kind, consisting of husband and wife and their children. With industrialization and modernization the nuclear type of family is becoming more common in India, but the traditional type of family, known as the joint or extended family, still retains an important place. In Hindu society, where descent is traced through males (patrilineal) the joint family consists of a man

[1] Kochanek's data confirm this proposition with respect to Congress M.P.s of the second Lok Sabha. Of the 224 M.P.s in his sample, 31·6% resided in villages (up to 10,000 population); 47·6% in towns (10,000–250,000 population); and 21·0% in cities (population 250,000 or more). 71% continued to reside in their birthplace.—Kochanek, *The Congress Party of India*, p. 393, Table XV—10.

and his brothers, all their wives, their married sons with their wives and children, and the unmarried daughters in each generation. Where descent is traced through females (matrilineal), as it is principally in Kerala, the joint family consists of a woman, her brothers and sisters, her own and her sisters' children, and the children of the women of the succeeding generations.[1] The laws of succession and inheritance in the patrilineal joint family provide that the ancestral property is held in common, although each male, on coming of age, has the right to demand partition and to receive his share. The head of the family is usually the eldest male of the earliest generation, but the headship may sometimes be vested in some other male if he has outstanding ability. Such a family, all eating food cooked in one kitchen, may consist of as many as 75 people, controlled by the head, who holds the whole family property.

Sociologists are divided on whether or not families in India are still predominantly of the joint type. In part, this disagreement arises because of the lack of an accepted definition of a joint family. In a period of transition something considerably less than the kind of family described above may still be regarded as joint. And what appears to be a simple family of the Western nuclear type may in India still be regarded as part of a joint family, if the husband continues to maintain property rights and obligations in the original family group. According to Dr Karve, the joint family is today most prevalent among cultivators who own land, and among merchants and trading communities. Recent surveys carried out by the Deccan College, Poona, however, have shown that 'over large areas the predominant pattern of family (up to 70 per cent) is the nuclear family. The incidence of nuclear families is large in urban areas, while joint families are more numerous but still in a minority in the rural areas.'[2] Even so, in most Indian families, of whatever type, aged parents are supported by the sons, sometimes living with only one son while the other sons contribute to their maintenance.

[1] I. Karve in B. N. Varma (ed.), *Contemporary India*, 1964, p. 52.

[2] ibid., p. 56. In 1961, 15·81% of a sample of rural households and 11·15% of a sample of urban households contained married relations.—*Census of India 1961*, Vol. 1, Part II c(i), Social and Cultural Tables, pp. 6–7. The presence of married relations might be taken as a rough indicator that the household constitutes a joint family. However, another sample survey undertaken in 1964–5 estimated that 51·6% of Indian families were joint families.—*All-India Consumer Expenditure Survey*, Vol. II, 1967, Table 3, p. 20.

In its attitude to the joint family, as in its attitude towards the village, Sarvodaya ideology is firmly committed to the traditional conception. Dr Bharatan Kumarappa, in his book *Capitalism, Socialism, or Villagism*, recently (1965) republished by Sarva Seva Sangh, expresses well the Sarvodaya view. Although ancient Indian economic organization was individualistic in the sense that each man owned his enterprise and had to earn through it whatever he required for himself, various devices, Kumarappa argues, were adopted to curb individual greed and to promote group interests. Among these devices was the joint family:

The joint family . . . was a little republic in itself where all the members shared things in common, with the oldest member as the head. It afforded training in group life, where selfishness was curbed, and the individual learnt to sacrifice his own desires for the well-being of the others. Whatever was earned by a member became the property of all, so that wealth made no difference exclusively to the one earning it. It was used for the good of all alike, thus indicating that the primary purpose round which family life was built was group welfare, wealth being but a means thereto. . . . It guaranteed a subsistence to every member, including the old, the infirm, the widow, the orphan, the decrepit and the maimed, thus doing away with organized charity such as prevails today. The joint family secured that from the cradle the individual was trained in controlling his desires in the interests of others, in protecting the weak and the helpless: and in so far as home-life is the training ground for character, it tended to produce an individual to whom altruism, gentleness, non-violence, and consideration for others were as second nature.[1]

The governing principle of the joint family, Kumarappa continues, was 'from each according to his ability, to each according to his need'—the principle of socialism. Socialism, therefore, might be regarded as a system of production and distribution based on the principles of joint family life. What distinguishes 'villagism' from orthodox socialism is its appreciation that 'the need principle' is more readily attainable in small groups such as the village and joint family. In the Gandhian ideal social order, the joint family will in effect be extended to embrace all members of a village: the village, in short, will become like a large joint family.[2]

In the light of this no doubt highly idealized account of the

[1] Kumarappa, op. cit., pp. 109–10.
[2] ibid., pp. 94, 187–9.

traditional joint family system, it is plausible to suggest the hypothesis that Sarvodaya leaders are recruited disproportionately from
people who have been brought up in joint families. Our data do in
fact support this hypothesis, since no less than 81 per cent of
respondents reported that they were brought up in a joint family.[1]
Even allowing for the rural class origin of many of the leaders, this
figure may be regarded as surprisingly high. It should be noted,
however, that no definition of a joint family was supplied. Respondents were left to give their own meaning to the term and it is
possible, therefore, that the figure includes some who were brought
up in a modified joint family. Further, given the favourable attitude
of the movement towards the institution, respondents are likely to
have interpreted the term in its widest possible sense.

IV. RELIGIOUS CHARACTERISTICS

For the purposes of sociological analysis, religion may be defined
as an institutionalized system of symbols, beliefs, values, and
practices focused on questions of 'ultimate meaning', i.e. matters
pertaining to the nature, significance, and purpose of reality.[2] In
this sense, religion provides for men a rationale for existence, a
view of the world, and a perspective, or frame of reference, for the
organization of their experience. Typically, if not invariably, a
religious perspective affirms the existence of a supernatural being
or force. In this respect it constitutes one of the alternative forms
of the more general phenomenon which may be designated as
'value orientation'. The other form is a humanistic perspective that
rejects the supernatural but provides the functional equivalent of
religion. In Western societies, where the growth of science has
contributed to a decline in belief in the supernatural, humanistic
or secular value orientations in the shape of ideologies, such as
Communism, appear to provide for many people an effective substitute for the traditional religions.

In classical sociological theory the institution of religion is related
to the general proposition that 'every society in order to maintain
itself must achieve some consensus around a set of basic values, an
agreement on ultimate meaning that affords an appropriate basis

---

[1] N = 212; 7% of the respondents did not answer this question.
[2] cf. C. Y. Glock & R. Stark, *Religion and Society in Tension*, 1965, p. 4.

for social organization and common action.'[1] From this standpoint, emphasis has been placed on the integrative functions of religion in society—an emphasis clearly apparent in Marx's celebrated dictum that 'religion is the opiate of the people', but an emphasis by no means confined to Marx. However, the relation between religion and social integration is too complex to be summarized in a single dictum. Institutionalized religion is not essential to social integration, and in societies where it conflicts with other moral authorities it may, on the contrary, contribute to 'social disorganization'.[2] Both historically and contemporaneously, in fact, religion in some of its manifestations has been associated not with social and political conservatism but with revolutionism and political extremism. As Engels, among others, noted, early Christianity and the early nineteenth-century revolutionary workers' movement in Europe had 'notable points of resemblance', particularly in their millennial appeals and lower-class social base.[3] In Tsarist Russia of the 1890s the young Trotsky successfully recruited the first working-class members of the South Russian Workers' Union from adherents to religious sects.[4] And recent research in Holland and Sweden suggests that Communist Party support is strongest in areas which were previously centres of religious revivalism.[5]

The existence of a relationship between religion and political radicalism would be sufficient to justify an exploration of the religious foundations of the Sarvodaya movement. But in any case such an exploration can scarcely be avoided, since, unlike comparable social movements in the contemporary West, the Sarvodaya movement presents to the world a visibly religious face. It is both a religious and a social movement. This characteristic it derives from its founder, Gandhi. Fundamental to an understanding of his life and work is the fact that he was first and foremost a religious man. 'Most religious men I have met', he once told a Christian friend, 'are politicians in disguise; I, however, who wear the guise of a politician, am at heart a religious man.' And again: '. . . at the back of every word that I have uttered since I have known what public life is, and of every act that I have done, there

---

[1] cf. C. Y. Glock & R. Stark, *Religion and Society in Tension*, 1965, p. 190.
[2] ibid., p. 180.
[3] S. M. Lipset, *Political Man*, 1960, p. 106.
[4] ibid., pp. 107–8.   [5] ibid., p. 108.

has been a religious consciousness and a downright religious motive.'[1] For most of Gandhi's followers in the contemporary Sarvodaya movement the same holds true. For them, the movement's social, political, and economic objectives are part and parcel of their religious and spiritual objectives. They share with Gandhi and some puritan sects in the Western Christian tradition the ideal of establishing 'The Kingdom of God on Earth'.

But if Sarvodaya is a religious movement, it is equally important to note that its religion is in no sense sectarian. As is well known, most Indians practise Hinduism—a creed which cannot easily be defined in terms of doctrinal beliefs, since these range from polytheism through monotheism and pantheism to atheism. Hinduism, however, is only the largest of India's religions. Islam is the creed of many millions, and in addition there are several small minority creeds such as Christianity, Sikhism, Jainism, and Buddhism. Gandhi himself was a devout Hindu and believed that he would find salvation only through Hinduism. But he also accepted all religions as being, in some fundamental sense, equally true. For him the significance of religion lay in the fact that it meant 'belief in the ordered moral government of the Universe'.[2] It did not really matter how a person defined God: 'there are innumerable definitions of God, because his manifestations are innumerable.'[3] God is Truth, he agreed, but, equally, Truth is God. It was even possible, therefore, in Gandhi's eyes, for an atheist who affirmed the Truth to qualify as a religious person.

This radically liberal and unsectarian attitude towards religion remains characteristic of the Sarvodaya movement, with the result that religious belief (or non-belief) constitutes no formal obstacle to participation as far as the movement itself is concerned. Nevertheless, our data suggest that there are factors operating which favour recruitment to the movement's leadership of persons of Hindu background rather than adherents to most other creeds in India. The following table shows the distribution of our respondents according to the religion of their parents, compared with the distribution of religions among the total population of India in 1961, and among members of the All-India Congress Committee, 1956.

[1] Both quotations cited in G. Dhawan, *The Political Philosophy of Mahatma Gandhi*, 3rd ed., 1957, p. 38.
[2] *Harijan*, 10 Feb. 1940, p. 445.   [3] Quoted in Dhawan, op. cit., p. 42.

It will be seen that Hindus (or, more strictly, the sons and daughters of Hindus) are over-represented in the Sarvodaya leadership to the extent of 10·5 per cent, while Muslims are under-represented to approximately the same extent, 9·7 per cent.[1] The Sikhs, belonging to a sect which may be regarded as originating in an attempt to reconcile Hindu with Muslim by getting rid of caste, superstition, and idolatry, while retaining the pantheistic ideas of higher Vishnuism (a form of Hinduism), are also slightly under-represented. In contrast, the smaller sect of Jains, whose religion

TABLE 3:8

Religion of parents of Sarvodaya leaders compared with Indian population and All-India Congress Committee, 1956

	Hindu	Muslim	Sikh	Jain	Christian	Buddhist	Others	%	N
Sarvodaya leaders	94	1	1	3	1	0	0	100	226
Indian population*	83·5	10·7	1·8	0·5	2·4	0·7	0·4	100	439M
A.I.C.C.**	91·5	3·8	4·4	—	0·3	—	—	100	636

Sources. *Government of India, *India 1964*, 1964, p. 18.
**Kochanek, *The Congress Party of India*, p. 365.

also has its roots in Brahmanism and who likewise reject caste distinctions, is more clearly over-represented. The difference in the representation of these two sects in the Sarvodaya leadership may, perhaps, be explained in terms of the contrasting attitudes of Sikhism and Jainism towards non-violence. Of all the sects of India, the Jains have been the most committed to Non-violence. For them the sacredness of all life is a fundamental principle, so much so that even insects must not be killed, and plants must be regarded as the brothers of mankind. In contrast, the Sikhs have a strong military tradition and have been an important source of

[1] It will be seen from the table that Muslims are also under-represented in the A.I.C.C., but not to the same extent. At the First Congress of the Communist Party of India, 1943, among the 139 delegates were 13 Muslims, 8 Sikhs, 3 Untouchables, 1 Christian, and 1 Jain. 'The remaining delegates were presumably of Hindu family background.'—Overstreet and Windmiller, op. cit., pp. 357–8. These figures suggest that the Communist leadership was more representative of the Muslim community than is the Sarvodaya leadership, although, of course, the Communist figures relate to the period before the establishment of Pakistan.

recruitment to the armed forces in India both before and since independence. It should be added, however, that a warrior tradition is not necessarily inimical to the acceptance of Non-violence: it was among the Pathans that 'the Frontier Gandhi', Khan Abdul Ghaffar Khan, built up an impressive non-violent army, the Khudai Khidmatgers or Red Shirts.

If cultural tradition may help to explain the over-representation of Jains, it might be thought that the Buddhists, who also have a strong commitment to Non-violence, would likewise be predisposed towards the movement. But in this case we may explain the absence of Buddhists in our sample by reference to the social basis of this sect in India. Buddhism, after practically dying out in the land of its birth, is now undergoing a revival—the increase of Buddhists in the period 1951–61 being no less than 1,670 per cent. But recent conversion to Buddhism has been largely confined to the lower ranks of traditional Hindu society, the Harijans. And, as we have seen, the latter—despite the movement's evident concern for their lot—are heavily under-represented in the Sarvodaya leadership, which consists predominantly of twice-born Hindus. The same social factor is relevant to the position of Christians. Apart from the Christian missionaries themselves and the Anglo-Indian community, Christianity in India has also been largely confined to the Harijan class. It is significant that the two Christians in our sample of Sarvodaya leaders are both of Western origin. In the Cuddapah District of Andhra Pradesh, Indian converts to Christianity, led by Shri V. Veerabramham of the Anandashram have made significant progress in persuading Harijan villages or hamlets to join the Gramdan movement; but these Harijan villagers do not yet occupy leadership positions and, therefore, are not included in our sample.

The most interesting disparity revealed by the figures in Table 3:8, however, relates to the position of Muslims. Gandhi, as is well known, worked throughout his life, with varying success, for the cause of communal harmony between Hindus and Muslims. He may, indeed, be regarded as a martyr to this cause, since his assassination was at the hand of a co-religionist who believed that Gandhi's efforts to achieve harmony were a betrayal of Hinduism. His followers in the Sarvodaya movement have been no less committed to the same cause. The Shanti Sena (Peace Army) wing of the movement has the maintenance of communal harmony as one of its major objectives, and Shanti Sainiks, again with varying degrees of success, have intervened in recent outbreaks of communal violence.[1] Vinoba himself has made great efforts in the direction of reconciliation, and his book, *The Essence of the Quran*, has achieved a wide circulation. Why, then, are Muslims still so rare in the movement?

Part of the answer undoubtedly lies with the Muslims themselves. Reconciliation is a two-way process, and the Muslims, as the minority party, must find it harder to take the initial steps. The difficulties inherent in the task of reconciliation are illustrated by the reactions of a few Muslims who saw in Vinoba's book a disparagement of Islam: why only the *essence* of the Quran? Muslim suspicions, even of liberal Hindus, are indeed hard to remove! Moreover, while there are many elements in the Islamic faith which are perfectly compatible with Sarvodaya doctrine, there are elements in the latter which may have little appeal to the orthodox Muslim. Among these elements are the equality of the sexes, the 'equal truth' of all religions, and, perhaps, the principle of Non-violence itself. These considerations would be sufficient to explain the apparent lack of appeal that the movement has for many of India's Muslims, although the presence of a Khan Abdul Ghaffar Khan suggests that Islam and Sarvodaya are not ultimately incompatible. However, it is also likely that the movement itself is partly responsible. No one who observes the movement at close quarters and participates in its activities can escape the feeling that it is pervaded with the ethos of Hinduism. The daily prayers and chants of Sarvodaya gatherings appear to be mainly Hindu in character, and the periodic symbolic gestures towards Islam (and also Christianity and other religions) are insufficient to remove the dominant impression.[2]

Religious views of the Sarvodaya leaders

Closer scrutiny of the religious views held by the leaders, however, might modify the impression that we are dealing with a movement

[1] B. B. Chatterjee, P. N. Singh, & G. R. S. Rao, *Riots in Rourkela*, 1967.

[2] As an example of the movement's gestures towards Islam, we may cite the attendance by previous arrangement of Sarvodaya workers at the mass prayer meeting of Muslims in Hyderabad on the occasion of Ramazan, 1968.—*Sarva Seva Sangh Monthly News Letter*, 2, 1 (Jan. 1968), p. 49. Shortage of Muslim workers in certain areas of Bihar where Muslims are a majority of the population is reported to have 'made it difficult to establish rapport with the Muslim community'.—ibid., 2, 2 (Feb. 1968), p. 5.

whose leadership is predominantly Hindu. Our data suggest that, if the vast majority do indeed come from Hindu families, they are now Hindus of a very special kind. These data derive from responses to a question asking the leaders to select a category which described the religious position which they currently held. The categories provided, based on responses to a pilot questionnaire, were: Orthodox; Liberal; Modern/Western; Non-religious; Humanist; Scientific Spiritualist; and Other. Definitions of these categories were not supplied, and some elucidation of their possible meanings to respondents is required.

'Orthodox' may be taken to mean, in the main, 'orthodox Hindu', signifying adherence not to any particular doctrine of that protean creed but rather conformity in respect of ritualistic practice and observances, such as temple worship and bathing, and food taboos. The two categories 'Liberal' and 'Modern/Western' may be collapsed together and taken to mean in this context that one's religious position is seen as departing to a significant extent from the orthodox and traditional Hindu one. 'Non-religious' is largely self-explanatory, and its selection might fairly be taken to signify that one positively rejected belief in a supernatural being, although, given the Gandhian latitude in defining God, it might be compatible with belief in some impersonal cosmic force. 'Humanist' is a term that presents more difficulty. In the Indian, and especially Sarvodaya, context, it does not have the connotation that it often has in the West, where the term often presents itself as the positive descriptive label of atheists and agnostics. It has more the connotation of the word as we find it in such expressions as 'Christian humanist', i.e. a Christian whose belief in the divine is combined with a deep concern for the human. As a choice for our respondents, it is fair to assume that it expresses a concern of religious intensity in the welfare of all humanity, irrespective of distinctions of caste, class, and creed. In this respect, it approximates, perhaps, to the Comtean Religion of Humanity. The category 'Other' called for specification, and from the answers given we derived the more specific Gandhian category 'Believer in the equality of all religions'.

The one remaining category, 'Scientific Spiritualist', is unique to Sarvodaya and calls for a more extended elucidation. 'Spiritualist' here has none of the connotation that the word has in the West when it is used in connection with belief in occult forces and the possibility of communication through mediums with the spirits of those who have 'passed over'.[1] Rather, what is involved is the wisdom derived from man's exploration of 'the inner life', of his Self. Spiritualism (or preferably spirituality) in this sense is regarded as a form of knowledge, the highest wisdom that men can achieve, and for Hindus it is rooted in the teachings of the Veda. Vinoba, however, insists that spirituality as a form of self-knowledge is no more complete than scientific knowledge. 'Just as science continues to advance with every new enquiry, so also should spirituality. The spiritual knowledge which is at our disposal is only a portion. It is not, therefore, right merely to read time and again the works of ancient authors or merely to repeat their words in different forms.'[2] Following his own injunction, Vinoba argues that spirituality demands that 'mind should transcend itself', and, like Aurobindo, he believes that men must seek to ascend to the 'supra-mental' level of consciousness. Taking as his text the Vedantic teaching that spiritual salvation or liberation involves giving up the 'I' and the 'mine', Vinoba invests it with new meaning. The search for individual liberation is a futile quest. Liberation must take a *collective* form, just as scientific knowledge takes a collective form. The 'I' can only be cancelled through the 'we', and the individual can find his own liberation only through the liberation of all men. 'Those who practise spirituality in our country', he says, 'have always emphasized that the "I" and the "mine" should be got rid of. But they have not sufficiently reflected on its significance.' In making their individual effort they have often acquired spiritual wisdom, in much the same way as a capitalist acquires money. 'The spirituality of Hindustan was full of subtle selfishness', and too often the spiritualist 'turns out to be a sort of capitalist'.[3] 'The Vedanta taught that nothing—neither

---

[1] This statement should be slightly qualified, since there is *some* interest in Sarvodaya circles in this kind of spiritualism. Vinoba Bhave's own position on the issue, however, is quite clear. Referring to the alleged spirit communications received by Sir Oliver Lodge, he said: 'All that, when it came from a scientist, had some value and could not be set aside as mere illusion or hallucination. It had some weight, but it was not spiritual and it did not much appeal to me, because I thought that just as science only looked to the *outer* world, this spiritualism only looks to the *other* world, so both are not so much concerned with the inner life and did not have much attraction for me.'—*Science and Spirituality*, n.d., p. 20.

[2] Vinoba Bhave, *Science and Self-Knowledge*, 2nd ed., 1961, p. 63.

[3] ibid., pp. 64–5.

this house nor this field nor even this body—was mine; likewise when we rise to the level of *Vijana* (science), we should say that this house, this property, this field, all these are *ours*.'[1]

Attempting a definition of spirituality, Vinoba sets out its 'minimum requirement'. Three things are involved: (i) 'faith in *absolute* moral values, not *relative* moral values, sometimes truth and sometimes falsehood, an opportunist attitude or a pragmatic way of thinking'; (ii) the unity and sanctity of life; and (iii) continuity of life after death: 'these three things are inseparable for spirituality.'[2] Absolute morality involves faith in at least three cardinal principles, truth, love, and compassion. But, of these three, truth is the more basic. However,

it is impossible to define Truth because Truth is the very definition of everything. We define everything on the basis of Truth. To me Truth is the simplest thing for anyone to grasp . . . we exactly understand what it is, all of us. I am not talking of the Ultimate Truth, the final Truth. That is a matter for search, and search for Truth is the definition of Life. If we want to define Life, it should be defined as—search for Truth. [Truth is] the basis of Life, the basis of common understanding, the basis of good conduct, of transaction, the basis of trade and commerce.[3]

However, none of the three things involved in spirituality is beyond debate. The scientist will certainly demand proof of all three. But the spiritually-minded person is not rationalistic like the scientist, pragmatic like the politician, or dogmatic like so-called religious people. 'Spiritual-minded people are transcendentalists.'[4]

The science in 'scientific spirituality' is more readily understood. While spiritual self-knowledge is concerned with the inner world, science is concerned with the outer; and literature mediates between the two. 'Science causes external changes, but also creates circumstances that influence [the] human mind. [But] science is not able to change the human mind directly.'[5] Science is nevertheless one of the great forces of the modern world. In contrast with the ambivalent or ambiguous attitude of Gandhi, Vinoba does not reject modern science and technology. On the contrary, he applauds their advances. 'Science has been marching ahead since ancient times and should continue this pace in [the] future. . . .

[1] ibid., p. 53.
[2] ibid., pp. 20–1.
[4] ibid., p. 28.

[3] ibid., p. 27.
[5] ibid. p. 42.

The more knowledge does man acquire, the better will he be able to grasp the nature of this creation.'[1] The discovery of atomic power is not to be deplored. 'In [the] future, factories may run with the help of atomic power and even decentralized industries may be run in the villages with its help.'[2]

There is, however, one fundamental condition that must be met. Modern science, with its unprecedented technological development, needs Non-violence as its guiding principle. The alliance of modern science and violence will lead to the destruction of science itself. Only the alliance of Science and Non-violence will lead to prosperity and the continued progress of science.

It is the appreciation of this truth which is at the heart of the doctrine of scientific spirituality. What is required in the modern age is neither science alone, nor spirituality alone, but a synthesis of the two. 'To me', says Vinoba, 'science is equal to spirituality, both should mean the same thing. One is more concerned with the *outer* aspect of the world, the other with the *inner* aspect, and both combined will give us *the whole world in ourselves*.'[3] In this sense, scientific spirituality can be seen, not as a religious doctrine, but as a step *beyond* religion. 'The days of religion and politics are over and the day of science and spirituality has come.'

Analysis of the leaders' responses to the question 'How would you describe your religious views *today*?' shows that several of the categories were not seen as mutually exclusive. A substantial proportion of leaders selected two or even more categories, 'Liberal and Humanist' and 'Scientific Spiritualist and Humanist' being the more popular combinations. The following table, however, presents the proportion of respondents selecting each category, so that those choosing a combination appear under more than one head. The table thus provides not a categorization of the leaders into distinct religious groups but a measure of the representation of various religious positions within the leadership as a whole.

It will be seen that the most popular choice was Humanist, followed by Scientific Spiritualist and Liberal and Modern/ Western. Together these account for the bulk of the choices. Of the remaining categories, the Non-religious is of interest. That one in twenty should have chosen it is perhaps surprising in a movement generally considered as essentially religious. Included in this

---

[1] Vinoba Bhave, *Science and Self-Knowledge*, 2nd ed., 1961, p. 12.
[2] idem.   [3] *Science and Spirituality*, p. 19.

minority is the well-known militant atheist Gora (G. Ramachandra Rao), author of *An Atheist with Gandhi*,[1] who is at present a Sarvodaya leader in Andhra Pradesh, and who has conducted in recent years a satyagraha campaign against pomp in politics and in favour

TABLE 3:9

Religious views of Sarvodaya leaders

	Proportion selecting a position (either separately or in combination) %
Orthodox	1
Liberal and Modern/Western	39
Humanist	58
Non-religious	5
Scientific Spiritualist	46
Equality of all religions	1
Miscellaneous	4

(N = 221)

of partyless democracy. Perhaps, however, the most striking feature of the table is that only 1 per cent of the leaders thought that their religious position could be adequately described as 'Orthodox'.

Type of religious upbringing

The significance of this finding is high-lighted when we consider it in relation to the type of religious upbringing that the leaders perceived themselves as having experienced. Data on this aspect of recruitment were derived from answers to the question: 'Would you describe your own religious upbringing as a child as: Orthodox . . . or Liberal . . . or Modern/Western?' For the purposes of analysis, the last two categories may be combined, interest centring on whether or not leaders saw their religious upbringing as an orthodox one. More than one in four (28 per cent) of the leaders selected, as an exclusive choice, the 'Orthodox' category.

Comparison of this figure with the figure of 1 per cent who now consider themselves orthodox suggests that almost all the orthodox

[1] Published 1951.

children have ceased to be so. At some point in their careers they have become more liberal or more radical in their religious views. Our data do not permit us to infer that this radicalization was either a cause or a consequence of their joining the movement. It seems likely that, for some of them at least, membership of the movement has been responsible for the radicalization; but it is possible that radicalization occurred in the period between childhood and joining the movement, and that the act of joining represented merely a step in the direction already taken.

That socialization within the movement played some part in

TABLE 3:10

Religious upbringing and current religious views of Sarvodaya leaders

Religious upbringing		Religious position currently held*			
		Orthodox	Liberal	Humanist	Scientific Spiritualist	
		%	%	%	%	N
Orthodox		3	34	44	51	59
Liberal		<1	45	62	47	150
	χ^2	N.A.	2·27	5·53	0·30	
	d.f.		1	1	1	
	p≤		0·20	0·02	0·70	

Notes. *The categories include all those who chose a particular position, whether alone or in combination with another position.
N.A. = Not subjected to chi-square test.

religious radicalization is suggested by the fact that the process does not appear to have been confined to those with an orthodox upbringing. If we may assume that 'Humanist' and 'Scientific Spiritualist' are more radical positions than 'Liberal' and 'Modern/Western', it is evident that many who had a non-orthodox upbringing do not now regard the latter two labels as descriptive of their present views, and that they have moved to a more radical position, one of which (Scientific Spiritualist) they are unlikely to have reached outside the movement, since it is very much the position developed by Vinoba himself in recent years.

Some hint of the path of religious radicalization taken may be derived from a comparison of the current religious views of those with an orthodox as opposed to those with a liberal upbringing.

The distributions in the table suggest that the orthodox are less likely than the liberal to describe their current religious view as 'Humanist'. It would appear, then, that a leader is less likely to adopt the position of humanist if he had an orthodox rather than a liberal religious upbringing.

Focusing attention on religious radicalization and the minority with an orthodox upbringing should not, however, lead us to overlook the fact that the great majority of Sarvodaya leaders originated from non-orthodox families. The precise significance of this cannot be determined, since we possess no comparable data about the Indian population as a whole. We do not know, in other words, what proportion of Indians would judge their religious upbringing to have been orthodox. It seems safe to assume that the proportion varies with age, and that modernization is leading to a decline in orthodoxy, although, of course, since we are dealing with *perceived* orthodoxy, what appears as 'liberal' to an older generation may appear as 'orthodox' to a younger generation. Even so, we would hazard the guess that there is a significant difference between the Sarvodaya leaders and the general population: that the leaders are more likely to perceive their religious upbringing as liberal. If further research were to prove this guess to be correct, the finding would be in line with the observation made at the beginning of this section that, in certain social situations, religious radicalism is associated with political radicalism. Historically, this association has taken two forms. Sometimes religious radicalism presents itself as an *alternative* to political radicalism: a person becomes, say, either a Jehovah's Witness or a Communist; or a person who would have become a Jehovah's Witness yesterday becomes a Communist today. Sometimes, however, as was notably the case with certain Christian sects, such as the Diggers of seventeenth-century England, religious radicalism is *combined* with political radicalism. When this occurs, the outcome is an aspiration, or an attempt, to establish 'the Kingdom of God on Earth'. From what we have learned of the religious background and views of the Sarvodaya leaders, it seems not unreasonable to conclude that we are dealing with a contemporary manifestation of what Walzer has conceptualized as 'The Revolution of the Saints'.[1] Consideration of what kind of revolution this is, however, we shall take up in Chapter Four below.

[1] M. Walzer, *The Revolution of the Saints*, 1966.

V. POLITICAL CHARACTERISTICS

In discussing the ideology of Sarvodaya we had occasion to observe that, unlike classical Western anarchism, Sarvodaya anarchism is committed to 'gradualism'. The Sarvodayites envisage no sudden 'leap into freedom', but a progressive development from 'good government' to freedom from all government. The movement does not seek to realize its objective through the machinery of government, since what is required is a fundamental change in people's values. No government, but only loving persuasion (both rational and emotional) can bring about that kind of change. However, given the perspective of 'gradualism', the movement does not reject legislative action which promotes its aims, and, in fact, it has actively sponsored Bhoodan and Gramdan Acts which are necessary to facilitate transference of property rights. At the same time, orthodox politics are subjected to severe criticisms and the movement seeks to shape and develop the existing Indian political system into one in which parties would have no place; in short, to develop a partyless democracy.

It must be remembered, however, that the movement grew out of the constructive wing of the movement for national independence which was led by Congress under Gandhi. Gandhi never broke with Congress, although in his last days he clearly wished Congress to develop in a way quite different from the way it has subsequently developed. Those associated with Sarva Seva Sangh see themselves as developing Gandhi's ideas in the spirit of his Last Will and Testament. Not all Gandhians, however, agree with 'the new politics' of Sarvodaya. Among these, to mention only those outside Congress, must be included the two veterans, C. Rajagopalachari, the founder in 1959 of the Swatantra Party,[1] and Acharya Kripalani, who argued that the movement should have a parliamentary wing of its own and in 1951 formed the Kisan Mazdoor Praja Party, which soon merged with the Socialist Party to create the Praja Socialist Party.

The constitution of Sarva Seva Sangh restricts membership to those who are not members of any political party; and the pledge of its Lok Sevaks contains the clause: 'I believe that real freedom

[1] The Swatantra Party represents an effort to build a 'non-leftist' opposition to Congress. For a full-length study of the party see H. L. Erdman, *The Swatantra Party and Indian Conservatism*, 1967.

can only be realized by the awakening of Lok-niti ("the politics of the people"). Therefore, I will not associate myself with party or power politics and will endeavour to seek the co-operation of all people and of all political parties.'[1] Notwithstanding this provision, it might be expected that the Sarvodaya leaders, because of the historical development of the movement, would have close affinities with Congress. In this section, therefore, we shall present our findings concerning the political characteristics of the leaders. According to Marxian theory, politics belong to the 'superstructure' of society and people's political allegiances are ultimately determined by their (economic) class position. There is much evidence to support this view, but for the purpose of analysis it is preferable to adopt the Weberian approach, which treats politics as an analytically distinct dimension of status, leaving open the question of the relationship between political position and class position. For this reason we propose to consider some of the basic political characteristics of the leaders in the context of a discussion of the social foundations of the movement.

In any case, there is no doubt that one party—Congress—must be regarded as a significant source of recruitment to the movement. Of our 228 respondents about one-third had been members of Congress, and at least ten had been active for Congress in national or state politics at a high level. Of these ten, two had been ministers in the Central Government, two had been chief ministers of a state or provincial government, a further two had been ministers in state governments, one was a former Speaker of a provincial legislative assembly, and the remaining three had been M.L.A.s (Members of Legislative Assemblies). These leaders provide the basis of the allegation that the Sarvodaya movement is a refuge for frustrated politicians, although no convincing evidence is produced to substantiate the implication that they joined for unworthy motives or are not sincere in their currently held political views. Personal contact with some of them has left us with quite the opposite impression, and it may be significant that only one of the ten volunteered the information that 'my defeat in the 1952 General Election perhaps to some extent contributed to my decision to leave politics'.[2]

---

[1] *Constitution of the Sarva Seva Sangh,* 1964 (in Hindi).

[2] The allegation that the movement is a refuge for frustrated politicians does not usually distinguish between Sarva Seva Sangh and other Gandhian organi-

Voting in national General Elections

The first political characteristic to be considered is whether or not
the leaders exercise their right to vote. Western anarchists have
not, as a rule, participated as voters in state elections, the act of
voting being deemed useless, and worse—a legitimization of the
political system that they wish to abolish. Sarvodayites do not
adopt this view, and the terms of the Lok Sevak pledge quoted

TABLE 3:11

*Reported voting behaviour of Sarvodaya leaders in
national elections*

| | Propor-tion who did *not* vote % | N* | Of those who voted and reported party vote, proportion who voted for: | | | | | N** |
			Con-gress %	Socialist %	Com-munist %	Swatan-tra %	Indepen-dent %	
1952 General Election	33	193	75	21	0	1	3	118
1957 ,, ,,	62	213	77	19	1	0	3	74
1962 ,, ,,	66	220	81	6	3	1	9	67

Notes.   *Those who were ineligible to vote because of age or nationality have been
         excluded.
       **The figures for N exclude those who voted but did not report the party for
         which they voted.

above do not explicitly forbid voting in General Elections, as distinct from other forms of active participation. From what we have
said, however, it may be anticipated that many Sarvodaya leaders
do in fact deliberately abstain from voting. This appears to be
borne out by the data presented in the above table.

It will be seen that, whereas one-third of the leaders eligible to
vote in the 1952 General Election did not vote, in 1957 and 1962
this proportion had risen to nearly two-thirds. In evaluating these
figures, it should be remembered that the turn-out of all electors

zations. In the latter, politicians, perhaps frustrated or otherwise, are much
more in evidence. There is no doubt, however, that Jayaprakash Narayan's
'defection' from the Socialist Party to the movement disconcerted many of his
colleagues, who for years refused to believe, without serious foundation, that he
had finally quit party politics. Indian political comment is notorious for its
questioning of the motives of politicians. As Morris-Jones has suggested, this
may be partly due to the persistence of 'the language of saintly politics', which
encourages feelings of distrust of, and disgust with, persons and institutions of
authority. If so, the 'saints' of Indian politics are subjected to the treatment
accorded to non-saintly politicians!

in the three elections covered was in the order of 50 per cent. It is possible that some of the leaders who did not vote were not deliberate abstainers, although—in the light of their relatively high social and educational status—one would expect, other things being equal, a higher-than-average turn-out by a 'population' of this kind. It seems fair to conclude that other things are not equal, and that the Sarvodaya leaders include many deliberate non-voters. This is probably *not* true of the 1952 General Election, since this was held before Sarva Seva Sangh developed its non-partisan political line. There seems little doubt, however, that it is true of the 1957 and 1962 elections, by which time the concept of partyless democracy had been promulgated. The fact remains that, even in 1962, one-third of the respondents did vote, a finding which underlines the difference between Sarvodaya and Western anarchism.

In interpreting the table, it should be noted that no account has been taken of whether or not the respondents were members of the movement at the time of the elections, although we know that most of them were. In interpreting the remainder of the table, dealing with party voted for, it should also be borne in mind that the figures relate to *reported* voting behaviour and are thus subject to errors of memory. It will be seen that only two parties proved significant: Congress and Socialist. However, the latter includes two separate parties: the Socialist Party and the KMP in 1952; and the Socialist Party and PSP in 1957 and 1962.[1] In all three elections at least three out of four of the leaders who voted reported voting for a Congress candidate. In 1952 and 1957 about one in five voted Socialist, and in 1962 one in twenty did so. In the latter year more reported voting for an independent candidate than for a Socialist. The preference for Congress of the Sarvodaya leaders who voted is thus very pronounced. The bias towards Congress of those leaders who voted may be judged from the fact that, in elections for the Lok Sabha, Congress polled 45 per cent of the votes cast in 1952, 47·8 per cent in 1957, and 46 per cent in 1962. The comparable proportions of the votes cast for the Socialist parties were 16·4 per cent, 10·4 per cent, and 9·3 per cent, respectively.[2]

[1] The SP and KMP merged after the 1952 election to create the PSP, but in 1956 a group led by Ram Manohar Lohia formed a new Socialist Party. In 1965 the SP and PSP merged to form the Samyukta Socialist Party, but PSP elements soon withdrew to reconstitute that party.

[2] W. H. Morris-Jones, *The Government and Politics of India*, 1964, p. 163, 2nd edn., 1967.

Thus, while there was a bias of about 30 per cent towards Congress among Sarvodaya leaders who voted in each of the three elections, there was also a smaller bias towards the Socialists in 1952 and 1957 and a small bias against them in 1962. The variations in the Sarvodaya leaders' vote for the Socialists is probably related to some extent to the political role of Jayaprakash Narayan. He joined the movement in 1952 after the General Election of that year, bringing with him many younger socialists. Although he had renounced party politics, he still remained strongly sympathetic towards the PSP in the 1957 election. By 1962, however, he had become much less sympathetic and much more committed to the non-partisan approach of Sarvodaya. It seems likely that some of the socialists recruited to the movement in the wake of Narayan's 'conversion' voted Socialist in 1957, but either did not vote at all in 1962 or had left the movement.

The leaders' perceptions of India's political parties

In constructing the questionnaire, it was anticipated that a substantial proportion of the respondents would not have voted. To enable us to determine the party preferences of *all* the respondents as distinct from those who voted, two further related questions were asked: 'Which political party, in your opinion, is most *sympathetic* to Sarvodaya ideals?' and 'Which party . . . is most *opposed* . . .?'

The answers to these questions may be interpreted as indicating not merely the broad party preferences of the Sarvodaya leaders but also how they perceive the various parties stand in relation to the movement's objectives. Although the Bhoodan movement began in the Telangana area of Andhra Pradesh as a non-violent alternative to a Communist-directed campaign to dispossess the landlords, and to establish a revolutionary base among the peasantry on Maoist lines, the Sarvodaya leaders have always sought the co-operation of the major political parties, including the Communist Party of India. The general line of the movement has been that, even if people are not yet prepared to give up their party affiliations, they should be encouraged to join together in programmes of action for the common good. At election times this has taken the form of trying to establish a code of conduct for electioneering and of calling on the parties to co-operate for the purpose of holding joint election meetings. The idea of a non-partisan government of 'the best men' is also held out as a possibility after the elections.

As might be expected, the responses of the parties to these suggestions have not been very favourable. However, a rather more favourable response has been made to the movement's programme of land reform. In September 1957 at Yelwal in Mysore State a conference was held which was attended by representatives of the Union Government, including the President and the Prime Minister, several state governments, other Congress leaders, and also Socialist and Communist leaders. The conference welcomed the Gramdan campaign and appealed to all sections of the Indian people to give it their enthusiastic support.[1] In the movement the Yelwal conference was hailed as an epoch-making event, signalling the general acceptance of the Gramdan approach to land reform. But the practical outcome proved disappointing. Some co-operation and co-ordination of activities have been achieved at the national level (notably the working party on Gramdan referred to earlier), and in a few states, particularly Madras. But, in general, support from the parties has been very patchy and largely confined to individual party workers.

With these prefatory remarks we may present the response of the leaders to the two questions about the parties (Table 3:12 below).

Since some of the categories used are not mutually exclusive, the table provides us with a measure of the relative strength of the leaders' attitudes to the parties, rather than a distribution of their party preferences. Taking the 'most sympathetic' column first, it will be seen that 15 per cent of the respondent leaders thought no party was sympathetic, while 2 per cent thought all parties were sympathetic. It seems improbable that the latter tiny minority really thought all parties were in fact sympathetic: their response may be fairly interpreted as an ideological one, expressing the spirit that was hopefully evoked at the Yelwal conference. The responses of the larger minority may be interpreted as expressing the feeling that no party as such (as distinct from individual party members) has evinced whole-hearted support for Sarvodaya ideals. As between the parties (or, rather, groups of parties) themselves, the proportions are in line with those already noted with regard to the party preferences of Sarvodaya voters. Congress, mentioned by 73 per cent, emerges as the party perceived

---

[1] Suresh Ram, *Vinoba and His Mission*, 3rd edn., 1962, pp. 209–11.

by the great majority to be the most sympathetic, with the
Socialists a long way behind at 15 per cent. It is perhaps of some
interest that preference for Congress is less marked among all
leaders than among leaders who voted in 1962, whereas preference
for the Socialists is more marked. This suggests that Socialist-
oriented Sarvodaya leaders were more likely to abstain in 1962 than
Congress-oriented leaders. It is more surprising than these findings

TABLE 3:12

The Sarvodaya leaders' perceptions of the political parties

In relation to Sarvodaya ideals, the party or parties seen as:

	MOST SYMPATHETIC %	MOST OPPOSED %
None	15	13
All	2	6
Congress	73	4
Socialists*	15	3
Communists**	3	34
Swatantra	< 1	21
Communal***	0	44
	N = 207	N = 189

Notes.   * Praja Socialist Party and Socialist Party.
        ** No distinction was made by respondents between the
           two Communist Parties, the 'Russian' and 'Chinese'
           factions which split in 1965. (In 1968 a third party was
           formed.) In the 'most opposed' column, the figure
           includes one respondent who listed the Revolutionary
           Socialist Party, a small Marxist party.
       *** Jan Sangh, Hindu Mahasabha, Ram Rajya Parishad,
           Rashtriya Swayamsevak Sangh. The percentages do
           not add up to 100, since some respondents named
           more than one party, falling into separate categories.

that *any* leader should have mentioned the Communist and
Swatantra parties. However, choice of the Communist Party is not
incomprehensible. Despite Communist criticism of the movement
as utopian, reactionary, and petty bourgeois, Sarvodaya ideology
might be easily interpreted as Communism minus the violence.
And in fact one of the six leaders involved commented: 'It is the
Communist party who want Sarvodaya but their method is different.' None of the six had actually voted Communist, four being

non-voters and two having voted for Congress (one of these only at the 1952 election), but one had been a member of the CPI from 1952 to 1956. Five of the six were non-graduates, the other being a postgraduate; three identified with the Peasants, one with the Lower Middle Class, and two with the Working Class. Choice of the Swatantra Party is also not incomprehensible. Swatantra presents itself as a right-wing conservative party, strongly committed to free enterprise in business and opposed to socialistic measures, especially co-operative farming. But its founder-leader is Rajagopalachari, an eminent former colleague of Gandhi; and there is a Gandhian element in Swatantra Party doctrine.[1] It may be significant that the respondent (only one) who mentioned Swatantra had an agriculturalist background and identified with the Peasant class.

Turning now to consideration of answers to the second question, 'Which party is most opposed to Sarvodaya ideals?', it might be expected that the responses 'None' and 'All' would be mirror images of the responses 'All' and 'None' to the first question. That is to say, it might be taken that if one thinks that no party is sympathetic, one must think that all are opposed; and, similarly, if all are seen as sympathetic, none will be seen as opposed. This, however, would only be the case if one accepted as true the maxim: 'He who is not with us is against us.' It is clear that at least some Sarvodaya leaders do not think in this dichotomous way.

As between the parties, the favourable attitudes to Congress and the Socialists are to be expected, with only 4 per cent and 2 per cent, respectively, seeing these as the parties most opposed. Given the open-ended nature of the question and the choice available, all that is remarkable is that *any* leader should single out one of these two parties. Of the seven leaders who mentioned Congress as 'most opposed', one was the respondent who thought the Communist Party 'most sympathetic' and who had been a member of the CPI. Another was a respondent who also mentioned Congress as 'most sympathetic'! Perhaps his inclusion in the group was due to a slip of the pen, since he had voted for Congress in all three general elections. The remaining six were all non-voters. One of the seven identified with the Middle Class, four with the Lower

---

[1] Erdman, op. cit., p. 191, states: 'The Gandhian element is not absent, but it provides only a thin veneer on this essentially liberal document' (a statement of the party's principles).

Middle Class, one with the Peasants (the Congress voter), and one
with the Working Class. The latter explained his answer thus:
'Congress party because they go against what they preach. Most of
them are hypocrites. Frankly they admit that what Vinoba says is
impractical. They give promise to the poor but up till now they are
on the side of the rich.'

Of the five leaders who mentioned the Socialists as 'most
opposed', four coupled them with other parties, either the Communist, Jan Sangh, or Swatantra, or a combination of these. One
had voted Congress in all three elections and three others had also
voted Congress in one or two elections. Three of the five were
graduates and their class identification included all our main self-
rated class categories.

Perhaps the more interesting feature of the 'most opposed'
column is the order of the preferences as between the three remaining parties or groups of parties: Communal 44 per cent, Communists 34 per cent, and Swatantra 21 per cent. The Communal
category includes four parties, but the great majority mentioned
only one of the four: the Jan Sangh, the largest and most influential of the parties generally regarded as communal.[1] It is
likely that many respondents found difficulty in choosing between
the Jan Sangh and the Communist Party for priority in this connection, and, indeed, some resolved the issue by mentioning both.
From the perspective of Sarvodaya, it is clear that Hindu communalism is perceived as even more of a threat than the espousal
of violence by the Communists. That the Swatantra Party is the
first choice of 21 per cent of the leaders is also noteworthy, in the
light of the Gandhian associations, already mentioned, of this party.
It is, however, explicable when one recalls that Swatantra is the
party on which right-wing conservatives in India have placed high
hopes. It is the party most unambiguously in favour of free business
enterprise and opposed to socialistic measures in agriculture, including even the imposition of land ceilings.

---

[1] In 1952, 1957, and 1962 the Jan Sangh obtained 3·1%, 5·93%, and 6·44%,
respectively, of the votes cast in elections to the Lok Sabha.—W. H. Morris-
Jones, op. cit., p. 163. The party denies that it is a Hindu party. Morris-Jones
comments: 'The views and motivations of many of its adherents would be
difficult to distinguish from those of the (Hindu) Mahasabha, but its being a
newer party, less burdened by memories of the past and more geared to an
electoral struggle, has helped to make its adumbration of policy and programme
rather more than a top dressing for a communal base.'—op. cit., p. 157.

In short, the Sarvodaya leaders share very much the basic political characteristics we might expect from our knowledge of the origins of the movement. Most of them do not now vote in national elections, but both those who do and those who do not vote retain a pronounced preference for Congress, while a small minority prefers the Socialists. However, as we shall see, relations of the movement with Congress are more complicated than this conclusion might suggest: the issue remains one over which the leaders are deeply divided.

CHAPTER FOUR

SOCIAL PSYCHOLOGICAL ASPECTS

EXCAVATIONS designed to reveal the social foundations of a movement constitute an essential step towards the understanding of it. But, however much of these foundations is uncovered, we remain a long way from answering the question 'Why do people join the movement?' It is never sufficient to say of a movement that its members are drawn from particular social categories, groups, classes, or statuses. Answering the question 'Who?' leaves the question 'Why?' unanswered. Social movements rarely draw their members from only one social group: they are usually drawn, albeit unevenly, from a variety of groups. Even if one makes the assumption—most common when the social group under discussion is a class—that people are motivated by conceptions of their own (class) interest, there remain the problems of explaining why *all* members of the group have not joined the movement and why members of *other* groups ('deviants') have joined.

In asking the questions 'Why do people join a particular social movement?' and 'Why, having joined, do they remain with it?' we are directing attention towards the social psychological, rather than simply social, aspects of the movement. For some movements, at least, the former may be more significant than the latter. Motivations for joining and staying with a movement, however, are only one element involved in the consideration of social psychological aspects. Other elements include: the texture of the movement, the kinds of bond that unite the members; the movement's 'embrace' of its participants, the kind and character of their act of participation; the content and quality of the members' commitment to the values of the movement; and the movement's ethos.

Dealing with the social psychological aspects of a movement is more difficult than dealing with its social foundations. This is most apparent in the case of motivations. Although we all know from our own experience what kinds of motive prompt particular kinds of social action, we also know that it is often impossible to determine accurately even our own motives in any concrete instance.[1] But, if

[1] Heberle lists the following difficulties in studying motives in social action:

motives are difficult to determine, so also are other social psychological aspects, such as the nature of the solidary relations between the members. Such relations involve attitudes. Isolating and measuring attitudes remains one of the less developed techniques of the social sciences. In recent years much progress has been made in developing these techniques, but the present authors are not equipped with the techniques necessary for a proper consideration of the social psychological aspects of the Sarvodaya movement. What follows, therefore, is a somewhat crude and fragmentary account of some of these aspects, based upon data derived from answers to a few simple factual questions and to one opinion question, and upon subjective impressions formed as the result of participant observation.

I. THE MOTIVATIONS OF THE SARVODAYA LEADERS

Following Heberle,[1] we shall employ a typology which reduces the motives of individuals in joining and supporting a social movement to four types. In the first, the value-rational type, the motivation is based on a conviction, after careful enquiry into the validity of the ideas and arguments used in support of them, of the desirability and rightness of the movement's goals. In the second, the emotional-affectual type, the member is motivated, not by rational considerations but by some experience which arouses his emotions against the persons and conditions which the movement attacks, or by his affection for the leaders and the masses in the movement. Sudden conversions to 'the cause' of the movement are characteristic of people experiencing this type of motivation. The third type is the traditional. 'By this term we mean that many individuals belong to a social movement because their parents or other relatives have belonged to it; because there is a tradition in the community or in the social status group or class to which the individual belongs, which demands adherence to certain ideals and support

(a) The real motives may be intentionally concealed by the actor. (b) The motives may not be clear to the actor: he may rationalize them, proclaiming them to be the expression of attitudes that are socially esteemed. (c) The real motives may not be recognizable to the actor himself because they lie buried in his unconscious self. And (d) the very complexity of motives makes any accurate determination difficult.—R. Heberle, *Social Movements*, 1951, pp. 94–5.

[1] Heberle, op. cit., pp. 95–9. The quotations in this and the following paragraph are from Heberle. The typology is derived from Max Weber, *The Theory of Social and Economic Organization*, 1947.

of the groups which uphold them.' 'Traditional' in this context therefore has no reference to the character of the value-goals of the movement. Participation in long-established progressive movements may be actuated by the traditional type of motivation. The fourth and final type is purposive-rational motivation. This type actuates individuals who join a social movement in expectation of personal advantages, such as the achievement of material rewards or position, although such motivation is seldom frankly admitted, and in the consciousness of the individuals concerned may be hidden or rationalized as value-rational motivation. Purposive-rational motivation occurs more frequently after a social movement has achieved a measure of power or influence, when it takes the form of individuals 'climbing on to the bandwagon'.

These are analytical distinctions. In the world of reality 'most men will be motivated not in one way or the other but by a combination of motives, and any movement will contain quite a variety of differently motivated adherents or followers'. Further, the motivations of any given individual member of a movement may change in the course of time. The originally enthusiastic member, who joined, say, for emotional-affectual reasons, may become disillusioned but remain in the movement out of habit or because he finds it to his personal advantage to do so. If the motivations of sufficient members change in this way, the social psychological complexion of the movement may be transformed; or the transformation may come about because old members with one principal type of motivation are replaced by new members with a different type.

From our survey we do not have the data necessary for an assessment of the motives which prompted the leaders to join the movement. However, we do have information that is relevant to this question. The information concerns family association with the movement, family attitudes towards the leaders' participation, and the leaders' reasons for joining the movement.

Family association with the movement

The data on family association are related to those on social foundations. Response to a social movement is likely to be on a family as well as on an individual basis. Members of a family are likely to find themselves in a similar social situation, such as their class situation, and, in addition, if one member joins, he becomes a potentially important source of information about the movement for other members of the family. Thus in many social movements, as in the British Co-operative Movement,[1] we often find that membership becomes a family affair and even a family tradition. In the Sarvodaya movement (interpreted for this purpose in its broadest sense, to include the pre-independence Gandhian movement) family association appears to be quite important. Nearly one out of every three (31 per cent) of the leaders reported that at least one other member of his family was, or had been, associated with the movement. 18 per cent reported that the member (or members) of his family so involved was either a parent or a sibling; 4 per cent reported that a close relation, such as a brother, was a co-worker; and 9 per cent reported that the member was a more distant relation.

Family attitude towards the leaders' participation

Given the relative strength of family feeling in India and, in particular, the widespread attitude of deference towards parents and elders, a further related factor which may be crucial in determining an individual's participation in the movement is the approval or disapproval of his family. Respondents were therefore asked to state whether the attitude of their parents (and/or close relatives) to their active participation in the movement could be categorized as one of the following: opposed; raised no objection; favoured. Fifteen per cent of the respondents did not answer this question but, of those who did,[2] only 17 per cent reported opposition. In this group is included one leader who wrote: 'They (my family) beat me and my wife who later died in hospital. They violently opposed our mixing up with Harijans and the disinherited.' One in three (32 per cent) of the leaders reported 'no objection', while no less than 51 per cent reported that their parents or close relatives favoured their participation.

For the great majority of Sarvodaya leaders, therefore, it may be fairly concluded that participation was not part of a syndrome of rebellion against parents that is sometimes alleged to be an important

---

[1] G. N. Ostergaard and A. H. Halsey, *Power in Co-operatives*, 1965, p. 90.
[2] N = 195. The proportion of non-respondents is relatively high, although the question would not appear to be a 'sensitive' one. It seems likely that for many of the non-respondents the question of family attitude did not appear relevant.

factor in Western protest movements.[1] Our findings probably reflect a widespread favourable attitude towards the movement among the public in India. The relatively high figure for positive approval is perhaps all the more notable when one remembers that participation in the movement offers very limited material rewards. On the other hand, it should also be noted that traditional Hindu culture places value on the dedication of at least one member of a family to a spiritual life. To have a son or daughter associated with the work of India's new saint, Vinoba, would thus be widely held to redound to the credit of a family.

The leaders' reasons for joining

Our data on family association and family attitude towards the respondents' participation suggest that the third type of motivation, the traditional, is present to quite a marked degree in the Sarvodaya movement. Our data are reinforced by answers to another question; but, at the same time, these answers suggest that traditional-type motivation is much less important than certain other types. The question was: 'Which of the following reasons influenced you most to join the Movement? Reading Sarvodaya literature; Personal contact with Gandhians; Parents; Friends.'

Of these four factors, 'Parents', despite the favourable attitude to participation of many parents noted above, ranked lowest, only 11 per cent of the leaders indicating this reason. Somewhat more important was the factor of 'Friends', selected by 19 per cent of the respondents. Both of these factors, however, were markedly less important than the remaining two. Thus, 59 per cent gave 'Reading Sarvodaya literature' as a reason while 74 per cent gave 'Personal contact with Gandhians'.[2]

That three out of every five leaders reported having been influenced by reading the movement's literature underlines the

[1] Recent research suggests that the allegation lacks firm foundation. In a sample of young activists in the British Campaign for Nuclear Disarmament 62% reported that at least one parent supported or approved of CND.— F. Parkin, *Middle-Class Radicalism*, 1968, p. 146. 'By and large, young [CND] supporters tend to have home backgrounds conducive to their own radical, activist orientations.'—ibid., p. 152. However, for a minority of young CND-ers, particularly anarchists, opposition to parental views may have been a significant factor in their participation.—ibid., p. 165.

[2] The percentages do not add up to 100 since some respondents ticked more than one category. Miscellaneous 'other' reasons were given by 9%. For this question N = 226.

importance of this as a factor in the recruitment process, and, undoubtedly, justifies the stress laid on it by Vinoba himself on many
occasions. No doubt, too, the high proportion reflects the relatively
highly educated character of the leadership. More important in
this context, it suggests the presence in a marked degree of the
value-rational type of motivation: the type based on a rational
conviction of the rightness of a movement's goals.

But of greater significance is the larger proportion influenced by
personal contact with Gandhians, since this suggests the presence
in an even higher degree of the emotional-affectual type of motivation, centred in this case on the persons of the movement's
leaders. In one sense the importance of this factor is not surprising.
From Gandhi onwards the movement has always expressed a
strong exemplary appeal. A large part of the image of a Sarvodaya
worker is that of a person who has identified himself with the
poorest and the lowliest and who expresses the non-violent social
revolution in his own way of life. In the context of traditional
Hindu culture such an image still has wide appeal. And when real
persons fit the image, as many Sarvodaya workers do, the appeal
can be very great indeed. More generally, however, the ranking of
this factor may be explained in terms of the charismatic quality of
the movement.[1] Its philosophy is embodied in the persons of its
leaders. They are seen as extraordinary individuals to follow whom
becomes a sacred duty of lesser mortals.

That charisma is involved in the recruitment process of the
movement is underlined by answers to the supplementary question:
'If there were any particular leaders other than Gandhiji, who
especially influenced your decision to join the Movement, who
were they?' No less than 188 respondents, i.e. 82·5 per cent, mentioned one or more persons by name. The complete list of names
was a lengthy one and included many persons who had achieved
a high reputation in their own state, if not at the national level.
The length of the lists suggest that charisma is not confined to a
single leader but is an attribute he shares with, or passes on to,
lesser leaders. But, as might be expected, it is one leader who stands
out. No less than 55 per cent of those mentioning an individual
listed Vinoba. Jayaprakash Narayan, the best-known leader after
Vinoba, was mentioned by 17 per cent; and Dada Dharmadhikari

[1] The concept of charisma will be discussed more fully in the next section.

by 8 per cent.[1] No other leader was mentioned by more than a handful of the respondents.

So far we have presented data which have an indirect bearing on three of the four types of motivation distinguished by Heberle. We have no hard data on the remaining type, the purposive-rational: the type based on expectations of personal advantage. One reason for this is the obvious difficulty of extracting from respondents by means of a postal questionnaire information which would have a bearing on this point. In general, one would not expect to find much evidence of purposive-rational motivation among Sarvodaya *leaders*, although one might expect to find it among villagers who join the Gramdan movement. For the latter, Gramdan may offer, and is said by its propagandists to offer, the prospect of personal material (as well as other) advantages. For the leaders, however, service in a movement which eschews the pursuit of political power, and which demands material sacrifice and dedicated self-discipline, can offer few obvious prospects of personal advantage. Nevertheless, it would be unrealistic to rule out *a priori* the possibility that purposive-rational motivation is present among *some* of the leaders in *some* degree. Comments by a few respondents to open-ended questions suggest this possibility. For example, one Representative wrote: 'There are three categories of workers in the movement. 1. The intellectual élite who joined the movement out of conviction. Their number is insignificant. 2. Secondly, the constructive workers who were engaged in various constructive work agencies from the very beginning. 3. Thirdly, those who consider Baba (i.e. Vinoba) as a great scholar and were led into the movement attracted by his great personality and out of devotion to him.'

In elucidating this comment, we may ignore the reference to

---

[1] Jayaprakash Narayan is the former Socialist leader who joined the movement after the General Election of 1952 and who initiated the procedure of jeevandan (dedication of one's life to the movement) in 1954. Despite his forswearing of party politics for 'the politics of the people', he was widely regarded for several years as the possible successor of Nehru. More recently his name was mentioned as a possible candidate for the Presidency of the Indian Republic in 1967. Dada Dharmadhikari, the author of several books (in Hindi), is recognized as one of the leading intellectuals of the movement and an authority on Sarvodaya thought and ideology. In the words of the historian of the movement, Suresh Ram, 'He has gone round the country several times and supplied the intellectual food to the workers. His lectures are very popular among the intelligentsia.'—S. Ram, *Vinoba and His Mission*, 3rd edn., 1962, p. 360.

'workers': in this context it would encompass our leaders as well as non-office-holders. The first and third of the Representative's categories clearly relate to value-rational and emotional-affectual type motivations, respectively. It is the second category which may be related to purposive-rational motivation. What, perhaps, is being suggested is that workers in the constructive work agencies participate in the movement for reasons unrelated to the movement's value goals or emotional-affectual concern for Vinoba and his cause. A possible implication is that such workers regard the movement as little more than a source of employment, an instrumental agency in their search for a livelihood. A similar suggestion was made in comments of two other respondents who specifically singled out Khadi workers for criticism. One of these wrote: 'It is only the honorary workers who can wholeheartedly work for the movement. Paid workers work for the pay. For instance, the numerous Khadi workers though expected to work for the Movement have severe limitations to give their whole time. They should resign their jobs in Khadi agencies.' The other wrote: 'They (Khadi workers) think themselves only employees and don't consider themselves as workers (for the movement).'

Khadi workers who treat the movement as an employer are not the only element subjected to adverse criticism. A few respondents echoed the allegation referred to in the previous chapter and complained of those who joined the movement to promote their own personal political ends. Thus one Representative wrote: 'The workers disgusted from Congress, not got any post there and they have joined it [the movement] only to recoup their position with the help of the Pope of Gandhian philosophy and Religious Guru [teacher], Vinoba Bhave, and in a disguised note these Congress workers are busy in corruption including some Khadi workers. And they are here only for the money making purpose not the real service of the poor people of the world, not even of the nation. . . .' Another Representative warned: 'We must be vigilant about the political workers who, frustrated in their efforts to gain leadership, join the Movement and then try to fulfil their frustrated desires by usurping leadership positions. It is they who have produced the worker-leader hierarchy in Sarvodaya.' Yet another, this time a member of the Prabandh Samiti, complained more generally of 'infiltration of undesirables into the organisation as the movement gains ground in the country'.

That the Sarvodaya movement has experienced something of 'the bandwagon effect' can hardly be doubted. It was particularly noticeable in the early enthusiastic years of the Bhoodan campaign, which attracted to the movement some politicians who joined it partly to gain from it the prestige which they hoped to cash later for political support. Vinoba's decision at Palni in 1956 to liquidate the movement's Bhoodan organizations, a decision which will be discussed later, was probably partly inspired by a desire to rid the movement of such 'undesirables'.

Too much should not be made of the comments we have quoted above. They present attitudes which are real enough but not the evidence required to justify them. All they point to is the possibility or probability that some of the movement's leaders and workers are motivated to some extent by purposive-rational considerations.[1] No precise assessment can be made, on the data we have, of the distribution of the various types of motivation among the leaders. Our subjective judgement, supported by limited evidence, is that in 1965 emotional-affectual motivations were most important, followed fairly closely by value-rational motivations, with both traditional and purposive-rational motivations a long way behind.

II. THE TEXTURE OF RELATIONS AMONG SARVODAYA LEADERS

The motives that prompt individuals to join a social movement, and more important, the motives that sustain their participation,[2] are closely, though not rigidly, correlated with what has been called its 'socio-psychic texture'. Groups, as distinct from categories such as the age and income categories considered in the previous chapter, 'exist as *social* phenomena in the minds and through the wills of the individuals who compose them'.[3] For individuals

---

[1] A few cases have been reported of individuals *impersonating* Sarvodaya workers and thereby fraudulently obtaining money from donees of Bhoodan land. One such impersonator presented himself as 'Vinoba's son'!

[2] Motives that sustain participation are more important than motives to join because the latter (recruitment motives) affect only *initial* involvement. Socialization—the acquisition of orientations necessary to function in any given role—and other subsequent experiences may modify or change completely the original motives.

[3] Heberle, op. cit., p. 128.

to be socially related, they have to become aware of each other, to develop mutual sympathy and confidence to some degree, and to recognize certain mutual obligations. The socio-psychic quality of a relationship depends on the quality of the volition by which it is formed and sustained. Two extreme cases may be distinguished: one in which the relationship is formed and sustained as an end in itself, a relationship exemplified in friendship; the other in which it is formed and sustained only as a means to an end, in order to realize similar interests of the participants, the kind of relationship exemplified in a business partnership. In the first, the personality of the participants is crucial; in the second, the purpose of the relationship is more important.

Applying these notions to the problem of seeking to understand the socio-psychological quality or texture of social movements, Heberle states: 'There exists a close inter-relation between the members' conception of what the movement means to them and their motivations in becoming and remaining members; these motivations and conceptions influence in their turn the attitudes which members of a movement develop towards each other.'[1] Although the motivations of individuals vary, it may be assumed that certain types of motivation or combinations of types predominate in any given social movement, and that therefore it has a distinctive socio-psychic texture.

For purposes of analysis three types of texture may be distinguished, each closely related to one of the types of individual motivation already mentioned, other than the traditional.[2] Following Heberle, these may be described as: (i) the purposive-rational or 'utilitarian association', (ii) the value-rational 'spiritual community or fellowship', and (iii) the emotional-affectual 'following' of a charismatic leader.[3] Although these are ideal types and in real social movements we find combinations of all three, the utilitarian (or rational) association is the type that is perhaps most familiar

[1] ibid., pp. 130-1.
[2] In theory the traditional type of individual motivation might be the basis of a fourth type of texture. In practice, however, traditional motivation is necessarily combined with other types of motivation: a movement could not be *initiated* by individuals all of whom had this type of motivation. In contrast, the other three types could exist in a pure form, although they rarely, if ever, do so. For this reason, a traditional-type texture may be ignored, although traditional-type motivations may well influence the texture of any given social movement.
[3] Heberle, op. cit., p. 131. See also his contribution on 'Social Movements' in *International Encyclopaedia of the Social Sciences*.

to modern Western man. It is exemplified in a wide variety of associations, such as business corporations, many (though not all) trade unions, and social clubs. When a social movement is of this type, the movement is a utilitarian, purposive association between otherwise independent individuals who see it as a means to the achievement of (usually fairly immediate) benefits for the members. The spiritual community or fellowship, while less common, is also quite familiar to modern Western man. It arises when devotion to a common cause is the prevalent motivation among the participants of a movement, and is associated with attitudes of fellowship, comradeship, or brotherhood among and between the members. This type is best exemplified in small political parties which emphasize ideological goals and doctrinal purity, and in certain religious sects whose members perceive themselves as a select minority of 'true believers' championing the cause of right-eousness in an unrighteous world. If such a sect succeeds in re-cruiting a large number of members, the attitudes and relationships between them tend to alter. The forms of intimate comradeship or fellowship may be retained but the spirit changes. The sect then becomes more like what sociologists of religion call a church.[1]

Least familiar of all to modern Western man is the third type, the 'following', in which attachment to a leader, perceived as possessing extraordinary qualities, is the predominant motivation of the members. In this type there is also, as in the second type, a strong sense of community, but it is generated indirectly: personal attachment to the leader who determines the goals and interprets the cause is the intermediate link.

In the literature on social movements it is often suggested that there is an historical relation between all three types, in the reverse order to the order of our presentation. The suggestion forms part of a theory of 'the natural history' of social movements, and, more generally, of a theory of social change. According to this view, expressed crudely and schematically, most social movements begin as a charismatic 'following' of a leader who defines the cause for which he lives; after the death of the original leader the cause remains, and members are related to one another directly in terms

[1] For a discussion of the sect-church theory of the origin and evolution of religious groups, a theory formulated by Weber and Troeltsch and refined by Richard Niebuhr, see C. Y. Glock & R. Stark, *Religion and Society in Tension*, 1965, Ch. 13.

of their value orientations; finally, the cause is lost sight of or relegated to the lower levels of consciousness, and what is left is a utilitarian association of members participating for 'rational', calculable, immediate benefits. This development constitutes the institutionalization of the movement. At the societal level the development is seen as part of the process of modernization associated with the spread of rational-legal authority, and a consequent 'disenchantment of the world', as social structures become increasingly rationalized and bureaucratic. There is much supportive evidence for the theory both at the level of social movements and at the societal level. Hence our suggestion that modern Western man is most familiar with utilitarian associations, less familiar with spiritual fellowships, and least familiar with charismatic followings. However, not all the evidence points one way, and, although the natural history of many social movements can be fitted into the schema of institutionalization, there is perhaps equally compelling evidence to suggest that the three ideal types are permanent elements of all human collectivities, even if in certain historical periods some elements are more obvious or visible than others.

According to what we have already said, the Sarvodaya movement, judging by evidence related to recruitment motivations, is primarily a combination of a spiritual fellowship and a charismatic following, the latter tending to predominate. It is time, therefore, to examine more closely the concept of charisma. In doing so, we may note Smelser's judgement that value-oriented movements are characterized by this particular type of leadership:

The main reason why leadership takes this particular form in the value-oriented movement lies in the character of the movement itself. Because it is oriented to values, the movement involves an envisioned reconstruction of an entire social order, from top to bottom. To follow the leadership of one man in such an adventure involves a diffuse, total kind of commitment on the part of the followers. Charismatic leadership is, in short, the most generalized form of leadership, for in such a leader is placed the hopes for a collective reconstitution of values.[1]

The term 'charisma' derives from Max Weber's classic analysis of the forms of domination. As reinterpreted by Bendix, Weber provided 'a three-fold division of the phenomenon of power: (1) power on the basis of constellations of interest, e.g., on the

---

[1] N. Smelser, *Theory of Collective Behaviour*, 1962, pp. 355-6.

market or in status groups; (2) power on the basis of established authority; i.e. legal, traditional, or charismatic domination; (3) power on the basis of leadership (the extraordinary qualities of a person and the identification of followers with that person).'[1] Weber himself defined 'charisma' as 'a certain quality of an individual personality by virtue of which he is set apart from ordinary men and treated as endowed with supernatural, superhuman, or at least specifically exceptional powers or qualities. These are such as are not accessible to the ordinary person, but are regarded as of divine origin or as exemplary. . . .'[2] With respect to the second division of power—that based on established authority—charisma constitutes the component which provides legitimacy for charismatic authority. In the case of traditional authority, legitimacy rests on 'an established belief in the sanctity of immemorial traditions and on the legitimacy of the status of those exercising authority under them'.[3] In the case of legal authority, it rests on 'rational grounds', 'a belief in the "legality" of the patterns of normative rules and the right of those elevated to authority under such rules to issue commands'.[4] As with other concepts of Weber, these are ideal types, and actual social formations are characterized by a mix, in varying proportions, of all three types.

In its original usage charisma was a 'gift of grace' bestowed by God; and leadership by a person possessed of such a gift was 'based upon a transcendent call by a divine being, believed in by both the person called and those with whom he has to deal in exercising his calling'.[5] Friedrich and others have criticized Weber for generalizing the concept and applying it in contexts where there is no question of a belief in the transcendent. The point is of

---

[1] R. Bendix, *Max Weber*, 1962, p. 299. Weber himself did not explicitly distinguish between domination as a result of charismatic authority and domination as a result of charismatic leadership. In social movements leadership rather than authority relationships are primarily involved. The leaders of such movements characteristically 'appeal' to their followers, rather than 'command' them as they do in organizations in which power has become institutionalized and transmuted into authority. cf. R. Bierstedt, 'The problem of authority' in M. Berger, T. Abel, & C. Page (eds.), *Freedom and Control in Modern Society*, 1954, pp. 67–81.

[2] Weber, op. cit., p. 329.

[3] ibid., p. 301.   [4] ibid., p. 300.

[5] C. J. Friedrich, 'Political leadership and the problem of charismatic power', *The Journal of Politics*, 23, 1 (Feb. 1961). Weber derived the term from the writings of the Church historian, Rudholf Sohm, who in turn derived it from the New Testament.

some importance, since the term is now used very loosely and applied to diverse types of leader, ranging from a Jesus through a Kennedy to an Adolf Hitler.

Wolfert has argued that much of what is today labelled 'charisma' is patently 'pseudo-charisma': a product manufactured by those who control, or have access to, the mass media of communication, an artifact of a very conscious form of rationality.[1] The outcome of a genuine charismatic leader, he asserts, is quite different from that of the pseudo-charismatic leader—the modern Caesarist.

The true charismatic leader carries within himself the seeds of what can become objectively absolute ends. He states in highly personalized terms a set of values which after his death may become generalized. Christ, who stands as the ideal type, carried a message which when scrutinized could find objective residence in the Church, even though there was a distortion of values in the process. The modern Caesarist, on the other hand, since he makes power the ultimate touchstone, cannot create values which are enduring. . . . [He] leaves no precipitate of value behind him, only refinement of technique and social and psychological wreckage.[2]

The Weberian might retort that, for the purpose of analysing social action, it is a matter of indifference *how* a leader acquires charisma. In the words of W. I. Thomas, 'If men define situations as real, they are real in their consequences.'[3] If the followers of, say, a Hitler ascribe to their leader 'exemplary qualities', then, for them, he *has* those qualities. From the perspective of the sociologist, it is unimportant whether the qualities are in some sense 'real'.[4]

For the purpose of the present discussion it is not necessary to take sides on the issue between Weber and his critics, because it is quite clear that the leadership of the Sarvodaya movement is of the 'genuine' kind.[5] Vinoba's charisma has not been consciously manufactured, and it manifests itself in the context of a belief in the

---

[1] J. F. Wolfert, 'Towards a sociology of authority', in A. W. Gouldner (ed.), *Studies in Leadership*, 1950.　　　　[2] ibid., pp. 692–3.
[3] Quoted in R. Merton, *Social Theory and Social Structure*, 1947 edn., p. 421.
[4] 'What is alone important is how the individual is actually regarded by those subject to charismatic authority. . . . It is recognition on the part of those subject to authority which is decisive for the validity of charisma.'—Weber, op. cit., pp. 329–30.
[5] Nevertheless, we would ourselves subscribe to a distinction between genuine and pseudo-charisma. There does seem something odd about a sociology which

transcendent. Indeed, we would hazard the judgement that of all contemporary social movements, other than perhaps the messianic cults of so-called primitive peoples,[1] Sarvodaya exhibits charismatic leadership in its purest form. In the person of Vinoba there is undoubtedly an element of the traditional leader. He is cast in the mould of the Vedas, and for many of his followers he conforms precisely to the ancient Indian ideal of the guru or inspired teacher. As we have noted, even his most revolutionary ideas are conveyed by traditional concepts which he invests with new meanings. But he is a traditional leader largely in the sense that charismatic leadership is itself a tradition in India. There are also, as we shall see, elements of rational-legal authority in the movement's organization, and, as we might expect from Weber's analysis, these are becoming increasingly evident. But it is highly significant that Vinoba himself occupies no position in the organization: he has consistently refused to vest himself with the trappings of rational-legal authority.

It is a mistake, however, to think of charisma as merely the quality of the individual 'top leader'. It is a quality possessed by many other leaders, perhaps all leaders to a certain degree; it occurs within a particular kind of social context; and a movement takes on certain characteristics as a result of being built around such leaders. These characteristics may be considered under three broad headings: the social psychological, the organizational, and the economic. With respect to the first, Turner and Killian point out that 'the nature and basis of adherence will affect the "texture" of the movement'.[2] An emotional form of communal (*gemeinschaft*[3]) relationship obtains between the members. They provide the top leader with 'a highly flexible body of adherents', who give support without questioning changes or inconsistencies in the move-

---

places a Jesus and a Hitler, a Kennedy and a Vinoba, in the same category. While accepting Thomas's dictum, we would agree with Wolfert that the long-term consequences of a genuine charismatic leader are likely to be different from those of a pseudo-charismatic leader.

[1] On modern messianic cults see V. Lanternari, *The Religion of the Oppressed*, 1963. On messianic movements in Indian religions see S. Fuchs, *Rebellious Prophets*, 1965. Fuchs does not deal with the movement of Gandhi and Vinoba but recognizes that these two leaders 'should probably be included'.—p. xiii. However, neither Gandhi nor Vinoba quite fits what is usually meant by the concept of a Messiah.

[2] R. H. Turner & L. M. Killian, *Collective Behavior*, 1957, p. 464.

[3] F. Tönnies, *Community and Association*, 1955.

ment's programme. At the same time, this support has an intense and unwavering quality which makes for a degree of commitment on the part of the followers that has no parallel in other forms of domination—the traditional and the rational-legal.

Participant observation has confirmed our view that the Sarvodaya movement, in this respect, *approximates* to Weber's ideal type. The emotional quality of the relations between the leaders we met was of the *gemeinschaft* type. Vinoba is revered by his colleagues as a contemporary saint, and darshan (vision or contact) of his person is one of the gratifications highly valued by them, as well as by other followers.[1] Support for his policies (among those for whom he continues to possess charisma) is intense and often unwavering. Successive developments in his vision of the meaning of Bhoodan have been accepted without open challenge and usually with evident enthusiasm. Covert criticisms of several of his policies are indeed sometimes made, but they are rarely brought into the open and made the subject of vigorous debate within the movement. The movement's journals are notable for their pious tone and their relative lack of controversial discussion of 'issues' within the movement. In Sarva Seva Sangh the movement does possess an organization. Vinoba appreciates the necessity of having this organization; but there is little doubt that his ideal organization is not an organization at all, but the body known, significantly, as the Sarvodaya Samaj—a fellowship of constructive workers, composed of 'members' who have selected themselves.

It is not possible to assess accurately the extent of 'the mix' in the Sarvodaya movement of spiritual community of believers in the cause and charismatic following of Vinoba. While Vinoba lives, the two are not readily distinguishable. Here it suffices to note that charismatic leadership has other consequences, particularly of an organizational character, which will be discussed in the next chapter.

III. THE MOVEMENT'S 'EMBRACE' OF THE LEADERS

Related to the types of texture of social movements is the way in which they 'embrace' their participants.[2] Some movements serve

---

[1] This is shown by the lower 'turn-out' at meetings of Sarva Seva Sangh when Vinoba is not present.

[2] The term 'embrace' is derived from A. Etzioni, *A Comparative Analysis of Complex Organizations*, 1961, p. 160. The analysis in the first part of this section

as collectivities in which many or most of an individual's activities take place, while others serve as a base for only one or a few specialized activities. Again, some movements attempt to regulate much of a participant's life, even 'outside' the movement, while in others little or no such attempt is made. Both variables are involved in the concept of 'embrace'. The first variable refers to what Etzioni calls 'scope': the number of activities in which participants of a movement are jointly involved. The scope of a movement (or organization) is determined by discovering the extent to which activities of its participants are limited to other participants, as against the degree to which activities involve non-participants as well. Movements may be either broad or narrow in scope. At the extreme, broad, end of this continuum are to be found 'total' movements in which all or most of the activities of participants are involved. The second variable refers to what Etzioni calls 'pervasiveness'. The range of pervasiveness is determined by the number of activities in or outside the movement for which the movement establishes, or seeks to establish, norms of behaviour for its participants. Pervasiveness may be either low or high, depending on whether the norms apply only to activities directly controlled by the movement's leaders or whether they extend to other activities carried on by the movement's participants.

Scope and pervasiveness, although analytically distinguishable, are inter-related. Pervasiveness may be more or less encompassing than scope; that is, the normative 'boundaries' of a collectivity (as measured by its pervasiveness) and its action 'boundaries' (as measured by its scope) do not necessarily coincide. Many Churches, for example, have relatively narrow scope but are highly pervasive, the Roman Catholic Church being a case in point. But in social movements, as distinct from organizations generally, scope and pervasiveness tend to go together. Social movements which are 'utilitarian associations' tend to be narrow in scope and low in pervasiveness. Social movements which are 'spiritual communities' or 'charismatic followings' tend to be broad in scope and high in pervasiveness.[1]

owes much to Etzioni. Although we have applied his concepts to movements rather than organizations, our empirical data relate to the leaders of the 'core' organization of the Sarvodaya movement.

[1] In terms of Smelser's types of movement, value-oriented movements tend to be both broader in scope and higher in pervasiveness than norm-oriented movements.

The degree to which a movement embraces its participants is, of course, inversely related to the degree to which they participate in other collectivities which constitute the social environment of the movement. Some measure of a movement's embrace may therefore be derived from data about the participation of its members in other movements and organizations. Before presenting such data with respect to the Sarvodaya leaders, however, it may be helpful to indicate briefly the theoretical significance of determining a movement's embrace.

Two points of interest, both deriving from the theory of 'mass society', may be mentioned. The first relates to social sources of recruitment rather than to social psychological character. It has been hypothesized that 'poorly integrated sections of the community are most likely to engage in mass action outside and often against established social institutions in times of crisis'. 'Within all strata, people divorced from community, occupation, and association are first and foremost among the supporters of extremism. The decisive social process in mass society is the *atomization* of social relations; even though this process is accentuated in the lower strata, it operates throughout the society.'[1] One important indicator of 'poor integration' and 'atomization' is lack of membership of those secondary associations[2] which collectively constitute the infra-structure of 'the pluralist society'. The hypothesis was developed to explain recruitment to mass movements in advanced industrial societies, but its application could be extended to developing societies in process of transition from 'communal society'. As modernization destroys or undermines traditional communal bonds, there is the danger that 'mass society' rather than 'pluralist society' may develop. The 'danger' arises from the fact that 'mass society' may easily lead to 'totalitarian society'.

Since Sarvodaya *might* be interpreted as an extremist mass movement (in the technical, not the ordinary sense of 'mass'), if the hypothesis is to be validated in the Indian context, we should expect its leaders (and other members) to have few associational ties outside the movement.

The second point of interest is related to the first but is more directly social psychological. On the assumption that isolation is psychologically intolerable for most human beings, it is hypo-

[1] W. Kornhauser, *The Politics of Mass Society*, 1960, pp. 66, 73.
[2] As distinct from primary associations, such as the family.

thesized that mass movements, recruiting atomized individuals, will seek to create for them a kind of *ersatz* community as a substitute for the community they have lost or from which they have been excluded for one reason or another.[1] In the literature on social movements Communist movements are often cited as examples confirming the hypothesis. Communist movements, it is suggested, attempt to create an organizational structure and climate which embrace all the important aspects of the lives of their adherents. To the extent that the attempt is successful, a person who joins a Communist Party enters into a new way of life, in which other relations, including family relations, are subordinated to his relations to 'the Party'. He begins to live and work in and for the party. 'The Party asserts control over every department of their (the militants') lives, and recognizes no dividing line between the political and the personal. . . . The Party is a movement to which he (the militant) belongs, a community in which he lives, a way of life in which he participates. . . . His personal interests and his personal feelings count for nothing in so far as they conflict with his duties that attach to his party membership.'[2] It is because the Communist Party becomes for many of its members a community-type collectivity that the act of quitting or renouncing the Party is often such a traumatic experience.[3]

Communist Parties are contrasted in this respect with the more usual kinds of party found in industrial societies. In 'liberal' as distinct from 'totalitarian' parties participation is segmental rather than integral in character. Membership in 'liberal' parties is seen as a relationship relatively distinct or separate from other social relationships. The conservative or modern social democrat, for example, votes for his party, perhaps attends its meetings, and

---

[1] The purpose of creating an *ersatz* community is not, of course, primarily related to providing personal satisfactions for the members but to creating a dedicated cadre of workers for the cause of the movement.

[2] A. Rossi, *A Communist Party in Action*, 1949, p. 102. Quoted in Heberle, op. cit., p. 350. Rossi's description refers to the Communist Party of France.

[3] Writing more generally on this point, J. R. Gusfield has observed: 'The socially alienated person finds in a movement a solution to his problems of "belonging". . . . In some movements, totalistic commitment is fostered by a round of life so controlled by organizational activities as to preclude interpersonal relations outside of the movement; where this happens, defection is tantamount to a complete reorientation of one's life. In more pluralistic movements, adherence to the movement does not cut the member loose from other competing and even conflicting roles.'—'Social Movements', *International Encyclopaedia of the Social Sciences*.

may be one of its activists; but his political activity does not embrace the whole of his life. He remains a conservative plus something else, a social democrat plus something else; and the 'something else' constitutes an important element in his sense of identity.[1]

The Sarvodaya movement is not a political party but it is an avowedly revolutionary movement aiming at a total reconstruction of society. In terms of a continuum ranging from 'liberal' to 'totalitarian', the Sarvodaya movement *might* be thought to come nearer to the latter. Although it resolutely eschews violent means to achieve its objectives and is not averse to 'social engineering' in some sense of that term, it does believe in the possibility of establishing a more perfect society, a heaven on earth, in which social conflicts will be finally resolved. Its radical criticisms of the existing social and political order and its determination to keep aloof from orthodox politics suggest a certain affinity with familiar totalitarian movements such as Communism. Again, therefore, if the hypothesis is to be validated, we should expect the Sarvodaya leaders to have few associational ties outside the movement.

In turning now to the presentation of our data about the leaders' participation in other movements and organizations, it should be emphasized that our findings are suggestive rather than conclusive. We lack similar data with respect to comparable social groups in India. In Western societies participation in associations is correlated with socio-economic status; the higher the status, the more likely are individuals to belong to associations.[2] Many middle-class persons, however, do not belong to any association. Since secondary associations are probably less well developed in India than in the West, we should expect fewer associational memberships among middle-class Indians than among their equivalents in, say, the U.S.A. In addition to the lack of comparability with other social groups in India there is the problem of the ambiguity of the

---

[1] Participation in social democratic parties and movements was formerly more 'integral' and less 'segmental' than it now usually is, although many of these parties still retain something of their former character. The change away from integral towards segmental participation is one aspect of the increasing integration of these parties in the socio-political systems of their societies. The change is also apparent in some Communist parties as they become more moderate and pursue their respective 'national' roads to socialism.

[2] 'Among Americans interviewed in 1955, in the lowest of five socio-economic classes only 8% belonged to any organization, as contrasted with 82% in the highest class.'—S. M. Lipset, *Political Man*, 1960, p. 195.

indicator. Absence of membership in associations may indicate *either* simply a lack of interest (perhaps because of the strength of traditional communal ties) *or* the possibility that participation in the Sarvodaya movement is 'integral' or 'total'. However, the presence of other memberships is a less ambiguous indicator, suggesting that participation is something less than 'total'.

Our major finding is that 58 per cent of our respondents held, at the time of the enquiry, at least one membership, usually at an official level, in some other organization than Sarva Seva Sangh, such as an educational society, co-operative, political organization, religious or cultural association. In the Indian context we should judge this figure to be remarkably high, suggesting that a substantial proportion of the leaders of the movement are not recruited from the 'socially isolated' and that their participation falls short of being 'total'. In other words, as far as the leaders are concerned, the Sarvodaya movement conforms more to the paradigm of the 'liberal' than of the 'totalitarian' movement. However, it should be added that the figure of 58 per cent includes memberships of organizations which might be considered part of the wider Gandhian movement. To take account of this we need a more refined analysis of associational memberships.

For purposes of analysis the organizations (other than Sarva Seva Sangh) which were mentioned by the respondents were divided into four categories: (i) 'Institutional Gandhian', such as the Gandhi Smarak Nidhi or a Gandhian ashram; (ii) 'Official Gandhian', which included mainly Khadi and village industries organizations; (iii) 'Political', comprising political parties, public legislative and administrative bodies, and peace organizations, such as War Resisters' International; and (iv) a residual 'Other' category which included co-operatives, trade unions, educational bodies, and cultural and religious associations. The following table summarizes the distribution of the associational memberships of the leaders between the four categories at two points in time: at the time of the enquiry and in the period before the year 1951 when the Bhoodan campaign began.

In more detail, of the 62 leaders who in 1965 held a position in an 'Institutional Gandhian' association, 32 per cent were members of the Gandhi Smarak Nidhi and 45 per cent lived in a Gandhian ashram. The latter group (about 12 per cent of all respondents) is of particular interest, since an ashram is an 'integral community', an organization approximating to what Goffman has called a 'total institution',[1] in which scope is very broad and pervasiveness is very high. Of the 11 leaders who in 1965 held a position in a 'Political' association, 6 were members of a peace organization, and, despite the movement's bar on membership of political parties, one belonged to Congress, one to the Communist Party, and 3 to other parties; none was a member of a legislative or administrative body. Of the 58 leaders who held a position in 'Other' associations, 53 per cent were members (almost all officers) of a co-operative, 26 per cent belonged to an educational society,

TABLE 4:1

Associational memberships of Sarvodaya leaders

Membership of at least one association in:	Institutional Gandhian	Official Gandhian	Political	Other — e.g. co-op., educational society	
	%	%	%	%	N
1965	27	15	5	25	228
Pre-1951	19	11	34	17	228

9 per cent to a religious society, 5 per cent to a cultural organization, 3 per cent to a trade union, and 26 per cent to miscellaneous associations.[2] Although we may regard the 'Political' and 'Other' categories as types of association clearly outside the Sarvodaya movement, it could be argued that co-operatives are closely related to the movement. Relations between the Co-operative Movement in India and the Sarvodaya movement are not as close as the leaders of the latter would like, but, as part of its programme of village development, Sarvodaya does sponsor co-operatives. If we exclude those who were members of a co-operative and also those who belonged to an 'Institutional' or 'Official' Gandhian association, a peace organization, or to Congress, the number of respondents

[1] 'A total institution may be defined as a place of residence and work where a large number of like-situated individuals, cut off from the wider society for an appreciable period of time, together lead an enclosed, formally administered round of life.'—E. Goffman, *Asylums*, 1961, p. xiii.

[2] The percentages do not add up to 100, since some were members of more than one type in this category.

with associational memberships outside the wider Gandhian movement in the broadest sense is 44 (or 20 per cent). In our judgement, this figure is still high enough to warrant the tentative conclusion that Sarvodaya does not conform closely to the picture of a mass movement as presented by political sociologists such as Kornhauser. It may be that the theory of mass society needs revision; it may also be that Sarvodaya is a deviant case. An argument could certainly be made out for the latter. Although Sarvodaya has several of the characteristics we associate with extremist mass movements, its mode of operation is not that of 'alienated man': its leaders may envisage a Kingdom of God on earth but, with their eyes fixed on heaven, their feet remain firmly on the ground; remoteness from the day to day interests of the people whom they seek to mobilize to change the existing order is *not* one of their traits.

The historical comparison presented in Table 4:1 permits us to judge whether the movement has changed its character in respect of becoming more 'totalitarian' since 1951, the year in which it was revitalized by the launching of the Bhoodan campaign. If we make allowance for the fact that one-third of the leaders have joined the movement since 1951, it would appear that the broad pattern of associational membership has not changed very much except in one significant feature: the decline in the proportion of leaders with memberships in 'Political' associations. This change, it may be safely concluded, is a direct consequence of the development of the movement's concept of partyless democracy, and its accompanying proscription on active association with political parties. Congress has borne the brunt of this proscription. In 1951, of the 77 respondents who then held positions in political organizations, 91 per cent belonged to Congress, 10 per cent to the Socialists, 5 per cent to other parties (including one who was a member of the Communist Party), 12 per cent were members of a local government body, and 8 per cent were members of provincial legislative assemblies.[1]

Our empirical data do not, we should emphasize again, provide the basis for an accurate assessment of the movement's 'embrace'. Despite the evidence of the 'liberal' as distinct from 'totalitarian' complexion of the movement, we should judge its scope to be

---

[1] The percentages do not add up to 100, since some were members of more than one organization in this category.

broad and its pervasiveness to be high compared with some other political movements in India. The withdrawal of the leaders since 1951 from political associations may be interpreted as involving a broadening of the movement's scope, an attempt to contain the political activities of the leaders within the movement as it sought to present itself as an alternative to orthodox political parties. There is also evidence that the pervasiveness of the movement has increased as a consequence of the introduction during the 1950s of various pledges prescribed for active participants. These pledges, however, may be most appropriately considered as measures of the kind and degree of commitment, a subject to which we now turn.

IV. THE COMMITMENT OF THE SARVODAYA LEADERS

To set out on a journey whose destination is the complete restructuring of the social order on the basis of a transformation of individual and social values calls for an intense and high level of commitment. Such a journey is not for faint-hearts or for those who prefer the satisfactions to be derived from the normal pursuits of what Beatrice Webb was fond of calling 'the average sensual man'. The Sarvodaya movement is no exception to this rule. In carrying out its non-violent social revolution, the role of the activists in the movement is crucial and the expectations attached to the role are many and demanding. The level of commitment called for by the movement is related, as in any other movement, to the question of selectivity. A movement demanding a low level of commitment (because its goals are restricted) can afford to be unselective in its recruits. A movement demanding a high level of commitment must either be highly selective, or, if it is unselective, provide for its recruits means which will effectively socialize them into its values and norms.

In principle, the universalism of Sarvodaya prescribes that it should be unselective. The movement appeals to all men and women, irrespective of caste, class, colour, or creed. Ideally, no distinction is to be drawn between the active participants in the movement (usually called its 'workers') and the general population. The movement seeks to elicit the loving and creative powers inherent in all men; to become a genuinely people's movement; and, finally, to liquidate itself as all men, women, and children become imbued with Sarvodaya values and the Sarvodaya society is established. In practice, however, the revolution can only begin if it is inspired and led by men and women of exceptional qualities, a moral élite who here and now in their own lives exemplify the spirit and values of Sarvodaya. All men *may* join; and it is believed that eventually all men *will* join; but, meanwhile, tests are prescribed for entry into the moral élite. These tests, consistent with the libertarian philosophy of Sarvodaya, do not take the form, as they do in certain ideological parties, of passing 'examinations' in doctrine. Instead, they take the form of voluntary adherence to pledges, a mode of seeking to ensure commitment familiar in religious organizations and part of the traditional culture of India.

Some impression of the general character of the ideal Sarvodaya worker may be obtained if we contrast him with the more familiar stereotype 'social worker' with which he is sometimes confused.[1] There are many resemblances between the two, but the differences are the more striking and revealing. One such difference is best symbolized by the image of Gandhi as the 'half-naked fakir', the man who chose deliberately to live the life of voluntary poverty and who identified himself with the masses of his fellow countrymen. Unlike the traditional voluntary social worker, the Gandhian is not a person who performs 'good works' from the vantage point of a privileged position in society, and who practises a benevolent paternalism prompted by charitable instincts or a nagging social conscience. Nor, unlike the professional social worker, is he a person who performs 'good works' because that is the job for which he has been trained and for which he is paid a professional wage. The Gandhian worker identifies—or at least makes a serious attempt to identify—with those he seeks to serve. This identification involves a willingness to adopt a standard and mode of life comparable with those of the masses. But it goes beyond the adoption of external symbols and involves also an acceptance of a community of spirit. The purpose of this identification is to create

[1] Sarvodaya workers often think of themselves as 'social workers' and are thought of as such by the general populace, although less frequently by 'professional' social workers. For a discussion of the relation between Gandhian 'constructive work' and social work in India see Sugata Dasgupta (ed.), *Towards a Philosophy of Social Work in India*, 1967. For a suggestive interpretation of the trends in modern social work which have some affinities with Gandhian 'constructive work' see Paul Halmos, *The Faith of the Counsellors*, 1965. The current interest of sections of the New Left in community action is very much in line with the Gandhian approach.

a vital bond between the worker and those with whom he works, thus providing a sound basis of communication between them. Identification also symbolizes the fact that the educative function of constructive work is a two-way process in which the worker is educated, as well as those who benefit from his work. Through identification the worker may achieve a degree of self-purification: in this respect, therefore, it contributes to his own personal salvation and transformation into a more moral being. But more important is the effect produced on those served, by the example the worker sets. 'A reformer's business', said Gandhi, 'is to make the impossible possible by an ocular demonstration in his own conduct.'

Identification may be represented as a novel and more effective version of the idea of 'propaganda by the deed' favoured by some violent Western anarchists in the late nineteenth century. The Gandhian worker, by his actions rather than by precepts, shows how people must behave if the Sarvodaya society is to be achieved. Describing the ideal worker, Gandhi once wrote:

He would be bound with the poorest in the village by ties of service. He would constitute himself the scavenger, the nurse, the arbitrator of disputes, and the teacher of the children of the village. Everyone, young and old, would know him; though a householder, he would be leading a life of restraint; he would make no distinction between his and his neighbour's children; he would own nothing but would hold what wealth he has in trust for others, and would therefore spend out of it just sufficient for his bare needs. His needs would, as far as possible, approximate to those of the poor; he would harbour no untouchability, and would therefore inspire people of all castes and creeds to approach him with confidence.[1]

It would, of course, be foolish to expect that the Gandhian ideal could ever be fully realized in practice. Neither Gandhi nor Vinoba would claim that they themselves approached near to the level of 'saintliness' demanded by the ideal. But there are undoubtedly many Sarvodaya workers, well known and little known, who do make a serious effort to live according to the ideal. As we have seen, a significant proportion of the Sarvodaya leaders, despite their relatively high social and educational status, reported having a standard of income approximating to that of the masses

[1] *Harijan*, 4 Aug. 1940, p. 235. Quoted in Pyarelal, *Mahatma Gandhi: The Last Phase*, vol. ii, 1958, p. 638.

of India. The level of personal commitment demanded of the Sarvodaya moral élite is clearly very high.

The Lok Sevak pledge

After these general observations we may turn to examine the content of the pledges used in the movement to encourage a sense of personal commitment to Sarvodaya ideals. One such pledge is that of the Lok Sevak taken by members of Sarvodaya organizations over the age of eighteen years, of whom there were in 1964, according to the Sangh's records, 8,621. Each of these should have signed a written statement, addressed to the Secretary of the Sangh and seconded by two other members, containing the following clauses:

1. I believe in the principles of truth, non-violence, non-possessiveness, bodily labour, and self-control. I will try to conduct my life on these principles.
2. I believe that the world can only know true peace when the common people are in direct control of their own affairs (through Lok-niti). I will, therefore, not take part in party politics or power-politics, but will do my best to get members of all political parties to help me in my work.
3. I will devote my whole mind to disinterested service of the people.
4. I will give no place in my life to any spirit of exclusiveness in matters of caste, class or religion.
5. I will give my whole time and my best thought to the work of the non-violent revolution of Sarvodaya, with its practical programme of Bhoodanyajna (Bhoodan offering or sacrifice) and village industry.[1]

In the *Constitution* of the Sangh this statement is further clarified as follows. A Lok Sevak who contests a seat in elections, either on a party ticket or as an independent, will cease to be regarded as a Lok Sevak. All those constructive trends that may help the cause of Sarvodaya will be regarded as coming within the compass of the movement for non-violent revolution. A person who, understanding the full importance of labour, leads his life accordingly and devotes his spare time to the work mentioned in the fifth clause above will be considered to be fulfilling the pledge of the Lok Sevak. And, finally, the condition applicable to the members of the Sangh is equally applicable to Lok Sevaks: they shall be

[1] Vinoba Bhave, *Shanti Sena*, 1961, Appendix I, p. 150.

habitual wearers of khadi, i.e. cloth made of self-spun or home-spun yarn or certified khadi.

The Shanti Sainik pledge

Very similar to the pledge of the Lok Sevak is that of the Shanti Sainik—a member of the Shanti Sena or Peace Army. The original pledge of the Shanti Sainik was identical with that of the Lok Sevak, except that it contained an additional sixth clause: 'Whenever and wherever I may be ordered to go for the work of the Shanti Sena, I shall be prepared to go, and, also, should need arise, to give my life in their service.'[1]

The pledge in use in 1965, however, took the following form and was open to any citizen of India above eighteen years of age:

I BELIEVE
1. in the establishment of a new society based on truth and non-violence;
2. that all conflicts in society can and should be solved, more so in this atomic age than ever before, by non-violent means;
3. in the fundamental unity of man;
4. that war blocks all human progress and is a denial of a non-violent way of life.
Therefore, I hereby PLEDGE that I SHALL
1. work for peace and be prepared, if need be, to lay down my life for it;
2. to do my best to rise above the distinctions of caste, sect, colour and party, etc., because they deny the unity of man;
3. not to take part in any war;
4. help in creating the means and conditions of non-violent defence;
5. devote regularly a part of my time to the service of my fellowmen;
6. accept the discipline of the Shanti Sena.[2]

The pledge of Jeevandan

The Lok Sevak and Shanti Sainik pledges are those currently used in the movement and of which records are kept for the purpose of estimating progress in increasing the numbers of workers. There is, however, also a third pledge, which at an earlier stage had considerable significance and publicity. This is the pledge of Jeevandan or dedication of one's life to the cause of the movement. It originated at the sixth Sarvodaya annual conference held in

[1] Ibid., p. 151.
[2] Shanti Sena Mandal, The Indian Shanti Sena, brochure, n.d.

1954 at Bodh-Gaya in Bihar, the place of the Buddha's enlightenment. The whole atmosphere of the conference was reported to
have been electrified by the announcement of the offer by Jayaprakash Narayan, the former Socialist leader, to dedicate his life
for the non-violent revolution. Vinoba responded by offering his
own life to the same cause, and more than five hundred of the
assembled workers followed suit, on the spot.[1] Subsequently, the
following rules for a Jeevandani were drawn up and approved by
Vinoba:

1. A Jeevandani in possession of land should give a reasonable portion
of his land in Boodan.
2. A Jeevandani should give part of his income or produce as Sampattidan (gift of wealth).[2]
3. A Jeevandani must believe in the dignity of labour; each person
should evolve a regular programme for productive labour which suits
him best.
4. A Jeevandani should wear khadi. Moreover, he should develop the
habit of spinning regularly. Members of his family should also take part
in spinning.
5. He should use articles produced by village industries.
6. He must give up intoxicants of every kind.
7. He must actively work for the removal of untouchability.

---

[1] Suresh Ram, op. cit., pp. 104–6.
[2] Sampattidan has provided the basis for yet a fourth pledge. It takes the
form of a signed letter to Vinobaji which includes the following terms:

I surrender the —th of my income to you and undertake to devote the same
every year to social welfare work in such a manner as you may desire me to do. I
will continue to send in regularly the annual account of my income to you or to
the agent or body which you may empower for the said purpose. I accept the
responsibility of keeping whatever amount of money may accrue to the donated
share in safe custody and to spend it according to your instructions. To this
pledge, willingly undertaken, I, as the *Antaryami*, i.e. the Inner Guide in me,
am myself a witness. I am conscious that I have to be faithful to my *Antaryami*.
May God help me. Attached herewith please find the statement of my wealth
and property.—S. Ram, op. cit., p. 510.

It will be noted that the proportion of income pledged is to be decided by the
pledger and that no money is to be sent to Vinoba. Vinoba had no intention of
saddling himself with the task of receiving and dispensing money so raised. In
the absence of instructions, it is left to the pledger to decide, according to his
conscience, how the proportion of his income devoted to Sampattidan should be
spent. The unusual form of the pledge is very characteristic of Vinoba. We were
unable to obtain from the movement's headquarters any information about the
numbers who have made this pledge. The general impression is that it has not
been a great success in raising money for the movement, although Sampattidan
remains one of the sources of financing workers.

8. He should actively cooperate in Bhoodan work.

9. Similarly, he should actively participate in constructive activity of every type.

10. A Jeevandani must not participate in elections as a candidate.

11. A Jeevandani should not go to a court of law; in case of dispute he should get it settled by a Panchayat (a judicial council traditionally of five members).

12. If he is a landlord, he should not evict his tenants.

13. A Jeevandani lawyer should not accept or plead false causes.

14. A Jeevandani should take fees only sufficient to make a simple living possible.

15. A Jeevandani businessman should not indulge in unfair practices or avoid taxes.

16. A Jeevandani intellectual should give some part of his time to propagate the Bhoodan movement.[1]

From this list of rules, with its fairly precise prescriptions of norms of behaviour, the attempt to extend the pervasiveness of the movement is plainly evident. The spirit of Jeevandan as envisaged by Vinoba, however, is not fully reflected in these rules. 'Those who enter the Jeevandan Yagna [sacrifice]', he said, 'will help, advise, and care for one another. This is not a herd of sheep requiring a shepherd. These are all lions who will work by their own, i.e. God's strength. None should think that he has submitted himself to any particular person. I am with all those who come with me. If anybody wants to part company, he can do so by all means. And I have the right to go onward.' And he concluded, 'Really there cannot be any class or caste of Jeevandanis. It cannot be said that such and such a person is a Jeevandani. Only *Antaryami* (God) can say that. . . . Therefore, the only statement that can be made is one *was* a Jeevandani, for it is only after a person's death it can be decided whether he or she has dedicated his or her life or not. A meeting of Jeevandanis can only be held in Heaven. On this earth only we ordinary folk, can meet or gather.'[2]

The pledges taken by Sarvodaya leaders

The following table presents our data concerning the pledges taken by the Sarvodaya leaders.

[1] Jayaprakash Narayan, *Jeevandan*, 1956, pp. 31-2.
[2] ibid., pp. 33-6.

It will be seen from section (a) of the table that nine out of ten of the respondent office-holders had taken the Lok Sevak and Shanti Sainik pledges and that one in three had taken the pledge of Jeevandan. The relative ordering of frequency of the three pledges is in line with what might be expected from a study of their content. The Shanti Sainik pledge is very similar in substance, as we have seen, to the Lok Sevak pledge, except that it involves an undertaking to go at any time to any place at the behest of the organization, and, if necessary, to lay down one's life for peace. (Few 'orders' of this kind have ever been made and no fatal casualties have been reported.) The Jeevandan pledge involved the highest degree of commitment and we might expect that fewer would subscribe to it. However, it should be noted that the

TABLE 4:2

Pledges taken by Sarvodaya leaders

(a) Proportion of respondents reporting having taken the:	%	(b) Proportion of respondents reporting having taken:	%
Lok Sevak pledge	90	All three pledges	31
Shanti Sainik pledge	88	Any one or two pledges	61
Jeevandan pledge	34	None	6
		Opposed to pledges	1
			99

(N = 223)

status of this pledge in the movement is now somewhat obscure. It has not been publicized for some years, no records are kept of numbers taking it, and recent recruits would probably not regard it as an 'option'. It may also be that some of the respondents who offered Jeevandan in 1954 or subsequently have taken Vinoba's words to heart and prefer to leave God to judge whether or not they are Jeevandanis.

From section (b) of the table we might have derived some measure of the distribution of degrees of commitment among the leaders if the status of the Jeevandan pledge had been less obscure. As it is, it is no more than probable that the 31 per cent who had taken all three pledges are more committed than the 61 per cent who had taken only one or two (mainly the Lok Sevak and/or Shanti Sainik pledges). Worthy of comment is the very tiny minority

opposed to pledges, an expression of an attitude to oaths characteristic of Quakers. The larger but still very small minority who
had taken no pledge might be thought to be the least committed.
But it is possible that all or some of those who reported no pledges
also had conscientious objections to taking pledges of this kind.
No attempt was made to verify whether or not a respondent had
taken a *formal* pledge, and it may be that some of this minority
had not, but considered themselves to be so committed informally.

The contributions of the leaders to Bhoodan

Pledges taken may provide a rough measure of the kind and degree
of commitment of the leaders to Sarvodaya values. Another rough
measure, possibly more important because it involves more than
words and habitual practices such as wearing khadi, is whether
or not the leaders have themselves contributed to Bhoodan.
However, this measure is subject to the difficulty that not all
leaders possessed land to donate. As we have seen, only 51 per cent
of the leaders reported that they possessed land *at the time of the
enquiry*. But Bhoodan is not the only kind of dan. There are no
have-nots, argues Vinoba, and everybody, however poor and
humble, has something which he can share with his fellow men.
Even if he has no property and no income, he can share his labour
and his talents. For this reason, respondents were also asked
whether or not they had contributed to dans other than Bhoodan.
The form of the question, however, made it likely that only the
more tangible kind of dan, such as a gift of wealth or a donation
of a portion of one's income (sampattidan) was considered. All
the leaders might well be regarded as donors of the less tangible
kinds of 'property': their time, their labour, and their talents.
Figures for 'other dans' must, therefore, be interpreted to mean a
donation, whether once and for all or regularly, of something on
which a cash value could readily be placed.

Of all the respondents, just over half (52 per cent) reported
having contributed one or more forms of dan. 43 per cent of all
respondents reported having contributed to Bhoodan and 18 per
cent to some other dan, 9 per cent contributing to both. The
proportion contributing to Bhoodan is rather less than the proportion owning land in 1965, but near enough to it to suggest the
conclusion that most leaders have behaved in an exemplary
manner, practising what they preach. However, the two groups—

the landowners and the contributors to Bhoodan—do not neces-sarily coincide. Some leaders are known to have donated *all* their land, so that they were no longer landowners at the time of the enquiry. The proportion of landowning leaders who have *not* con-tributed to Bhoodan is therefore higher than 8 per cent (the differ-ence between landowners and Bhoodan contributors). But it is possible that such leaders *share* in the ownership of land as mem-bers of a joint family, and consequently were not in a position to make a donation unilaterally.

The proportion of leaders who had contributed to other dans might be considered relatively small. But it should be recalled that our data on incomes showed that two-fifths of the leaders had a *per capita* income below, or not much more than, that of the average Indian. The proportion contributing to other dans (18 per cent) is about the same as the proportion (17 per cent) reporting a household monthly income of over Rs. 400/-, although the two groups do not necessarily coincide. When one considers the rela-tively high social and education status of most Sarvodaya leaders, it seems likely that many of them could, if they so chose, earn a higher income than they now receive. In a sense, then, it is possible to argue that, even if they have made no formal contribution to other dans, they may have contributed a *notional* share of their income, i.e. the amount of the difference between what they *could* have earned outside the movement and what they do in fact earn inside it. In the case of some leaders, such notional contributions would undoubtedly be considerable.

V. A REVOLUTION OF THE SAINTS?

In their personal lives, in their attitudes to social behaviour, and in the content of the various pledges instituted as mechanisms of commitment to the movement's values, the Sarvodayites conform in many ways to the popular Western stereotype of the puritan. As is well known, asceticism is a deeply rooted element in the Indian cultural tradition. As far back as the Atharva Veda it is mentioned that a person can obtain supernatural powers by the practice of austerities; and, in one of the hymns of this Veda, Brahma is described as born from 'austere fervour' or tapas. In the Kena Upanishad the mystic way of knowing Brahman (Truth, God) is described thus: 'Austerity (*tapas*), restraint (*dama*), and

work (*karman*) are the foundation of it [viz. the mystic doctrine].'[1]
Tapas are thus seen as capable of producing great inner strength.
Gandhi fully accepted this doctrine; and his fasts, his vow of
brahmacharya, and his other rules of bodily discipline were merely
the outward means to the attainment of this inner strength.[2] The
'puritanism' of Sarvodayites, therefore, is neither their own in-
vention nor an accidental feature of the movement: it is not the
expression of the personal 'fads' of Gandhi or Vinoba, but something near to the heart of their being and quite central to their
spiritual approach to life and to politics.

In contemporary India the ascetic tradition and the austere
puritanical approach to life remain very much alive, alongside
their exact contrarieties, the former providing standards by which
men in public life are often judged. But the processes of modernization are undermining the ancient tradition, especially among the
Westernized and educated élites, with the result that asceticism
is frequently placed on the defensive. Even such a sympathetic
observer as Frank Moraes can so misinterpret Gandhi's teaching
on this point as to write that it was the expression of 'a repressive
attitude which saw life as a series of taboos'.[3] Moraes ignored what
Gandhi always tried to make clear: that self-denial and self-
restraint were only means to the larger end of self-realization.[4]

Attitudes to 'puritanism'

In an effort to assess the strength of 'puritanical' attitudes among
the Sarvodaya leaders, respondents were asked to state whether
they agreed or disagreed with the following statement: 'The movement will have to change some of its traditional attitudes to things
like smoking, drinking and birth control if it hopes to attract young
people today.' Although this statement is worded in such a way

[1] R. E. Hume, *The Thirteen Principal Upanishads*, 1951, p. 340. Quoted in
I. Rothermund, *The Philosophy of Restraint*, 1963, p. 59.
[2] Rothermund, op. cit., p. 59.
[3] F. Moraes, 'Gandhi Ten Years After', *Foreign Affairs* (Jan. 1958); quoted
in Rothermund, op. cit., p. 59.
[4] The spirit of Gandhi's asceticism is revealed in such statements as: 'Abste-
miousness from intoxicating drinks and drugs, and from all kinds of foods,
especially meat, is undoubtedly a great aid to the evolution of the spirit, but it is
by no means an end in itself. Many a man eating meat and with everybody, but
living in the fear of God, is nearer his freedom than a man religiously abstaining
from meat and many other things, but blaspheming God in every one of his
acts.'—*Young India*, 6 Oct. 1921, p. 318. Quoted in N. K. Bose (ed.), *Selections
from Gandhi*, 2nd edn., 1957, p. 252.

that, logically, someone who shared the traditional attitudes in question might agree with it as a matter of factual judgement, it is more likely that answers to the question expressed the respondents' own attitudes of approval or disapproval to smoking, drinking, etc. The three items mentioned are illustrative of what would commonly be regarded as the 'puritanism' of the movement. Most Sarvodayites follow Gandhi in regarding smoking as an unhealthy, degrading habit; they are staunch supporters of Prohibition, even to the extent of apparent inconsistency, since they affirm the necessity of State legislation on the subject; and they believe that the only moral form of birth control is one which rests on the restraining of physical desires.[1] Other items might have been included: for example, watching modern films, the 'indecent posters' for which was the subject of a notable campaign led by Vinoba and his followers at Indore in 1960.[2] Behind all the manifestations of Sarvodayite puritanism, it must be emphasized, lies the insistence on the need for self-discipline and self-restraint. The Kingdom of Heaven is realizable on earth, but it will be entered only by men and women who have schooled themselves for the journey. The Sarvodayites are a band of the chosen, but it is a band open to all who care to enter. None is predestined for Hell. The self-imposed vows and rules of behaviour are conceived as pointing to the preconditions of the new social order, an order which can only be made by new men.

These preconditions, however, cannot be stated precisely. Even within the context of a puritanical attitude, there is room for debate on each particular. Is the occasional intoxicating drink, for example, really the first sign of damnation? The statement, therefore, may be interpreted as questioning the full rigours of puritanism, not necessarily puritanism itself, at least in some modified form. It is highly unlikely that those who agreed with the statement envisaged a drastic revision of the traditional Gandhian attitudes.

---

[1] Gandhi's views on contraception were even more outspoken (and absurd) than those of the present Pope: 'If contraceptives are resorted to, frightful results will follow. Men and women will be living for sex alone. They will become soft-brained, unhinged, in fact mental and moral wrecks.'—quoted in Bose, op. cit., p. 281. Such views are, perhaps, more understandable if one also accepts Gandhi's judgement: 'Realization of God is impossible without complete renunciation of the sexual desire.'—ibid., p. 248.

[2] Notable not only for the subject of the campaign but also because it was one of the rare occasions on which Vinoba has countenanced 'negative' satyagraha. See S. Ram, op. cit., pp. 314–15.

It is much more likely that they felt the need for some modification which could enhance the attractiveness of the movement without sacrificing its essential principles. It is probably all the more significant, therefore, that only 36 per cent of the respondent leaders agreed with the statement.[1] In other words, about two out of every three did not agree that traditional attitudes of the movement on such matters as smoking, drinking, and birth control needed changing.

Sarvodaya and the revolution of the saints

Puritanism we may conclude is strong among the Sarvodaya leaders, and, on the assumption already noted that this is a vital aspect of the movement, it is instructive to compare these 'saints' of contemporary India with the English Puritans of the seventeenth century. In a recent study Walzer has outlined a model of radical politics, based on the history of the English Puritans and designed to reveal the crucial features of radicalism as a general historical phenomenon.[2]

Walzer's model encompasses the following features. (1) At a certain point in the transition from traditional to modern society there appears a band of 'strangers' who see themselves as chosen men ('saints') and who seek a new order and an impersonal ideological discipline. (2) These men are distinguished from their fellows by an extraordinary self-assurance and daring. They not only repudiate the routine procedures and customary beliefs of the old order but they also cut themselves off from the various kinds of 'freedom' (individual mobility, personal extravagance, self-realization,[3] despair, nervousness, vacillation) experienced amidst the decay of tradition. The band of the chosen seeks and wins certainty and self-confidence by rigidly disciplining its members and teaching them to discipline themselves. (3) They confront the existing world as if in war. The members of the chosen band interpret the strains and tensions of social change in terms of conflict and contention. (4) The organization of the chosen suggests the nature of the new order they seek. Men join the band by

---

[1] On this question, N = 212.

[2] M. Walzer, *The Revolution of the Saints*, 1966. Walzer's model is outlined on pp. 317–19, and the précis of it that is given here follows closely Walzer's text.

[3] By this term we take it that Walzer means something more akin to self-aggrandizement than self-realization in the Idealist or religious sense.

subscribing to a covenant which testifies to their faith. Their new commitment is voluntary, based upon an act of will for which men can be trained, but not born. The commitment and zeal of the prospective saints must be tested and proven. Hence, it is not easy to choose sainthood and the band of the chosen remains exclusive and small, each of its members highly 'talented' in virtue and self-discipline. Within the band of the chosen, all men are equal; status counts for little, and men are measured by their godliness and by the contributions they can make to the work at hand. (5) The acting out of sainthood produces a new kind of politics. The activity of the chosen band is purposive, programmatic, and progressive, in that it continually approaches or seeks to approach its goal. This activity may be defined as an organized effort to universalize sainthood, to reconstruct or reform the political or religious worlds, according to objective criteria, without any regard for the established forms. Politics is made into a kind of work, to which the chosen are required to commit themselves for long periods of time. At work they must suppress all personal feelings and behave in a disciplined fashion. They must learn to be patient and to concern themselves with detail. Above all, they must work regularly and hard. The violent[1] attack upon customary procedures sets the saints free to experiment politically. The saints are entrepreneurs in politics. (6) The historical role of the chosen band is two-fold. Externally, as it were, the band of saints is a political movement aiming at social reconstruction. It is the saints who lead the final attack upon the old order, and their destructiveness is all the more total because they have a total view of the world. Internally, godliness and predestination are creative responses to the pains of social change. Discipline is the cure for freedom and 'unsettledness'. As romantic love strengthens the bonds of the conjugal family, so ideological zeal establishes the unity of the non-familial brethren and makes it possible for men to feel secure outside the traditional system of connections.

Enough, perhaps, has been said in the preceding pages to suggest that there is a *prima facie* case for arguing that Walzer's model is applicable to the Sarvodayites.[2] The fit, of course, is not

---

[1] In the sense of 'forceful', not, we presume, necessarily physically violent.

[2] In Walzer's view his model would 'make possible a systematic comparison of Puritans, Jacobins, and Bolsheviks (and perhaps other groups as well)'— op. cit., p. 317.

exact. The model emphasizes ideological bonds and does not include the role of charismatic leaders. The concept of predestination is not one that figures in the philosophy of Sarvodaya. The novelty of the 'strangers' does not accord with the traditional garb in which the Sarvodayites, at least partly, present themselves. But of the six crucial features, only the third may be questioned as clearly inapplicable to the Sarvodayites. The Indian saints, with their emphasis on the universal values of Truth, Love, and Compassion, do not give the appearance of 'confronting the existing world as if in war'. And, if they interpret the tensions of social change in terms of conflict, they emphasize the common interests of mankind; and their primary endeavour is to resolve all conflicts non-violently and to demonstrate that, in the final analysis and under the right conditions, men can live without conflict. But even here there is some hint of resemblance. The movement organizes a Peace *Army*, Gramdan is presented as a *defence* measure, and, even more to the point, satyagraha is regarded as William James's 'moral equivalent of *war*'.

It is not, however, our purpose here to pursue the question of the applicability of Walzer's model or to attempt to refine it. We have referred to it because it is suggestive, and provides an imaginative link between our English reader's past and the Indian present, which is such a confusing picture of the traditional and the modern. It is a model also which offers for the Indian saints themselves a glimpse into their future. In this respect Walzer is not encouraging. Elaborating the historical role of the saints in politics, he suggests that the security which the chosen band has achieved for itself outside the traditional system of connections eventually 'becomes a habit, and zeal is no longer a worldly necessity. Then the time of God's people is over. In this world, the last word always belongs to the worldlings and not to the saints. It is a complacent word and it comes when salvation, in all its meanings, is no longer a problem.' But, he adds,

the saints have what is more interesting: the first word. They set the stage of history for the new order. Once that order is established, ordinary men are eager enough to desert the warfare of the Lord for some more moderate pursuit of virtue. . . . Hardly a moment after their triumph, the saints find themselves alone; they can no longer exploit the common forms of ambition, egotism, and nervousness; they can no longer convince their fellow men that ascetic work and intense repression are necessary. . . .[1]

In more prosaic terms, Walzer is postulating the inevitability of the institutionalization of the movement of the saints. The attempt to reconstruct the world ends up in a purposive-rational utilitarian association! These revolutionaries, he is saying, are doomed to go down to defeat. They may set the stage for a new kind of human drama, but the play that is finally put on is not the one they themselves have written.

Walzer may well be right: much historical experience, perhaps, suggests that he is. But no saint, of course, will admit it. The saint will continue to believe with Gandhi that his task is to make the impossible possible. Against all the evidence of the historian and the social scientist, he will maintain the faith that man can and will transcend his present self.[2]

[1] Walzer, op. cit., p. 319.

[2] Social scientists are now beginning to appreciate that the problem of institutionalization is more complex than the 'natural history' theory of social movements allows.

There would appear to be no inherent tendency either in organization or in the sources of organizational commitment to move towards accommodation and compromise and thus to weaken the ardor of the membership and the definiteness of the program. Not all unions lose their factional characteristics; not all sects become church-like as they become regularized and stable; not all organized movements become accommodative. The fate of a movement is dependent upon many factors, among which are the contingencies which affect resistance, as well as those which change the character of the initial adherents.—J. R. Gusfield, op. cit.

CHAPTER FIVE

ORGANIZATIONAL ASPECTS

I. ELEMENTS OF ORGANIZATION THEORY AND THE SARVODAYA MOVEMENT

THE collectivities that we call 'social movements' are not themselves 'organizations'.[1] But most movements contain a 'core' organization which serves as the skeleton of the movement's body. Sarva Seva Sangh is the 'core' organization of the movement of 'revolutionary Gandhism'.

A movement that was a pure 'charismatic following' would require either no organization, or one of only the most rudimentary kind. But if such a movement is serious in its attempts to change the world, and if it is not chiliastic enough to believe that the change can be brought about overnight, or at least within the lifetime of its leader, it must acquire independence of the actual people who compose it. All men are mortal, even charismatic leaders and their followers! And if a movement is to escape the bonds imposed by this fact, it must do at least two things to maintain its continuity and stability: (i) its informal procedures must become standardized as norms; and (ii) the various roles performed by its members must become standardized as statuses. It is the institutionalization of informal procedures into norms and roles into statuses which transforms unorganized into organized groups.[2] And with organization comes authority as distinct from leadership. In the typical organizations of the modern world this authority is primarily of the rational-legal type. Norms are attached to statuses and not to the persons who occupy those statuses. The paradigm of the rational-legal organization, however, can be misleading if it is assumed that all organizations conform to this type. Most, if not all, organizations are infused with the two other kinds of authority distinguished by Weber, the traditional and the charismatic, and also with the phenomenon of (charismatic) leadership. And some organizations are heavily infused with

---

[1] cf. A. Etzioni, *A Comparative Analysis of Complex Organizations*, 1961, p. 53.
[2] See R. Bierstedt, 'The problem of authority', in M. Berger, T. Abel, & C. Page (eds.) *Freedom and Control in Modern Society*, 1954.

the charismatic authority and leadership. Where this is the case, as we suggest it is in Sarva Seva Sangh, the constitution setting out the structure of *formal* organization may be a poor guide to how the organization actually works.[1]

An organization usually consists of several statuses, the main distinction in 'voluntary organizations' being between 'the officers' and 'the members'. In complex organizations the officers are divided into several statuses and are aided in their duties by clerical and technical 'staff'. Attached to the various statuses are the norms which prescribe the actions of the organization's participants, the ways in which decisions should be made, and the procedures by which they are to be carried out[2]. In complex organizations the main norms are usually codified and laid down in the organization's constitution, statutes, and standing orders.

Among the main activities of most organizations is the function of recording the actions of the officers and of other participants. The importance of this function increases with the size and complexity of the organization. Control of this function, which is closely related to communication between participants, is usually central to control of the organization—a fact underlined by Michels in his specification of the conditions leading to oligarchy.[3] Another main function is financing the organization's activities. In business organizations this is done chiefly by selling goods and services to customers; in typical 'voluntary organizations' the ways are more various: by membership fees, donations, collections, contributions from affiliated organizations, grants from foundations and the Government, and by selling publications. Financing an organization is not simply a 'technical' problem of raising money: *how* an organization finances its activities will vitally affect its organizational character, the relations between parts of the organization and between statuses, its goals and its programme, and its relations with other organizations.[4]

[1] Even in predominantly rational-legal organizations, constitutions are notoriously misleading on this point. This fact alone points to the presence of other types of authority and/or leadership, giving rise to 'informal' organization.
[2] R. Heberle, *Social Movements*, 1951, p. 270.
[3] R. Michels, *Political Parties*, 1915.
[4] Heberle, op. cit., p. 272. If the local parts of an organization are permitted, for example, to retain a portion of monies raised locally, rather than required to transmit them to the centre for redistribution, power within the organization is likely to be more decentralized. As we shall see, this is the position in Sarva Seva Sangh.

Finally, a further main type of activity of organizations concerns recruitment of participants and their subsequent socialization. Control over recruitment and dismissal—hiring and firing—is crucial in business organizations. In typical 'voluntary organizations' dismissal is not much of a problem: dissatisfied members can usually resign without severe sanctions—imposed by them on the organization, or by the organization on them. Recruitment is much more of a problem, since, as we have seen, *who* it recruits is directly related to the texture of an organization and the commitment of its participants. 'Voluntary organizations' rarely reject potential recruits, but they vary in their selection procedures. The problem is often partially solved by creating a kind of probationary status of sympathizers and supporters who have no formal rights in decision-making. For the active participants mechanisms of commitment are provided to ensure that they subscribe to the values and norms of the organization. The activists are also often subjected to formal socialization procedures in the shape of training, education, and indoctrination to achieve the same purpose. The efficacy of such procedures is usually an important determinant of the efficiency of the organization in carrying out its programmatic activities.

So far, we have discussed organization generally without specifying clearly types of organization. On this point we shall follow Etzioni, who provides a three-fold classification of organizations according to the predominant compliance pattern they exhibit.[1] Compliance patterns are a function of two variables: kinds of involvement, and kinds of power. Involvement ranges from 'alienative' through 'calculative' to 'moral', while power may be 'coercive', 'remunerative', or 'normative', depending on whether the means employed are physical, material, or symbolic.[2] The first two kinds of power are familiar enough to require no elucidation here. 'Normative' power, however, is a less recognizable type. Etzioni defines it as resting on 'the allocation and

---

[1] By 'compliance' Etzioni means 'a relationship consisting of the power employed by superiors to control subordinates and the orientation of the subordinates to this power'—op. cit., p. xv.

[2] 'Involvement' Etzioni defines as 'the cathectic-evaluative orientation of an actor to an object, characterized in terms of intensity and direction'—ibid., p. 9. 'Moral' involvement is the zone of positive orientation of high intensity. By 'power' Etzioni means 'an actor's ability to induce or influence another actor to carry out his directives or any other norms he supports'—ibid., p. 4.

manipulation of symbolic rewards and deprivations through employment of leaders, manipulation of mass media, allocation of esteem and prestige symbols, administration of ritual, and influence over the distribution of "acceptance" and "positive response" '.[1] Each of the three kinds of power tends to be associated with one of the kinds of involvement: coercive power with alienative involvement, remunerative with calculative, and normative with moral. And all three kinds of power *may* be regarded as legitimate by those over whom it is exercised, although normative power is most likely, and coercive power least likely, to be so regarded, remunerative power falling in between.[2]

According to their predominant compliance pattern, organizations may then be classified into three types: (i) *coercive*, in which coercion is the main means of control and involvement is highly alienative; (ii) *utilitarian*, in which remuneration is the main means of control and involvement is calculative (mildly alienative or mildly committed); and (iii) *normative*, in which the main means of control are normative and commitment is high.

Etzioni's distinction between utilitarian and normative organizations is obviously related to the distinction referred to in the previous chapter when we discussed textures of social movements: the distinction between the 'utilitarian association', on the one hand, and the 'spiritual community' and the 'charismatic following', on the other. In dealing with textures we were concerned with the nature and quality of commitment. In dealing with organizations Etzioni has added the further dimension, central to all organization, the dimension of power.

Core organizations of social movements tend to be of the normative type, although in some movements remunerative and even coercive power may be important elements. From all that we

---

[1] A. Etzioni, op. cit., p. 5. 'Normative power' is further subdivided into (a) 'pure normative power' based on manipulation of esteem, prestige, and ritualistic symbols—the kind most frequently used in 'vertical relations' between actors of different rank; and (b) 'social power' based on the allocation and manipulation of acceptance and positive response—the kind used in 'horizontal relations' between actors of equal rank. Etzioni believes his typology of power to be exhaustive. For a more complex but related typology see A. de Crespigny, 'Power and its forms', *Political Studies*, XVI, 2 (June 1968).

[2] That all forms of power *may* be regarded as legitimate appears to have been overlooked by those like de Crespigny, op. cit., who distinguish legitimate power as a separate type.

have said previously, we should expect Sarva Seva Sangh to be an organization of the normative type. This implies, of course, that it is a collectivity in which *power* is exercised. To Sarvodayites this might seem fallacious. Sarvodaya ideology is opposed to 'power', abhors 'power politics', and the movement aims to 'abolish all centres of power'. But the language of Sarvodaya is ambiguous on the subject of power. The 'power politics' of the State is to be dispensed with, but it is to be replaced by 'the politics of the people' when the people themselves have generated and realized their own 'power'. The ambiguity of Sarvodaya language in this respect, like that of similar radical and pacifist groups elsewhere, stems from a loose usage of the term 'power' and a failure to make necessary distinctions. Behind all the castigations of 'power politics' is the not uncommon assumption— often promoted by hard-boiled politicians and political scientists who regard themselves as 'realists'—that the coercive and, to a lesser extent, the remunerative are the only kinds of power. It is indeed true that in State politics, and especially in the sphere of inter-state relations, coercive and remunerative power are both highly visible; but even in these spheres normative power is also present. For the sake of clarity in thinking, it must be insisted that the normative is a kind of power, no less important intrinsically than the other kinds.[1]

Nothing needs to be given away by Sarvodayites (or other radical pacifists) in recognizing this. All that is involved is the acquisition of a more precise and informative vocabulary. The objectives of Sarvodaya can be readily translated into the new language. Instead of talking of 'abolishing power', one talks of abolishing coercive and remunerative power, or, better still, of replacing coercive and remunerative relationships by purely normative relationships. This is not to say that *all* normative power relationships are necessarily acceptable. It may be that, once we have rid ourselves of linguistic confusions, we shall be able to

[1] A distinction is sometimes made between 'power' and 'influence', on the ground that only the former involves 'sanctions' (usually coercive). From this perspective, Sarvodaya would countenance 'influence' but not 'power' relationships. The distinction, however, is unsatisfactory since influence relationships often involve sanctions which, while not physically coercive, may be as severe as, or even more severe than, physical sanctions. An example would be: depriving a loved one of love or esteem in order to induce him to act in a certain way. Among the followers of a charismatic leader, even a frown might be experienced as a severe sanction.

focus attention on distinguishing morally acceptable from morally unacceptable forms of normative power. For Sarvodayites such a distinction would centre upon the concept (odd though it may seem to most Western readers in this context) of love: a positive concern for the integrity, dignity, and self-respect of others. Only normative power relationships consistent with love for others would, in the last analysis, be acceptable. In this sense, but only in this sense, the politics of Sarvodaya is not 'the politics of power' but 'the politics of love'.[1]

Clarification of the Sarvodaya perspective on power in general is not irrelevant to a discussion of Sarvodaya organization. This is because the organization of a social movement tends to reflect the kind of social order the movement is trying to bring about or to maintain. Fascist organizations, for example, exhibit 'the leadership principle' to be applied in the Fascist society; Communist organizations show the blend of democracy and centralization, with an emphasis on the latter, found in Communist states; while modern Conservative parties display a mixture of aristocratic, élitist principles tempered with democracy characteristic of the kind of social order they wish to preserve. Similarly, Sarvodaya organization provides in microcosm a picture of the organization of the ideal Sarvodaya society.[2] In other words, the organization is marked by decentralization, dispersal of power, and a looseness of structure characteristic of images of a stateless, anarchist society. In the Sarvodaya movement, however, special problems arise. Since the ideology does not countenance power relationships, organization is seen as presenting special difficulties. Basically, these concern answers to the question: How far, if at all, is the

[1] G. Ostergaard, 'Sarvodaya, the politics of love', *Bharat*, Birmingham University India Society, 2 (Jan. 1967). In Etzioni's language, 'pure normative power' would *not* be compatible with 'the politics of love'. 'Social power', the power used between equals, *would be*, provided that the manipulation of acceptance and rejection focused on the qualities of a person, not on the person himself. In Gandhi's language, one rejects the sin but not the sinner.

[2] The 'fit' between principles of the organization and principles of the ideal social order is often not exact, especially in 'utopian' movements with long-term objectives. Thus, the principles of Communist party organization do not fit its ultimate objective of a stateless society. In regard to the short- and middle-term objective (the dictatorship of the proletariat), the fit is more exact. Less frequently, perhaps, some organizations, for reasons of expediency, adopt principles which they reject for the long-term. In general, however, the envisaged 'future' is mirrored in the 'present' of a movement's organization.

principle of Non-violence consistent with any kind of organization?[1]

Some Sarvodayites have been inclined to argue that violence is inherent in all organization. On occasions Vinoba has uttered statements—such as St Francis's injunction, 'Do not get yourself entangled in organizations'—which suggest that he subscribes to this point of view. In fact, he does not. The possibility of violence, he believes, is inherent in all men, so associations of men are certainly liable to lead to violence. But the task of creating non-violent organizations, while difficult, is in principle possible. Among the conditions necessary for a non-violent organization is that it must rely on the self-discipline of members and not impose 'external' sanctions.[2] Top-level leaders of the Sarvodaya movement are certainly very conscious that adherence to the value of Non-violence presents special problems that the movement has not yet satisfactorily solved. And in this context they are fond of quoting Gandhi's dictum: 'Organization is the test of non-violence.'

The problems of organizing Non-violence might be even more difficult than they in fact are if the movement were not highly charismatic. We must consider, therefore, some of the implications of charisma in so far as these relate to organization. As we have already observed, charisma is not to be thought of as merely the quality of an individual leader, since it occurs within a particular kind of social context, and a movement (including its organization) takes on certain characteristics as the result of being built round such a leader. The social psychological characteristics we have previously mentioned; there remain the organizational and the economic.

Among the organizational, Weber emphasizes the following features which contrast with those of traditional and rational-legal organizations. The administrative staff of the charismatic leader does not consist of technically-trained officials, nor is it chosen on the basis of social privilege, or of domestic or personal

[1] In a different form, this is the question that has plagued Western anarchists who have not subscribed to Non-violence as a principle. Opponents, sensing the difficulty, have ridiculed as inconsistent the notion of 'anarchist organization'. For anarchists themselves, however, the real question has been: What kinds of organization are compatible with anarchist principles?

[2] In sociological terms, the norms of the organization must be completely internalized by the members.

dependency. Instead, it is chosen on the basis of the charismatic qualities of its members.

> There is no such thing as 'appointment' or 'dismissal', no career, no promotion. There is only a 'call' at the instance of the leader. . . . There is no hierarchy. . . . There is no such thing as a definite sphere of authority and of competence. . . . There is no such thing as a salary. . . . Disciples or followers tend to live primarily in a communistic relationship with their leader on means which have been provided by voluntary gift. There are no established administrative organs. In their place are agents who have been provided with charismatic authority by their chief or who possess charisma of their own.

In short, unlike both traditional and rational-legal authority, charismatic authority and leadership are 'outside the realm of every-day routine and the profane sphere'.[1]

This is also evident in the economic aspects of a charismatic movement.

> Pure charisma is specifically foreign to economic considerations. . . . It disdains and repudiates economic exploitation of the gifts of grace as a source of income, though, to be sure, this often remains more an ideal than a fact. . . . What is despised . . . is traditional or rational every-day economizing, the attainment of a regular income by continuous economic activity devoted to this end. Support by gifts, sometimes on a grand scale, involving foundations, even by bribery and grand-scale honoraria, or by begging, constitute the strictly voluntary type of support. . . . From the point of view of rational economic activity, charisma is a typical anti-economic force. It repudiates any sort of involvement in the everyday routine world.[2]

These characteristics, it must be remembered, apply to an ideal type to which actual movements will only more or less conform. In describing the Sarvodaya movement and its organization as charismatic, we do not imply that it necessarily exhibits all the features mentioned, or that features of other ideal types are not also present. To what extent a movement is charismatic is always a matter for empirical determination. To this question we now turn, and, in so doing, we shall look first at the *Constitution* of Sarva Seva Sangh, a document which in itself is evidence that the movement is not wholly charismatic but contains rational-legal features.

[1] M. Weber, *The Theory of Social and Economic Organization*, 1947, pp. 331–2.
[2] ibid., pp. 332–3.

II. SARVA SEVA SANGH: ITS CONSTITUTION AND WORKING

The Foreword to the *Constitution* of the Sangh in use in 1965 describes it as 'a united organization of constructive agencies (which) has become a country-wide co-ordinating organization of Lok Sevaks'.[1] 'The organization, founded on Non-violence, lays stress on mutual love and confidence, traditions and healthy conventions, rather than on laws, democratic procedures, representative democracy and majority rule. Reliance on the general goodness of man and the process of change of heart by mutual contact will form the basis of the co-ordination, work, and ideology of the Sangh.' In the *Constitution* proper the objective of Sarva Seva Sangh is defined as: 'to evolve a social order which is free from exploitation and the rule of man by man'.

Eradication of the sense of superiority or inferiority based on caste, class, colour and sex differences; promotion of mutual cooperation and harmony between classes; and removal of economic inequalities by developing Khadi and village industries will be the policy of the Sangh. By arousing the feelings of peace, love, friendship, and compassion, and by making use of scientific and spiritual techniques the Sangh will create an independent public opinion for non-violent revolution.

The members of the organization are the Lok Sevaks, men and women over the age of 18 years, who have taken the pledge quoted previously in Chapter Four. The basic units of the formal organization are the Primary Sarvodaya Mandals (Circles) comprising at the most ten Lok Sevaks. The area of a Mandal is not to exceed that of a district of the Indian Union. With the increase in the number of Lok Sevaks and Primary Mandals, the intensity of work done is expected to increase and the area covered by each Mandal to decrease. The long-term objective is to provide one Lok Sevak to every village and to establish one Mandal for every ten villages. Each Primary Mandal has a Convenor, who is to be appointed unanimously by its constituent Lok Sevaks. In addition to the Primary Mandals, the *Constitution* also permits the establishment, where desired, of District Mandals and Regional (or

---

[1] Sarva Seva Sangh, *Constitution* (in Hindi) 1963. The first part of the quoted phrase refers to the fact that four specialized Gandhian organizations merged with the Sangh.

State) Mandals, both of which may frame rules for themselves provided they do not contradict those of the Sangh.

The Sarva Seva Sangh itself comprises the following two classes of person: (i) Representatives (one for each district) elected unanimously by the Lok Sevaks of the District Mandals, or the Primary Mandals operating in a district; (ii) those nominated by the President of the Sangh. Membership of the Sangh is restricted to those who accept its objectives, habitually wear Khadi, spin regularly, and are not members of any political party. Any Lok Sevak, however, can take part in the Sangh's meetings as a member. Specifically, the functions of the Sangh include: (i) to provide opportunities for mutual contact and exchange of thought between the Lok Sevaks and agencies engaged in the programme of social reconstruction; (ii) to indicate the way ahead in the light of past experiences; (iii) to seek solutions of the difficulties and problems arising in the implementation of the programme of social reconstruction; and (iv) to undertake, as needed, experimental constructive programmes, the training of workers, and the publication of material related to the movement.

The term of office of members of the Sangh, both elected Representatives and nominees of the President, and of the President himself is three years. The members of the Sangh, collectively and unanimously, elect the President of the Sangh. The President then, 'according to conventions', appoints the Prabandh Samiti (Executive Committee), a body of not less than 11 and not more than 25 persons, from among the members of the Sangh. The President also appoints the Secretary, the Joint Secretary, and other office-bearers, according to need.

The movable and immovable properties of the Sangh are vested not in the Sangh itself but in a Trustee Mandal of between 3 and 7 persons appointed by the Sangh. The Trustee Mandal, to the meetings of which the President and Secretary must be invited, represents the Sangh on legal occasions and is entitled, as is the Prabandh Samiti, to frame laws and by-laws in accordance with the Sangh's policy and constitution to further the work of the Sangh. It is also the body entitled to invest the funds of the Sangh.

The Sangh meets once every six months, and at such other times as called for by the President or Secretary. The quorum for such meetings is 25, and for meetings of the Prabandh Samiti one-third of its members with a minimum of 5. Amendments to the

Constitution of the Sangh must be made by resolutions adopted at two successive meetings for which prior notice has been given.

Clause 13 of the *Constitution* states that 'The decisions of the Sangh, Prabandh Samiti and other committees and sub-committees shall be arrived at unanimously or on the basis of a consensus of opinion.' This clause is clarified by the statement that a unanimous decision is one in which all the members (presumably those present at the meeting) vote for a proposal. A decision based on consensus, however, is one in which a few members disagree with a proposal but do not vote against it.

Appended to the *Constitution* are rules applicable to members of the Sangh. These include the four conditions of membership mentioned above, and in addition the obligation to use 'for personal and family requirements': home or self-spun or certified Khadi; hand-pounded rice; hand-ground or animal-ground flour; oil produced by bullock-driven means; sugar made by village industries; and leather goods made by such industries. Members of the Sangh are, further, proscribed from contesting 'any election for Parliament, Assembly, Council, District Board, Municipal Board or any such Government or semi-government institutions', and from accepting any posts therein without election. Finally, the general demand addressed to landowners for one-sixth of their land as the first instalment in Bhoodan is 'equally applicable' to the members of the Sangh, although it is believed that members may wish to contribute more.

The Sarvodaya Samaj (Brotherhood or Fellowship) is distinct from the organization of Sarva Seva Sangh, though connected with it. Its general object is the same and its 'basic principle' is defined as 'insistence on the purity of the means as well as that of the end'. A Sevak's register is kept of those who, subscribing to the general object and basic principle, enrol in the Samaj by informing its Secretary of their name and address. For the intensive propagation of Sarvodaya ideology, members of the Samaj must undertake every year: (i) observance of the 30th January (the day of Gandhi's assassination) as Sarvodaya Day; (ii) holding Sarvodaya Melas or fairs on the 12th February, the day on which Gandhi's ashes were immersed; and (iii) the calling of the Sarvodaya Sammelan or annual conference. The nature of the Samaj is defined as that of an advisory, not executive, body. Sarva Seva Sangh is responsible for maintaining the register of Sevaks and for providing information about relevant matters, including the Sammelan.

Of the formal organization of Sarva Seva Sangh as set out in its *Constitution* several preliminary comments may be made. The emphasis on ideological commitment and on norms taken to indicate such commitment is great. The central organization, Sarva Seva Sangh, is conceived not as the apex of a hierarchical structure but as a co-ordinating agency for basic local organizations, which, within the general framework, possess a large measure of autonomy. The organization, taken as a whole, is weakly articulated: the relations between the several parts are not clearly delineated. The functions and powers of the more important officers, President, Secretary, and Joint Secretary are not clearly defined. Hierarchical relations between members, though they exist, are minimal. The *Constitution* contains no statements concerned with the means of financing the organization's activities. Its most distinctive feature is its decision-making procedure, based on the principles of unanimity and consensus. In general the constitution of Sarva Seva Sangh reflects its ideal of a new social order which might be described as a radically decentralized communitarian democracy in which all adult members participate as decision-makers of equal status.[1]

We have already suggested, however, that the constitutions of formal organizations in which charismatic leadership comprises a large element may not be good guides to the way the organizations actually work. In Sarva Seva Sangh the disparity between form and content is most striking in relation to the decision-making procedure, which will be the subject of the following section. In the remainder of this section we shall deal with other aspects of the organization's working.

---

[1] It should perhaps be noted that, although the constitution reflects the ideal of the new social order, it is not related in any direct way to the new social order which is, we venture to hope, actually emerging in the Gramdan villages. In other words, the organization is still an organization of Sarvodaya workers and does not encompass the Gramdan villagers themselves, except in so far as some of them may also be Sarvodaya workers. Vinoba has recently suggested that the entire structure of Sarva Seva Sangh must be changed, the Gram Sabhas of the Gramdan villages replacing the Primary Mandals of Lok Sevaks as the basic units of the organization. Such a change might be seen as a necessary organizational condition for transforming the movement into a genuine 'people's movement'. To date, however, no steps have been taken to implement Vinoba's suggestion. See *Sarvodaya*, XVIII, 2 (Aug. 1968), p. 57.

One relatively unimportant point may be made briefly. Most of the Primary Mandals in existence are in fact District Mandals. It is the latter which constitute the main locus of the organization's day to day power. State Mandals also exist in most states, the main exceptions being Uttar Pradesh and Bihar, in which the movement is particularly strong. A State Sarvodaya Mandal did exist in Bihar, but, at the suggestion of Vinoba, was dissolved in 1963. The suggestion was prompted by the presence of conflicting views, partly based on generational differences, among the Lok Sevaks in Bihar about the working and financing of the movement in their state. There was a feeling among the younger workers, many of them ex-socialist followers of Jayaprakash Narayan, that the substantial financial contribution of the State Khadi Samiti to the State Sarvodaya Mandal was not being distributed fairly or effectively to the District Mandals. Under the present arrangement the District Mandals in Bihar deal directly with Sarva Seva Sangh.

The State Sarvodaya Mandals comprise, if the Andhra Pradesh Mandal may be taken as a guide, the Presidents and Secretaries of the Primary and District Mandals in the state, and the Representatives and nominated members of Sarva Seva Sangh in the state.[1] State Mandals elect their own officers and hold an annual meeting, attended not only by the members but also by sympathizers, including donors and donees of Bhoodan. Programmes for the state are developed at such meetings. However, another important function of State Mandals is to maintain relations between the movement and the various State Governments. Such relations are important in obtaining, for example, Bhoodan and Gramdan legislation and assistance in distributing Bhoodan land and registering Gramdans. Some top leaders of the movement would argue that State Mandals, where they exist, are often too important, in the sense that they tend to detract from the work of the District Mandals. The energies of the ablest workers are often devoted to work at the state level in the state capitals, when their energies might be more fruitfully employed in constructive work in the localities. For this reason, those who hold this view would prefer to see an extension of the arrangement now instituted in Bihar.

---

[1] Although secretaries of District Mandals are not, like the District Representatives, *ipso facto* members of Serva Seva Sangh, they are often more influential, at least in their districts. They are generally full-time workers, whereas Representatives quite frequently are not.

The Prabandh Samiti, formally selected by the President, con-
sisted in 1965 of 25 persons, including the Secretary, the Joint
Secretary, and the President himself. Among the remaining 22
were three Presidents of State Sarvodaya Mandals, three Regional
Secretaries of Sarva Seva Sangh, the Secretary of the Shanti Sena,
the head of Sarva Seva Sangh Prakashan (its publishing agency),
the Secretary of the Khadi and Village Industries Commission, and
the head of Gandhi's ashram at Sevagram. But in addition to these
25 there were 25 persons listed as 'permanent invitees' of the
Prabandh Samiti. This list included some of the prominent intellectual leaders of the movement, the Chairman of the Khadi and
Village Industries Commission, the Secretary of the Gandhi
Smarak Nidhi, the Secretary of the Kasturba Memorial Trust, and
the Secretary of the Gandhi Peace Foundation, who was also the
principal founder of Gandhigram, an important Gandhian training
centre in Madras State. A further 25 persons, designated
'nominated members of the Sangh', may be regarded as 'top
leaders', although they were not members of the Prabandh Samiti.
This group included some prominent former associates of Gandhi
and some of the more active Sarvodaya workers in the field.
Vinoba, as previously mentioned, is not included in any of the
above lists.

The Prabandh Samiti meets every three months as required by
the *Constitution*, but the statutory meeting is insufficient: there is
a need for the Samiti to express its views more frequently on
matters of urgent interest. As a consequence, a small inner committee of ten members, consisting mainly of those involved in work
at the headquarters of Sarva Seva Sangh, has been set up and
empowered to act in between full Samiti meetings.

The *Constitution*, it will have been noted, does not provide what
might be called an integrated system of representative democracy.
The 'top leadership' is, of course, representative, in some sense, of
the various interests and groups within Sarva Seva Sangh and also
of the wider Gandhian movement, but they are not spokesmen,
much less delegates, of the groups they 'represent'. The Prabandh
Samiti is clearly conceived not as an arena where diverse interests
and viewpoints are reconciled but rather as an assemblage of 'the
best men'. In other words, the underlying conception is 'élitist' in
the original sense of that term. The Sangh itself, apart from those
nominated by the President, is composed of Representatives of the

district organizations. But the term 'Representative' is misleading if it suggests that the Representatives see their role as spokesmen for the near-autonomous organizations which have chosen them. Again, the underlying conception is élitist. The absence of what in the West would be understood as a representative element in their role is underlined by the provision that any Lok Sevak who is not a Representative or a nominee of the President may attend, as a member, meetings of the Sangh. If the district organization has not chosen 'the best man', he can, so to speak, choose himself! And in practice Sangh meetings are frequently attended by ordinary Lok Sevaks who participate on an equal footing with Representatives. Among certain members, especially younger ones and those with experience in more conventional political organizations such as Socialist parties, there is a demand for a representative structure. In fact this is almost a perennial topic of discussion at Sammelans, which suggests a certain discontent with existing procedures, particularly as they relate to selection of 'top leaders'. There is some support for the demand among the 'top leaders' themselves, but to date the demand has been successfully resisted. It is clear that the adoption of a more conventional representative structure would be likely to change radically the character of the organization.

The administrative 'staff' of the organization, apart from the bare mention of the offices of 'Secretary, Joint Secretary and other office-bearers', do not figure in the *Constitution*. Although the offices are of the kind we should expect to find in rational-legal organizations, and the chief officers are formally appointed by the President, the roles attached to them are not carefully prescribed. There is, of course, a rough division of labour between the main offices; and the 'lower administrative staff' employed in the head-quarters have fairly specific roles and tend to regard themselves as 'employees'. But there is a diffuseness of roles at the higher administrative levels. Perhaps partly as a consequence, the central office of the organization does not present what a Western observer, used to rational-legal organizations, would regard as a picture of efficiency. By Western standards many Indian organizations, including Governmental and business ones, would not be judged very efficient, and it is to be expected that 'voluntary organizations', employing low-paid staff, would be even less efficient. Our own personal dealings with the staff of the headquarters of Sarva Seva Sangh have led us to conclude that, although they are men of abundant good will, some of them are not notably efficient at their jobs. Even as a co-ordinating agency, the central office appears to lack much of the information and statistics that might fairly be regarded as necessary for rational decision-making. The fault, of course, is not wholly or necessarily mainly attributable to officers at the centre, since the local organizations are often lax in supplying information when it is called for.

Some of the 'top leaders' would probably agree with our judgement on the efficiency of the central organization: a flair for organization is often seen as a Western rather than an Indian characteristic.[1] In part, at least, the relative lack of efficiency might be attributed to the low value placed on organizing ability in the movement. The movement is still a crusade, and the laurels are accorded not to 'organization men' but to the prophets and the effective propagandists 'in the field'.[2] On the other side, it should also be said that men in the movement can on occasion display remarkable organizing ability. The arrangements for annual conferences, for example, which often involve housing and feeding five thousand delegates in temporary camps, are usually most impressive, displaying a marked flair for simple but practical organization.[3]

The financial aspects of Sarva Seva Sangh, a subject hardly treated at all in the *Constitution*, are difficult to determine precisely and no aggregate figure of financial resources is available. In general, Sarvodaya organizations derive funds to finance their activities from five main sources: (i) grants from foundations and from Gandhian organizations of an offical or semi-official status, such as the Khadi and Village Industries Commission and local Khadi bodies; (ii) individual donations, which include regular contributions in the form of sampattidan; (iii) profits from the sale of publications; (iv) revenue from sales of Khadi yarn hanks made by workers and sympathizers (sutranjali); and (v) proceeds from Sarvodaya patra (pot). In the early enthusiastic years of Bhoodan the Gandhi Smarak Nidhi (National Memorial Trust) made sub-

---

[1] At the same time Gandhi's abilities as an organizer are often commented on, usually in contrast to Vinoba's lack of these abilities.

[2] One leader, wishing for a change of environment, agreed to leave to Vinoba the decision where he should go. Chosen for high administrative office, he insisted on combining it with a teaching role. In the Shanti Sena there is a rule that officers should work both in the organization and in the field.

[3] cf. Gaston Gerard, 'The Saints in Session', *Anarchy*, 42 (Aug. 1962).

stantial annual grants to Sarva Seva Sangh, which were sufficient to support directly or indirectly about 2,000 workers.[1] Misunderstanding arose between the two organizations, and these formed part of the background to the decision taken at Palni in 1956 to forgo such subsidies in the future. The Nidhi, however, continued until 1961 to contribute Rs. 100,000/– per annum to Sarva Seva Sangh, although not asked to do so, as part of its general policy of making grants to Gandhian organizations. Grants from other Gandhian bodies remain important, and in 1963, before the Mandal was dissolved, the Bihar Khadi Samiti was contributing Rs. 100,000/– per annum to the Bihar State Sarvodaya Mandal. Individual donations are usually made to the local organizations, and there is no provision that any proportion of them must be forwarded to the central organization. The latter, through its Prakashan (publishing body), derives revenue from its publication of books, pamphlets, and periodicals, the sales of which have averaged about Rs. 250,000/– per annum since 1955, although the policy of the Prakashan is to cover its costs rather than to make a profit.[2] Sales of publications, however, are quite an important source of income for individual Sarvodaya workers, for some of whom it is their main source of subsistence.[3] Revenue from the sales of Khadi yarn hanks is used to support the local organizations. Hanks are made throughout the year by workers and sympathizers, spinning on the takli or charkha being the equivalent of knitting in the West, as a secondary occupation of many who attend the often lengthy Sarvodaya gatherings. Once a year, during the Sarvodaya Fortnight, there is an intensive spinning drive to obtain Khadi yarn donations (sutranjali).

There remains to be mentioned the Sarvodaya patra, a characteristic device invented by Vinoba in 1958 and forming part of

[1] In these early years the Nidhi is estimated to have contributed Rs. 5 million to the Bhoodan movement in various ways. Without this contribution the movement would have had serious teething troubles.

[2] For an account of the publishing work of the movement see Sarva Seva Sangh, *Ten Years of Our Publications (1955 to 1965)*, 1965. In the ten years covered by the report 447 new books and pamphlets and 256 reprints, totalling nearly 4·3 m. copies, were published. Twenty-two weekly, tri-monthly, fortnightly, or monthly periodicals in the various Indian languages and in English were also published. The circulation for each of these in 1965 varied from 500 to 25,000. While book and pamphlet publishing covers costs, a loss is made on the periodicals.

[3] A discount of 33½% is allowed to workers on the movement's publications.

his design to make Sarvodaya a people's movement. He explained the device in the following words:

Let there be a Sarvodaya patra (pot) in every home. The children of the house should drop one handful of grain into it daily before taking their own meals. We do not want a handful of grain from the adult that would bring in much, for I have no desire for large quantity. I want only a child's handful of grain. Children will learn that they must not eat till they have contributed something to the society. There will be no burden on any one on account of this Sarvodaya patra. This should be in the home of the poor as well. The children in the poor homes will also drop their handful of grain in the patra for the sake of peace and of those poorer still.[1]

In some areas of the country Sarvodaya patra is an important institution. In Vijaywada in Andhra Pradesh, for example, a dedicated doctor who is active in the movement has been largely responsible for introducing it to some 20,000 or more households.[2] The grain (or where paisas—the smallest coins—are substituted for it, the money) is collected monthly by Sarvodaya workers who use it to support themselves and the movement's activities. The general impression, however, is that Sarvodaya patra has not yet proved the success Vinoba hoped it would be. Collection is time-consuming and the amounts collected often not economically worth while, although the importance of personal contact between workers and donees should not be ignored.[3]

Over-all, finance is the most pressing problem of Sarvodaya organizations, particularly from the workers' point of view. Sarva Seva Sangh is able to pay a subsistence allowance of up to Rs. 250/– per month to some workers, but many receive no allowance and have to find other sources of livelihood. Lack of adequate pro-

---

[1] S. Ram, *Vinoba and His Mission*, 1962 edn., p. 215.

[2] The collection amounts to the equivalent of about Rs. 8,000/– per annum, of which one-sixth is remitted to the Andhra Pradesh Sarvodaya Mandal and one-sixth to the centre. The remainder helps to support 120 workers. The total annual budget of the A. P. Sarvodaya Mandal in 1965 was about Rs. 20,000/–.

[3] In the Jhansi District a variant of Sarvodaya patra has been tried which involves collecting grain collectively from some 60 villages at harvest time. The grain collected is sold and, in the light of the amount of money raised, the year's programme of activities is arranged. Although our informant agreed with Vinoba that the variant was not so good as Sarvodaya patra, he argued that it was much more effective. In his area, only Rs. 30/– had been raised in Sarvodaya patra in the previous year, compared with Rs. 4,000/– under the alternative scheme. He estimated that only two out of three patras were being 'filled' continuously.

vision for maintenance of workers and their families is, as we shall see later, perceived by the leaders as one of the main obstacles to the further extension of the movement.

In an effort to probe the leaders' perceptions of other aspects of the organization several 'opinion statements' were included in the questionnaire and they were asked whether they agreed or disagreed with them. Two such statements may be dealt with here. The first relates to the question of centralization and took the following form: 'The movement needs a stronger central organization than it has at present.' The statement, it will be seen, is very general and not much can be inferred from the responses to it. The concepts of centralization and decentralization are by no means simple, and it is possible to want both greater decentralization and more centralization, if one thinks of the latter as implying more effective co-ordination at the centre. From some of the comments made by respondents to the statement, it is clear that they were looking for precisely this: no abandonment of decentralization (a principle firmly rooted in Sarvodaya ideology) but more effective central co-ordination. Whether such effectiveness can be achieved without greater central control of local organizations is not a question which has been clearly answered. Some of the top leaders, certainly, are very conscious that one of their biggest problems is the development of an effective non-violent but also decentralized organization.

It is probable, therefore, that agreement with the statement does not imply for many respondents a desire for an organization in which decision-making is more centralized and the higher bodies exercise tighter control of lower bodies. Some respondents indicated as much by suggesting that the movement needs both stronger central organization and stronger local organization. The fact that 65 per cent of the leaders agreed with the statement[1] may be interpreted as indicating a large measure of general dissatisfaction with the organization as it operated in 1965, particularly with the headquarters at Varanasi.

A second 'opinion statement' relates to the matter of training, an important aspect of formal socialization procedures in organizations. The statement was framed as follows: 'While the Movement's workers are generally dedicated people, they often lack the training to carry out their jobs effectively.'

[1] N = 215.

One of the organizational features of a charismatic movement according to Weber, it will be recalled, is that the administrative staff of the leader does not consist of technically trained officials: the staff is chosen in terms of the charismatic qualities of its members, there being no such thing as appointment or dismissal, career or promotion. For our purpose, all Sarvodaya workers (not merely those occupied in administration) might be regarded as the administrative staff responding to the 'call' of the charismatic leader.

We have already presented evidence which suggests that the Sarvodaya movement is not *purely* charismatic in respect of absence of technical training: 12 per cent of our respondent leaders possessed a Gandhian-type professional qualification. The qualifications reported were mainly connected with Khadi and village industries and involved attendance at courses provided by 'official' and 'institutional' Gandhian bodies such as the Khadi Commission and the Kasturba Memorial Trust.

Sarva Seva Sangh itself, however, does make some provision for what, in the broadest sense, may be called training of its workers. One important mode of training is that provided by ashram life. In the scores of Gandhian ashrams scattered throughout India, workers are initiated in the disciplines demanded of constructive non-violent revolutionaries. In Gandhi's day such ashrams played a vital role in the life of the movement.[1] Under Vinoba's leadership new ashrams have continued to be formed, but some of the older ashrams are in decay—monuments and museums of the Gandhian era, rather than throbbing centres of activity. In general, in the judgement of some of the present top leaders, the ashrams, old and new, no longer provide the kind of training that they did in the past. They touch only a minority of the workers, and, as we have already noted, only 12 per cent of the respondent leaders reported that they were living in ashrams at the time of our enquiry.

In addition to periods, long or short, spent in ashrams, the movement provides, as the occasion seems to demand, a variety of short courses, seminars, and training camps. At these, selected groups of workers assemble to discuss the practical problems they face and to listen to talk from leaders on the philosophy and practice of Sarvodaya. Vinoba himself often addresses regional and national conferences of constructive workers. A common theme of

[1] cf. M. K. Gandhi, *From Yeravda Mandir: Ashram Observances*, 1957, and *Ashram Observances in Action*, 1955.

his talks on such occasions has been the need for greater self-reliance and self-education on the part of the workers. In 1957, for example, he said: 'I have a feeling that the constructive workers all over India are suffering from some kind of deficiency. They seem to lack that sturdy self-reliance which used to be their hallmark. . . . Workers are depending on the Government far too much in the development work of Gramdan villages. Our workers have begun to look to the Government for taking up the responsibility of development work. This is bound to weaken the movement.'[1]

The wing of the movement which, perhaps, has paid the most serious attention to training is the Shanti Sena. The Shanti Sena Mandal has organized several training courses at its national headquarters at Varanasi in recent years, in addition to summer camps for its youth section. In 1963 it produced *A Hand Book for Shanti Sainiks*,[2] which recognized that 'to organize an effective Shanti Sena involves training of members in large numbers. This will have to be done in camps, study groups, workshops and other courses of training. The training will be most successful if all Shanti Sainiks realize the importance of continuous self-education and self-equipment.' Something of the flavour of the training involved may be gathered in the following extract from the chapter concerned with work in the villages:

D. Remember you life is being watched:
1. Do not forget to have a waste paper basket, a place to put your used datoons (twigs used for cleaning teeth).
2. Make a latrine and a bathroom at the earliest possible opportunity.
3. Keep compound clean and, if possible, decorated.
4. Do not have too many pictures or photographs in your room.
5. Do not write too many slogans on the wall.
6. Always remember simplicity and beauty.
E. Greet visitors:
1. Smilingly.
2. Do not worry about the language, the language of the heart can very well be understood by villagers.
3. Ask him about his own self and his family. Do not talk too much yourself, learn to listen, do not interrupt.
4. Have sincere interest in the subject he is speaking about.

---

[1] *Bhoodan*, 14 Aug. 1957.
[2] Written by Narayan Desai, published 1963. In preparing the handbook, Desai acknowledges his debt to the pamphlet, *Organizing for Non-violent Direct Action*, by the American peace worker, Charles Walker.

Apart from listening to the homilies of leaders at large gatherings, it seems likely, however, that most Lok Sevaks have not received any formal training for their work. The general mode of training continues to be training-on-the-job in the form of working with a more experienced worker. The long list of names of persons who were mentioned as having influenced the respondents to join the movement is perhaps indicative of this. The novice in the movement attaches himself or is attached to one or other of the more prominent local or national leaders. He may become the leader's secretary or 'right-hand man'. The informal structure of the movement might in fact be described, not too misleadingly, as consisting of sets of leaders and their followers, all united by their common allegiance to *the* national leader, Vinoba. Or, to change the metaphor, a galaxy of moons, centred on Vinoba's sun, each moon possessing a varying number of secondary planets of its own.[1]

The training of the majority of Sarvodaya workers is thus, probably, mostly practical, as distinct from formal, technical training. Given the objectives of the movement, such practical training is probably the most important kind of training they could acquire. It is difficult to envisage revolutionary non-violent social action being reduced to a technique which can be effectively transmitted through formal training courses. This is not to say that non-violent revolutionaries are born and not made. Rather, it is to say that they are made in a special kind of way.

Having stated this point, however, it is also necessary to add that there are many tasks that confront the workers which call for technical expertise that *can* be acquired by what is commonly understood as training. We are not concerned in this study to attempt an assessment of the impact of Bhoodan and Gramdan on village India. But any such assessment would undoubtedly highlight serious shortcomings in the movement's workers. The relative failure in the distribution of Bhoodan land is partly attributable to the incompetance of the movement's workers: they often lack the special skills required for such a complex task.[2] The failure of Gramdan to make more impact than it has is not only due to

---

[1] The moons are illuminated by Vinoba's sun but, unlike the earth's moon, possess a light of their own, i.e. the lesser leaders also possess their own charisma.

[2] This has been recognized in some instances, as in Bihar, where the State Government in 1965 sanctioned its own technical staff's help with Bhoodan.

shortage of man-power and resources. Some villages, selected to be shining examples of the new social order, have not lacked either manpower or financial resources: nevertheless they have become tarnished. But for development work, as the official Community Development Programme has shown, manpower and resources alone are not sufficient. Successful development work demands an order of skills in social engineering which is most exacting and which many Sarvodaya workers, however dedicated, simply do not possess.

Responses to the statement under discussion—'While the Movement's workers are generally dedicated people, they often lack the training to carry out their jobs effectively'—were most revealing. They showed that the great majority of respondent office-holders were aware of the workers' shortcomings in this respect, no less than 90 per cent agreeing with the statement.[1] Clearly this points to a need for a radical rethinking by the leadership of what is involved in training and for a reshaping of its existing training programmes.

III. DECISION-MAKING IN SARVA SEVA SANGH

The formal procedure for taking collective decisions in Sarva Seva Sangh at all levels is, as we have noted, based either on the principle of unanimity, in which all participants positively agree, or on the weaker principle of consensus, in which 'the few' who disagree do not register their dissent by voting against. For brevity, we shall refer to both as 'the principle of consensus'.

Although it is most unusual to find the consensus principle written into the constitutions of rational-legal organizations of the kind we are most familiar with in the West, it is by no means unknown in the practice of many *committees* in such organizations, as distinct from larger meetings of members. Putting questions to the vote and deciding by the majority is often avoided in committees, especially in those which do not see themselves as 'arena'

---

distribution. The movement's workers were slow in recognizing their lack of the required expertise, wishing to retain distribution (usually for quite honourable reasons) in their own hands.

[1] N = 220. For the record, it should be noted that a few respondents did *not* agree with the first part of the statement, i.e. that workers were 'generally dedicated people'. Such comments should not be taken too seriously. The evidence of the dedication of the majority of the workers is too overwhelming.

bodies representing several interests, in those which have administrative as distinct from policy-making functions, and in those in which the decisions to be taken concern external rather than internal relationships.[1]

The British Cabinet is perhaps the best known example of a committee which rarely puts matters to the vote.[2] Many university committees, and even the occasional board of directors of a business firm, practise the consensus principle. As an *explicit* principle of procedure buttressed by ideological arguments, however, the principle is much less common. In this form it is found in Quaker organizations, in which taking 'the sense of the meeting' is the standard procedure, the idea being that all participants consult their 'inner light' in a serious effort to arrive at the right decision. It is also found in non-religious organizations, principally in those inspired by anarchist or near-anarchist ideology.

It is safe to say, however, that, despite contacts between Quakers and the movement, the procedural principle in Sarva Seva Sangh has been inspired not by Western practice but by native Indian tradition, or at least interpretations of that tradition. This much is evident from Vinoba's discourse on the tradition of unanimity in the ancient Indian village *panchayat* (council):

The Indian idea of a village panchayat holds a special place among the political ideas of the world. It included the principle of 'God speaks through the five', which was accepted throughout India. This meant that the five members of the Panchayat must reach a common mind, and then only the decision was made. But now we 'pass' a decision by a majority of four to one or three to two, as though God now speaks in three! I contend that such proposals are not really passed, so long

---

[1] F. G. Bailey, 'Decisions by Consensus in Councils and Committees', in *Political Systems and the Distribution of Power*, 1965, p. 13. Bailey distinguishes between 'élite' and 'arena' councils as follows: 'Élite councils are those which are, or consider themselves to be (whether they admit it openly or not), a ruling oligarchy. The dominant cleavage in such a group is between the élite council (including where appropriate, the minority from which it is recruited) and the public: that is to say, the dominant cleavage is horizontal. The opposite kind of council is the arena council. These exist in groups in which the dominant cleavages are vertical. The council is not so much a corporate body with interests against its public, but an arena in which the representatives of the segments in the public come into conflict with one another' (p. 10).

[2] The practice of voting in the Cabinet, however, varies with the Prime Minister, and also, no doubt, with the kind of decision to be taken.

as they fail to convince even one person. Only that proposal deserves to 'pass' which commends itself to all. We must revive this ancient Indian tradition, for a people's democracy can only be built on mutual trust and cooperation.[1]

In speaking thus Vinoba no doubt over-idealized the ancient village panchayat: there is no hard evidence that historical practice conformed even approximately to his picture of it.[2] But equally, there is no doubt that in appealing for the principle of consensus he was appealing to a deeply-felt element in the Indian cultural tradition, an element which, incidentally, is present in other Oriental and also in African countries.[3] Whatever may be the reasons for it, consensus appears to be defined by many Indians as more legitimate than conflict: the value placed on conflict (as well as consensus) by Western theorists of pluralism appears strange to Indians. Even when modern Western political forms, thriving on institutionalized conflict, namely political parties, are adopted, the search for consensus in some shape affects their working. Congress, for example, though a party riven by factions, is still seen by some of its adherents not as a party but as a 'movement' which seeks, or ought to seek, to embrace every citizen and every group of citizens in its fold. And, although it is recognized by most politicians that consensus is impossible in national and provincial politics, there is a strong feeling that it ought to be possible in local politics. In the new structure of statutory panchayats introduced as organs of the Panchayati Raj programme, several state governments have provided special grants to those panchayats in which elections of their officers and members are unopposed.[4] Such grants have, apparently, had some effect, for in the panchayat elections in Andhra Pradesh in 1965 over 40 per cent of the elections were uncontested.

The Sarvodaya movement, with its concept of partyless democracy, actively supports all steps to promote consensual politics. It believes that in its own organization it has demonstrated that the consensus principle is a practical mode of procedure. But how in fact does the principle work in Sarva Seva Sangh?

[1] Vinoba Bhave, *Democratic Values*, 1962, pp. 112–13.

[2] Bailey writes: 'So far as I know there are no accounts of events in village councils in ancient India which give the same substantial detail that we get from our own experience. We have no means of knowing how consensus was reached in those days, or on how many occasions it was not reached.'—op. cit., p. 4.

[3] See, e.g., R. A. Scalapino & J. Masumi, *Parties and Politics in Contemporary Japan*, 1962, p. 145.   [4] Bailey, op. cit., p. 1.

In attempting to answer this question, it should be noted that we are dealing with an organization which is still in the process of development. This is particularly relevant to any judgement about the role of Vinoba, who, as we shall see, has distinctive views about leadership. Bearing in mind this caution, we may begin by considering decisions relating to the selection and election of officers.

As far as the principal officer, the President of Sarva Seva Sangh, is concerned, the *Constitution* formerly provided for his election by the Samiti. He is now elected by the Sangh at a meeting which any Lok Sevak may attend. In practice, three informal procedures have been adopted to ensure that only one candidate is presented to the meeting. One procedure is for the Samiti to consult Vinoba, whose advice is accepted without question. A second is to remit the matter to a small committee of experienced leaders who are not themselves candidates. The third procedure is to invite all those who have been suggested for the office to meet together to decide among themselves which one of them should go forward to election. The latter procedure, combined with discussion in small groups participated in by the members of the Sangh who were present, was the one adopted in the election of 1969. On that occasion there were, at the outset, no less than twenty-seven nominations, but, after one half-hour of discussion, a consensus emerged in favour of the Tamilnad leader, Jagannathan. The Sarvodaya doctrine on power, of course, facilitates the development of consensus in such situations: it encourages nominees to withdraw in favour of someone else.

The other chief officers, the Secretary and Joint Secretary, are appointed by the President. Since their terms of office are not fixed, a new President may not be called on to make an appointment. When a President does make such an appointment, he seeks the advice of his colleagues, including, no doubt, Vinoba. In selecting the Prabandh Samiti, the President has a choice roughly comparable, perhaps, to that of a British Prime Minister. In other words, the choice is limited because most 'top leaders' almost 'choose themselves': they are so well known or influential that they cannot be left out. There are usually, however, a few changes in the composition of the Samiti, of the permanent invitees, and of nominated members of the Sangh, every three years.

The officers of the local organizations, the Primary, District, and State Mandals, are elected by the Lok Sevaks in the organizations concerned in a manner similar to the Sangh's election of its President, except that Vinoba would not usually be consulted. One President of a State Sarvodaya Mandal described the procedure thus: 'people respectfully ask one to serve on the committee and to guide them'. At the local levels of organization rival candidates for particular offices are not uncommon, but such differences are usually resolved before the formal election meeting. In the case of election of Representatives there is an organizational sanction promoting unanimity. If the Lok Sevaks cannot agree unanimously, the district is not represented in the Sangh, although, of course, Lok Sevaks in the district are still free to attend Sangh meetings.

The procedure of elections in the local organizations differs from the one that used to obtain only a few years ago. The old procedure was akin to that employed by Gandhi in respect of the various Gandhian organizations, such as the All-India Spinners' Association. It was Gandhi who appointed the trustees and boards of management, although usually with a provision that one-third of the appointees should retire every three years. Boards of provincial organizations were then appointed by the management boards of the central organization. The organizations in Gandhi's days often acted in an autocratic manner, in the sense that ordinary members of the associations they managed were not consulted, even in decisions which vitally affected them. In the early years of the Bhoodan movement Vinoba took over the practice of Gandhi, and it was he who in effect selected the leading members of the various Bhoodan committees and organizations that sprang up in the wake of his padayatra. In December 1956 at Palni the decision was taken to liquidate these Bhoodan organizations, in many of which local politicians were taking an active role. The idea was that there should be no local organizations for Bhoodan work, but that individual Lok Sevaks should work in their own areas and earn their subsistence from the people by selfless service. In furtherance of this idea Vinoba selected certain of his followers who were accompanying him on his padayatra to return to their states to take charge of the work there.

A remarkable account written at the time by one of the present leaders describes the decision and the ethos in which it was taken; it merits quotation at length. The whole atmosphere of the conference, she writes, was surcharged with new enthusiasm when

Vinoba announced the decision to dissolve the provincial and district committees and to dispense with the subsidy from the Gandhi Smarak Nidhi. Despite earlier trepidation and the knowledge that the decision would put them all to the test, 'the decision clicked with everyone . . . there was a spontaneous feeling of joy. Everyone felt that the decision taken was right.' Vinoba, happy to see the workers in tune with the spirit of the movement, slept little that night but sat up pondering the decision taken. After morning prayer Rajamma, a devoted worker from Kerala, saw him and asked his permission to return to her place. He asked her to sit down and then read to her the passage in the New Testament (Matthew 10:5–20) reporting Christ's address to his disciples when they were leaving him. The passage begins: 'These twelve Jesus sent forth, and commanded them, saying, Go not into the way of the Gentiles. . . . But go rather to the lost sheep of the house of Israel. And as ye go, preach, saying, The Kingdom of heaven is at hand . . .', and ends with the words: 'For it is not ye that speak, but the Spirit of your Father which speaketh in you.' The account continues:

As he read this, tears trickled from his eyes and he had to stop reading as his voice was choked and he could not speak. All of us sat in silence for a time. It was drizzling outside. But at the stroke of six he got up and the trek started. On the way he said to Radhakrishnaji, 'I have been thinking all the night on the resolution you have passed. I know it will test many of our workers. Organizationally we shall have to face new difficulties. Ultimately our object is to create a large cadre of workers who have the Fourfold faith in Non-violence, Truth, Non-possession, and Lok-niti. We have broken the skeleton organization that came into existence. The movement now rests on the people entirely. I would like to ask some one person to consider himself responsible for the work of each state. He should become a Zero; that is, he will have no authority. He will be the first servant. But I will consider him as my representative and keep in touch with him. For instance, I am thinking of asking Prabhakarji to do the work in Andhra-desa, as Rajamma may do it in Kerala.' Prabhakarji was walking with us. He came forward. He said, 'I have dedicated myself to the movement and I would do my humble best and be worthy of your confidence.' Vinobaji said, 'I know you are a volunteer and not a leader. Just as an earthquake does greater damage to big mansions, this step we have taken may upset plans of people who had become bosses and leaders. For all our difficulties we shall have to look within and purify ourselves more and more. I know that some of our workers may discontinue to work but I have no doubt that the general quality will improve. . . .'

After reaching the next village, Vinobaji called Rajamma in the afternoon and said to her, 'I am hoping that you would be our representative in Kerala. Have faith. You come from the land which produced Shankaracharya[1]. . . . Keep your heart pure and simple. Remember what Christ had told his disciples. He had said: Never make an effort to speak and God will speak through you. . . . Meditate deeply and keep the heart pure. The discourse on the *Gita, Shitapradnya-Darshan* and *Ishavasya-Vritti* contains everything that I would like to give you.[2] Read the books again and again. Neither consider yourself low nor high. Work with faith and humility. He who inspires you, will guide and support you. He, who points out the way, will give you the strength.' Rajamma left that evening for doing work in the province of Shankaracharya.

How can I possibly convey what all this meant to her. She was overwhelmed with devotion and had surrendered herself completely to her God and was praying that she may be worthy of it. Prabhakarji and Rajamma are the new type of revolutionaries which the Bhoodan movement has thrown up. . . .[3]

This graphic account of the charismatic leader appointing his disciples conveys more clearly than any words we could have chosen the ethos of the Sarvodaya movement, an ethos redolent of Galilee 2,000 years ago. The Palni decision, however, did not quite work out in the way intended. The existing local Bhoodan committees were dissolved, but it soon became apparent that some local organization was necessary. In the next few years the local organizations already described were developed, along with the Lok Sevak pledge and the concept of partyless democracy which effectively ensured that party politicians would be excluded from participating in them. The development of the Primary, District, and State Sarvodaya Mandals meant that a new procedure for

---

[1] A Vedanta monist, *c.* A.D. 788–820 or 850, credited with making the first commentary on the *Gita*. Vinoba regards Shankaracharya's teachings on property as anticipating those of Sarvodaya: 'Wealth and enjoyment are the property of none; they are for the benefit of all. They belong to all alike.' cf. S. Ram, op. cit., p. 196.

[2] Vinoba has written several works on the *Gita*, of which *Talks on the Gita* is perhaps the most popular. The second work referred to is Vinoba's philosophy of the man of steadfast wisdom, a collection of lectures on the behaviour and characteristics of the perfect sage. The third work is Vinoba's commentary on the Ishavasyapanishad. See V. Nargolkar, *The Creed of Saint Vinoba*, 1963, Ch. III.

[3] Nirmala, *Bhoodan*, 12 Dec. 1956.

appointing local leaders was instituted, a more democratic procedure, in the sense that, formally at least, appointment was to be from below by the Lok Sevaks rather than from above by Vinoba. As might be expected, the new procedure did not lead to dramatic changes in the composition of the leadership. Generally, the Lok Sevaks elected the leaders who had been singled out by Vinoba to carry on his mission (although it should be added that Vinoba did not appoint missionaries in all the states). Prabhakarji, for example, remains the leading worker in Andhra Pradesh, where he is President of the State Sarvodaya Mandal. However, this happy coincidence did not occur in all areas. Thus, in Uttar Pradesh, where Vinoba had appointed a Sarvodaya Mandal, a new Mandal was set up as the result of elections; but those who were appointed by Vinoba continued to think that *they* were the Mandal. The outcome was a confusion that persisted for several years. In another state there was in 1965 a person who still thought himself the Convenor because at one stage Vinoba had appointed him, even though there was a regular Mandal appointing its own Convenor.

In short, one may conclude that, in the decisions involving elections, Vinoba's opinion on candidates for the chief offices at the national and, perhaps, state levels has played an influential, if not wholly determining, role. In the elections of officers at lower levels, except in most (but not all) cases where Vinoba's wishes are known, the actual procedure conforms more closely to the procedure outlined in the *Constitution*. Even here, however, it is unlikely that in practice the opinion of each Lok Sevak counts for one and no more than one. The opinions of the older and more experienced leaders, provided they can agree among themselves, are likely to be determining. In this respect, of course, elections in Sarvodaya organizations do not differ in essence from more conventional democratic elections: in the latter, too, 'opinion leaders' carry more weight in practice than ordinary voters. This is not to say that the procedure of conventional democratic elections, if it were adopted, would make no difference to the outcome. Control of democratic elections by élites where choice of candidates is institutionalized is rarely complete. Such elections usually result in a regular 'circulation of the élite', bringing new men to the top, replacing some of the former incumbents. The principle of consensus, when applied to elections, does not itself provide for this kind of circulation. Circulation occurs *only* through co-optation by the existing élite of new members; and these, of course, will generally be persons sharing the values and attitudes of the existing élite. The consensus principle, therefore, operates in a basically conservative direction. Applied to statutory pan-chayats, it is likely to help preserve the political position of the existing dominants in a village—a point that Sarvodayites, seeking radical change, appear to overlook or, at least, not pay sufficient attention to.[1] In an organization such as Sarva Seva Sangh, how-ever, as in other structures which are *already* satisfactory, con-servatism is no bad thing. Conventional democracy can, in the long run, be disastrous for the objectives of a social movement. The British Co-operative Movement, with its open membership and one member, one vote, is a case in point. Whatever other worthy objectives it may be pursuing, the Co-operative Movement is not now seeking to establish the voluntary communist society which was the objective of the Owenite pioneers! And this change of objective is directly attributable to, or at least made possible by, its democratic principles, particularly that of open membership. A movement which seeks to change the world cannot afford to be too democratic, if that means giving equal rights and an equal voice to those who wish to preserve the existing order. *Some* kind of élitism or oligarchy is essential, at least in the transition stage. It could certainly be argued that the élitist, oligarchical, aspects of Sarvodaya elections have not demonstrably produced a leadership inferior to one that might have been produced by more conven-tional democratic procedures: the probability is that the reverse is the case. However, even if élitism is justified by its results in this instance, it is important to note that a price has to be paid for it. Democracy is not merely a means; it is also an end, the end being the self-development of individuals. And *any* limitation of demo-cracy is a hindrance to the full development of men.

Turning now to decisions other than those involving election of officers, our judgements on how the consensus principle works in practice are even more crudely based and impressionistic. There are decisions and decisions: not all decisions are equally important; participants themselves disagree about which are important; and

---

[1] cf. Bailey, op. cit., pp. 18–19. Morris-Jones's conclusion on this point is that 'Consensus is a fair name for what may be an ugly reality.'—W. H. Morris-Jones, 'The unhappy utopia—J. P. in Wonderland', *Economic Weekly*, 25 June 1960.

there is the problem of deciding *when* a decision has been taken. Determining who are the decision-makers in any organization is no light undertaking. For our purpose, we shall limit ourselves to consideration of decisions of strategic importance for the movement, such as decisions about the structure of Sarva Seva Sangh itself, about the movement's mode of operation—whether or not, for example, it should use 'negative' satyagraha to achieve its objectives—and policy statements issued by Sarva Seva Sangh at Sammelans.

In quoting above the account of the Palni decision of 1956 we have already indicated what the broad conclusion must be: Vinoba is the principal decision-maker; no crucial decisions are taken which either do not emanate from him or are not in some way sanctioned by him, although there are occasions when the Samiti has not followed his advice.[1] There is no doubt that the Palni decision was crucial and was recognized as such by the workers in the movement at the time. They could scarcely think otherwise, since for many of them the ending of the subsidy from the Gandhi Smarak Nidhi meant that they had to find alternative means of financial support if they were to continue working for the movement. Ideologically, the Palni decision was justified on the ground that it marked the transformation of Sarvodaya into 'a people's movement', although purging the Bhoodan committees of political and other opportunists by abolishing the committees—a drastic remedy, indeed!—was clearly another consideration in Vinoba's mind. In the event, the decision was neither a complete success nor a complete failure. In the following years Sarvodaya did not succeed, and has not yet succeeded, in becoming a people's movement, in the sense intended—although it is probably much nearer to being so than if it had continued on its existing course. After the initial enthusiasm for the decision had subsided, the workers had to face hard reality. Many of them, and not always the least able or least dedicated, fell by the wayside. They had to find jobs other than promoting Bhoodan full-time in order to support themselves and their families. Some, completely disillusioned, left the movement altogether; others found refuge, so to speak, in 'official' and

---

[1] Examples of instances when Vinoba's advice has not been accepted are: (i) a suggestion that Khadi organizations should increase the wages of weavers by 50%; (ii) the advice that Shanti Sena should not accept a grant from the Gandhi Smarak Nidhi for work in the Northern border areas.

'institutional' Gandhian organizations, from which bases they could continue working for the general objectives of Sarvodaya and, occasionally, participate part-time in Bhoodan or Gramdan activities. The main point to be noted here, however, is that the Palni decision was essentially Vinoba's decision. It was not exactly an overnight revelation; and constraining features apparent for some months beforehand contributed much to the form, character, and timing of the decision. Nevertheless, it was a decision whose likely consequences were neither fully thought out nor thoroughly discussed by other top leaders. It was almost, if not quite, as much a surprise for them as it was for the ordinary Lok Sevaks. At the same time, the decision was formally taken by the Sangh: it was proposed at a regular meeting of the Sangh; *any* single Lok Sevak *could* have prevented the decision by voting against it. If it was an autocratic decision, it was autocracy by consent.

The same qualification applies to the policy statements drawn up by the Prabandh Samiti which are discussed and passed at Sammelans.[1] Their substance is undoubtedly discussed with Vinoba, although Samiti members play an important part in framing them. In deciding the terms of the statement, the consensus principle does operate in such a way as to give real power to individual Samiti members. On one occasion a resolution was drafted after three days of discussion. One Samiti member, unable to attend the earlier part of the discussion, arrived late and objected to certain passages in it. Although some of the other members were, perhaps understandably, annoyed, the resolution was amended to meet the late-comer's objections. The procedure adopted does not, however, permit amendments to a resolution when it is presented to the meeting of the Sangh: the resolution must be either accepted or rejected. In other words, there is a mechanism promoting consensus in the larger gathering. Nevertheless, *any* Lok Sevak can, by voting against it, block the adoption of the Samiti's statement or resolution. At the Raipur Sammelan, December 1963, an observer reports that several Lok Sevaks did raise objections to the resolution (the one proposing The Triple Programme), on the ground that it should have included mention of some particular items they favoured (prohibition being one candidate for inclusion). After discussion, however, 'the objectors

[1] For the policy statements or resolutions passed, 1952–61, see S. Ram, op. cit., Appendix B.

agreed either to have their points made in an additional, not the main, statement or to postpone consideration of them until a later conference'.[1] In this way the principle of consensus was maintained.

In other kinds of policy decision there is scope for satisfying in some degree different viewpoints simply by not taking up an 'official' line. In this case adherents of differing policies proceed to pursue their various courses. The issue of whether or not to adopt the tactic of 'negative' satyagraha—a subject which will be discussed later—can serve as an illustration. Sarva Seva Sangh has no policy on this: if individual Lok Sevaks and local organizations wish to use the tactic, they are free to do so, although, if they do, they will not necessarily be supported by other Lok Sevaks. Some local organizations have in fact used 'negative' satyagraha; and Gora, a Representative in Andhra Pradesh, has even formed a Satyagraha Sangh specifically for the purpose of campaigning against ministerial pomp and for partyless democracy. Gora's campaign, however, illustrates an important aspect of this kind of solution to the problem of maintaining the consensus principle. He has tried, without marked success, to obtain Vinoba's public sanctioning of his campaign. If he were to obtain that sanctioning, his particular policy would almost certainly become the policy of the Sangh. In other words, the advocates of differing policies compete with one another to obtain Vinoba's blessing. If they do not get it, they will not be fully satisfied; but, on the other hand, they will not be quite inhibited either—unless Vinoba actually pronounces against their policy. As might be expected in this situation, Vinoba is spare with his blessings. His role demands that he should display a cautious reserve in respect of controversial issues within the movement. And in displaying this reserve he is as liable as any conventional political leader to be regarded as equivocal.

Bailey, in discussing the consensus principle in general, states categorically: 'a decision by consensus cannot be reached in a council where *active* members number more than about fifteen. A unanimous decision in a council of one hundred men is, in fact, an act of acclamation or legitimation: the actual decision has been taken elsewhere. The very complicated and subtle process by which consensus is reached is not possible where large numbers are involved.'[2] Since the Prabandh Samiti (with invitees) numbers

[1] Gaston Gerard, 'The Saints in Session', *Anarchy*, 42 (Aug. 1964).
[2] Bailey, op. cit., p. 2.

fifty and meetings of the Sangh some 300, with the possibility of a much larger number if other Lok Sevaks choose to attend, Sarva Seva Sangh is clearly an organization in which decisions 'cannot be reached by consensus': its consensus principle must be a fake, if Bailey is right. From what we have said, there is clearly much truth in what Bailey says as far as Sarva Seva Sangh is concerned. Certainly, resolutions unanimously passed at Sangh meetings are, to a large extent, acts of acclamation or legitimation for decisions taken elsewhere. But, equally clearly, Bailey's statement is much too simple and vague (how active is '*active*'?) to be the whole truth about decision-making in Sarva Seva Sangh. Bailey's conception of consensus is a Western conception of rational, independent, self-activating men of varied viewpoints reaching unanimous agreement: it does not fit the kind of consensus we find present among the followers of genuine charismatic leaders; and it is probably not what most Indians mean by consensus.

In the Sarvodaya movement, we repeat, Vinoba is *the* decision-maker; but any notion that consensus is somehow spurious because men follow the lead of a man they define as a saint, a man who has displayed 'exceptional qualities' in persuading landowners in a peasant country to part with millions of acres of land, is a shallow notion. Granted a firm commitment to the values such a leader stands for, it is not unreasonable for a follower to accept his lead, on the ground that the leader probably has greater insight into the problems of realizing those values than anyone else. There is nothing forced or fake about a consensus reached in this way. Nevertheless, there is a large element of paradox in Vinoba's leadership. Every turn of events in the movement confirms that he is the movement's leader; but he does not appear to seek leadership and he does not believe in the principle of leadership. His is a leadership truly made by his followers. It is a kind of leadership which, oddly enough, can achieve success, according to his own lights, only by a demonstration of its failure. Only when he has ceased to be the leader and his erstwhile followers have become their own leaders, can he be said to have succeeded. 'Not success but failure is my aim,' declared Vinoba on one occasion.

I never had the sense of being a leader of a movement. No leader would desire failure. A leader has hardly any colleagues, he has only followers. I desire failure, and success to my colleagues. . . . My ambition is to fail completely in my mission. There can be no deliverance for me unless this happens. And deliverance is the aim of my life. If I succeed, desire will pursue me. So what I need is failure. I am deliberately working for it. I am only anxious that my colleagues should succeed.[1]

That such a viewpoint is sincerely held by Vinoba cannot be doubted. In recent years he has progressively withdrawn from an active leadership role in an effort to wean the movement from its dependence on his personal presence. In his own terminology, he has switched from the grosser to the finer, more subtle, form of Karma Yoga. Or, as some of the Sarvodayites themselves put it, he is deliberately 'dying before his death', so that he may see for himself how the movement will fare without him.[2] As a consequence, although it would still be correct to describe him as *the* decision-maker in the movement, he is now no longer, as was formerly the case, the sole important decision-maker. Increasingly, the movement's decisions are being made by his colleagues, Vinoba giving advice only when asked.

Having made the point that there is something genuine in the consensual decision-making of Sarva Seva Sangh, that it is not the kind of mechanical or forced consensus sometimes found in totalitarian movements,[3] it is necessary to add that in 1965 we found a strong dissatisfaction among office-holders about the process of decision-making. Some top leaders in fact used the terms 'authoritarian' and 'autocratic' in describing the process. Such leaders were perhaps conscious that they and their colleagues did not measure up to the standards Vinoba set before them. They were aware that in Samiti deliberations most new ideas originated with Vinoba or were mooted by three or four of their number. Some were conscious, too, that Vinoba's presence at Sangh meetings has an inhibiting effect on discussion: the debate is more genuine when the ears of the gathering are not cocked to catch the

---

[1] *Bhoodan*, 27 Nov. 1957.

[2] One indication of Vinoba's withdrawal from an active leadership role was his announcement in October 1969 that he would make no more speeches to large public gatherings, including Sarvodaya Sammelans.

[3] Totalitarian movements do not explicitly adopt the consensus principle, but many of the decisions taken are 'unanimous'. In such movements, there is strong psychological pressure on minorities to conform to the majority (or purported majority), and also the sanction of expulsion of dissidents. In Sarva Seva Sangh the psychological factor is present, although probably in a much weaker form, but the sanction of expulsion barely exists at all.

latest revelation from the lips of the master. Others made invidious comparisons between Sarvodaya consensus and the kind of consensus they believed occurred in Quaker meetings, where, they thought, real face-to-face relations exist and all participants are honestly striving to reach the truth.

In order to determine in some measure the extent of general dissatisfaction among office-holders with the working of the consensus principle, they were asked whether they agreed or disagreed with the following statement: 'All the workers in the Movement can join in making decisions on policy but in practice the decisions are made by only a few leaders.' The 'few leaders' might be Vinoba himself; the Prabandh Samiti—those with greatest access to Vinoba; the leading members of the Primary and other Mandals; or all or some of these. The finding is quite clear: no less than 75 per cent of the respondents agreed with the statement.[1] This result might be held to confirm the suspicions of those who think that consensual decision-making in an organization like Sarva Seva Sangh must be spurious. Undoubtedly, it does indicate that there is a large gap between the ideal and the real. But it is only fair to add that the level of expectation is probably high, so that the organization is judged by the highest standards, quite possibly unrealizable. From comments made by respondents there certainly appeared to be very little support for the abandonment of the consensus principle and its replacement by the more conventional majority principle. It seems fair to conclude, therefore, that, despite widespread dissatisfaction among office-holders with the decision-making process, and despite the difference between form and actual content, the consensus principle does in some real sense 'work' in Sarva Seva Sangh. To the extent that it 'works', it does so because it is based on a high degree of consensus about values *already* present among the members, and on their strong attachment to Vinoba, the charismatic leader. Whether it would continue to work if the movement ceased to possess a charismatic leader is another question.

IV. CHARISMA AND THE PROBLEM OF SUCCESSION

To raise such a question is to point to a further outstanding feature of charisma and its consequences. This feature is its instability.

[1] N = 210.

Because the social relationships directly involved are strictly personal and based on the validity of personal qualities, charisma is
necessarily a transitory phenomenon. Indeed, as Weber puts it, 'in
its pure form charismatic authority may be said to exist only in the
process of originating. It cannot remain stable but becomes either
traditionalized or rationalized, or a combination of both.'[1] This
process of transformation is what Weber terms 'the routinization
of charisma'. Typically, routinization proceeds in the directions
indicated, but Weber also recognizes another option: the deper-
sonalization of charisma and its transmission to members of a
family or the incumbents of an office or institution regardless of
the persons involved. Familial charisma as an aspect of domination
on the basis of authority has been, in Weber's judgement, particularly important in Indian society, where it formed a component
in the development of the caste system. In Western societies
'familial charisma' took the form of hereditary kingship 'by the
grace of God', but in India it spread throughout society.[2]

The inherent instability of charisma has special implications for
'the problem of succession'. In systems of traditional and rational-
legal domination, with their everyday routine, crises of succession
are frequent enough, but they possess procedures designed to
minimize disturbances. Even so, a new leader (king, president,
prime minister, or party chief) often experiences trouble until, as
the saying goes, he has 'established his authority'. In systems of
charismatic leadership, however, succession invariably brings a
crisis—indeed a crisis within a crisis situation. 'Charismatic
leadership', in the words of Bendix, 'is a uniquely personal
response to a crisis in human experience; those who succeed the
charismatic leader therefore face the problem of preserving a personal charisma after the leader and the crisis have passed away and
everyday demands have again come to the fore.'[3]

Weber indicates several ways in which charismatic movements
attempt to solve the problem of succession:

(1) The search for a new charismatic leader on the basis of criteria of
the qualities which will fit him for the position of authority.

---

[1] Weber, op. cit., p. 334. As already noted, Weber did not clearly distinguish
between charismatic leadership and charismatic authority. His point applies to
the former rather than to the latter. If 'authority' is defined as institutionalized
power, it is possible to conceive of stable charismatic authority. The authority
of the Pope is largely of this kind, although it also contains a traditional element.

[2] R. Bendix, *Max Weber*, 1962, p. 146.   [3] ibid., p. 301.

(2) By revelation manifested in oracles, lots, divine judgements or other techniques of selection.

(3) By the designation on the part of the original charismatic leader of his own successor and his recognition on the part of the followers.

(4) Designation of a successor by the charismatically qualified administrative staff and his recognition by the community.

(5) By the conception that charisma is a quality transmitted by heredity; thus that it is participated in by the kinsmen of its bearer, particularly by his closest relatives.

(6) The concept that charisma may be transmitted by ritual means from one bearer to another or may be created in a new person.[1]

All these solutions, however, lead away from charismatic leadership in the sense of a uniquely personal mission. Charisma becomes routinized, and the movement becomes more traditional or more rational, or both. A charismatic element nevertheless remains: the exercise of leadership or authority is still bound up with a specific person and his distinctive qualities.

The problem of succession is thus seen as fundamental. But, according to Weber, it is not the *most* fundamental problem. Rather, the latter is the problem of making a transition from a charismatic staff and corresponding principles of administration to one which is adapted to everyday conditions. The original administrative staff tend to develop an interest in routinization, since only a small minority of enthusiasts will be prepared to devote their lives idealistically to their mission. The great majority, Weber opines, will in the long run 'make their living' out of their calling in a material sense as well. If *this* problem is solved, then the 'revolution' is over and the movement has become institutionalized.

If we apply Weber's ideas about the problem of succession to the wider Gandhian movement in India, it is clear that the problem created by Gandhi's death was partially solved by the choice of the third method. Gandhi designated Nehru as his 'political heir' and the choice was widely accepted. Part of Gandhi's charisma was thus transmitted to a leader who made good use of it, while at the same time encouraging the development of rational-legal authority. But it is important to insist that Nehru was Gandhi's *political* heir. Although Nehru espoused some of Gandhi's policies, he was opposed—and Gandhi knew that he was opposed—to others. To the extent that some of the Gandhian programmes were capable of

<hr>

[1] Weber, op. cit., pp. 334-6.

being effected by governmental action, the rational-legal authority of the new state was used to promote them. Part of Gandhi's charisma was also transmitted in an institutional form to the various independent voluntary Gandhian associations, such as the Harijan Sevak Sangh and the Gandhi Smarak Nidhi. There still remained, however, an important residue which could not be taken up by Nehru, the Government, or the Gandhian associations. An important position remained to be filled by a person who could be designated as Gandhi's 'spiritual heir'. This position was eventually filled by Vinoba.

There is no doubt that Gandhi's assassination did create a crisis and one that was particularly severe in that part of the movement —the constructive as distinct from the political and nationalist— concerned with the realization of Sarvodaya values. For the constructive movement the period 1948–51 constitutes an interregnum during which a search was on for the charismatic successor, and various well-known constructive work leaders were, in a sense, competing for the vacancy. In this period Vinoba, whose spiritual qualities had long ago been recognized by Gandhi,[1] was emerging as the favoured candidate of many workers; they were looking to him for leadership and initiative. But he was a genuinely reluctant candidate. By temperament he was not, and did not consider himself to be, a 'natural leader' of men. He was, indeed, an innovator, given to experiment, but he believed that his role was that of small-scale experimenter—the kind of person capable of demonstrating in his own ashram at Paunar, for example, how selfless service should be performed and how a moneyless economy could be run. But this very modesty singled him out for greater things. Pushed by his disciples, he made the trek on foot in March 1951 to the Sarvodaya Sammelan at Shivarampalli, near Hyderabad. From there on 15 April 1951 he proceeded to make a 'pilgrimage of

---

[1] Vinoba joined Gandhi at the latter's ashram in 1916 when he was 21 years of age. Shortly afterwards, Gandhi wrote to Vinoba's father, 'Your son has acquired at so tender an age such high-spiritedness and asceticism as took of me years of patient labour.' Ram., op. cit., p. 16. In 1940 Gandhi selected Vinoba as the person to offer satyagraha first in the campaign of Individual Satyagraha.— ibid., p. 24. Mahadev Desai, Gandhi's secretary, is reported to have predicted as early as 1936 that Vinoba would one day lead the movement. Desai wrote of Vinoba: 'Vinoba has something which others have not. His first characteristic is to resolve his decision into action the moment it is made. His second characteristic is continuous growth. Besides Bapu (Gandhi), I found this quality in Vinoba alone.'—ibid., p. 29.

peace' through Telangana, an area in which the Communists were attempting to build the base of a peasant revolution. And it was in the village of Pochampalli on 18 April that a talisman was discovered: the first gift of Bhoodan land.[1] The Bhoodan movement had begun and the new charismatic leader had been designated. The first gift of 100 acres by Shri V. R. Reddy was thus not merely a gift of land to the Harijan villagers of Pochampalli but the visible sign of the bestowal on Vinoba of a divine 'gift of grace'.

For the constructive movement, therefore, the method adopted to solve its problem of succession was of Weber's first type: a search—informal in character—for a new leader on the basis of criteria of the qualities which will fit him for the position. But the sixth type of method was also involved: not, it is true, the transmission of charisma by ritual means, but rather the creation of charisma in a new person. It is necessary to insist on this, because the accession of Vinoba did *not* bring with it a routinization of charisma. On the contrary, it reversed the tendency towards routinization evident in the movement prior to Gandhi's death. It is incorrect to think that Vinoba simply 'inherited' part of Gandhi's charisma. He possesses in addition his own genuine charisma. It may even be said that Vinoba consciously sought to *destroy* his inheritance, which he rightly divined could prove to be an encumbrance that would, unless removed, undermine the mission of Gandhi. We thus find him, even in the period of the interregnum, *opposing* 'Gandhism', albeit in the spirit of the Gandhi who had said, 'There is no such thing as "Gandhism" and I do not want to leave any sect after me.' As we have already noted in our first chapter, Vinoba exhorted his colleagues in 1949 to 'forget Gandhi', to think for themselves about ahimsa, and to have the courage to make new experiments on their own account. And the same message was repeated in different forms after his accession, particularly in the early years before his own charisma had been firmly established, i.e. recognized.

Vinoba's conduct of the leadership suggests that he has an intuitive grasp of what charismatic leadership demands and of the dangers (from the movement's point of view) inherent in its routinization. His campaign has been marked by successive dynamic charges, adoption of new programmes, new targets, new objectives, often in the short run bewildering to his disciples, all of which can

[1] Significantly enough, Vinoba himself refers to the first land gift as a talisman.
TGA—P

be interpreted as efforts at the continuous creation of charisma or, at least, as efforts to demonstrate his possession of it.[1] Programmatic targets constitute a potential threat to the leader of a charismatic movement, since, if they are not achieved, the leader may be felt to have lost his gift of grace. Targets have been set and they have not been achieved—for example, the objective of 50 million acres of Bhoodan by 1957, heralded as the Year of Land Revolution. But the movement has not suffered great damage from such misses. As soon as one target is in danger of being missed, another is put in its place. The result is a constantly moving target. The latest instance of this technique occurred in 1965. At that time the movement for Gramdan appeared to be slowing down, and there was a feeling among a section of the members that the movement should consolidate its position and concentrate on the development of existing Gramdan villages. Instead of choosing this 'safe' (but also dangerous) path, Vinoba proceeded to launch a new toofan (whirlwind) campaign for Gramdan, which resulted in a spectacular increase in the number of Gramdan declarations. His continued possession of charisma was thereby unquestionably confirmed.

Vinoba's efforts have not, as might be anticipated, prevented all routinization, and the movement is in the process of developing a rational-legal structure. But it may be predicted with some confidence that, so long as he remains leader, the movement will retain its strong charismatic flavour. Nevertheless, even inspired saints are mortal. In 1969 he celebrated his 75th birthday, and he is subject to recurrent illnesses which have finally compelled him to give up the padayatra, though not his mission. The problem of succession may, we hope, not arise for some years yet, but it cannot be avoided. Just as the question 'After Nehru, who?' was asked in the years before Nehru's death, it is possible to ask 'After Vinoba, who?'

In an attempt to probe the leaders' views on the problem of Vinoba's successor, they were asked the following question: 'Vinobaji has been the principal leader and guide of the Movement since Gandhiji's death. When Vinobaji himself eventually passes on, which three persons, in your opinion, would be able to give the

---

[1] Referring to value-oriented movements, Smelser writes: 'Changes of direction and bursts of enthusiasm occur as one set of tactics appears to be losing its effectiveness and another appears to show more promise.'—N. Smelser, *Theory of Collective Behaviour*, 1962, p. 358. However, Smelser does not relate these features to the dynamic of charismatic leadership.

best general guidance to the Movement?' The following table summarizes the answers given.

The first point to notice about section (a) of the table is the
relatively high level of non-response to the question. Despite an
attempt to frame the question in an inoffensive way, it clearly
proved to be a sensitive one—as sensitive as the question on
ownership of property. One can only speculate about the reasons
why such a large minority of respondents did not answer the
question. Several reasons may be suggested. (i) The question presupposed the death of a revered leader and was deemed improper
or even impertinent. (ii) The question was regarded as a kind of

TABLE 5

Views of the leaders on Vinoba's successor

(a) All respondents:

	%
No response	17
'Collective leadership'	4
'Leader to emerge'	2
First name listed:	
Jayaprakash Narayan	59
Some other individual	18
	100

(N = 228)

(b) Of respondents naming one or more individuals, proportion who listed:

	%
Jayaprakash Narayan	86
Dhirendra Mazumdar	46
Dada Dharmadhikari	36
Manmohan Choudhury	13
Narayan Desai	12

(N = 189)

'straw vote' and the respondents did not wish to commit themselves, despite assurances about the confidentiality of the questionnaire. (iii) The question involved selection from a large number of
possible candidates and any choice between them was difficult or
invidious. (iv) The question was hypothetical and consequently
difficult to answer. (v) The question presupposed a situation in
which the respondents had no interest, since for them the movement would not exist without Vinoba. (vi) The respondents did
not know the answer or did not care about it. Of these possible
reasons, we guess that the first was the most important and that the
second also operated. Whatever the reason, it is undoubtedly
significant that one in six of the leaders were not prepared to
answer the question.

It will further be seen that 6 per cent of the respondents
rejected the form of the question and replied in terms other than

naming individuals. The 4 per cent who opted for 'collective leadership' constitute an interesting minority. The phrase— actually used by some respondents—has gained currency in recent years, particularly with reference to the post-Stalin ideal of leadership in the U.S.S.R. For some of these respondents the application of the idea to the post-Vinoba period of the Sarvodaya movement might be seen as the expression of a desire to get away from a system of 'one-man' leadership. It might then be said to represent a desire for a more rational (in the Weberian sense) form of leadership. The phrase might also be interpreted as in line with Vinoba's own ideas. As we have already noted, Vinoba has often insisted that he is *not* a leader and that he does *not* want followers. He does not wish to be looking continually over his shoulder to see if anyone is following him. He wants what every anarchist wants: every man to be his own leader, or, what amounts to the same thing, no leaders and no followers. His position is very similar to that of the American socialist leader, Eugene Debs, who is reported to have said: 'I don't want you to follow me or anyone else. . . . I would not lead you into the promised land if I could, because if I could lead you in, someone else would lead you out.'[1] It is more probable, however, that the 'collective leadership' minority was composed of leaders who felt that they themselves had a legitimate claim to at least a share in the heritage of Vinoba and that no single individual could take his place as leader.

The even tinier minority of 2 per cent who answered that the leader would emerge might reasonably be interpreted as consisting of those who, consciously or unconsciously, realized that the movement was a charismatic one and that there was no way of forecasting the person on whom 'the gift of grace' would be bestowed. They may have had in mind the fact that, immediately after Gandhi's death, no one could have predicted with confidence that Vinoba would emerge as Gandhi's 'spiritual heir'. It is also possible, however, that this kind of answer was a way of responding

---

[1] Or, to take a more contemporary example, Daniel Cohn-Bendit ('Danny the Red'), student leader of the May–June revolt in France, 1968: 'Power corrupts. I think I'm corrupted. It's time I left my position and disappeared back down into the movement. . . . If you lead people they place faith in you. This corrupts. If you say or do something good then people will lean on you and say, "He's okay—he'll do." This is corruption. In any case we don't believe in lasting management.'—Interview with A. Mitchell, *Sunday Times*, London, 16 June 1968.

positively without having to indicate a choice between individual leaders.

With regard to the majority (77 per cent) of respondents who did name one or more individuals, it should be noted that the form of the question did not ask for a ranking of preferences, although it may have suggested this. In order to avoid embarrassment, three names were asked for. Each leader therefore, had three chances of appearing in the list and no special weight should necessarily be attached to the name of a person mentioned first. Nevertheless, it is probably significant that Jayaprakash Narayan was listed first by 59 per cent of the leaders who returned a questionnaire and that quite a few listed only Narayan.

The preference for Jayaprakash Narayan is underlined when we turn to section (b) of the table. Of the 189 respondents who did name individuals, Narayan was listed by 86 per cent, most of whom, of course, listed him first. Four other leaders were mentioned by more than 10 per cent of these respondents. Dada Dharmadhikari (along with Jayaprakash) figured prominently after Vinoba among the names of individuals who influenced respondents to join the movement.[1] A brief word is in order about the remaining three. Dhirendra Mazumdar is a constructive worker of long standing, the author of several works (in Hindi) on the movement, and a former President of Sarva Seva Sangh. According to the historian of the movement, Suresh Ram, he is 'known for his wonderful capacity to train workers. As he himself says, he is a *mistri* (an expert) to turn *huzoors* (intellectuals) into *mazdoors* (those devoted to body labour).'[2] Narayan Desai is the son of Mahadev Desai, the one-time devoted secretary of Gandhi who died in jail in 1942. Narayan Desai is thus one of the (relatively few) leaders of whom it can be said that they were 'born into the movement'. He was brought up in the Sabarmati Ashram, near Ahmedabad, and counts Gandhi as one of his teachers as a child. In recent years he has been secretary of the Shanti Sena Mandal. He belongs to a younger generation than the three previously mentioned leaders, all of whom are over 60 years of age. Manmohan Choudhury belongs to the same generation as Narayan Desai, and he, too, comes from a family with very strong Gandhian associations. He is the nephew of Nabakrushna Choudhury,

---

[1] See Chapter Four, pp. 141–2 above.
[2] S. Ram, op. cit., p. 360.

former Chief Minister of Orissa, who resigned office to dedicate his life to the movement. Manmohan Choudhury at the time of the enquiry was President of Sarva Seva Sangh.

To the extent that the answers to our question may be taken as a guide to the future of the Sarvodaya leadership, it seems clear that the majority of leaders believe that Jayaprakash Narayan is the person able to give the best general guidance. It should be remembered, of course, that the question was not a direct question about Vinoba's successor, that opinions change, and that, in any case, the Sarvodaya movement does not elect its leaders by majority vote. It is possible that the opposition of a minority to Jayaprakash, perhaps because of his political background, or for other reasons, might make him unacceptable as Vinoba's successor. But it seems more likely that, provided there is no unforeseeable event, such as the demise of Jayaprakash before that of Vinoba, he will inherit Vinoba's mantle and that the next problem of succession in the movement will not be an unduly critical one. However, if Jayaprakash is accepted as Vinoba's successor, this does not mean that the character of the leadership (and of the movement) will remain unchanged. Jayaprakash undoubtedly has his own personal charisma, and it has been demonstrated on many occasions, most notably on the occasion of his declaration of Jeevandan. His renunciation of chances of high political office, and many personal qualities, mark him out as a worthy successor of India's greatest contemporary saint. Indeed, many of the Sarvodaya workers already regard him as a saint.[1]

But he is a saint with a difference. He is not cast in the same mould as Vinoba. In Weberian terms, he is a much less traditional and a much more rational figure. He is more of a *modern* saint than either Gandhi or Vinoba could ever be. He has written at length on Sarvodaya doctrine and, although he has developed rather than originated some of its basic concepts, he has done so in a way which appeals most strongly to those familiar with Western modes of thought. He challenges at many points the received opinion of most Western or Western-oriented intellectuals, but at the same time he has succeeded in linking Sarvodaya thought with a train

---

[1] One witticism coined by a Western participant who was less than impressed by what he regarded as Vinoba's ambiguous stand on the issue of India's relations with Pakistan in 1965 ran as follows: 'There are two leaders in the movement: one a saint and the other a politician. Vinoba is the politician.'

of dissenting radical thought in the West. As a self-declared communitarian socialist, he would have found the company of, say, a G. D. H. Cole thoroughly congenial. It is symbolic of his position that, unlike Vinoba, he does not reject the possible contribution of Western social science. On the contrary, as the principal founder of the Gandhian Institute of Studies, he has initiated one of the more interesting and possibly significant developments in the movement in recent years: the attempt to marry Gandhian thought with social science. And in so doing, he has sought not a Gandhian social science but rather an appreciation on the part of the Gandhians of 'the need and value of modern social science and its methodology for attaining the ends of the Gandhian movement'.[1]

Many sympathetic observers of the movement in the West may agree, as we do, that this is what the movement needs. Nevertheless, this should not blind them to the fact that something of value may be lost in the process. The magic of charisma and all that it involves may tend to disappear in the cold light of social science, with its emphasis on cause and consequence and on rational criteria. What can be fairly confidently predicted is that the accession of a person like Jayaprakash to the leadership will hasten the routinization of charisma and the development in the movement of rational-legal authority and procedures. Whether revolutionary Gandhism can survive as revolutionary in such circumstances is problematical, if past experience is any guide. For the Sarvodaya movement this may be *the* problem in the years immediately ahead: how to prevent its becoming transformed into one more expression of 'institutional Gandhism'.

[1] Gandhian Institute of Studies, *Report, 1961–1963*, n.d., p. iii.

CHAPTER SIX

STRATEGY AND TACTICS

I. THE CONCEPTS OF STRATEGY AND TACTICS IN RELATION TO SARVODAYA

THE terms 'strategy' and 'tactics' are often used to denote the ways and means by which political organizations and social movements seek to achieve their goals.[1] The concepts derive from military science, one of the great masters of which, Clausewitz, defined 'tactics' as the theory of the use of force in battles, and 'strategy' as the theory of the use of battles for the conduct of war. According to these definitions, both terms refer to the *principles* concerning methods or techniques of action, not the ways of action as such. Strictly speaking, therefore, they should be applied only to movements which have a consciously developed set of principles concerning ways and means. However, the terms are often used to refer to observable patterns of action, whether these are based on developed principles or not, and it is in this sense that they will be used here.

The extended use of the terms outside military science can be justified by reference to Clausewitz himself, who pointed to the inherent sociological relationship between war, commerce, and politics.[2] However, when applied to social and political movements, the terms lose something of the precision they have in military science. In war, military goals can usually be defined precisely, as can the ways and means to achieve these goals. The same is not so true in politics, with the result that it is often difficult to distinguish sharply between strategy and tactics.

In a social movement, the principles of strategy and tactics are included in its 'ideology', in the sense in which we have used this term. A movement's ideology contains statements concerning not only its ultimate goals but also ways and means of achieving them; and the goals may be defined in such a way that they prescribe certain broad ways and means to be adopted and proscribe others. The strategic ideas of a movement may often be more important

---

[1] R. Heberle, *Social Movements*, 1951, p. 359.
[2] ibid., pp. 360–1. The point is apparent in Clausewitz's famous dictum that 'War is a mere continuation of [the state's] policy by other means.'

in some sense than its ultimate goals, since many movements share the same ultimate goals but are sharply divided from one another over the question of ways and means. The differences between democratic socialist and Communist movements, for example, centre largely, though not entirely, on questions of strategy and tactics.

A movement's strategy and tactics are also related to its organization. 'Certain forms of action require certain forms of organization; on the other hand, the choice of action patterns is limited by the form of organization.'[1] For example, if a movement's strategy is directed towards the capture of the offices of the government of states, if necessary by the use of force, then it is likely to develop a highly centralized organization which imposes tight discipline on its members. On the other hand, a movement, like Sarvodaya, whose organization is decentralized and loosely structured is not geared for making, say, a *coup d'état*. From this perspective, organization is part of the ways and means of a movement, and the type of organization chosen expresses a fundamental strategic decision.

In *The Politics of Nonviolent Action*[2] Gene Sharp has made the most systematic attempt to date to adapt the military concepts of strategy and tactics to the theory of non-violent action. Following Liddell Hart,[3] Sharp distinguishes between 'strategy' and 'grand strategy'. The latter serves 'to co-ordinate and direct all the resources of the nation or group toward the attainment of the political objectives of the conflict'.[4] It involves the distribution of economic, moral, manpower, and other resources to the various groups carrying on the struggle, and also the allocation among such groups of particular tasks in the conduct of the struggle. The rightness of the cause, considerations of winning the immediate conflict, and consideration of the likely long-term consequences of the struggle are all included in grand strategy. 'Strategy' is then seen as operating within the scope of the grand strategy. It is largely but not exclusively concerned with the means of conducting the struggle. 'Not exclusively' because, as Liddell Hart has emphasized, it is within the realm of strategy to seek to develop a strategic situation so advantageous that it may bring success without the necessity of open struggle, or will make success certain in

[1] ibid., p. 361.
[2] Published 1970. References below, however, are to his unpublished D.Phil. dissertation, Oxford University, 1968.
[3] Liddell Hart, *Strategy: The Indirect Approach*, 1955.
[4] Sharp, op. cit., Appendix One.

the event of open struggle. Strategy is thus the broad plan of action for the over-all struggle. Involved in the formulation of strategy are consideration of the objectives, resources, and strength of both one's own and the opponent's group; the various possible courses and means of action of both groups; and the actual or possible roles of third parties. In particular, strategy involves consideration of the results likely to lead from particular actions; the development of a broad plan of operations; provision for whatever means may be needed for the battles; decisions about the deployment of combat groups in various smaller actions; consideration of requirements for success in the operation of the chosen technique of action; and making good use of success.

'Tactics', again following Liddell Hart,[1] are 'the application of strategy on a lower plane'. Tactics are thus concerned with the more limited courses of action which fit within broad strategy. Tactics are applied for a shorter period of time, or in a smaller geographical area, by a more limited number of people, or by some combination of these. 'In the case of nonviolent action the specific issue or issues on behalf of which the struggle is conducted, and their relation to the political situation, may be significant factors also in distinguishing between tactics and strategy in the struggle.'[2]

Sharp's discussion may appear more relevant to movements concerned with the three major classes of methods of non-violent action that he distinguishes—non-violent protest, non-violent resistance, and non-violent intervention—than to a movement concerned to promote non-violent revolution. However, a movement for non-violent revolution may use any or all of the methods of non-violent action. What distinguishes non-violent revolution is not the methods it uses but its grand objective, which is not limited to changing the policies of the existing power-holders but seeks the replacement of the regime.[3] A non-violent *political* revolution aims at replacing the existing by a new political order; a non-violent *social* revolution has the even more ambitious objective of changing the social as well as the political order.

---

[1] Liddell Hart, op. cit., p. 335.   [2] Sharp, loc. cit.

[3] In Sharp's terminology 'non-violent revolution' is a type of principled Non-violence, not a technique of non-violent action, although he recognizes that non-violent intervention may have as its objective the setting up of a parallel government as a prelude to a change of political regime. The philosophy of satyagraha precludes the Sarvodaya movement from using certain methods of non-violent action, notably those designed to coerce or harass the opponent.

Certain 'key elements' or general principles of non-violent strategy and tactics are singled out by Sharp for special attention.[1] These include: (i) the indirect approach to the opponent's power. This may be regarded as an application of 'the indirect approach' to military strategy as formulated by Liddell Hart, who argues that such an approach is militarily more sound, since it helps to ensure the opponent's unreadiness to meet a plan of action based on it. (ii) Psychological elements are as important in non-violent as in military action, maintaining morale of one's 'troops' being a case in point. The element of surprise, often so important in military encounters, is, however, generally achieved in non-violent action simply by the adoption of a technique different from the one used by the opponent. (iii) Geographical and physical elements, though not unimportant, are generally less important in non-violent than in military action, since success in the former depends more on human beings than on the possession of geographical positions. (iv) The element of timing, however, is extremely important in non-violent action, as it is in military action. The success of tactical moves is usually heavily dependent on choosing the right time to make them. (v) Numbers and strength are important in non-violent action, but, as in military action, they are not the only important factor and they are not always decisive. (vi) Much more crucial is the element of concentration of strength, which includes choice of the issue on which to fight. 'The principles of war, not merely one principle,' states Liddell Hart, 'can be condensed into a single word—"concentration". But for truth this needs to be amplified as the "concentration of strength against weakness".'[2] This statement applies equally to non-violent action: 'war without violence'. Finally, (vii) obtaining and keeping the initiative is a key element in both military and non-violent action. The point was well appreciated by Gandhi, who wrote: 'An able general always gives battle in his own time on the ground of his choice. He always retains the initiative in these respects and never allows it to pass into the hands of the enemy.'[3]

This quotation suggests what was in fact the case: that Gandhi had a lively appreciation of the importance of strategy and tactics,

---

[1] Sharp, op. cit., Part Four, Chapter 9.
[2] Liddell Hart, op. cit., p. 150. Quoted by Sharp.
[3] N. K. Bose (ed.) *Selections from Gandhi*, 2nd edn., 1957, p. 235. Quoted by Sharp.

even though he nowhere systematically set out the strategy and tactics of satyagraha. His views on these matters take the form of practical advice and passing observations, expressing his intuitions of what should be done. In the Sarvodaya movement since Gandhi, considerations of strategy and tactics can also be found. But there is, perhaps, less overt discussion of these matters, partly because the movement operates in a post-independence situation, where tactical decisions of the kind Gandhi had to make are not called for; and partly because most of the leaders are less involved in day-to-day politics than in constructive work, and also lack experience in 'practical politics'. This, however, is not the whole explanation of the difference. The Sarvodaya movement today is more 'moralistic' than the movement led by Gandhi. Under the leadership of Vinoba, the movement has clarified its attitude to political power, although its attitude still remains ambiguous. This clarification has been achieved to some extent by paying the price of reduced political acumen. In rejecting 'power politics', the movement sometimes gives the impression that its major operational principle is 'Speak Truth to Power'; a principle which, if acted on with sufficient vigour, it is believed, will dissolve Power, leaving Truth triumphant. In the last analysis, this may indeed be the ultimate principle that will conquer Power, if such a conquest is at all possible; but it is not a principle which will achieve such a result merely by being trumpeted. The trumpeters must also show an awareness of the subtleties of Power, and this awareness is not always plainly evident in the utterances and activities of the Sarvodaya leaders today.

It should, of course, be observed that conscious consideration of strategy and tactics is an expression *par excellence* of the rational mode of thinking—thinking in terms of cause and consequence. This mode is not the dominant mode of Sarvodayites. If it were, these saints of Indian politics might never have started out on their journey. A sublime indifference to consequence, an insistence on non-attachment to the results even of one's own actions, are perhaps necessary prerequisites for making such a journey. A conviction that one has the truth and that truth will prevail, come what may, is perhaps part of the saint's armour; without it, there would be no 'holy fools' persisting in their 'folly', no 'absurd' attempt to make the impossible possible.

No general plan into which specific actions fit as parts of a com-

prehensive whole is to be expected, therefore, of the Sarvodaya
movement. Nevertheless, the movement has a strategy and makes
tactical decisions, or at least decisions which may be interpreted
as tactical. 'Act rightly, for the good of all!' is the moral imperative
in Sarvodaya decision-making; but, as Sharp observes, in a given
situation there may be several possible courses of action which may
all be morally right. Choices, therefore, have to be made, and
Sarvodaya has made them.

In outlining the ideology of Sarvodaya, we have already referred
to elements of the movement's strategy. Sarvodaya, the Welfare of
All, a casteless, classless, stateless, free society of equals being the
ultimate social objective, the grand strategy to achieve it is a
revaluation of values on the part of individuals and groups, leading
to progressive changes in social structure and social institutions.
Commitment to non-violence as both a means and an end rules out
certain courses of action. It obviously rules out the use of physical
force, armed resistance, and guerrilla warfare; less obviously,
perhaps, it also rules out the conventional democratic alternative
to these: political action designed to capture the power of the state.
The state is seen as the organization of institutionalized violence;
in the long term, therefore, it must be dispensed with, and in the
interim one works for its 'withering away'. In the place of conventional political action is substituted direct non-violent action by
the people themselves, a form of action which, contrary to received
opinion, is seen as a more democratic form of action. For Sarvodaya this is a strategic rather than merely a tactical decision. It is
a decision conducive to retaining initiative in the movement's own
hands, since it involves 'fighting' on the movement's chosen
'territory' rather than on that of its principal opponents, the
political power-holders, who know how to win elections but are
less sure of how to counter 'the power of the people'. The psychological element of surprise is also involved in this strategy; and it
exemplifies very clearly a principal characteristic of non-violent
action: the indirect approach to the opponent's power. To the
extent that power is won by the people (more accurately, retained
in the hands of the people),[1] the politicians and other rulers are
disarmed, almost without their realizing it.

---

[1] A major assumption of non-violent action, as Sharp clearly demonstrates in
Chapter 8 of his book, is that all power ultimately rests on the consent, active or
passive, of the people. The problem, therefore, is to get the people to take back

The decision to appeal to all men, rather than to a particular class or sectional group, is also a strategic 'decision'. In the short run, the decision has certain disadvantages: it is always easier to mobilize a class or a sectional group than a whole society. But the disadvantages are offset, even in the short run, by obvious advantages: no man and no group is defined as an enemy. And those who might see themselves cast in such a role, and who stand to lose, at least materially, by the adoption of the movement's programme, find it all the harder to fight back at an opponent who refuses to be regarded as such but insists that he is a friend. In the absence of a clear enemy-friend dichotomy, opponents of Sarvodaya tend to be reduced to employing the less satisfactory weapon of ridicule and to ignoring the movement: it is either childishly utopian or it is too insignificant to be worth bothering about. To date, the Sarvodaya movement has not gained as much as it hoped from its policy of being a friend to all, but it has probably gained more than it would have done with a different policy. Within the scope of this strategy, Sarvodaya has made a tactical decision to direct its activities to uplifting a particular class in society: the landless. As the most depressed class in Indian society, the landless do *not* possess, at least at the outset, great revolutionary potential: revolutions are rarely, if ever, made by the most depressed class. But the choice of the landless as a focus for the Bhoodan campaign displayed great tactical insight: this was an issue around which general support could be readily mobilized in the 1950s.

The rural orientation of the movement is a direct consequence of its adoption of Gandhi's vision of genuine swaraj. But following this vision has resulted in a strategy of revolution which, in broad outline, bears distinct affinities with a far more widely known strategy of revolution: that of Mao Tse-tung. Central to the latter is the notion of mobilizing the peasantry, especially the poor and middle peasants, behind 'the working class', in effect the Communist Party, which, whatever its members' social origins, sees itself as embracing the vanguard of the working class. The power of the revolution is then built up in the rural areas; rural bases in the form of soviets are established; from these the forces of revolution wage a protracted guerrilla warfare against the enemy; and,

---

the power they have *given* to their rulers. *Pace* Mao Tse-tung, political power does *not* grow out of the barrel of a gun. As Talleyrand observed to Napoleon: 'Sire, one can do anything with bayonets, except sit on them!'

as support for the revolution increases and the area under Communist control is extended, the cities are gradually encircled by the countryside. The Sarvodaya movement likewise seeks to mobilize the peasantry behind a moral élite, the movement's workers; in establishing Gramdans it is establishing the non-violent Indian equivalent of the Chinese village soviets; from these bases the non-violent guerrillas[1] conduct their protracted operations, gradually extending the movement's control of the countryside; and eventually—to project into a hypothetical future—the cities, dens of iniquity sucking lifeblood from the villages, are surrounded and fall to the revolutionary forces. In this analogy, Bihar, the first Gramdan state, is clearly designated as India's North Shensi. The general analogy is not without its irony: the Bhoodan campaign began as a non-violent alternative to a violent Communist-inspired peasant uprising on Mao-ist lines in the Telangana area of Andhra Pradesh. The movement announced itself as such at the time, and it is apparently living up to its initial promise!

The analogy cannot, of course, be stretched too far, but it extends also to the level of tactical decisions. Perhaps the most important single tactical decision taken by Mao was the one which resulted in the famous Long March of the Red Army.[2] Writing of it later, Mao stated:

We say that the Long March is the first of its kind ever recorded in history, that it is a manifesto, an agitation corps, and a seeding machine . . . we encountered untold difficulties and great obstacles on the way, but by keeping our two feet going we swept across a distance of more than 20,000 *li* through the length and breadth of eleven provinces. . . . The Long March is also a manifesto. It proclaims to the world that the Red Army is an army of heroes and that the imperialists and their jackals, Chiang Kai-shek and his like, are perfect nonentities. . . . The Long March is also an agitation corps. It declares to the approximately two hundred million people of eleven provinces that only the road of the

---

[1] The parallel between the movement's workers and guerrilla armies has been explicitly drawn by Satish Kumar, who in 1969 organized the London School of Non-violence. Earlier, 1963–5, Kumar, with E. P. Menon, undertook a world peace march. The two young Sarvodaya workers set out with Vinoba's blessing and a characteristically Vinoban piece of advice: to take with them no money, and to remain strict vegetarians. The first would compel them to seek the support of the people, while the second would provide an opening for discussion.

[2] The decision appears initially to have been taken for tactical reasons, but its success led to the new, distinctively Mao-ist strategy. Even in military matters, the distinction between strategy and tactics is not always clear.

Red Army leads to their liberation. . . . Without the Long March, how could the broad masses have known so quickly that there are such great ideas in the world as are upheld by the Red Army? The Long March is also a seeding-machine. It has sown many seeds in eleven provinces, which will sprout, grow leaves, blossom into flowers, bear fruit, and yield a crop in the future. To sum up, the Long March ended with our victory and the enemy's defeat.[1]

Vinoba's padayatra, his 'Long March' throughout the length and breadth of India, covering an average of ten miles per day, summer and winter, was less spectacular than that of the Chinese Red Army. It was less 'heroic': no one was killed or lost on the way. It lasted much longer, over fourteen years in fact, to be ended only by his illness, which eventually compelled him to settle in his Yenan, in Bihar. But, in its own way, it was the first of *its* kind in history, a manifesto, an agitation corps, and a seeding machine. Intuitively, India's new saint spurned the obvious ways of spreading his message, rejected 'modern' means of transportation, and chose the traditional path of the Indian sage.[2] Like Mao's, it was the tactical decision of a genius. And, although it is much too early to speak of victory, the seeds sown by Vinoba and his army on their march are already beginning to flower and to bear fruit.

The principle of concentration is also evident in Vinoba's tactical decision to emphasize the three elements of The Triple Programme, when a less wise tactician, in order to mobilize support, might have been tempted to yield to pressures to extend rather than to limit the movement's programme. There has never been any shortage of issues for inclusion in the programme: there are many workers in the movement eager to press the claims of their favourite panacea, or, if this is too harsh a term, their own favoured item in the Constructive Programme. But for Vinoba, the movement might easily have been lost in a medley of activities ranging from village sanitation and cow-service to nature cure and prohibition. Without rejecting any of them, Vinoba has insisted on the essential ones, Gramdan, Khadi and village industries, and

[1] Speech made by Mao Tse-tung on 27 Dec. 1935, quoted in J. Ch'ên, *Mao and the Chinese Revolution*, 1965, pp. 199–200.

[2] This statement requires qualification. Although Vinoba and his colleagues chose to walk themselves, jeeps and lorries have been used to carry baggage and equipment. He also makes use, where possible, of the modern device of the microphone. Vinoba does not reject modern technological devices as such, but, on the contrary, makes use of them when, but only when, they serve his ends.

Shanti Sena, especially the first. For Vinoba, concentration on essentials and a single-mindedness of purpose have become as second nature, even though it is combined with a capacity for innovation, the sparking off of new ideas, which his followers have often found bewildering. The decision to make Bihar first the Bhoodan, then the Gramdan state also exhibits an application of the principle of concentrating strength, as well as a concern for geographical position. Bihar, in the heartland of India, is the state where the infrastructure of Gandhian organizations is perhaps best developed. Vinoba's 'generalship' has sometimes been criticized by his 'captains' and 'troops' (rarely openly, more often in the 'mess'), and invidious comparisons drawn between it and that of Gandhi. But Vinoba conducts a very different 'war without violence' from the war that Gandhi fought; and the new war is not only more difficult but calls for different strategy and tactics. It is by no means plainly evident that in his basic decisions Vinoba has shown a capacity for generalship less than equal to Gandhi's.

In this section we have discussed the concepts of strategy and tactics and their relation to the Sarvodaya movement in general terms. In the remainder of this chapter we shall discuss particular (mainly tactical) decisions or issues in greater detail, and at the same time report the opinion of the leaders on these issues. The issues to be discussed are, of course, only a selection of the issues the movement has faced, although we believe them to be the more important ones. Consideration of them throws additional light on the character and working of the movement. For convenience, the issues may be grouped into two broad categories: those involving relations with the Congress, Government, and conventional politics; and those concerned with the deployment of the movement. These categories, however, are somewhat arbitrary, since many of the issues involve several aspects of the movement.

II. RELATIONS WITH THE CONGRESS, GOVERNMENT, AND CONVENTIONAL POLITICS

The grand strategy of the movement, as we have seen, is designed to generate the power of the people by developing radically decentralized self-governing institutions, working by consensus, which will eventually replace the state. The Sarvodaya revolution, however, is not seen as a cataclysmic event, and it is far removed from the Mao-ist conception of revolution as 'an uprising, an act of violence whereby one class overthrows another.'[1] In one sense the Sarvodaya conception is more sociological: revolution is seen as a fairly lengthy period of rapid social change, involving not merely a redistribution of power between social classes and strata but a change in the entire system of social stratification. Given this conception, which implies an acceptance in some form of 'gradualism', the problem arises of the movement's relations with, and attitude to, the existing power-holders who constitute the Government. In India since independence these belong principally to the Congress party, although non-Congress governments have held office in various states of the Union.

Relations with the Congress

In discussing the social foundations of the movement, we have presented data which confirm, what might have been expected from a knowledge of the historical origins of the movement, that the leaders have a strong bias towards the Congress, three out of every four of them seeing Congress as the party most sympathetic to Sarvodaya ideals. At the same time, we observed that relations with Congress are more complex than this finding might suggest.

The constructive work programme, in which the present Sarvodaya movement has its roots, was initiated by Congress under Gandhi's leadership when Congress was the spearhead of the campaign for national independence. Since taking over the reins of the Union Government, Congress has continued, although not very effectively, its own constructive programme. In addition, Congress—a party noted for its ideological diversity—remains committed in some measure to Gandhian ideas and has actively promoted several of them. At the Yelwal Conference of 1957 Congress, along with the Socialist and Communist parties, officially endorsed the Bhoodan-Gramdan campaign. Today the Congress Party's commitment to Gandhism is symbolized by the maintenance of the rule that its active members should wear Khadi—'the livery of freedom'.

On the other hand, the political ideas of Sarvodaya are opposed to all parties, Congress included. Indeed, one might even say 'especially Congress', since, as we have noted, it was Gandhi's

[1] Mao Tse-tung, quoted in Ch'ên, op. cit., p. 212.

last wish that Congress should disband as a political party and transform itself into a social-service organization of the kind that Sarva Seva Sangh now is. Further, the commitment of Congress to Gandhism is by no means certain. Pro-Gandhian policies, such as the encouragement of Khadi and village industries, have been 'balanced' by policies, such as the development of large-scale urban-centred industries, which would have been anathema to Gandhi. For these and other reasons the Sarvodaya movement has been a constant critic of Congress governments on many points. At the same time, personal relations between many Congress leaders and leaders of the Sarvodaya movement have generally remained good. Nehru, for example, on several occasions 'paid court' to Vinoba, who invariably responded in a sympathetic way, rarely voicing outright condemnation of Nehru's policies, even when he strongly disapproved of them.

One drawback of the movement's ambivalent relations with Congress is that, in the public mind, the movement is often identified in some way with Congress. In a period when Congress has been steadily losing popular support throughout the country this identification has presented a severe handicap. Taking steps to dissociate itself more clearly from Congress is clearly a tactical option that the movement might have taken and still could take, although taking it would have involved a revision of the strategic policy of seeking to work with all parties. In order to test the leaders' opinions on this matter, they were asked whether they agreed or disagreed with the statement: 'The Movement has become too closely identified in the public mind with the Congress Party.' Agreement with the statement might be fairly held to imply that a stricter separation between the two would benefit the movement.

Analysis of the replies showed that slightly more than half (52 per cent) of the respondent leaders agreed with the statement.[1] The leadership, therefore, is fairly evenly divided over this tactical issue, some, even of those who see Congress as the most sympathetic party, wishing for less identification. The finding, of course, relates to the year 1965 when the survey was made, and it is possible that the subsequent fortunes of Congress, notably the

[1] N = 212. Non-respondents to particular questions have usually been excluded from the calculation of percentages, except in cases where the level of non-response was particularly high (over 10%).

split which took place in 1969, have strengthened the feeling for stricter separation. It may be confidently predicted, however, that firm steps to dissociate the movement from Congress would still lead to deep divisions within the movement. Until an overwhelming majority of the leaders and other workers favour it, it is unlikely that the movement will seriously change, unilaterally, its relations with Congress.

Partyless democracy

Closely related to the issue of its relations with Congress is the more general issue involved in the movement's concept of partyless democracy. The movement, it should be noted, is not the only group in contemporary India espousing this idea: it has long been advocated by the late M. N. Roy and his associates in the Radical Humanist Movement.[1] From the perspective of the ultimate anarchistic goal of Sarvodaya—the stateless society and freedom from all government—partyless democracy may be viewed as an interim objective, applicable to the second stage of political development distinguished by Vinoba, that of the decentralized self-governing state. Since Sarvodayites believe that India is now entering this second stage, propagation of the idea is part of the movement's work, particularly at election times. As we have already noted, propagation has taken the forms of advocating Voters' Councils to select candidates on a non-partisan and, if possible, unanimous basis, and of calling for the formation of non-party governments. The latter idea was elaborated at the Non-Party Democratic Convention, sponsored by the Sarva Seva Sangh and the All-India Panchayat Parishad and presided over by Jayaprakash Narayan, which was held in Delhi in December 1966. Arguing that the parliamentary system did not suit the genius of the people and present conditions, Jayaprakash proposed a National Government. Although the abolition of political parties was desirable, he continued, it was impossible in the present circumstances. The parties, therefore, should contest the election as parties, trying to get their own candidates elected. But after the election the representatives of the parties should function within the legislatures as non-party men. They should collectively 'select or elect' a leader to form a Cabinet and the leader so chosen should select his Cabinet colleagues out of the members of Parlia-

[1] See M. N. Roy, *Politics, Power and Parties*, 1960.

ment, irrespective of their party affiliations. Outside Parliament the parties should function as educators of the public.[1]

In order to gauge the support among the leaders for the policy of partyless democracy, they were asked whether they agreed or disagreed with the statement: 'While partyless democracy is the ideal to be aimed at, the Movement cannot ignore that parties now exist. Sarvodaya workers, therefore, should help good candidates at election times, even if they have been given a party ticket.' Jayaprakash's views cited above are in line with the first part of this statement. There has been no shift, however, in the movement's policy with respect to support of party candidates. The terms of the Lok Sevak's pledge still hold good: not to take part in party or power politics. The second sentence of the statement may thus be seen as providing a test of the extent to which the leaders agreed with the movement's policy in this respect. On any straight interpretation of the pledge not even 'good' candidates may be supported if they stand as party men.

Analysis of the replies showed that almost half (49 per cent) of the respondent leaders in 1965 held a view contrary to the movement's official policy and agreed that 'good' party candidates should be helped by Sarvodaya workers.[2] In view of the party preferences of the leaders, it may be assumed that most 'good' candidates would be found to be Congress men. Perhaps not too much weight should be given to the actual percentage figure: the question was persuasive in form and it might have required reflection to disagree that 'good' party candidates should not be helped. But, even allowing for this, the finding suggests a large degree of uncertainty among the leaders about the wisdom of promoting partyless democracy in the way the movement was then doing. It may also suggest uncertainty about the wisdom of the movement's policy in abstaining from participating in elections itself. Development of the movement in recent years has made this policy more questionable. The whirlwind campaign for Gramdan has had as

---

[1] *Sarvodaya*, XVI, 7 (Jan. 1967), p. 299. More recently, Jayaprakash has actively sponsored the idea of a Council for National Consensus, a non-official body representative of the main political parties and of leaders from other walks of life, which would have as its object 'creating national consensus on matters of urgent public importance'. The idea was mooted at the First National Convention on National Unity and Democracy, February 1969. See *Sarva Seva Sangh Monthly News Letter*, 2, 2 (Feb. 1968); 2, 9 (Sept. 1968); and 3, 1 (Jan. 1969).
[2] N = 218.

one of its more significant results the bringing of extensive areas of the country, particularly in Bihar, within the movement's fold. Gramdan villages are no longer scattered throughout the countryside. Assuming that the movement can influence the political choices of Gramdan villagers, the possibility therefore arises that it might be able to influence the elections in several significantly large areas. In this situation the temptation for the movement to move into conventional politics and put up its own candidates, or at least candidates known to favour the movement, has increased. This issue has in fact been the subject of recent discussion in the movement, Jayaprakash taking a leading role. No decision to depart from previous policy has been taken but it cannot be ruled out as altogether improbable. It should be evident, however, that the issue is a crucial one for the movement: abstention from electioneering is not merely a tactical decision; it is a strategic one. Changing course in this respect would radically change the character of the movement as it has developed to date. On the side of maintaining the existing course is the strong probability that a venture into conventional politics would reveal painfully the 'political weakness' of the movement even in Gramdan areas.

The issue of taking up current problems

The idea that the Sarvodaya movement might be tempted to move into conventional politics receives additional support from the leaders' responses to another statement: 'The Movement should make more effort than it has done so far to take up urgent current problems such as high prices and evictions as a way of rousing the masses.' No less than 74 per cent of the respondents agreed with this statement.[1]

The connection between views on this statement and disposition towards conventional politics may not be obvious at first sight, and was probably not obvious to most respondents; it requires therefore some elucidation. The statement was included in the questionnaire because it was apparent in 1965 that there was dissatisfaction among Sarvodaya workers about the existing policies of the movement and its progress. The dominant mode of mobilizing support for the movement adopted by Vinoba has been simply a persuasive appeal in the name of Sarvodaya values. Where these values can be readily related to a practical and pressing problem, such an

[1] N = 219.

appeal—by a person like Vinoba—can be very effective. In the context of an incipient Communist uprising, and, more generally, in a climate of opinion favourable to land reform, Vinoba's appeal for Bhoodan met with a truly remarkable response. The appeal for Gramdan, as distinct from Bhoodan, proved less effective. Gramdan was a much more revolutionary objective and involved a more far-reaching transformation of existing values. By 1960 the pace of the movement had slackened considerably and it began to look as though Gramdan declarations would be increasingly difficult to obtain.

In this situation the feeling grew among Sarvodaya workers that the movement should pay more attention than in the past to 'current problems'. This feeling implies that the central programmatic objectives of the movement—Gramdan, Khadi, and Shanti Sena—are in a sense too remote to serve as effective instruments of mobilization. The whole of the constructive programme—including the above items—can, of course, be regarded as a list of 'current problems'. The general Sarvodaya strategy of revolution is geared to the idea that the new values can best be nurtured in tackling such problems. There can be no sudden 'leap into freedom'; the revolution is a gradual piecemeal process which reveals itself in the successful solution of social problems. But the items in the list vary in importance and in their degree of urgency. All of them may be judged in some sense important and urgent, but many of them are also perennial problems. They have existed for a long time and fail to elicit *special* attention. Bhoodan did so in the 1950s when land reform was 'in the air'; but land legislation, however ineffectively implemented in parts, has taken the edge off the issue of the landless labourers. No item in The Triple Programme or in the constructive programme as a whole now enjoys the status of such immediate relevancy. It is just this quality of immediate relevancy that lies behind the feeling that the movement needs to do more to solve current problems. The feeling was well expressed by a Representative who, in reply to the question on the goals of the movement, stated: 'There is a need to give a new orientation to the Movement so that it concentrates on giving immediate relief to the people from the many problems that beset their lives.'

The leaders have in fact responded to this feeling to some extent. From time to time Sarva Seva Sangh has issued policy statements expressing its views on current issues such as rising prices, evictions of tenants, and corruption. To the extent that it has done so, it finds itself behaving rather like a political party. The taking up of current problems and their 'exploitation' is, of course, a standard procedure adopted by political parties to mobilize opinion in their favour: the public is invited to invest support in a party in exchange for a promise to solve the problems. But Sarva Seva Sangh is not a political party. It has deliberately chosen not to enter the electoral arena; at the most, it can be no more than an additional pressure group, bringing its influence to bear on the politicians. It is thus in a very weak position, having little or nothing to exchange directly with the public. It cannot in the nature of things promise to solve the kinds of problem that politicians trade in. To ask that it should do more to take up current problems comes near, therefore, to asking that it should act more like a political party. If it were to accept the demand, it would find itself being propelled in the direction of conventional politics.

It can be argued that to take such a step would not only change the character of the movement but also detract from its real, if limited, strength. For the movement does have an important 'weapon' in its arsenal that the orthodox political parties do not possess, at least in the same degree. This is the weapon of 'selfless service': practical service freely given to all and undertaken without any thought of reward. The movement uses this weapon continually but especially in times of great emergency. Its special use was well demonstrated in 1967 in Bihar, where, under the leadership of Jayaprakash Narayan, the movement was in the forefront of famine relief work. We do not suggest that there is any ulterior motive in such activity. Quite the contrary. It is the absence of an ulterior motive which makes this kind of activity such an effective method of mobilization. It is likely to enhance the standing of the movement as an incidental consequence of a practical demonstration of Sarvodaya values. At the same time, it must be noted that not all 'selfless service' is accompanied by rewards. In particular, the movement's interventions to reduce communal tensions and conflicts often earn more kicks than halfpence.

As far as one can judge from his public pronouncements, Vinoba's own position on the issue of taking up 'urgent current problems' is quite clear. He does not ignore them but neither does he encourage taking them up. And when he does mention them, he seeks to relate them as directly as possible to the items of The Triple Programme, particularly Gramdan. In reply to the question 'How should Bhoodan workers tackle day-to-day questions?' Vinoba advised that they should not get involved in all the innumerable questions of injustice they see around them. Their main task was to bring about the transformation of values that would encourage the people to solve their own problems. He added, 'It is idle to think that a Brave New World can ever be created in which everything is perfect and there are no problems.... It is nice to think of creating heaven on earth, but let us understand clearly that questions will arise and demand a solution even in an ideal society.'[1]

In holding to this position it may be concluded that Vinoba displays greater tactical sense than the 74 per cent of the respondent leaders who agreed with the statement in our questionnaire. It is one mark of good generalship not to be diverted from the central objective by the prospect of winning minor victories which might not contribute much to the main end.

The issue of Kashmir

As an illustration of a current problem of a rather different kind from those discussed, we may take the issue of Kashmir, on which the movement has been urged to adopt a tactical position. In discussing this issue it is important to remember not only the universalistic values of Sarvodaya, symbolized in Vinoba's slogan 'Jai Jagat!' (Victory to the World!), but also that the movement had its origin in the Indian nationalist movement. The association with Indian nationalism remains strong and undoubtedly colours the reactions of some Sarvodaya workers to a number of issues. In general, Sarvodaya universalism is not seen as antipathetic to a restrained nationalism. Vinoba has suggested that 'Jai Jagat!' includes the more familiar 'Jai Hind!', that nationalism is good up to a point, and that, although 'Jai Jagat!' commands the respect of Indians, it has not yet won their affection.[2]

The issue of Kashmir touches most sensitively on Indian national consciousness, although it is also, of course, bound up with the question of communal relations between Hindus and Muslims.

[1] *Bhoodan*, 5 Feb. 1958.
[2] *Sarvodaya*, XIII, 12 (June 1964), p. 445.

No attempt will be made here to sketch, except in outline, the origin and complex character of the Kashmir issue. It may be sufficient to remind the non-Indian reader at this point that Kashmir is populated mainly by Muslims, and that the status of the state (now divided *de facto* between Pakistan and India, but with India retaining control of the greater part) has been a chronic source of friction between the Indian and Pakistan Governments from the time of the partition of the sub-continent to the present day.

In January 1964, in the wake of communal rioting in Kashmir that followed the theft of a holy Muslim relic, Jayaprakash Narayan took the initiative in publicly advocating conciliatory steps designed to resolve the Kashmir issue. With the tacit encouragement of Nehru, he formed the Indo-Pakistan Conciliation Group, which sought to influence leaders in both India and Pakistan. He judged, quite correctly, that little progress in resolving the issue could be made until the Indian Government, supported in this respect by the bulk of Indian public opinion, modified its position on the status of Kashmir. The Indian Government, with strong legal justification, argued that Kashmir had become part of the Indian Union as a result of the declaration of accession made in 1947 by its ruler, the Hindu Maharaja, Sir Hara Singh. Pakistan refused to accept the decision, armed conflict ensued, and the issue was referred by the Indian Government to the Security Council. A Truce Commission was set up and a cease-fire line agreed in July 1949, but the Indian Government rejected the Commission's suggestion to appoint an arbitrator whose decision would be binding on both sides. Arbitration was rejected because it would have involved a plebiscite by the people of Kashmir, the result of which would undoubtedly have favoured Pakistan, since it may be assumed that the voting would have closely followed religious lines. Nehru, at the time of accession, had made an informal promise to refer to the will of the people of Kashmir on the accession issue after Pakistan had called off the invasion. No plebiscite has in fact been held, but the Indian Government argues that the promise was conditional on a Pakistani withdrawal, and that, in any case, subsequent elections in the Indian-held part of the state have confirmed that the majority of Kashmiris regard the state as an integral part of the Indian Union.

In several public statements made early in 1964 Jayaprakash

Narayan questioned the moral, if not the legal, validity of the Indian Government's stand. Urging the release of the then imprisoned Kashmiri leader, Sheikh Abdullah, he pointed out that the Government of Kashmir (a notoriously corrupt administration) did not enjoy the confidence of its people. And, in the course of developing his argument, he flatly disagreed with those who spoke and acted as if the Kashmir issue had been settled once and for all, and as if the people of Kashmir had put their seal of consent upon that settlement.[1] For these pronouncements Jayaprakash was subjected to vociferous attacks by sections of the Indian press, by politicians, and by members of the public.

It is necessary to add that Jayaprakash has modified the position he adopted in 1964. The death of Nehru ended, temporarily at least, any chance of pursuing far the path of conciliation. At the time of the Indo-Pakistan armed conflict of September 1965 Jayaprakash expressed his 'full support' for the Indian Government's action in dealing with Pakistan's 'aggression'. By its 'deliberate and blatant action, Pakistan had forfeited whatever place it had obtained in the Kashmir issue'. The plea for a plebiscite had been only 'a smoke-screen behind which Pakistan had been making tireless plans to annex the State of Jammu and Kashmir. . . . Therefore, Pakistan and the world should understand now that recent events have established the truth that if there is any issue now in Kashmir, it is between the people of Kashmir and the Government of India.'[2]

In an attempt to probe the opinion of the Sarvodaya leaders on the Kashmir issue, they were asked whether they agreed or disagreed with the following statement: 'It is not true to say that the people of Kashmir have already decided to integrate themselves with India. The accession of Kashmir to India is not final and irrevocable.' This statement is in fact a close paraphrase, if not the actual words, of Jayaprakash's pronouncements of early 1964. His later statement, quoted above, still leaves open the 'final and irrevocable' nature of Kashmir's accession and the consent of the people of Kashmir to union with India. But there is little doubt that he no longer regards the issue in the same light as he did in 1964. And it is probable that other Sarvodaya leaders have also subsequently modified their views. Nevertheless, responses to our

[1] *Bhoodan*, 29 Feb. 1964, pp. 345–6.
[2] Press statement, republished in *Sarvodaya*, XV, 5 (Nov. 1965), pp. 215–16.

statement provide a pointer to the state of opinion among Sarvodaya leaders in mid 1965, a few months *before* the border conflict of that year.

The first point to notice about our findings is the rate of response to the question. No less than 22 per cent of the leaders did not answer that they agreed or disagreed, most of these leaving the question blank, but about one-third of them replying either that they did not know or that they were unwilling to answer the question.[1] The remaining 78 per cent comprised 46 per cent who agreed with the statement and 32 per cent who disagreed. For Sarvodaya leaders Kashmir was obviously as sensitive an issue as it was for most Indians in 1965, although it is very unlikely that one could find a political group, other than Muslim, which contained such a high proportion of leaders sympathetic to the cause of conciliation.

The division among the leaders on the Kashmir question underlines the difficulties of the movement's taking a stand on such issues. It cannot, of course, avoid taking *some* stand: the Kashmir issue was such that it could not avoid doing so, without being accused of cowardice and betrayal of its values. Its way of 'resolving' the dilemma in such circumstances is to propose a solution to the substantive problem which is morally unobjectionable, but equally clearly not feasible or 'practical politics', at least in the short run. In this particular instance Vinoba 'resolved' the dilemma by advocating, at the time of the armed conflict, the confederation of India and Pakistan. It should be noted that pronouncements of Jayaprakash in 1964 were made in his *personal* capacity, not as a spokesman of the movement. He sought support among Sarvodaya leaders for his conciliatory moves, and certainly received some, but not as much as he would have liked. From the point of view of preserving the cohesion of the movement, if not its moral integrity, there is much to be said for its way of 'resolving' such dilemmas and for allowing personal initiatives by leaders which do not commit the movement as such. *The* leader, i.e. Vinoba, cannot take such initiatives without risking disruption of the movement, but a Jayaprakash Narayan can—although in doing so he may take considerable risks with his reputation. Whatever one's final moral judgement on the Sarvodaya movement in

[1] N = 228. The average non-response to all other opinion statements reported in this chapter was 7%

respect of its stand on such issues, it remains a fact that it provides an important source of conciliatory movement within Indian politics. Jayaprakash's perhaps somewhat less abortive move on the issue of the Nagas is another example of this role of the movement.

Non-co-operation with the Government's military efforts

The Sarvodaya movement had to take some position on the Kashmir issue, if only because it is a movement dedicated to peace. As the spearhead of the Indian peace movement, it is also faced with the problem of defining its position in relation to the Government's efforts to make the country strong militarily. Under Nehru India's military build-up proceeded apace, but at a rate rather slower than might have been the case if his policy had not been influenced by the Gandhian philosophy of restraint.[1] The Sino-Indian war of 1962 and the subsequent armed conflict with Pakistan have resulted in a redoubling of efforts to maintain and to increase India's military power. Gandhi's vision of a free India, without an army and relying on non-violence for its defence, has faded fast among Indian politicians and the public at large.

The position of Western pacifist movements with regard to their governments' military defence preparations is essentially simple and straightforward: the preparations are opposed, the expenditures on them deplored, and the radical elements proceed beyond protest to active resistance to their governments' efforts. The Sarvodaya movement's position in relation to the Indian Government's military preparations are less simple, and illustrate an important difference between India's advocates of non-violence and Western pacifists.

The general Sarvodaya position starts from the assumption that 'Protest is not enough.' But this does not mean that one proceeds at once to resistance. The real task of non-violent revolutionaries is to build up the power of non-violence among the people, so that they will no longer feel it necessary to rely on military defence. Until that power has been generated, India will continue to defend itself by military means and it is useless to oppose efforts to strengthen the armed forces. On the other hand, no Sarvodayite can himself be a party to such efforts.

[1] For figures on the rise of defence expenditure in India since independence (up to 1958), and a critique of Indian defence policy, see V. V. Ramana Murthi, *Commonsense about Defence*, 1959.

This position is expressed in the following statement included in the questionnaire: 'Until we have a real non-violent alternative to offer, we should not ask people to non-co-operate with the Government's efforts to make India strong militarily.' 'Non-co-operation', of course, could be interpreted in this context to include a wide range of behaviour, from the exercise of peaceful persuasion and propaganda to acts of positive disassociation from government policy, such as tax refusal, resignation from government bodies, and satyagraha campaigns designed to focus attention on the issue. With their Gandhian understanding, however, it is likely that the term was interpreted as implying more militant forms of action than propaganda and protest, i.e. as implying active non-violent resistance. The movement has in fact issued statements deploring increased expenditure on military defence; but it has not sanctioned anything resembling the kind of non-co-operation practised by the independence movement against the British Raj. Restricting itself to the mildest general form of non-violent action, the movement has played some part in stiffening the Government's determination—if such it be—not to embark on an atomic-weapons programme. But compared with, say, the peace movement in Britain, its protests against militarism have been exceedingly mild. It has not even attempted to make an effective protest against the introduction of compulsory National Cadet Corps training for university students. Vinoba, in fact, deprecated any such move, on the curious ground that service in the NCC helped to instil a sense of discipline among students. Individual Sarvodaya leaders and workers have suggested that service in the Shanti Sena should be recognized as an alternative to NCC service, but the movement has done almost nothing to press for the adoption of this suggestion.

In judging the movement's position on this general issue, it should in fairness be pointed out that Sarvodaya leaders are convinced that the Indian Government has only pacific intentions, and that there is little likelihood that a Congress Government would radically depart from the kind of policy pursued by Nehru. It is probably also true that, in a situation of mounting nationalistic fervour following the Sino-Indian and Indo-Pakistan armed conflicts of recent years, a vigorous anti-militarist campaign would serve to inflame rather than to damp down public opinion.

Analysis of the responses of the leaders to the statement in the questionnaire on this issue shows that a majority of the respondents accepted the 'official' Sarvodaya line. But the question was second only to the Kashmir question in degree of 'sensitivity', judging from the proportion of non-respondents and 'don't knows'. 12 per cent fell into this category, 62 per cent agreeing with the statement and 25 per cent disagreeing.[1] The one in four of the leaders who disagreed can be regarded as constituting a militant minority who would like to see the movement taking a firmer line on this issue, more comparable to the line adopted by radical pacifist and anti-war groups in the West. It is possible that since 1965 this minority has grown in strength, as the Indian Government's military policy has hardened and as the influence of Western radical pacifism among the leaders has increased.

Attitude to Panchayati Raj

If active non-co-operation is not favoured by the movement with respect to the Indian Government's military preparations, much less is it to be expected in relation to those government policies which can plausibly be seen as inspired by Gandhian sentiments. Among the more important of these are the related programmes of Community Development and Panchayati Raj. The Community Development Programme, launched symbolically on the anniversary of Gandhi's birth on 2 October 1952, may be seen as an expression of what we have called 'official Gandhism'. Extended by phases throughout the country, it has been described by the Government itself as 'a programme of aided self-help to be planned and implemented by the villagers themselves, the Government offering only technical guidance and financial assistance. Its objectives are to develop self-reliance in the individual and initiative in the village community.'[2]

It would be wrong to judge the programme a complete failure. In the face of inadequate financial resources and lack of trained personnel, much has been achieved. Nevertheless, over-all the results are disappointing. The emphasis has been placed on the material aspect of development, especially agricultural production, rather than on the harmonious blending of both material and moral development that Gandhi envisaged. Even so, with all the physical

---

[1] N = 228. Rounding to nearest whole figure results in an aggregate total of 99%.

[2] Government of India, *India 1964*, 1964, p. 166.

improvements that could be cited, the programme thus far has hardly made a perceptible dent in the human suffering, the grinding poverty, and the primitive conditions of Indian village life.[1] The Government's own Programme Evaluation Organization, in a report issued in 1957, stressed two main shortcomings of the programme: 'that the contact established by the Government through its officials had not been with communities but with a few families in the various villages assigned to development, and that the richer cultivators had benefited disproportionately, if not indeed at the expense of the poorer ones.'[2] The report concluded that Community Development had failed to become a people's movement in which the mass of the population identified themselves with the objectives of the community projects.[3]

Responding to the report, the Government began in 1959 to introduce a new pattern of local government in the rural areas, popularly known as Panchayati Raj. Launched again on Gandhi's birth anniversary, this new programme of 'democratic decentralization' evokes something of the Gandhian vision of an Indian polity based on village republics. Though all states do not have the same pattern, its salient feature is a three-tier structure comprised of local authorities at the village, block, and district levels, known respectively as Gram Panchayats, Panchayat Samitis, and Zilla Parishads. In the same year as Rajasthan was enacting the first Panchayati Raj legislation Jayaprakash Narayan produced *A Plea for Reconstruction of Indian Polity*.[4] The *Plea* develops an argument for reconstructing the Indian polity as a participating communitarian democracy, in effect a 'classical' democracy of government

[1] cf. R. W. Poston, *Democracy Speaks Many Tongues*, 1962, pp. 86–7. For a general account of the programme see B. Mukerji, *Community Development in India*, 1961. For an evaluation of the programme from the perspective of planning at the 'grass roots' see A. H. Hanson, *The Process of Planning*, 1966, Ch. XI. For highly critical observations on the programme see B. Moore, *Social Origins of Dictatorship and Democracy*, 1966, pp. 393–408. For a discussion of community development as an effort to mobilize mass support for modernizing India see R. Bendix, *Nation-Building and Citizenship*, 1964, Ch. 7.

[2] R. Segal, *The Crisis of India*, 1965, p. 214.

[3] Government of India, *Report of the Team for the Study of Community Projects and National Extension Service* ('The Balvantray Mehta Report'), Vol. II, 1957, p. 53. See also the contributions of Shiviah and S. R. Nanekar in G. S. Halappa (ed.), *Dilemmas of Democratic Politics in India*, 1966.

[4] Paper published for private circulation, 1959. An abridged version has subsequently been published in Jayaprakash Narayan, *Socialism, Sarvodaya and Democracy*, 1964.

by the people, in place of the system of competitive oligarchy called parliamentary democracy. Jayaprakash's practical proposals bear a strong resemblance to the Panchayati Raj structure at the lower levels of government, although, of course, he also proposed that the reconstruction should be extended to the state and Union levels. Not surprisingly, therefore, he was greatly encouraged by the development of Panchayati Raj, and he has subsequently devoted much of his attention to trying to shape the new institutions in the way he envisaged in his *Plea*.[1]

Jayaprakash himself would be the first to admit that the official programme of democratic decentralization is not developing on truly Gandhian lines. He has suggested that many of those concerned in the programme lack faith in the ideal of self-government, with the result that the decentralization and devolution of powers have been grudgingly conceded and heavily circumscribed. He is also pained to see how, despite professions to the contrary, the political parties are using the new institutions as a means of building up their power in the rural areas. As a result, the already divided rural communities are further divided on party lines, and the politicalization of caste and village factions is accentuated. Jayaprakash is aware of the danger that, far from flowering into a unique kind of people's democracy, Panchayati Raj may be developing into a convenient administrative arrangement under which the traditional local bosses, the dominant castes and factions, and the new economic dominants in the villages can maintain and extend their rule.

Nevertheless, it can be argued that the official programme continues to offer considerable potential for political development on Gandhian lines, and an opportunity to promulgate within a context of living institutions the principles and values of Sarvodaya. From the movement's point of view, the greatest danger is that too much involvement in the promotion of Panchayati Raj may result in compromising its political principles. If the movement

[1] See his *Swaraj for the People*, 1961, republished in *Socialism, Sarvodaya and Democracy*, op. cit.; 'Decentralized Democracy: Theory and Practice', *The Indian Journal of Public Administration*, VII, 3 (July-Sept. 1961); *Seminar on Fundamental Problems of Panchayati Raj*, 1964; and, more generally, the journal, *Avard*, now *Voluntary Action*, published by the Association of Voluntary Agencies for Rural Development, New Delhi. J. P. Narayan was formerly the president of the All-India Panchayat Parishad, a non-official, non-political, and non-party voluntary organization of Panchayati Raj institutions, devoted to the spreading of the concept of Panchayati Raj and to strengthening them.

becomes too much identified with a set of institutions in danger of developing into just another structure of local government, the image of the movement may be gravely blurred. Oddly enough, Vinoba, the spiritual leader, appears to be more conscious of the danger than Jayaprakash, the experienced ex-politician. Anticipating the critic of 'romantic Gandhian nostalgia', Barrington Moore, who argues that 'To democratize the villages without altering property relationships is simply absurd',[1] Vinoba, before the Panchayati Raj programme was launched, pointedly placed Gramdan as the first step to be taken before the introduction of gram panchayats (village councils). 'Then alone', he said, 'it can be a force for good and work for the welfare of the whole village. With the present inequalities a panchayat too often becomes an instrument in the hands of a few and they boss it over [the rest]. It is a formal democracy. . . . The decentralization of power has become an attractive slogan. We must understand the implications clearly. It should not mean entrusting power to the few, however close they may be to the people. It really means opportunity for service. . . .'[2] Since uttering this warning, Vinoba has not discouraged the activities of Jayaprakash and other Sarvodaya workers who share Jayaprakash's views. But he has not encouraged them, either. For him, Gramdan—and, more generally, The Triple Programme—remains at the centre of the movement's activities.

From responses to a statement in the questionnaire: 'The Movement should pay more attention to the Government's programme of Panchayati Raj as a means of achieving the Sarvodaya Society', it would appear, however, that there is strong support among the office-holders for Jayaprakash's lead on this issue. No less than 70 per cent of the respondents agreed with the statement.[3] It may be that this relatively high figure reflects a certain feeling of frustration among the leaders about the Gramdan programme in early 1965 and a desire for an alternative way ahead. When the survey was made, the view was current among Sarvodaya workers that the movement was grinding to a halt as far as securing Gramdans was concerned. The launching of the whirlwind campaign shortly afterwards proved this to be false, and the success of the campaign rapidly dissipated any feeling of frustration. Even allowing for this, however, support for the Government's programme of

---

[1] Barrington Moore, op. cit., p. 394.
[2] *Bhoodan*, 19 Dec. 1956.   [3] N = 217.

Panchayati Raj as a road to the Sarvodaya society was remarkably strong. It underlines, once again, the difference between Sarvodaya and Western anarchism.

The general conclusion which emerges from consideration of various aspects of the movement's relations with the Congress, Government, and conventional politics is that Sarvodaya strategy and tactics are much more complex than those of most Western anarchist movements. Almost totally alienated from the social and political order in which they live, Western anarchists have tended to exhibit a 'purist' approach to strategy and tactics. They have operated so to speak, 'outside' the existing order, hoping and working for a spontaneous and dramatic collapse of that order from the ruins of which they believe will emerge the new order of anarchy. From this stance, they have rarely been called upon to make compromises which might endanger their principles.[1] But their 'purism' has been achieved at the expense of effectiveness. They have struck, and they continue to strike, at the existing order, occasionally dealing it swingeing blows; but they have never conquered. Their movement waxes, then wanes, withering for want of successful deeds. The Sarvodayite anarchists, in contrast, are far from being totally alienated from the Indian social and political order. There is much that they dislike about that order, both the traditional order and, more especially, the 'modern' order that is emerging; but they feel that they belong to that order; and they work 'inside' it. Their historical origins and their resolute adherence to Non-violence have endowed their movement with the blessing of legitimacy. The state that they wish eventually to dispense with is not wholly evil; it responds to some extent to their demands; and, in any case, it is not an abstract horror: at any given time, its appearance, good, bad, or indifferent, merely reflects the level of consciousness of its citizens. The state will disappear, 'wither away', as and when men become capable of living without it. In addition, the constructive approach of Sarvodaya precludes a 'purist' strategy. Creating the new social order within the womb of the old, they need the assistance of the Government to help bring the new order to birth: they need, for

[1] There have been some notable instances of 'compromise' by Western anarchists; Kropotkin, for example, supported the Allies in World War One; and leading anarchists, including Garcia Oliver, joined the Republican Government in 1936 during the Spanish Civil War. When anarchists lack influence the temptation to compromise is correspondingly less.

example, legislation to effect the piecemeal changes of property relations which are designed to lead to complete communism.

Those who chart Sarvodaya strategy and tactics, therefore, face a more demanding task than most Western anarchists have faced. Steering a course in the waters of non-conventional politics presents many hazards. Whether they will reach their final port is problematical. The great danger, from this point of view, is that they will be tempted into the smoother waters of conventional politics. The history of the British Co-operative Movement provides a warning of the hazards. Setting out 150 years ago on the same journey to voluntary communism, with the same joyful word 'Community' on their lips, the British co-operators have failed to reach Owen's 'New Moral World'. Instead, they put in at a safe and accessible harbour, and then succeeded in building a 'Co-operative sector' of the economy which has progressively accommodated itself to the private and state capitalist sectors. In the process their movement has served the function of integrating the working class into a social and political order which, whatever else it may be, is a whole world away from the vision which inspired Owen and his followers.

III. ISSUES RELATED TO THE DEPLOYMENT OF THE MOVEMENT

In the preceding section we were concerned with issues of strategy and tactics which involved, principally, the relation of the Sarvodaya movement with external bodies and forces. In the conduct of external relations any organization tends to have less freedom of manœuvre than it has in the conduct of internal relations. Necessarily, in the external sphere even the most powerful organization often finds itself responding to the activities of others. It may seek to capture and maintain the initiative, but in the nature of things it can never completely succeed. In the internal sphere, in contrast, an organization is not called on to respond to the activities of others, and decisions can be governed largely by its own judgement of what is the best use of its resources.[1] In this section we propose to con-

---

[1] The distinction between external and internal relations is analytical: in practice they do not give rise to two sharply separate spheres. In some instances decisions which might appear to be exclusively internal to an organization are defined by other organizations as external. Nevertheless, in general an organization has greater control over internal than external relations.

sider a select number of issues, decisions on which are largely in the hands of the movement itself. Among the more important matters falling within this category are those concerned with the movement's programme—the issues on which it chooses to fight— and its choice of 'technique' in fighting. The movement's current programme focuses on three items: Gramdan, Shanti Sena, and Khadi; and its technique of fighting is that of satyagraha.

Khadi

The content of The Triple Programme we have already discussed in considering the ideology of Sarvodaya. Here we are concerned not with the content of the three items but with problems arising from their selection as programmatic objectives. We begin first with Khadi, the oldest of the three. This item, along with other related village industries, was inherited, so to speak, from the Gandhi era. For Gandhi it had both a symbolic and a practical importance: Khadi symbolized the renaissance of the Indian village economy, provided work for the unemployed and under-employed, and constituted a means for the generation of disciplined non-violence. In the post-Gandhi era Khadi has lost none of these attributes. Local self-sufficiency in the basic essentials of food and shelter remains a key instrument for the achievement and mainten-ance of a non-violent social order. Even if it wanted to, the move-ment, therefore, could not, so long as it remains true to its purpose, dispense with Khadi, or something equivalent to it. In addition, although the Khadi industry has not progressed at the rate desired by Gandhi and is beset by numerous problems, it is now an established industry once again in India, employing hundreds of thousands of workers and giving rise to a network of co-operative organizations throughout the country. These organizations, as already noted, constitute a large part of the infrastructure on which the Sarvodaya movement is based. The 'revolutionary Gandhians' are faced with a continual struggle to convince Khadi workers that they are more than simply workers in a revived industry, but the movement regularly draws on the 'more conscious' Khadi workers as a source of recruitment to its cause.

From the perspective of a movement seeking to revolutionize the world, however, Khadi suffers from one major drawback: it can readily be labelled as a Gandhian 'fad', an atavistic attempt to put back the clock of technological progress. Mill-made cloth is

more durable and cheaper than Khadi; it already supplies the
large bulk of the market's demand;[1] it requires no comparable
government subsidy: what reason, other than sentimentality,
could justify the continuance of Khadi? The answer, of course,
is not to be found within the framework of conventional economics,
although even within this framework a case can be made supporting a limited role for cottage industries.[2] Within an economics
that recognizes the importance in developing countries of what
E. F. Schumacher has called 'intermediate technology' the case
is stronger still.[3] The real answer, however, as we have already
suggested, lies outside economics: the promotion of Khadi and
other village industries can be justified as a *political* decision designed to assist the establishment of a particular kind of structure
of social power. The economic costs of making such a decision are
not irrelevant, but, equally, they are not necessarily decisive. To
decide against Khadi on economic grounds does not avoid a
political decision: it is to decide for a structure of power determined by the market and by those who can influence market forces.

Nevertheless, the conventional wisdom of professional economists and the forces of the market make the promotion of Khadi
a difficult task. We have already seen that, of the items in The
Triple Programme, Khadi (including other village industries) was
perceived by the leaders as the least important item. To explore
further their attitudes to Khadi, they were, therefore, asked
whether they agreed or disagreed with the following statement:
'The production of Khadi will be important for some time to come
but we must expect that it will eventually give way to mill-made
cloth.'

Responses to this statement cannot be taken as more than suggestive of the leaders' commitment to Khadi, and of their understanding of the relationship between it and the Sarvodaya theory

[1] According to Vinoba, only 1·25% of the cloth requirement of the country is
met by Khadi.—Suresh Ram, *Towards a Total Revolution*, 1968, p. 52.

[2] cf. J. P. Lewis, *Quiet Crisis in India*, 1963, p. 60: 'In the light of Indian
factor endowments, it is perfectly possible that, with product adaptions and a
selective, indigenously innovated modernization of their techniques, some of
the traditional industries will be able to compete unassisted in Indian markets
for many years to come. I suspect that this may be the case, for example, with
some types of handlooming, although emphatically not with home-spinning.'

[3] E. F. Schumacher, *Roots of Economic Growth*, 1962, and *Sarvodaya*, XVII,
3 (1967). The Intermediate Technology Development Group, London, is now
actively engaged in promoting Schumacher's concept.

of social organization. The terms of the statement do not make this relationship clear. Clarity, in any case, is not possible on this issue, because of uncertainty about the precise nature and level of technology that is consistent with the ideal of local self-sufficiency. As some of the qualificatory comments of a few of the respondents made evident, Khadi in its present form—where spinning is done on the takli, the charkha, and the more recently introduced ambar charkha[1]—might disappear but be replaced by cloth produced in small, decentralized village factories using, as Vinoba himself has envisaged, power derived from atomic energy. However, the statement, juxtaposing as it does Khadi and mill-made cloth, was probably interpreted by most of our respondents as raising the issue of whether Khadi *in any form* could survive and not be displaced by cloth made in large, centralized, and urban-situated factories. Agreement with the statement may, therefore, be taken as signifying a lack of confidence in the movement's ability to achieve its programme in this respect, in the face of the continued development of conventional modern factory production.

Since 24 per cent of the respondent office-holders agreed with the statement,[2] we may conclude that there is a sizable minority, one in four, who lack confidence in the long-term prospects of the Khadi industry. Although we have no comparable data on confidence in the prospects of the other two items, it seems likely that, if the movement does change its programme in the future, Khadi may be the first item to go or to be substantially revised. No jettisoning of Khadi in the near future, however, is to be expected, for the reasons already given; and, if it is ever jettisoned, the problem of ensuring local self-sufficiency as the underpinning of a non-violent social order will remain.

Shanti Sena

In the case of Khadi the major tactical question is its place in the movement's programme. In the case of the Shanti Sena the major question is the purposes for which the army should be deployed. We have already noted that the main object of the Shanti Sena is

---

[1] The takli is a small hand-spinning tool, about 7 inches long; the charkha is a spinning-wheel which, unlike the traditional spinning-wheels used in the West, rotates horizontally rather than vertically; the ambar charkha is a more complex spinning-wheel with four spindles.

[2] N = 210.

to help prevent or to quell communal violence within India; in other words, the army is seen as having police rather than defence functions. However, its objects also embrace the latter, since they include helping to create such an atmosphere of non-violent strength that war may be outlawed from the international field; and the Shanti Sainiks pledge themselves not only not to take part in war but also to create the means and conditions of non-violent defence.[1]

The incursion of Chinese military forces across the disputed Macmahon line and in Ladakh in October 1962 not only presented the movement with the need to define its position on any war in which India herself was involved but also raised sharply the question of the deployment of the Shanti Sena. Within the wider Gandhian movement in India the Sino-Indian border war led to widely different reactions. Some well-known 'political Gandhians', such as the former President of the Republic, Rajendra Prasad, supported the Government's policy of armed resistance on the ground that non-violent resistance was simply infeasible. Quoting statements of Gandhi condoning participation in war, they often conveniently omitted to mention his view that the practice of non-violence is always superior to the use of violence. For Gandhians who could not accept such a line several other choices seemed available.[2] One was to investigate the merits of the case, and, if the investigation showed the Indian Government to be in the right, to give moral support to the war, but to refrain from direct participation in the war effort. Another was to try to organize and to offer non-violent resistance in defence of the country's territorial integrity. Yet a third choice was that of the war resister. Such a person would not be concerned with the rights and wrongs of the conflict. He would, says Vasant Nargolkar, an adherent of this view, 'simply throw himself in between the combatants so far as physically possible and try to stop the insensate mutual killing through the spiritual force generated by his willing self-immolation. His stand would be that war is an unmitigated evil and, no matter whether it is started by a nation or thrust upon it, it leads to total disaster and hence more rational methods of settling

[1] A number of the Sarvodaya leaders are members of the War Resisters' International and have participated in the largely abortive World Peace Brigade. Jayaprakash Narayan is a co-Chairman of the Brigade and Siddharaj Dhadda is Secretary of its Asian Council.

[2] See Vasant Nargolkar, 'Himalayan War', *Seminar*, 46 (June 1963).

disputes or resisting aggression have to be investigated and pursued.'[1]

The reaction of Vinoba and Sarva Seva Sangh to the conflict was rather different from any of these. The Chinese action was defined by Vinoba as aggression and labelled 'absolutely wrong';[2] and a resolution of the Sangh declared: 'although we remain firm in our fundamental faith of non-participation in war, our full sympathy is with India.'[3] Further, Vinoba repeated his assertion first made in 1957, that 'Gramdan is a defence measure', adding: 'I hold that at this time the more we can develop our programme of Gramdan, the more we shall contribute toward world peace and unity in India. It may even check China's programme of expansionism. It may not affect the Chinese policy . . . but Gramdan will certainly check the strength of their aggression.'[4] Vinoba also confessed that he had not been happy about the work of the Shanti Sena so far, and he continued: 'I hope that all the Shanti Sainiks will recognise their true function at this juncture and make their full contribution towards the maintenance of *internal* peace. This will be our special responsibility the fulfilment of which will lead towards non-violence and make the nation strong.'[5]

In its resolution passed at the 14th Sarvodaya Conference, at Vedchi, Sarva Seva Sangh in effect endorsed Vinoba's view and urged every believer in Non-violence to 'devote all his energies to the task of increasing the people's power of non-violent resistance'. It added, however, an explicit reference to the role of the Shanti Sena: 'The thought of non-violent resistance immediately brings to mind the idea of going to the front and facing the aggression. It is a matter of joy and congratulation that many Shanti Sainiks have expressed their eagerness to offer their lives for such a programme. However, in present conditions a programme of this nature could be undertaken only after serious consideration.' Instead of the Shanti Sena itself undertaking a symbolic act of non-violent resistance, the Sangh proposed a programme designed to 'awaken the *capacity* for non-violent resistance *among the people of the border area*'.[6] This moderate

---

[1] ibid.
[2] *Sarvodaya*, XII, 6 (Dec. 1962), p. 204.
[3] ibid., p. 209.
[4] ibid., p. 205.
[5] loc. cit., emphasis added.
[6] ibid., p. 210, emphasis added.

proposal was implemented; Shanti Sainiks were asked to volunteer for constructive peace work in the border area; and several Peace Centres have subsequently been established.[1]

Not all Sarvodayites were satisfied with such a limited programme. With volunteers from peace groups in other countries, some of them participated in the Delhi–Peking Friendship March (March 1963 to January 1964), sponsored by the World Peace Brigade and the Shanti Sena Mandal, and led by Shankarrao Deo, a former General Secretary of Congress and the first Secretary of both the Sarvodaya Samaj and the Sarva Seva Sangh. The March received the blessing of Vinoba and the active support of Jayaprakash Narayan. But, although it did useful propaganda work in the face of a largely hostile Indian press, it ran into many difficulties, and was abandoned when the Chinese authorities refused it permission to enter China.[2] Other Sarvodayites, including some of the most active leaders, such as Jagannathan, Thakurdas Bang, Harivallabh Parekh, and Gora, took the initial steps at the Vedchi conference to organize a new body, the Shanti Dal, whose objects were to include explicit reference to organized efforts at war resistance. Vinoba's reaction to this step was to agree that such resistance was one possible mode of action open to the non-violent revolutionary, but that it was not the mode he himself favoured. As he jokingly put it to one of the organizers, those with no head may go ahead! In the event, the new body proved abortive, although the spirit behind it undoubtedly represented a not insignificant current of thought in the movement.

In order to probe the leaders' attitudes to the general issue of the Shanti Sena's role, the questionnaire included the statement: 'If China renews her aggression, the Shanti Sena should be asked to go to the battle areas to offer non-violent resistance.' Agreement with the statement could fairly be taken to imply favouring a more militant course of action than the one approved by Vinoba, the Sarva Seva Sangh, and the Shanti Sena Mandal.

The issue between the 'moderates' and the 'militants' may be partly a difference of judgement about what is tactically expedient. It is clear that, given its present strength, non-violent resistance by the Shanti Sena is most unlikely to prove effective. Any idea

[1] See Kusum Nargolkar, *In the Wake of the Chinese Thrust*, 1965.
[2] For accounts of the March see *Sarvodaya*, XII, 2 (Aug. 1963); XIII, 8 (Feb. 1964); and XIII, 9 (Mar. 1964).

that a group of Shanti Sainiks could physically get to the point of interposing themselves between the Chinese and Indian armies is out of the question. Nehru was prepared to permit and even to encourage constructive peace work in the border areas, but no Indian government is likely to permit activity of the kind envisaged by those who wished to form the Shanti Dal. In addition, there is no doubt that attempts to organize non-violent resistance by the Shanti Sena would arouse widespread public hostility and react on the movement's other activities. But it is not simply a question of the tactical expediency of deploying Shanti Sena forces in acts of non-violent resistance in situations such as that of October 1962. A much broader issue is also involved: the issue of 'negative' versus 'positive' satyagraha. This issue will be discussed later in this chapter. Here it suffices to note that the 'positive' satyagraha favoured by Vinoba questions the value of some symbolic acts of non-violent resistance. They may easily become no more than gestures to salve the conscience—a way of demonstrating that one's own hands are clean. In themselves they may do little or nothing to achieve the really important objects: the generation of the power of Non-violence among the people at large and the elimination of the conditions which give rise to violence. The difficulty, of course, is that the 'moderate' approach may be interpreted as—and may in fact be—simply a rationalization for doing nothing that is likely to offend the government or the chauvinist public. The 'militants' are conscious of the difficulties inherent in a policy of organized non-violent resistance, but they are suspicious of the motives that prompt at least some of the 'moderates'. They feel that, unless the movement is prepared to risk offending the government and the chauvinists, it will be discredited as the vanguard of the non-violent revolution.

Analysis of the leaders' responses to the statement that the Shanti Sena should be sent to the battle areas to offer non-violent resistance shows that this was an issue over which the office-holders were almost equally divided: 51 per cent of the respondents agreed with the statement.[1]

Gramdan

The third item of The Triple Programme, Gramdan, raises two

[1] N = 206. 9% did not answer this question, two respondents expressly stating their unwillingness to answer it.

important tactical questions: one is the issue of whether to deploy the movement's resources in spreading the Gramdan idea by obtaining more Gramdan declarations, or to concentrate on the development of existing Gramdan villages; the other issue relates to the redefinition of Gramdan in the shape of Sulabh Gramdan.

On the first issue the choice can be interpreted as one between different methods of propaganda: spreading the Gramdan idea by maximizing the number of Gramdan declarations, so that a strong feeling of movement towards the ultimate social objective is generated throughout the country; or spreading the Gramdan idea by providing examples of the superior results of Gramdan organization, a form of 'propaganda by the deed'. The arguments for choosing either course are strong. For the first it can be argued that, unless the movement spreads rapidly and extensively, it is likely to become bogged down. In favour of concentrating on development it can be argued that example is always more persuasive than precept, and that, in any case, there must be some development, some follow-up, in villages that have declared for Gramdan, otherwise there is a danger that the situation of the villagers will be *worsened*. Experience has shown that a typical reaction to a Gramdan declaration is overt and covert hostility on the part of opponents, including often the immediate withdrawal by traditional moneylenders of sources of credit, on the ground that the borrowers in a Gramdan village no longer own land to offer as security for a loan. If something must be done, then, it can be argued, it is better that much should be done.

By 1956, when the Bhoodan campaign was being superseded by the campaign for Gramdan, the movement had already 'acquired' nearly 2,000 villages, some 1,500 of them in Orissa, principally in the Koraput District. This number, it could be argued, was more than enough for the movement to cope with. If they could be developed they would serve as models of the new social order. Just as the Sarvodaya workers exemplify the new man, the Gramdan villages would exemplify the new social order. Further, it could be argued that not to concentrate on development would be to repeat in another form the weakness of the Bhoodan campaign—the failure to follow up, speedily and effectively, the donation of land by its redistribution. As Achyut Patwardhan pointed out, Vinoba's words go to the heart of his listeners. 'But when one visits the area which has given thousands of acres of land in Bhoodan, after six months, what does one find? A few landless have got land, but there is no trace of the new society whose song Vinobaji is singing. Life there is drab and stagnant as before.'[1]

On the other side, in favour of concentrating on getting more declarations of Gramdan, it could be argued that Gramdan is essentially a symbol of Sarvodaya values. As such, the important thing is to get it accepted, however gropingly, by as many people as possible in the shortest possible time. Success in this respect will breed success, so that within a foreseeable future the general climate of opinion in the country will be changed for the better. Furthermore, propagating Sarvodaya values in the form of persuading villagers to declare for Gramdan is the work for which the movement is uniquely well equipped and which only it can do. The movement, however, does not possess the resources of either finance or trained personnel to undertake development work. Such work, therefore, is better left to the Government, which, in its Community Development programme, has shown itself to be conscious of the need and aware of its responsibility. In any case, a central idea of Sarvodaya is that the people should be encouraged to take the initiative themselves rather than to rely on 'outside' help.

As can be seen, the issue is not clear-cut and the movement has in fact tried both to spread the Gramdan idea and to develop existing Gramdan villages. It remains, however, an issue in the sense that the movement has emphasized one more than the other at different times and that individual workers tend to lean one way rather than the other. At the end of 1955, when enthusiasm ran high, the 'development' protagonists, led by Annasahab Sahasrabudhe, came to the fore. For the three years 1956–9 a concentrated effort was made by the Sarva Seva Sangh to develop the Gramdan villages of Koraput. Annasahab, who headed the 'experiment', attracted several hundred workers to the area, many of them from 'outside' the movement, and substantial funds for development work were obtained from the Gandi Smarak Nidhi and the Khadi Commission as well as from Sarva Seva Sangh. The experiment, however, encountered many difficulties. The relations between the workers involved in the project were not always harmonious. There were several sources of friction, but

[1] *Bhoodan*, 16 Oct. 1957.

Annasahab himself complained of the 'unhealthy and unscientific' tendency to make a distinction between development work and propaganda for getting Gramdans—the former being regarded as 'reformist' and the latter as 'revolutionary'.[1] More important, relations with the Orissa State Government and its administrators were frequently strained. Annasahab, in a notable bout of self-criticism, took the blame for this on himself and his co-workers, but undoubtedly the faults were not all on one side. Friction in any case was inherent in a situation where the movement could be interpreted as aiming to set up a 'parallel government'. Some important results were achieved,[2] but, over-all, the experiment proved disappointing. In 1959, therefore, the Sarva Seva Sangh decided to call it off, leaving behind only a score or so workers to continue development efforts on a much more modest scale.

The Yelwal Conference of 1957, at which Union Government representatives publicly endorsed the Gramdan programme and undertook to promote co-ordination between Community Development work and the work of the movement, provided a justification for playing down the developmental and emphasizing the educative role of the movement. It could henceforth be argued that development was primarily the responsibility of the Government agencies. Practical results of the Government's decision have been slow to materialize, partly because Community Development is primarily a state rather than a Union Government responsibility and not all state governments are equally enthusiastic about Gramdan. Playing down the movement's developmental role does not, of course, mean that it makes no effort at all in this direction. Developmental work of its own is being done, much of it financed in recent years from funds raised by the War on Want organization in Britain. But such work by no means embraces all Gramdan villages. In 1965 a member of the Prabandh Samiti, in an interview with one of the authors, gave his opinion that 'real' development work was proceeding in no more than 500 of the then 8,000 or so Gramdan villages. Even this number was stretching the movement's resources to the limits.[3]

---

[1] *Bhoodan*, 2 Apr. 1958.

[2] A. W. Sahasrabudhe, *Report on Koraput Gramdans*, 1960.

[3] It was clear in talking to some leaders engaged in development work that in 1965 they were deliberately not encouraging further declarations of Gramdan, on the ground that they already had more than they could effectively cope with. This suggests that a reservoir of potential Gramdans was building up which

Vinoba's own position on this issue has varied, but his main emphasis has been on spreading the Gramdan idea. In 1957 when the 'development' protagonists were in the ascendancy, he endorsed the idea of the movement's building up a new social organization in selected Gramdan villages, as 'a laboratory experiment' and as an example to others. But, at the same time, he was careful to point out that 'the responsibility of reconstruction does not rest on us alone. It is a national responsibility and must be shared by the Government, the other political parties, and the people.'[1] A few months later, by which time the difficulties in Koraput were becoming apparent, he was even more explicit. Development work, he insisted, was not 'our prime responsibility'. How could it be, when the movement was trying to persuade the 500,000 villages of India to declare for Gramdan? The Community Development Programme had shown that crores (tens of millions) of rupees could achieve no commensurate results if the people played only a passive role. 'In a gramdan village the dynamics must be provided by the people themselves. Their urge to bring about a change can be the only effective agent of development. . . . Development work has its own importance but a spontaneous gift of thousands of villages would affect the people more than the development work of a few villages.'[2] With specific reference to the Koraput experiment he insisted, later, that the movement's capacity to cope with the problems of development need not circumscribe the limits of Gramdan. In spite of the movement's 'best efforts for development work', it had not been able to approach more than 250 of the 1,200 Gramdan villages of Koraput. The conclusion, therefore, was obvious: 'Our main objective is to realize the latent creative capacity of the people and to harness it for village development.'[3] Since these words were spoken in 1958, he has not changed his position in any essential, and the call for a whirlwind campaign in the Autumn of 1965 in Bihar and elsewhere may be seen as the clearest expression of his view on this issue.

In order to determine how many of the office-holders shared Vinoba's view, they were asked whether they agreed or disagreed

could fairly readily be released when the call for the whirlwind campaign came later in that year.
[1] *Bhoodan*, 23 Jan. 1957.　[2] *Bhoodan*, 3 Apr. 1958.　[3] *Bhoodan*, 1 May 1958.

with this statement: 'The Movement should now concentrate on the development of existing Gramdan villages rather than on getting more declarations of Gramdan.' Our findings were as follows: 50 per cent agreed; 33 per cent disagreed; and 17 per cent rejected the alternatives posed and replied in effect that both development and more declarations were essential.[1]

In interpreting these findings it must be remembered that the questionnaire was administered just *before* the launching of the whirlwind campaign. The remarkable success of that campaign in multiplying the number of Gramdan declarations is virtually certain to have changed the views of many respondents on this issue. Indeed, it may be suggested that the success has finally decided the issue, since, given the movement's resources, it is plainly impossible for it to cope itself with the reconstruction of 140,000 Gramdan villages: the villagers themselves, as Vinoba had previously insisted, must be motivated to undertake this task.[2] But the issue is not, of course, resolved so simply. What has been called 'modelism' may now be at a discount, but even the protagonists of propagating the Gramdan idea are conscious that the overwhelming number of recent Gramdan declarations are no more than, in Jayaprakash's phrase, 'declarations of intent'. If they are to become more than 'paper Gramdans', the movement must take action to encourage the villagers to proceed rapidly to the second or pushti stage of Gramdan, even if this involves distribution of land to the landless and the setting up of Gram Sabhas on a *de facto* rather than on a *de jure* basis. Vinoba himself endorsed this view at the Rajgir Sammelan, October 1969, when he called for an ati-toofan (super whirlwind) campaign to consolidate Gramdan villages.[3] With the virtual achievement of Bihardan, it has become crucial for the movement to show that it is succeeding in generating, among the people of at least one state of the Union, a spontaneous enthusiasm for social reconstruction in the direction of the ideal of Gram Swarajya. The minority of our respondents who stated that both development and more declarations were essential might be thought, therefore, to have made the most sensible judgement. But, of course, deciding for 'both' does not

---

[1] N = 215.
[2] See *People's Action*, 3, 7 & 8 (July–Aug. 1969, special number on Gramdan Development), pp. 7–9.
[3] *People's Action*, 3, 11 (Nov. 1969), p. 28.

avoid the dilemma altogether. The movement's resources *are* limited, and there is always the question of how best to deploy them. In 1965 Vinoba inspired the decision to deploy them in one way rather than the other, to concentrate on spreading the Gramdan idea rather than on developing existing Gramdans. The results of the whirlwind campaign have not yet fully demonstrated that it was the wisest course of action for the movement to take. If many of the new Gramdans are not consolidated, if too many 'declarations of intent' are not followed by observable acts of social reconstruction, disillusionment with the whole concept of Gramdan may become widespread, and the movement may experience a severe and perhaps irreversible set-back. But this much at least may already be said in justification of the whirlwind campaign: it did lead to an *expansion* of the movement's resources, particularly of workers, even if that expansion proved to be considerably less than was hoped for.[1]

The second issue related to Gramdan, that of its redefinition in the form of Sulabh Gramdan, presents the most obvious appearance of being a pure tactical issue. We have already[2] discussed the substantive differences between Sulabh Gramdan and Gramdan in its original form, and remarked that the former represents an important concession to the principles of private property, particularly in the provision that 19/20ths of donated land may be retained in the possession of the donor and passed on to his heirs. There remain for discussion here the reasons for the concession and the attitude of the leaders to it.

To take the latter point first, the respondents were presented with the categorical statement: 'Sulabh Gramdan involves too many concessions to the principles of private property.' It should be noted, again, that the questionnaire was administered in 1965, before the whirlwind campaign for Sulabh Gramdan, and that opinions may therefore have changed markedly since then. Nevertheless, it is striking that nearly two-thirds of the leaders (64 per cent) agreed with the statement.[3] Less than 10 per cent

---

[1] One notable feature of the campaign for Bihardan was the involvement in it, on a part-time basis, of large numbers of teachers and Khadi workers who had not previously been active participants. It remains true, however, that Sarvodaya is still a long way from becoming what it sets out to be, a 'people's movement', as distinct from a movement largely confined to the Sarvodaya workers.

[2] Chapter Two above.

[3] N = 216.

of those replying to the question qualified their agreement or disagreement in any way; and those who recognized that Sulabh Gramdan does involve concessions to the principles of private property, but added that they were necessary concessions, were counted as disagreeing. The finding suggests a remarkable disparity between the views of most office-holders and the official policy of the movement on a matter quite central to the Sarvodaya programme. This would certainly appear to be an instance in which an important decision taken by the movement did not correspond with the real views of those who were a party to it, although, of course, given the decision-making procedure in Sarva Seva Sangh, any one member could have prevented its adoption.

It seems likely that the success of the whirlwind campaign has confirmed in the eyes of most office-holders the wisdom of the revision. The pace of Gramdan declarations in the early sixties had slowed up considerably, and the adoption of Sulabh Gramdan can be seen as a necessary preliminary to the further advance of the movement. This was a case of 'One step backwards, two steps forward', a tactical principle which Gandhi had in mind when he said, 'Sometimes a step back is a prelude to a step forward.'[1] As a result of the 'step back', the movement in the space of four years increased more than fifteen-fold the number of Gramdan declarations, and, in so doing, moved from Gramdan through Blockdan and Districtdan to Statedan. Whether the expansion of the movement has been bought at too high a price, the dilution of the content of Gramdan not compensating for the extension of Gramdan, it is too early yet to judge. Much depends on whether the revolutionary objectives can be kept clearly in sight. If they are not, Sulabh Gramdan may in retrospect mark a significant step by the movement towards accommodation with the world as it is, a step comparable to the British Co-operative Movement's progress from community-building to storekeeping.

There is no evidence at all that Sulabh Gramdan represented a *conscious* attempt at accommodation. Nothing more than considerations of tactical expediency are necessary to explain the decision to adopt it. However, it would be a mistake to think that calculated foot-stepping is all that was involved. The decision may also be seen as an application of Vinoba's distinctive approach to

[1] N. K. Bose, op. cit., p. 193. The statement was made in 1942.

satyagraha, an approach which reverses the typical application of
coercive power from 'harsh to harsher to harshest' and proceeds
instead from 'gentle to gentler to gentlest'. To a consideration of
this approach we shall now turn.

Satyagraha: 'negative' and 'positive'

As is well known, the term 'satyagraha' was coined by Gandhi as
a more accurate description of his 'method' than the term 'passive
resistance'. It is often translated as 'non-violent resistance', although its literal meaning is 'holding fast to Truth'. 'Truth force'
perhaps comes nearest to Gandhi's meaning, since the search for
Truth was central to all his ideas and activities. Non-violence,
in the positive sense of Love, he saw as Truth's twin-principle: *the*
way to Truth. And Sarvodaya, the Welfare of All, was the term
which best expressed Truth in social relations.

Although his was clearly an integral philosophy, in which the
values of Truth, Love, and Sarvodaya were inextricably interwoven, interpreters have often overlooked the fact. Perhaps the
most common approach to Gandhi is to ignore his metaphysics, to
dismiss lightly his social ideas, and to proceed to abstract from
him a technique. Satyagraha is then presented as Gandhi's principal contribution to political action, a novel technique of resolving
conflict without the employment of physical violence. Those who
interpret satyagraha in this way sometimes, but not always,
realize that it is not a technique to be taken up and put down at
will. They appreciate Gandhi's insistence that the commitment to
Non-violence should be on the basis of principle rather than of
expediency. And they may also recognize that he saw satyagraha
as involving persuasion rather than non-violent coercion. The object of a Gandhian satyagraha campaign—in Gandhi's eyes at
least—was to convert the opponent, not to compel him to grant
concessions against his will.[1]

Looked at in this way, satyagraha as a form of non-violent
action is seen as a potentially powerful weapon—a weapon whose
power was frequently demonstrated by Gandhi, and which has
been employed with varying degrees of success in countries other
than India since his death, particularly in the U.S.A., where

[1] Of course, Gandhi's satyagraha campaigns were often experienced by his
opponents as 'coercive'. To intend to persuade is no guarantee that one's
actions will not be felt as coercive.

it has been used by the followers of Martin Luther King. The
questions then arise: Why has it not been used by the Sarvodaya
movement to achieve its objectives? Why has Gandhi's successor,
Vinoba, not employed it to promote Bhoodan, Gramdan, and the
abolition of landlessness? Why has he apparently disavowed this
most celebrated Gandhian technique? Even to sympathetic Western
observers of the movement these questions are at first sight puzzling. Coming as they often do from backgrounds of radical social
and political protest, it appears to them that the movement lacks
militancy. And, searching for an explanation of this, they attribute
it, not implausibly, as we have seen, to the ambiguous relations
that exist between the movement and the ruling Congress party.

In considering such questions, it should, however, be pointed
out that it is incorrect to say the movement has not employed
satyagraha in its characteristic Gandhian form. We have already
mentioned Gora's campaign against pomp and power in politics. But,
Gora and his associates apart, it is also true that local satyagraha
campaigns have been conducted occasionally by other Sarvodaya
leaders. One such occasion was a campaign against evictions of
tenants in Bihar in 1955. At the Sarvodaya Sammelan of that year
Vinoba had drawn attention to the problem. 'We have made it a
point in our movement', he said, 'to approach landlords, explain
to them the wrong they are doing, ask for land-gifts from them, and
rehabilitate the evicted peasants. If the landlords do not respond
we will have to ask the peasants to stick to their land, whatever the
consequences.'[1] Taking this as their cue, various Sarvodaya
workers offered satyagraha with and in behalf of evicted tenants;
but the campaign was not persisted in. More recently, Jagannathan, the leader of the movement in Tamilnad (Madras State),
initiated in July 1965 a satyagraha campaign directed towards
securing for a group of tillers in the village of Vilampatti the lease
rights of cultivation of land worked by them but owned by a large
absentee landowner who sub-let his land to intermediaries.[2]

The movement, therefore, has not completely set its face against
the use of non-violent resistance. Nevertheless, it remains true

[1] Suresh Ram, *Vinoba and His Mission*, 1962 edn., p. 143.
[2] About 700 people were involved in the campaign, 350 of whom were
arrested, including the Reverend Ralph Keithahn, a former American missionary
and now a leading Sarvodayite and nominated member of the Sangh. For
accounts of the campaign see articles by Jagannathan and Keithahn in *Sarvodaya*,
XV, 2 (Aug. 1965) and XV, 3 (Sept. 1965).

that it has not used it to promote its central programmatic objectives. One reason why it has not is eminently 'tactical'. It is
argued that an essential prerequisite of the successful use of
satyagraha is that the consensus of public opinion should clearly
support the resisters. In the case of tenant evictions public opinion could be fairly held to support the claims of the tenants, while
in the Vilampatti campaign the rights claimed were consistent
with the Government's land reforms aimed at the abolition of
intermediaries in land-holding. However, with respect to both
Bhoodan and Gramdan, and also the more general object of
abolishing landlessness, there is as yet no favourable public
consensus. Opinion may be moving in favour of land for all tillers
and common ownership, but it has not yet reached the point where
a consensus on these principles may be said to exist. In this cir-
cumstance, the use of satyagraha would be unsuccessful. That there
is wisdom in this 'tactical' argument is suggested by the frequently unsuccessful uses of 'satyagraha' by various groups in
post-independence India, a most notable failure being its use by
the Lohia Socialists, who believed that 'satyagraha' could be a
principal weapon in their armoury.[1]

In defending the movement's line on the use of non-violent
resistance, however, Sarvodayites go beyond simple tactical arguments. Moral considerations are also involved. In the absence of a
favourable public consensus, satyagraha, it is suggested, would be
unjustified in promoting the movement's programme, because it
would be an attempt to compel the unpersuaded majority to
adopt the principles of the minority. This argument is in line
with Gandhi's warning that civil disobedience would cease to be
a normally appropriate technique once responsible government
with proper channels for the expression of grievances had replaced the alien rule of the British.[2]

[1] cf. M. Weiner, *Party Politics in India*, 1957, p. 40.

[2] W. H. Morris-Jones, *The Government and Politics of India*, 1964, p. 37
See also his 'Mahatma Gandhi—political philosopher?' in *Political Studies*
VIII (Feb. 1960). Vinoba has elaborated this point. Questioned on the use of
satyagraha in post-independence India, Vinoba points out that people forget that
'the whole context has changed after freedom. (1) We could then (i.e. before
1947) say "Quit India" to the British. We can never say this to any group or
interest in India. (2) There was then no democracy in India. (3) The British did
not have the moral right to rule here. So a "negative" satyagraha was permissible
against them. Now we have to bring about a change of heart in our own people.'
He adds: 'Universal friendliness and absence of bitterness and enmity is the

But there is more to it than this, and to understand the 'more' it is necessary to look afresh at the whole concept of satyagraha as generally understood.

It can be argued that Vinoba's major contribution to the evolution of Non-violence lies precisely in his clarification of the difference between Non-violence as a technique and Non-violence as a principled way of life. When Non-violence is used as a technique in conflict situations, it is often simply another way of overpowering the opponent. Because it seeks to avoid or to minimize violence,[1] it may be morally superior to other ways, but it still belongs to the realm of (coercive) power politics. Such Non-violence is, in fact, not satyagraha but what Gandhi called duragraha—stubborn resistance in a cause that is prejudged.[2] In duragraha the objective is to change the policy of the opponent by applying pressure with skill and in sufficient strength to force him to stand down or, at least, to make concessions. Duragraha focuses on the misdeeds of the opponent, assumes that right is on the one side only, and that the proper outcome of the struggle is a result which acknowledges the rightness of those who practise it. It is thus clearly a form of non-violent coercion. Satyagraha, in contrast, is not. Not only is it not coercive in intent but, to the extent that the opponent makes concessions because he feels coerced, it is not genuine satyagraha. The objective of satyagraha is a constructive transforming of relationships in a manner which not only effects a change of policy but also assures a restructuring of the situation leading to the conflict. It does not assume that the right is all on one side; it is always an 'experiment with truth'; and the outcome is always educative to both sides. While duragraha involves harassment and possible distress to the opponent, satyagraha is fundamentally supportive and reassuring to him. If necessary, the satyagrahi will call off the struggle, if he sees

---

first quality of a satyagrahi. This is being forgotten by people who resort to law-breaking on any excuse.'—*Bhoodan*, 2 Apr. 1958.

[1] Violence is rarely avoided altogether in non-violent action: the opponents typically respond by using violence, often in the hope that it will provoke the resisters to respond violently and thus legitimize the opponents' use of violence.

[2] For an illuminating analysis of the distinction, to which we are indebted, see Joan Bondurant, 'Satyagraha versus duragraha: the limits of symbolic violence', in G. Ramachandran & T. K. Mahadevan (eds.) *Gandhi—His Relevance for Our Times*, 1964. For a more general explication of satyagraha see J. Bondurant, *Conquest of Violence*, 1965.

that it is harming his opponent, and perform positive services to help him. The satyagrahi will do this because he recognizes that even his opponent is his brother, who must be accorded the dignity and respect that is the right of all men.

From this perspective satyagraha appears not so much as a special technique in the politics of power but rather as an expression of a new kind of politics—the politics of love. The revolution Vinoba is engaged in is a revolution to be achieved by love and not by coercive power, however non-violent.[1] He rejects, therefore, the suggestion that he has abandoned satyagraha, that he is no longer a satyagrahi. Explaining his conception of satyagraha, he asked: 'What kind of power is it which we believe inheres in true satyagraha and what is its form?' 'Its characteristic mark', he answered, 'is that it disarms the opponent . . . the very sight of it compels a man to think where he had been unwilling to think, and to purify his thinking where his thoughts had been running on different lines. Where this doesn't take place, and some form of pressure is used, satyagraha loses its power. The greater the element of pressure, the weaker will be its power.'[2]

In Vinoba's view, satyagraha can be distinguished from both violence and 'tactical' non-violence by the direction in which it moves. 'In the domain of violence', he explains, 'men proceed from the gentle weapon to the sharp and sharper ones. But the process of the working of non-violence is entirely different. If our gentle Satyagraha does not yield the desired fruit, we must infer that there is something wanting in our gentleness itself and we must, therefore, render it finer, gentler. If Satyagraha evolves in this manner, its vitality and effectiveness would grow.'[3] Thus, since satyagraha is always to be practised *with* someone and not

---

[1] We have argued (Chapter Four above) that some elements of normative power are involved in Sarvodaya politics. But the disjunction between the politics of love and the politics of power, expecially in view of most people's conceptions of power, conveys perhaps most strikingly the difference between Sarvodaya and ordinary politics, both conventional and non-conventional. It is the mark of a new idea that it is difficult to express in familiar concepts.

[2] Quoted in Bjorn Merker, 'Vinoba's Vision', *Peace News*, 9 July 1965. This article represents a succinct presentation of Vinoba's approach. Interestingly enough, it also represents a revision of its author's earlier views, which were highly critical of the 'gentle, gentler, gentlest' approach and in favour of 'negative' satyagraha. See 'Gandhians or Gandhi?' in *Peace News*, 16 & 23 Apr. 1958. As with some other Western radicals, Merker's initial espousal of 'militancy' dissolved in a fuller appreciation of Vinoba's philosophy of action.

[3] Quoted in Suresh Ram (1962), op. cit., pp. 140-1.

against someone, if the original effort fails, we should look for more gentle methods. For example, if landowners refuse to admit the injustice of their position, instead of organizing non-violent pressure, the poor and the landless could unilaterally initiate actions, such as providing their services free to the landowners, which would undermine the basis of private property. Or, to take another example, if Gramdan in its original form is seen by landowners as hostile to their interests, Sulabh Gramdan, in which what they believe to be their legitimate interests are safeguarded, may be substituted. Such an approach, it is suggested, would be 'gentler' but not weaker; it would be more and not less persuasive; and it would bring about changes likely to prove lasting and meaningful.[1]

Vinoba has epitomized his conception of satyagraha by suggesting that it involves an emphasis on non-violent *assistance* rather than non-violent *resistance*. The 'gentle, gentler, gentlest' approach, however, does not mean that the satyagrahi should quietly submit to evil. It is not a version of, or reversion to, the doctrine of 'non-resistance'.[2] The maxim 'resist not evil' is interpreted to mean: do not let evil *condition* your actions. It is futile for the satyagrahi to respond to the evil of violence by resisting its outward and obvious manifestations. His task is the more fundamental one of eliminating the conditions which give rise to violence. If, for example, people are still wedded to the notion of violent defence of their country, a campaign of anti-militarism will achieve nothing positive. They will cease to be so wedded only when they have come to realize that they have the moral power within themselves to rely on non-violent defence.

On the basis of this approach, Vinoba, therefore, has refused to be deflected from his main course into protest and resistance campaigns against the Indian Government and the landowners. The possibility of using 'negative' satyagraha in the future to achieve the movement's programmatic objectives cannot be ruled out altogether. But if it is used, it will be used only when the consensus of public opinion is overwhelmingly behind the movement. By

[1] The approach displays psychological insight. An opponent is likely to react most wildly when he feels himself threatened or isolated.

[2] A principled form of pacifism whose adherents generally seek not to act against evil situations, even by non-violent methods, but to ignore them. The doctrine is espoused by various Christian sects, such as the Mennonites or Amish.—Sharp, op. cit., Appendix One.

the time that point is reached, if it ever is, the forces of love may be so strong that the last-ditch defenders of the old order may well surrender before the battle is joined.

If this is a correct explication of Vinoba's approach to Non-violence, how well is it understood by his followers in the Sar-vodaya movement? In an attempt to determine this point, the leaders were asked whether they agreed or disagreed with the statement: 'While persuasion should be used as much as possible, the Movement should also be prepared to organize satyagraha campaigns as a means of abolishing landlessness.' The statement is not unambiguous, since, as we have seen, Vinoba regards him-self as being engaged already in a genuine satyagraha campaign. But it may be fairly assumed that, in this context, 'satyagraha' was interpreted in the 'negative' sense of active resistance or inter-vention rather than in the 'positive' sense characteristic of Vinoba. It is significant, therefore, that no less than 66 per cent of the respondents agreed with the statement.[1] This is a surprisingly high proportion, and the finding suggests that a substantial major-ity of leaders in the summer of 1965 were dissatisfied with the strategy of the movement and would have preferred a more mili-tant approach. The time factor, however, may have been significant. At that point in the movement's career there were signs that a feeling of the need for greater militancy, for some dramatic forward move, was building up. If so, this feeling soon found expression for some in the Vilampatti (negative) satyagraha cam-paign. For most Sarvodaya workers, however, it probably found ample expression in the whirlwind campaign for Gramdan launched a few months later.

In concluding this excursus of Sarvodaya strategy and tactics, it is perhaps as well to repeat the point made in the opening section: the mode of thinking of most Sarvodayites is not conducive to thinking in terms of strategy and tactics. This is true of Vinoba, though less so of Jayaprakash Narayan, with his political exper-ience and background. In making 'decisions' affecting strategy and tactics, Vinoba's influence, as in most other decisions, has un-doubtedly been preponderant. The issues that we have selected for discussion do not suggest that no 'mistakes' have been made, but the overwhelming impression is that of 'generalship' of a very high order. It is very doubtful whether the movement would have

[1] N = 209.

achieved so much if its strategy and tactics had been in the hands of a lesser person than Vinoba. The conclusion is somewhat para-doxical when we remember that we are referring to a 'saint' and not a general or a politician. But such an apparent paradox lies at the heart of the Gandhian style of politics: what is morally the right course of action frequently turns out to be also the most expedient course of action in the long term. It is not without reason that Gandhi sometimes appears to the less perceptive to present the face of his polar opposite: Machiavelli. For Gandhian Non-violence is nothing less than Machiavellism redeemed.[1]

As the movement's 'general', Vinoba certainly seems to have been reasonably successful to date in maintaining one of the most important assets of any army: a high morale among the troops. Having assembled his army in the enthusiastic years of Bhoodan, he inevitably lost some followers when the going became more difficult. But morale among those that stayed with him has re-mained high, judging from the responses of the leaders in 1965 to the statement: 'The Movement has had its ups and downs but we may confidently expect that it will take a new surge forward in the next few years.' 88 per cent of all respondents agreed with the statement, 4 per cent disagreeing, and 8 per cent replying 'don't know' or leaving the question blank.[2] The statement echoed a widely reported statement of Vinoba himself. At the Raipur Con-ference in December 1963 Vinoba, in explaining the new ap-proach of Sulabh Gramdan, said: 'There are ups and downs in a man's life. There are also ups and downs in societies and nations and they also get tired as individual men do. Then it seems as though they have become passive. This is equally true of move-ments. The period of our downward tendency is, however, over and that of our onward march is coming. We should, therefore, rededicate ourselves to our mission with a new zeal.'[3]

The Raipur Conference at which these words were spoken is generally regarded in the movement as one of the more successful

---

[1] See the illuminating study by Simone Panter-Brick, *Gandhi against Machiavellism*, 1966.

[2] N = 228. Responses to the statement provide, of course, only a very crude indicator of morale. The statement was the last of a series, and included partly as a way of striking an optimistic rather than a pessimistic closing note. There is no reason, however, for believing that this unduly affected the nature of the responses.

[3] *Sarvodaya*, XIII, 8 (Feb. 1964), p. 286.

of recent years. A Western observer who was present throughout reported thus:

Vinoba's presence and inspiration clearly gave a much needed lift to the movement. The year 1969, the centenary of Gandhi's birth, was set as the target year for the accomplishment of the basic structure of Gramswaraj (village self-government). It is a significant date and one which conveniently fits into the current myth among Sarvodaya workers. It is now twelve years since Vinoba publicly assumed the mantle of Gandhi by launching the Bhoodan movement. The first six of these were fat years during which enthusiasm ran high and many new workers, including not a few disillusioned politicians, were swept into the movement in the wake of its initial successes. Then followed six lean years as it became evident that the movement would not achieve in the time set its declared objective of 50 million acres of Bhoodan land. During this period the pace of the movement slackened, new recruits were slow in coming forward, and some of the former enthusiasts found reasons for concentrating on other matters. On the assumption of some kind of natural rhythm in the life of social movements, it is anticipated that in the six years 1963–9 the Sarvodaya movement will wax fat once again. Whether this view will prove to be anything more than a self-sustaining myth remains to be seen. . . . But the Raipur conference convinced at least this observer that (Gandhi's) spirit is still alive in India and may yet provide through Vinoba the inspiration for the realization of that apparently impossible dream—a non-violent social revolution.[1]

Whether the foundations of Gramswaraj may be said to be truly laid, now that the Gandhi Centenary has come and gone, may be doubted, but it is clear that the Raipur Conference did mark the beginning of a revival of the movement. Eighteen months later the revival had gone sufficiently far to permit the launching of the successful whirlwind campaign for Bihardan. Perhaps the propagation of the myth of the six fat years to follow the six lean years is an instance of a self-fulfilling prophecy.

[1] Gaston Gerard, 'The Saints in Session', *Anarchy*, 42 (1964).

CHAPTER SEVEN

ACHIEVEMENTS, OBSTACLES, AND PROPOSALS: THE LEADERS' PERCEPTIONS

IN the preceding chapters we have discussed: what the Sarvodaya movement is seeking to achieve (its ideology, including programme); who leads the movement (as far as can be judged from the social characteristics of its principal office-holders); the social psychological relations that obtain among the leaders; the organization that has been developed to carry forward the movement; and other ways and means (strategy and tactics) that have been adopted to achieve its ends. The main focus throughout the discussion has been on the leaders as a single collectivity; and the major source of our empirical data has been information supplied by the leaders in response to a questionnaire, most of the questions in which were 'closed' rather than 'open' ended, calling for the respondent to select one or more of several answers provided.

The discussion has covered some of the more important aspects relevant to the study of any social movement, but it has by no means covered them all. In particular, we have not considered, except incidentally, what the movement has actually achieved; for example, the impact of Bhoodan and Gramdan on village life in India, and the part the campaigns for them have played in actually bringing about the non-violent social revolution for which the movement stands. Discussion of this important aspect is outside the scope of the present study and would call for different, and also more difficult, research techniques. However, by using the questionnaire method we can obtain information about the leaders' *perceptions* of the movement's achievements. These perceptions may be very different from the *actual* achievements (although not irrelevant to them); and they may tell us more about the leaders, their opinions and their feelings, than about the actual course of the non-violent revolution. In addition, by the same method we can obtain information not about the actual obstacles the movement faces but about the leaders' perceptions of those obstacles. And, arising naturally from such perceptions, we can find out what proposals the leaders have for overcoming the perceived obstacles. In this chapter, therefore, we shall be concerned to present our findings with regard to these three matters: the leaders' perceptions of the movement's achievements; their perceptions of obstacles to the further progress of the movement; and their proposals to make the movement more effective. The discussion will inevitably involve aspects of the movement already considered, but in so doing it may help to integrate parts which belong to a single whole but which have been separated for purposes of analysis and presentation.

Two general points may be made about the material presented in this chapter. First, it is based on answers to open-ended questions. This means that the respondents had greater freedom in answering than they had in replying to the more structured questions. In a sense, in dealing with such a question the leaders 'speak for themselves' without clear guide-lines from the researchers, although the form of the question and its position in relation to other questions may influence to some extent the answers given. The absence of systematically structured response, however, makes analysis more difficult. Some respondents used their freedom to expound their views at length; others chose to be laconic. Again, some obviously gave a great deal of thought before replying; others may have replied, so to speak, 'off the cuff'. But content analysis, however crude, requires that each reply should be given, in some sense, equal weight, if we are to use the answers as indicating views of leaders, or groups of leaders, as a whole rather than as simply the interesting expressions of individuals. For these reasons this part of our study should be regarded as largely exploratory, designed to reveal points which may merit further, more systematic, investigation. Apart from this, the material may be of use in the evaluation of responses to some of the more structured questions. For example, the use of 'negative' satyagraha was recommended by some respondents as a proposal to make the movement more effective. All respondents were asked (at a later stage in the questionnaire) to express an opinion on this point. But only a small minority of leaders made the point in replying to an open-ended question. It may be fairly assumed that those who, without prompting, proposed satyagraha felt most strongly about it, but they were still only a minority. The fact that a majority of the leaders favoured satyagraha, when asked to express an opinion, then appears in a somewhat different light. The majority may have been made up largely of people who did not feel *very* strongly about it, certainly not strongly enough to bring it to the researchers' attention.

The second general point concerns the mode of analysis. In this chapter, although we are still concerned with the leaders as a whole, we extend the analysis further by distinguishing groups or categories within the leadership. Previously we have been concerned mainly with 'external' comparisons: comparisons between the Sarvodaya leaders and the general population or leaders of other movements. Such comparisons are not practical in dealing with the material used in this chapter. But 'internal' comparisons between different groups of leaders are. In differentiating the leaders, however, only one variable will be employed here: level of office held. This variable is related to the constitutional structure of Sarva Seva Sangh. Although the organization exhibits a very low degree of hierarchical structuring, it is possible to distinguish three levels within the group of office-holders who compose our population. The first (top) level comprises members, including permanent invitees, of the Prabandh Samiti and nominated members of the Sangh; the second level includes Secretaries of State Sarvodaya Mandals and the District Representatives; and the third level is made up of District Convenors. Some individual leaders occupy offices at more than one level. Where this is the case, they have been placed in the level appropriate to the highest office they hold. For convenience and brevity, the three levels are referred to in the text by the title of the office whose holders predominate at each level: Samiti, Representative, and Convenor. These preliminaries behind us, we may now turn to consider the perceptions of the leaders.

1. PERCEPTIONS OF ACHIEVEMENTS

The data under this general heading were obtained from answers to the question: 'Which in your opinion are the most important achievements of this Movement since Independence?'

Examination of the answers suggested eight broad categories, not necessarily exclusive of each other, which might perhaps be better seen as clusters of items which shared a common orientation.

One further category was reserved for answers which denied that the movement had any achievements to its credit. The answer of only one respondent fell into this category. It may, therefore, be eliminated from the analysis as an oddity, along with a few answers of a residual, miscellaneous kind. The eight categories were as follows:

1. *Promotion of land reform*

Included in this category are answers relating to the movement's achievements in the fields of Bhoodan and Gramdan, both answers in general terms and those specifically in terms of number of acres donated and number of Gramdan declarations. Answers quoting the number of workers engaged in Bhoodan and Gramdan work are also included. In addition, references to the concept of Gramswarajya (village self-government) fall into this category. Among the phrases used were: 'obtained 4,500,000 acres of land through love and persuasion', 'birth of Gramdan as a means to Gramswarajya', 'to have got over 6,000 Gramdans and nearly 5,000 full-time workers is a big thing', and 'attempt made to solve the land problem through non-violent means'.

2. *Promotion of Khadi and other village industries*

Answers placed in this category stressed the achievements of extending the production of Khadi and promoting other village-based industries. Typical phrases used included: 'village-oriented khadi', 'emphasis on village industries', and 'has brought good village industries'.

3. *General economic achievements*

Although closely related to the previous category, the answers placed here were those claiming that the movement had helped to reduce both the number of unemployed and the incidence of poverty. Examples of phrases used are: 'generate programmes to solve problems of poverty and unemployment', and 'showed the world a new method of eradicating poverty'.

4. *Promotion of peace*

This is a category which interprets 'peace' in a comprehensive sense. All achievements which might be regarded as contributing to the promotion of peaceful conditions in any area were included.

This category, therefore, covers answers mentioning the promotion of peace in India, the Nagaland peace mission, Shanti Sena work, the universal realization of peace, and the familial approach to world politics. Also classified here are answers mentioning the movement's part in the containment or prevention of violent revolution, in combating 'Communist threats' in specific areas, and, more generally, in providing an alternative to Communist-initiated social change. Among the phrases used were: 'peace mission in Nagaland', 'efforts to end forces of violence in India and abroad', 'Shanti Sena', 'Communist menace in Hyderabad in 1951 removed', and 'stemmed the growing menace of Communism and showed the alternative', 'containment of bloody revolution', 'idea of Jai Jagat against narrow nationalism', and 'Vinoba's attempt to lift the movement from narrow nationalism to an international world outlook'.

5. *Changes in the social climate and social values*

This is another very broad category, one which includes references to changes in attitudes to property holding, to wealth, and to land legislation. A further group of answers referred to the rousing of the masses from their inertia, apathy, and hopelessness. The raising of moral standards generally is included here, as are answers claiming for the movement success in decreasing caste and class tensions and, more specifically, in removing the stigma of 'untouchability'. Examples of replies placed in this category are: 'made the landlord to think that their land one day or other will go to the hands of the poor landless', 'giving a new set of values with regard to land ownership', 'the partial change brought about in the content of the body politic and society as a whole', 'the awakening of the people', and 'increased inter-religious, inter-caste and international contact'.

6. *Propagation of Gandhian ideology*

This category includes answers referring both to the propagation of Gandhian principles in general and to specific components of the ideology. References to such achievements included, for example: 'it has proved that Gandhi still lives in India', 'creation of faith in non-violence', 'raising the spirit of non-violence and Gandhian ideology', and 'evolution of the concept of Dan as a means to social change'.

7. Formation of a cadre of workers

In this category are included answers claiming as an achievement of the movement the formation of a cadre of devoted workers. Such answers can be distinguished from those in which numbers of Bhoodan-Gramdan workers were cited as an index of success in promoting land reform. Phrases used included: 'raising a cadre of devoted workers', and 'a nation-wide organization of Lok Sevaks'.

8. Changes in attitudes to the role of government and the state

The final category groups together answers suggesting that the Sarvodaya movement has begun to re-structure attitudes and ex-pectations with regard to the role of government and the state. Two sub-categories of answers may be distinguished. One type stresses the growth of Lok-niti (people's politics) and the strength-ening of the forces of democratic socialism, emphasizing both the participation of the masses and moves towards decentraliza-tion. The other type cites as achievements people's disillusion-ment with reliance on the government and its agencies, and the growing recognition that the movement has shown itself to be an agent of social change providing an alternative to state initiative. Examples of phrases from answers included in this general cate-gory are: 'undermining people's faith in the present system of Government', 'mass consciousness for democratic socialism', 'Lok-niti has strengthened the roots of democracy', 'the direction given to the people to look for themselves rather than look up to the Government', 'reducing the omnipotence of the State', and 'disillusionment of politics and Government authority as a means of social reform'.

Although the above categories may be useful, if relatively crude, tools of analysis, a certain richness in the material may be lost by analysis in these terms only. Answers given by some respondents must be quoted in their entirety in order to give some indication of the quality of replies received. A Samiti member wrote:

The common man has realized in spirit that Sarvodaya is the only movement that can deliver the goods. But to deserve this confidence we have yet to go a long way. Vinobaji's life and movement have released for service a genuine band of workers which is hardly sufficient to meet the needs of the society. Vinobaji's Bhoodan, Gramdan and

Sarvodaya Patra work have revealed a potentiality that could be canalized for bringing about an equalization in society. But even here we are still far off from the ideal. People have lost glamour in claiming that they own much land or wealth.

A Convenor gave the answer,

Although no revolutionary achievement is drawn to the forefront of this movement, still no doubt it rendered a great inspiration to the mass mind at least to meditate upon a certain gospel of the Universe. And such musing upon a true and ideal utopia developed the mass mind to think something in a mode something different from the mode of thinking led by the narrow party politics. The correlation of scientific knowledge with divinity has been neared to by this movement. As a result of which the 'modern intelligentzia' is charmed by the principles of the movement. Like all countries in all ages, the intelligentzia can win over its cause very soon in this country.

Another Representative listed the achievements as follows:

1. Lakhs (hundreds of thousands) of acres of land were received in Bhoodan, which for the first time jolted people out of their attachment to individual ownership, and make them to realize the fact that it did not have that much sanctity after all. 2. From Bhoodan to Gramdan— the process showed the way to a decentralized social order. 3. The movement contributed to growth of peace and amity in the country. 4. The development of the idea of 'greatest good of all' rather than 'greatest good of the greatest number'. 5. Sarvoday ideology is far more revolutionary than communism. Instead of nationalization it aims at socialization and even in that socialized system it gives great importance to the individual.

The following table (7:1) summarizes the analysis of the answers in terms of the categories previously defined, using level of leadership as a variable.

From the table it will be seen that the Sarvodaya movement's activities in the sphere of land redistribution and, from this base, the evolution of Gramdan and the lodestar of Gramswarajya were the achievements most frequently claimed. Seven out of every ten respondents focused on a component in the Bhoodan-Gramdan complex. The two top levels of leadership were more likely (by a margin of about 15 per cent) to give such answers than were Convenors.

If we look in detail at answers in this category, the perception

The Sarvodaya leaders' perceptions of the movement's achievements

Percentage of respondents giving answers in each category:

Leadership level:	Promotion of land reform %	Promotion of Khadi, etc. %	General economic achievements %	Promotion of peace %	Changes in the social climate %	Propagation of Gandhian ideology %	Formation of cadre of workers %	Changes in attitudes to Government %	N
I Samiti	77	2	0	33	40	14	7	23	43
II Representative	76	15	6	39	33	21	7	10	103
III Convenor	61	19	3	33	33	24	9	6	67
All respondents	71	14	4	36	34	21	8	11	213
x^2	4·96	6·64	N.A.	0·86	0·66	1·63	2·39	8·31	
d.f.	2	2		2	2	2	2	2	
$p \leqslant$	0·10	0·05		0·70	0·80	0·50	0·90	0·02	

Note. In calculating the percentages in each cell, the answer of a respondent who made more than one reference falling within a category is counted as one unit only. Since respondents often mentioned more than one general type of achievement, the percentages in the rows add up to more than 100.

N.A. = Not submitted to chi-square test.

of Bhoodan and Gramdan as the most important achievement is clear. About six in ten of all respondents gave this answer. In contrast, only 7 per cent mentioned progress towards Gramswarajya, although it is probable that those who stated simply 'Bhoodan-Gramdan' often used the term as a convenient shorthand for all that is hoped for from the initial land-gift. A tiny minority (5 per cent) asserted that the activities of the movement had focused attention on the land problem, publicized it, and in so doing, had helped long-term prospects of amelioration.

Land-gift and villages reborn in the new hopes generated by the ideas of common ownership and co-operation are, of course, the most visible symbols of the progress of the movement since independence. As such, they are easily recognizable in achievement terms. The targets, the facts, and the figures published in Sarvodaya literature must continually reinforce pride of achievement in these areas. Further, Bhoodan-Gramdan now operates under Government aegis, secure in a legal status. Certainly, progress in this area has not been unspectacular in the comparatively short period since the first land-gift at Pochampalli in 1951.

No other type of achievement comes anywhere near to Bhoodan-Gramdan in the perceptions of the leaders. The 'Promotion of peace' and 'Changes in the social climate, were next in line, both types being mentioned by about one in three of the respondents. In both cases the variations in perceptions between the leadership levels are not statistically significant.[1]

Looking at the components of the category 'Promotion of peace' in more detail, we find Shanti Sena, concerned with the promotion of peace in India (particularly communal harmony), most frequently mentioned. About one in five at all levels answered in terms of Shanti Sena. Sarvodaya's contribution to world peace was less frequently mentioned, by slightly fewer than one in ten. A similar low figure was recorded for claims to have provided an alternative to Communism.

More detailed examination of the components in the category 'Changes in the social climate' shows that changes in attitude to property and land-holding, and hence to land legislation, were the most frequently mentioned. About 15 per cent of all respondents made a comment which fell into this subdivision. Even within this

---

[1] For an explanation of our use of the term 'statistically significant' see Chapter Eight, pp. 314–15 below.

small proportion, however, there was a clear difference of approach. Some maintained that landowners were now accepting the inevitability of a major change in the pattern of land-holding; others took the more positive view that the old attachments to wealth and to land were becoming less intense, and that other 'human' values were replacing predominantly materialistic ones. Some respondents, for example, suggested the appearance of different criteria for the evaluation of people, so that property and prestige were no longer virtually synonymous. Closely connected with this subdivision is another, namely, that values have so changed that feelings for the poor have been aroused. This point was made by one in ten of all respondents, but twice as frequently at the Samiti level.

The 'Propagation of Gandhian ideology' was seen as an achievement by about one-fifth of the leaders. As to the components that make up this general category, the most frequently cited achievement is that of the spread of Non-violence, mentioned by one in ten respondents. The other components—propagation of Gandhian-principles generally, spread of the idea of Sarvodaya, and giving new meaning to the concept of dan—were less frequently mentioned.

At a still lower level of perception came the 'Promotion of Khadi and village industries', mentioned by one in seven. Frequency of answers referring to these items was inversely related to level of leadership, with a notable divergency between Samiti members and Convenors, the latter being almost ten times as likely as the former to refer to them. The relationship might be explained by the hypothesis that lower-level leaders, working at the village level, are more likely than higher-level leaders to perceive as an achievement developments which increase employment opportunities in the villages. It is also possible, however, that the top leaders are more informed than others about the problems of Khadi production and more sceptical of its long-term prospects; in which case, they would be unlikely to perceive its promotion as an achievement.

Only a tiny minority of answers (4 per cent) fell into the separate but related category of 'General economic achievements'. If the two categories are collapsed, the same pattern of divergence between top leaders and other leaders still holds good. None of the Samiti members perceived the provision of employment and the reduction of poverty as achievements of the movement.

References to the movement's success in changing or modifying people's attitudes to government and the state are isolated as a separate category in our analysis, although there are clear, if indirect, links with two other categories: changes in the social climate, and propagation of Gandhian ideology. Specific references to changes in attitudes to government and its agencies were made by just over one in ten of the leaders as a whole. But within this small minority there is a very clear relationship: the higher the level, the more likely is a respondent to make this point, Samiti members being four times as likely to do so as Convenors. The explanation of the difference may lie in the hypothesis that top leaders are, in some sense, closer to government and more aware than other leaders of the differences between the movement's and the Government's approach to building a new social order.

The remaining general category is the one stressing as an achievement the formation of a dedicated cadre of workers. References of this kind were made in 8 per cent of the answers, with insignificant differences between the leadership levels.

Having presented an account of the data resulting from our analysis of the leaders' perceptions of the movement's achievements, and having indicated rather than answered various questions inherent in the material, we are still left with the task of considering what this analysis can contribute to our understanding of the movement. While nothing that might with justification be termed 'conclusions' should be drawn from such an analysis, a few comments may be made.

On the whole, the respondents were less expansive on the achievements of the movement than they were in answering the other open-ended questions to be considered below. In part this may be attributable to the useful 'shorthand' of the term 'Bhoodan-Gramdan' which, as we have already suggested, may leave unstated but implicit the wider connotations it bears for people in the movement. In part, however, the explanation may be linked with the tendency of respondents to concentrate on self-criticism as a means of making the movement more effective, and on 'internal' deficiencies and short-comings seen as obstacles to the movement's progress. This impression is reinforced by the fact that, in the space for 'additional comments' at the end of the questionnaire, achievements barely figured at all: overwhelmingly, criticisms of the movement and suggestions to improve effectiveness were the topics discussed.

A point that is perhaps more clear from reading the answers than from our presentation of the analysed material is the essential realism of the respondents. Wishful thinking was certainly not entirely absent, but there was a general lack of extravagant or exaggerated claims.

Further, to introduce a point to be made in more detail later, it is clear from these data that Sarvodaya workers do not see themselves as a separatist group, a small society encapsulated within a larger one, and succeeding merely in bringing more 'converts' into their own 'sect'. Instead, the answers underline the essentially universalistic and comprehensive outlook of the movement. Gramdans are not seen as private utopias.

Finally, and related to this point, consideration of these answers is interesting in terms of the role of a social movement in effecting social change. Characterization of Sarvodaya as essentially a value-oriented movement has been fully discussed already. In this connection it is worth pointing out that many of the leaders were measuring achievement in the sense, if not the terminology, of a regeneration of values. The movement is perceived as a powerful agent for change, a force seeking both institutional and individual regeneration. Sarvodaya is seen, especially, as that vehicle of change which stands in opposition both to the Socialist-cum-welfare-state approach and to the Communist solution. In this sense, Sarvodaya presents itself as the revolutionary vanguard, marching into the future under the twin banners: Forward from Democratic Socialism! Forward from Communism!

II. PERCEPTIONS OF OBSTACLES

The leaders' perceptions of obstacles are derived from their answers to the question: 'What in your opinion are the most serious obstacles to the further progress of the Movement?' Again, an element of arbitrariness enters into any formal analysis of the content of the answers. In addition, in this instance it is possible to interpret the answers on at least two levels of analysis. On one level may be found simple straightforward appraisals of the difficulties facing the movement in terms, perhaps, of the perennial problems of most voluntary organizations: shortage of staff and shortage of money. On the second level may be found a further dimension of the leaders' perceptions, in so far as there is some degree of correspondence between the obstacles they cite and the type of movement which they believe they serve.

In illustration of the responses a few answers may be quoted verbatim. A Samiti member wrote:

In spite of the living examples set by Bapu and Baba (i.e. Gandhi and Vinoba), people in general still make a difference between Swardha (selfishness), Parardha (helpfulness to others), and Paramardha (dedication to the Almighty). Unless and until we decide once and for all that true selfishness is achieved in being useful to others in a spirit of dedication, there is no room for progress and for collective goodness. Besides we have to realize that in sticking to the path of righteousness through thick and thin despite any seeming outward reverses, there is a real growth of the Soul within. The unknown man in the large majority of cases is not only neglected but allowed to dwindle by paying a deaf ear to the call of conscience and running after the immediate material benefits that accrue from the compromise of the cardinal virtues of truth, love and compassion. It is a matter for deep regret that the lives of great men that lie before us do not open our eyes to the realities of the true eternal values of life. Compromise of one vital virtue leads man into a vicious circle when he falls from one virtue to another, till he falls flat. Development of collective goodness has, therefore, become a very difficult issue. Man, without acquiring sufficient self-control begins to disagree with the opinions of great men who have made themselves embodiments of sacrifice, service, devotion and humility. Thus man seems to have decided for himself that he could grow only through trial and error, while apparently he pays homage to acknowledge the great men only in name. In this way the messages from the top do not reach the common man whose pulse has been rightly studied and understood by Bapu and Baba. Men may doubt what we say but they cannot disbelieve the perseverant righteous actions of well-meaning friends who act as the liaison workers between the common man and the great leaders at the top. So if through right understanding the liaison-workers mend themselves into proper form and convey the messages not only through words but through their remodelled lives, much could be done in the growth of collective goodness which is *sine qua non* for all-sided development. The Danadhara (Gift Movement) initiated by Baba through Bhoodan, Sarala Gramdan, Sampattidan, and Sammatidan through Sarvodaya patra if properly understood and carefully implemented will lead to a revolution in Society more powerful and sustained than the most powerful violent revolutions.

The vast number of Khadi workers and workers in all allied institutions are to a large extent utter strangers to the philosophy and life of

Mahatma Gandhi with the result that they are not able to assert their own in their own homes before their own wives and children and their kith and kin. It is a matter for shame that even in the Sarvoda field, some of the workers wish to bring about reformation in society without influencing their own near and dear ones for whose welfare they live, move and have their being. In this way a vast body of workers which could easily act as a ferment in society and bring about revolution is thus leading an inert life.

The following reply came from another member of the Prabandh Samiti, who listed the obstacles:

1. People's disillusionment from Swaraj and its leadership. People distrustful of change.
2. Welfare state—its numerous agents, agencies and management of facts—loss of perspective—no urge for self-expression.
3. Absence of dedicated leadership in the Movement.
4. Cynicism in middle class youth. Loss of values.
5. Institutionalization of constructive work.
6. Absence of national progressive outlook.
7. No funds, no workers.
8. Our appeal has only just started reaching the masses.

A District Representative wrote:

1. The government does not take any effective interest in the Movement.
2. The people are also uninterested to some extent. 3. Weakness of the workers; e.g. (a) lack of desired co-operation among the workers, (b) there are no means to support their families, (c) they do not receive effective guidance when needed, (d) the leaders are busy in hair split-ting, but don't try to stick to the field and create models for others to see and know. At least this is true of Uttar Pradesh.

As these quotations may make clear, elaborate analysis, a coding procedure with exact and exclusive categories, would be unrealis-tic and do less than justice to the quality of the replies received. Answers were, therefore, assigned to broad categories which are not exclusive, and which are identified below. A fairly clear dis-tinction emerged between certain categories. There was an obvious division between replies which indicated that the obstacles lay in factors intrinsic to the personnel, policy, programme, and organization of the Sarvodaya movement itself, and those which suggested that the obstacles to success lay in the outside world, the context in which the movement had to work. Identification of the categories used in this analysis will, therefore, be considered in turn, within each of the two major fields, 'internal' and 'external'. The 'internal' field may be divided into five major categories.

1. *The Workers*

This category includes answers regretting the lack of workers both in purely numerical terms and qualitatively, emphasizing a lack of dedication and idealism, the advanced age of some workers, the infiltration of undesirables into the movement, and a lack of fellowship among the workers. Answers in this category include such terms as 'lack of imaginative and devoted workers', 'need of active workers having faith in Sarvodaya ideals', 'lack of people who could entirely devote themselves to the movement and love Sarvodaya ideals in their personal life', 'lack of a feeling of kinship among the workers'.

2. *Leaders*

Leaders were sometimes regarded as obstacles to the success of the movement in that they were found wanting in moral calibre and dedication. Other answers suggested that leaders of the movement lacked effectiveness and that the leader–worker relationship needed redefinition. Also included in this category are references to a personality cult, and specific references to the leadership of Vinoba. Answers were phrased in terms which included: 'some of the leaders themselves do not follow the Sarvodaya principles', 'love of ease and comfort by top persons of the movement', 'blind following of Vinoba', 'its commander is good and sincere but not so its lieutenants', 'lack of dedicated efficient and effective leadership'.

3. *Organization*

Answers in this category range from general criticism of the organizational side of the movement (inadequate co-ordination of its facets, including deployment of personnel and finance) to specific references to the problem of maintaining the workers and their families, and the inadequacy of training methods. Some answers on training specify approaches such as the use of residential centres or camps, or on-the-job-training by attachment to an experienced worker. Among the phrases used here are: 'lack of effective organization', 'no proper organization', 'deficiency in training programme of adequate numbers of workers', 'lack of training', 'lack of funds', 'no means to support their families'.

4. *Policy and programme*

This category includes answers suggesting that the Sarvodaya movement is unduly idealistic, its goals unattainable and too diffuse. The movement is also criticized for its failure to appeal to the intelligentzia, its failure to follow up and develop Gramdan, and its failure to reach the masses. Included here are such comments as: 'too much high ideal', 'too high ideals which prohibit the common people from joining', 'has not yet reached the lowliest and the low', 'not geared to reach the minds of the intellectuals', 'though Gramdan is principal item of Sarvodaya movement they don't concentrate on it'.

5. *Strategy and tactics*

Within this category fall answers criticizing the movement's over-reliance on the Government and its failure or reluctance to oppose the Government. Included here also are replies stressing the need for the movement to use 'negative' satyagraha to solve some of the problems it tackles. Phrases used are: 'tendency to consult the Government and act with their help', 'tendency of the Sarvodaya leaders to depend on the state', 'reluctance to displease the Government', 'indifference towards Satyagraha'.

Factors external to the movement are divided into four further categories as follows:

6. *The social and economic context*

Included under this heading are references to the traditional social structure of India, to caste and communalism, for example; to the economic determinants of social inequalities, the system of land-holding; and the influences on social values of such factors as Western modernizing agents and the educational system. Associated with these factors and included here are references to ignorance, illiteracy, and apathy of the mass of the population, and the materialistic outlook. Classified in this section are answers using phrases such as 'existing social and economic structure of society', 'poverty', 'individual ownership', 'ignorance and illiteracy of the masses', 'unharnessed capitalism', 'present materialistic trend of society'.

7. *Political and governmental factors*

This is a comprehensive category and includes those answers mentioning the increasing area of governmental activity, the welfare-state function, and, conversely, those mentioning government opposition to the movement or reluctance to come to its aid. Answers relating to political parties, including specific references to Congress, the electoral system, and to the problem of corruption, are all included here. Typical of this category are such phrases as 'extension of Government Sector', 'the intrusion of the Union and State governments in all spheres of people's lives', 'political parties', 'political competition', 'present election system', 'insincerity of the Congress party', 'corruption rampant in the national polity', 'the Government does not take any effective interest in the movement'.

8. *The threat of Communism*

Within this category are included references to the threat of Communism. Phrases used, for example, are 'Communist threat', 'the menace of Communism'.

9. *The threat of war*

Under this heading are included answers relating to external threats to peace. Answers are phrased in such terms as 'world tension' and 'war menace at the borders of India'.

The table opposite (7:2) summarizes our analysis of the answers in terms of the above categories, using level of leadership as a variable.

The first point to notice about the table is the emphasis of the answers on 'internal' as opposed to 'external' obstacles. Many respondents, as might be expected, referred to both, but the weight, as measured by number of references, was on the former. Detailed analysis (not shown in the table) reveals that 76 per cent of all respondents referred to at least one 'internal' obstacle, compared with 52 per cent referring to an 'external' one. Analysis in terms of leadership level reveals a further interesting divergence: with respect to 'internal' obstacles, the higher the level, the more frequent the reference; with respect to 'external' obstacles, in contrast, the relationship is inverse—the higher the level, the *less* frequent the reference. The divergence is such that

TABLE 7:2

The Sarvodaya leaders' perceptions of obstacles to the further progress of the movement

Percentage of respondents giving answers in each category:

Leadership level	'INTERNAL' OBSTACLES					'EXTERNAL' OBSTACLES				
	Workers %	Leaders %	Organization %	Policy and programme %	Strategy and tactics %	Social and economic context %	Politics and government %	Threat of Communism %	Threat of war %	N
I Samiti	70	30	35	33	12	12	17	0	11	40
II Representative	53	11	24	19	9	36	33	2	15	102
III Convenor	42	20	38	22	0	39	39	1	14	69
All respondents	53	18	30	22	7	33	32	1	14	211
x^2	7·95	6·43	4·40	3·21	N.A.	8·06	5·53	N.A.	N.A.	
d.f.	2	2	2	2	N.A.	2	2	N.A.	N.A.	
$p \leqslant$	0·02	0·05	0·20	0·30	N.A.	0·02	0·10	N.A.	N.A.	

Note. The percentage figure in each cell shows the proportion of answers which made *at least one* reference to a topic falling within a general category. Since individual answers often contained references classifiable in more than one category, the figures in the rows add up to more than 100.

N.A. = Not submitted to chi-square test.

at the lowest level (Convenor) answers are fairly evenly balanced between the 'internal' and 'external' fields, while at the highest level (Samiti) frequency of mention of 'internal' obstacles is over three times as great as mention of 'external' ones.[1]

In attempting to explain the emphasis of the leaders as a whole on 'internal' as opposed to 'external' obstacles, two points may be made. The first is that introspection and self-criticism were probably encouraged by the format of the questionnaire. The respondents had been led, on fairly well defined lines, to describe their careers, to appraise the movement in certain respects, and (in a later section) to express their attitudes towards various 'issues' within the movement. That they should carry over a critical approach in answering open-ended questions is hardly surprising. The second point is that introspection and critical appraisal do not necessarily imply despondency or a general lack of faith in the movement. Rather, they may reflect exceptionally high standards.

In attempting to explain the divergences of emphasis between the various leadership levels, it may be hypothesized that lower-level leaders are likely to have more recent field experience than others. Then, the immensity of their task, the conditions under which they work and the immediacy of the problems they face may make them more aware of 'external' obstacles. An alternative or supplementary hypothesis is that a basic function of top leaders in any organization is to preserve the organization itself. From this perspective, top leaders are likely to be more conscious of problems of organization in the widest sense, decisions on which are to a large extent within their own control: they would then be more likely to perceive 'internal' than 'external' obstacles.

[1]

Leadership level	Percentage mentioning at least one		N
	'internal obstacle' %	'external obstacle' %	
I	92	27	(40)
II	75	55	(102)
III	68	62	(69)
χ^2	8·40	12·91	—
d.f.	2	2	—
$p <$	0.02	0.01	—

To turn now to a detailed commentary on Table 7:2, it will be seen that the most frequently perceived obstacle was the movement's workers. Just over one-half of all respondents gave answers critical of, amongst other things, the numbers of workers, their calibre, their spiritual quality, and their practical capabilities, the emphasis being on quality rather than quantity. In terms of leadership levels, the pattern of response in answers of this kind is quite clear: the higher the level, the more likely are respondents to express dissatisfaction with the workers of the movement. This pattern is not surprising: one would expect less criticism the nearer one got to the grass roots of the movement. Nevertheless, criticism among Convenors is still marked, two out of every five of them making a reference of this type.

The shortcomings of leaders as distinct from workers were referred to by less than one-fifth of all respondents. In the 'additional comments' of a Representative whose answer fell into this category the authors were informed:

Sarvodaya is a revolutionary ideology and complete in itself. But, barring Vinoba and a few others, most of the workers are extremely weak. I would say that those who are expected to be the real messengers of Vinoba's revolution are incapable people and they are ineffective. That is the reason that it is not becoming a people's movement. It would not be an exaggeration to say that the direction of the Movement is in the hands of 'mediocres', with the result that there is more a 'mirage' than a 'revolution'. These so-called leaders are more interested in self-projection.

Thus, on the face of it, we have leaders criticizing workers and workers criticizing leaders. But the leader–worker distinction is not nearly so clear-cut as it may appear superficially, and to regard the movement in leader–worker terms may at best be somewhat artificial and at worst misleading. Our respondents are all office-holders, 'leaders' in some obvious sense. The 'leaders' referred to in answers in this category are 'top leaders' or a smaller group within the first level of leadership. But even with respect to the latter all leaders are also workers and regard themselves as such. This identification may be clearly seen in the answer of a Samiti member: 'Failure to de-class ourselves and lack of consistent efforts. We workers are quite shallow.' The criticism is self-criticism, the strictures introspective. A sharp leader–worker dichotomy typical of many voluntary organizations does not exist in the Sarvodaya movement: even the 'top leaders' may take a turn, as Gandhi did, at cleaning out the latrines! It should be added that in voicing criticism—criticism of workers and criticisms of leaders—respondents are following a cue often given by Vinoba himself. It may, indeed, be said that an aptitude for self-criticism is a hallmark of the satyagrahi: his philosophy enjoins him to remove the mote in his own eye before casting out the beam in another's.

But if the leader–worker dichotomy is blurred in the Sarvodaya movement, it nevertheless exists; otherwise it would have been impossible to discern in the material two categories instead of one. As might be expected, the clearest indications that a leader–worker distinction is perceived came in answers of Representatives and Convenors. One in twenty of respondents at these two levels referred to defects in communication between leaders and workers. A Secretary of a State Sarvodaya Mandal wrote: 'Those working at different levels of the society of Sarvodaya ideology—from the village to the international—are not feeling as if they are in the same movement, and the effort of the Bhoodan worker in the village does not reinforce the work of bringing amity between conflicting interests, say between India and Pakistan, or in Kashmir and Nagaland and vice-versa.'

Another facet of the leader–worker relationship is that which concerns the unique position of Vinoba. 2 per cent of the replies of all office-holders referred directly to this point, in such phrases as: 'blind following of Vinobaji' and 'there are no leaders created by Vinoba as Gandhi created in his day'. In addition, an almost equally tiny proportion were critical of the leadership in general terms, suggesting lack of moral and spiritual qualities, and alleging lack of effectiveness.

Of the five categories concerned with 'internal' obstacles, the one concerned with organizational defects ranked second to that dealing with the workers. Three out of ten of all respondents referred to organizational obstacles. Two subdivisions were discernible in these answers, one concerned with financial matters, the other with organization generally. 12 per cent of all respondents referred to the problem of inadequate provision for the maintenance of workers and their families, the proportion being nearly 20 per cent at the Convenor level. Just under 10 per cent of all respondents deplored the absence of a sound financial basis for the movement, the higher leadership levels being more likely to make this point. About the same proportion (one in ten) mentioned lack of sound organization generally, the distribution of such answers being roughly the same, proportionately, at all levels. A similar proportion drew attention to inadequacies in arrangements for training, Convenors being the most likely to make such a point. A minute proportion, which included no Samiti member, commented unfavourably on the alleged lack of co-ordination between various wings of the movement.

Just over one in five of all respondents made some reference (in many cases more than one) to aspects of the movement's policy and programme which, they felt, militated against success. The proportion rises to one in three at the top leadership level. Included in answers coded in this general category were those (about 6 per cent of all respondents) making a criticism of the movement that strikes deep to its roots. The obstacle here is seen as the 'excessive idealism' of the movement, which is regarded as precluding 'practicality'. A quotation from the answer of the Secretary of a State Sarvodaya Mandal illustrates this somewhat unexpected perspective:

Too much high ideal, i.e. 'Land belongs to God' and 'land is the common property of the village community', does not catch the imagination of the common people, or, in other words, people are not bold enough to swallow or cherish the idea and still less ready to put it into practice. The landlords and the rich who are not ready to give it up in favour of the community by persuasion. Moreover, too many ideals also are often placed before the volunteers or staff and stress is often being given variously. Less ideals (or practical ideals such as 'Action against eviction from land'), steps to implement land reform enactments should be taken up, organize the tillers without putting too much conditions and achieve the goal one by one. That will infuse confidence in the minds of the people and help further progress.

The remaining answers grouped under the 'Policy and programmes' heading include a tiny proportion making the point that the movement's goals are too many, ill-defined, or diffuse; an even smaller proportion that refer to the movement's failure to attract the intelligentsia; those which criticize its failure to tackle immediate problems; and those which criticize results in the Gramdan field. Answers referring to Gramdan, it may be noted, were too few to allow differentiation between those respondents dissatisfied with the rate of numerical expansion of

Gramdan declarations and those criticizing the lack of adequate development work in existing Gramdan villages.

The last of the general categories concerned with 'internal' obstacles—'Strategy and tactics'—covers the answers of 7 per cent of all respondents who criticized the ways and means currently being adopted. No Convenor, it should be noted, was included in this group. In this category were placed the answers of those who felt that the movement's failure to resort to 'negative' satyagraha was an obstacle. Strongest support for this tactic came from Representatives, but this stood at only 4 per cent. As we shall see later, however, support for such satyagraha figures more prominently in answers to the questions asking for proposals to make the movement more effective.

The four categories in the 'external' sphere include all answers of respondents who perceived as obstacles to success such factors as the existing social structure, the educational system, economic institutions, modernizing and Westernizing forces, the roles of the state and the political parties, and the general threats of war and Communism. The whole field is, therefore, something of a summary of the total environment which the movement challenges. Two categories in this sphere—the 'Social and economic context', and 'Politics and government'—were especially important, about one-third of all respondents giving answers classifiable in each of these categories.

Within the first category the most frequent answers were those referring to the economic structure, including capitalism, individual ownership, and economic equalities, and those referring to the ignorance and apathy of the masses. The problems of India's traditional social structure were less frequently mentioned. Top-level leaders were three times less likely than other leaders to perceive obstacles in this category.

Political parties and the election system figured prominently within the second category. About one in five of all respondents made such references, including a tiny proportion who singled out the activities of the Congress party for criticism. Just under one in ten referred to over-dependence on the Government and what was perceived as the 'encroachment' of government activity in everyday life. A slightly smaller proportion, mainly respondents at the Representative and Convenor levels, cited as an obstacle government opposition to, and slowness in helping, the movement.

In the remaining categories in the 'external' sphere, answers referring to the threat of Communism were numerically inconsiderable. The threat of war, however, was seen as an obstacle by one in seven of all respondents.

The nature of the material analysed above does not permit firm conclusions. But two general comments appear to be warranted. The first is that the most serious obstacles are perceived as lying within the movement itself, and, moreover, with the workers. Looking at the movement dispassionately a detached observer would not wish to deny that 'internal' obstacles are important: the qualities of its leadership, the calibre of its workers, the soundness of its organization, the attractiveness of its policy and programme, and wise strategy and tactics are important in any social movement. But, considering the nature of its goal, a total revolution, a complete regeneration of values, it can scarcely be open to doubt that the most serious kinds of obstacle facing the Sarvodaya movement are 'external' ones. However successful the movement were to be in overcoming 'internal' obstacles, the 'external' ones would remain immensely formidable. The predominant character of the leaders' perceptions, therefore, probably tells us more about their psychology than about the actual situation. This psychology may be a distinctive feature of this kind of social movement. Individuals who blame themselves rather than others for any shortcomings are rare enough: social movements whose leaders tend to do the same must be rare indeed. Much more typical in the world of social movements are those which perceive outside forces as the devils responsible for all ills, devils to be vanquished by the angels of light. For the Sarvodaya movement, however, emphasis on 'internal' obstacles serves a useful function: it serves to concentrate attention on matters within the control of the movement. In striving to overcome such obstacles the members of the movement are likely to find themselves all the better equipped to overcome the more formidable 'external' obstacles.

The second general comment relates to the movement's attitude towards, and relationship with, the Government. Indications illuminating the position of the movement *vis-à-vis* the Government may be found in many answers. But these indications are not consistent; instead they point to a certain ambivalence of attitude on the part of at least some members of the movement.

On the one side we find those who castigate the movement's

over-reliance on the Government, lament its failure to oppose the Government, and regret its neglect of 'negative' satyagraha. On the same side are those who see as an impediment to the movement's progress the proliferation of governmental activity, penetrating into all aspects of people's lives. This is seen as the corollary of people's dependence on the Government and their willingness to leave the initiative to the Government, so further sapping the will to individual and collective self-help. In other words, the issue here is to be seen basically as the ideal of the stateless society versus the approaching reality of the welfare state. Then the increase in governmental activity in the direction of a welfare state is interpreted as a disincentive to the development of that Lok shakti (self-reliant power of the people) which is an essential component of the stateless society.

On the other side, and in complete contrast, we find those (a smaller proportion, including only one Samiti member) who feel that an obstacle to the movement's success is the Government's failure to help the movement effectively, and who are obviously hurt by what they see as the neglect of the movement by Congress.

The possible significance of the ambivalent attitude of the movement towards the Government may be seen in two ways: it may be seen in the historical context which makes such ambivalence understandable, and it may be seen as having implications for the future of the movement.

In our opening chapter we referred to the institutionalization of Gandhism evident in both the independent Gandhian associations and certain programmes of the Government. 'Revolutionary Gandhism' has also been subject to institutionalization, most notably in the granting of a legal status to Bhoodan and Gramdan. The process is a continuing one and there is nothing novel about it: the roots of a modern Western welfare state, such as twentieth-century Britain, may be traced to small-scale nineteenth-century voluntary organizations and movements. To some extent, therefore, the movement's aims are consonant with those of the Indian Government, and attempts to pursue these aims may well proceed within the framework of an increasingly welfare-oriented state. But from the perspective of the future of the Sarvodaya movement, there is a crucial division between the type of social movement which works for the amelioration of conditions with government support and under government auspices, and the type of movement, value-oriented and radical, which ameliorates social conditions in the process of building a stateless society based on truth, love, and compassion. The relationships which the latter kind of movement comprehends are quite other than those of social worker to client, or civil servant to citizen. Immediate results for each kind of movement may be similar. The difference lies in the perspective; but perspective in this case may be all-important.

III. PROPOSALS TO INCREASE EFFECTIVENESS

The final open-ended question was: 'What proposals would you make to ensure that the movement becomes more effective in its work in the future?' In part, then, this question is complementary to the preceding one: respondents, having described the obstacles they saw in the path of the movement, were now asked, in effect, how they would overcome the problems they had exposed. A few respondents answered directly in terms of their previous replies. But the majority made use of this question for something more than merely balancing positive proposals against the negative obstacles already mentioned. As might be anticipated, the proposals varied greatly in their degrees of specificity. In this context norm-oriented responses might be expected to predominate—the norms involved being primarily those of the movement—but some respondents replied in generalized value-oriented terms.

The procedure adopted in the analysis is the same as that for answers to the other open-ended questions: the material was examined to see what general categories were inherently discernible in it. Before setting out these categories and proceeding to the analysis, with the inevitable loss of colour and intensity that run through many of the answers, it may be useful to quote verbatim a few of the replies.

A Samiti member wrote: 'One who has (been) convinced of this movement should spread to ten, ten to hundred, hundred to thousands and so on. Gramdan lived will spread the Movement (more) than Gramdan preached, because Gramdan lived will not only teach and preach but also reach the horizon.' A lengthier answer came from another Samiti member:

It is easy to wake a sleeping man, but an attempt to wake a man who pretends to sleep is an overwhelming task. But the few genuine workers have to take up this hard task and work up if we are to retain the freedom won through truth and non-violence. The sincere workers should form into groups and work along the constructive channels and gather round them more kindred souls. The work thus begins to gather momentum and the collective goodness built in this way will bring about revolutionary changes. But the real stumbling block to progress even among the genuine workers is lack of mutual regard and trust among themselves. Charity, if it is to bear any fruit, should begin at home. Workers should vow to love and like each other. Satyagrahi should learn to live the life of a Satyagrahi and look upon his fellow workers with faith and love. Unilateral effort in love is sure to pay in the long run. This aspect assumed, hatred towards the neighbours and later hatred towards even the person who considers us his enemy may be converted to love. Ultimately, truth, love and compassion are bound to deliver the goods. There is no other way. It may take time.

A Representative replied:

1. Due to the limited human and other resources we have to limit the movement to the triple programme only. It should be broad based to touch all spheres of people's life, so that people take more interest in it. 2. Consolidation of the Movement's achievement with the help of workers trained in rural development. Such training should not be restricted to particular field only—'total training'. If we can build a cadre of trained Sarvodaya workers a social order freed from state control will be possible. 3. Peasants, workers, and artisans (technicians) are the *real workers*. They need to be educated and drawn into the movement. Much of the thinking for the movement today is done by the intelligentsia. People have not been participating in it. It will be necessary to pick up the real workers and train them for the Sarvodaya.

A Convenor wrote:

1. It should be effectively organized throughout the whole country. 2. It should have a clear leadership. Vinoba may be a good counsel but not an effective leader. 3. It should concentrate on Gramdan movement more effectively and thus make these real centres of democracy. 4. It should associate itself in Government sponsored movement. 5. To propagate its ideals, its workers who have faith in the programme should try to find more and more places in the Government offices.

From such answers nine general categories were derived. Most of these are related to categories used in the analysis of perceived obstacles, but in this instance the major division between 'internal' and 'external' is hardly relevant. Almost all the proposals refer to areas of decision-making within the competence of the movement to carry out, even when they concern its relationship with 'external' bodies or forces. A few answers, however, did make proposals which implied other agencies to carry them out. The categories were as follows.

1. *Workers*

Proposals placed in this category include suggestions to increase the number of workers, to improve and widen recruitment, to raise the standards of the workers morally and spiritually, and, a corollary of the latter, to exclude 'undesirables' who were alleged to have penetrated the movement. Among the phrases used were: 'more fulltime workers', 'draw young blood into the movement', 'eliminate undesirables', 'emphasis on moral development', and 'reducing the gap between profession and practices of Sarvodaya workers'.

2. *Leaders*

In this category come proposals in general terms for more effective leadership as well as specific proposals that leader–worker relations should be closer and that leaders themselves should engage in constructive work. Phrases employed were: 'clear leadership', 'co-operation between the field workers and the leaders', and 'leaders should show an example'.

3. *Organization*

Answers placed in this category were often, of course, closely related to answers in other categories. Included here are proposals about the financing of the movement in general as well as specific references to the provision of adequate financial maintenance for workers and their families. The provision of training, both spiritual and technical, for the workers is also included. Within this category come suggestions for the better ordering of relations between the levels of organization and more co-ordination and co-operation between various sectors of the movement, and specifically between all agencies engaged in Gandhian constructive work. The proposal to spread the movement by a chain of 'cells', to be discussed more fully below, also falls into this category. Phrases used in the answers include: 'more effective co-ordination', 'make organization more responsible to the movement', 'build up cells', 'heavy financing of the movement', and 'active participation by the institutions known for their constructive activities'.

4. *Policy and programme*

This category covers an extensive range of answers. Proposals involving The Triple Programme itself or any of its components are included. So, too, are suggestions that there should be intensive activity in selected areas, or that a number of villages should be developed as examples of the Sarvodaya society. More effective tackling of problems outside The Triple Programme, for example, problems in the urban industrial sector, national defence, corruption, and other 'urgent current problems' are further topics in this category. Other proposals included here are: making the movement a people's movement, developing the movement at the international level, and the tactical suggestion that 'negative' satyagraha should be used to achieve the movement's aims. Typical phrases found in the answers in this category are: 'carry on threefold programme', 'concentrate on Gramdan movement more effectively', 'start immediate follow-up in new Gramdan villages', 'intensive work in some selected district', 'have Sarvodaya workers throughout the world', and 'revival of Gandhian technique of mass satyagraha'.

5. *Propaganda*

This category includes all answers containing proposals for the development of propaganda and publicity techniques. Specific suggestions included: making more use of padayatras (walking tours), seminars, and facilities in existing educational institutions. Extension of both the quality and the availability of Sarvodaya literature was another proposal. Phrases used in these answers included: 'padayatras', 'cheap Sarvodaya literature', 'more literature in national and regional languages', and 'Sarvodaya should be made a compulsory subject' (in schools, etc.).

6. *Redefinition of relations with the Government*

Within this category were to be found two opposing kinds of proposal: (i) those for working in closer association with the Government and its agencies, and (ii) those for disassociating from and, in an extreme form, opposing government activities.

Typical answers assigned to this category were, on the one hand, 'admit the Government officials into the Sarvodaya family as its friends', and 'active co-operation from central and state governments', and, on the other hand, 'non-co-operation with the Government', and 'the Movement should give up all its compromising attitude with Government'.

7. Redefinition of relations with political parties

Proposals for reappraisal and redefinition of relations with political parties again involved divergence of opinion. Within this category, then, are included suggestions from some for closer relations between the movement and political parties, and also contrary suggestions from others to avoid close relations with the parties, and specifically with Congress. Phrases used were: 'some of the existing political parties should take up the Sarvodaya programme' and 'the movement will become more effective . . . if the leaders . . . function independent of the Congress party and its big guns'.

8. Changes of ownership by agencies outside the movement

This category includes suggestions of government action to end individual ownership and to abolish the large landlord system. A phrase used in such answers is 'abolition of private ownership'.

9. Changes in the social climate

Changes in the values of the population at large is the theme of proposals placed in this category. 'Change in film industry', 'make people conscious . . . that there are other values (human values) which are necessary to fulfilment' were among the phrases used.

The following table summarizes the answers in terms of the above categories, with level of leadership as a variable.

In contrast to the two previous tables, the analysis by levels of leadership does not reveal any large differences between the groups of leaders, except with regard to the organization category. The greater frequency of organizational proposals by top-level leaders may be explained by hypothesizing that one of the basic functions of such leaders is special concern for organizational issues.

It will be seen that the kind of proposal most frequently made by the respondents related to the policy and programme of the movement, more than one in two making at least one proposal of

TABLE 7:3

The Sarvodaya leaders' proposals to increase the movement's effectiveness

Percentages of respondents making proposals in each category:

Leadership level	Workers %	Leaders %	Organization %	Policy and programme %	Propaganda %	Relations with the Government %	Relations with political parties %	Changes of ownership (other agencies) %	Changes in social climate %	N
I Samiti	35	7	49	56	26	12	2	0	2	43
II Representative	39	14	31	50	24	9	7	3	6	101
III Convenor	27	12	31	58	18	15	10	3	4	67
All respondents	34	12	35	54	22	11	7	2	5	211
x^2	2·49	1·37	4·84	1·34	1·34	1·45	N.A.	N.A.	N.A.	
d.f.	2	2	2	2	2	2				
$p \leqslant$	0·30	0·70	0·10	0·70	0·70	0·50				

Note. The percentage figure in each cell shows the proportion of answers which made *at least one* proposal within a general category. The categories are not exclusive.
N.A. = Not submitted to chi-square test.

this kind. Of the various components in this category, proposals urging steps to make Sarvodaya a mass movement, and related proposals urging that attention be paid to current problems, figured most prominently. Just under one in ten of all respondents proposed that 'negative' satyagraha should be used to achieve the movement's objectives. The difference between this proportion and the proportion (66 per cent) who, when asked specifically later, favoured satyagraha for this purpose may reflect variations in intensity of feeling about this issue. Or it may reflect differences over the question of timing. While two-thirds of the office-holders would be *prepared* to organize satyagraha campaigns, only a small minority would favour it as a general and possibly immediate approach. The answers in this category also confirm the previous findings that Gramdan is perceived as the most important item in The Triple Programme. Proposals involving Gramdan were made by 7 per cent of the respondents, compared with the 3 per cent referring to Khadi and the 1 per cent mentioning Shanti Sena. Additionally, another 7 per cent proposed steps to follow up Gramdan declarations and develop Gramdan villages. Yet a further 7 per cent suggested concentration on Gramdan without indicating whether increased declarations or development of existing Gramdans was intended. Of the remaining components in the 'Policy and programme' category, only educational proposals were made by more than 5 per cent of the respondents. These proposals envisaged a mass education programme, an idea clearly related to transforming Sarvodaya into a people's movement. There was also a small amount of support for the idea of intensive activity by Sarvodaya workers in selected areas, to provide as it were an exemplar of the work of the movement.

Just over one-third of all respondents suggested changes in the organizational field as a means to increase effectiveness. Within this category by far the most emphasis was laid on the provision of training for workers. Proposals of this nature were made by 13 per cent of the respondents, but came most frequently from Samiti members, about one in five of whom proposed training schemes in some form. It is evident from the answers that training for Sarvodaya workers is envisaged as something more than technical: moral and spiritual development are also included. The remaining points on organization were made by far fewer respondents. 8 per cent of all respondents, but more at the Samiti level, proposed that the general financial basis of the movement should be stabilized. A similar proportion, but with more at the lower leadership levels, proposed adequate financial provision and living conditions for workers and their families. An interesting proposal for extending the movement came from 5 per cent of the respondents, mainly Samiti members. This was the suggestion of establishing 'cells' of activists, seen as either proliferating at all levels or spreading by contagion at the grass roots of the movement. Other points made in this category by a few respondents called generally for stronger, more effective organization and improved co-operation and co-ordination, and greater initiative from below. Additionally, 5 per cent specified co-ordination of all constructive work agencies. With the main exception of the idea of 'cells', it is perhaps significant that the tenor of organizational change proposed is towards systematization, training of personnel, and a limited programme backed by a propaganda system and on a sound financial base. Only one respondent specified organizational effectiveness without centralization.

Ranking almost equal with proposals in the organization category were proposals concerning the workers. In some respects, of course (for instance, training and maintenance), the two categories are scarcely distinguishable. Within the category related to workers the demand for an improvement of their calibre was most marked. A minute proportion went further and proposed the elimination of 'undesirables' from the movement by some unspecified, non-violent, process. Another tiny proportion proposed that the workers themselves should close the gap between practice and precept by donating a proportion of their own lands. It was a Representative who took the opportunity in the 'additional comments' section of the questionnaire to offer the following piece of cogent self-criticism:

1. If we want the movement to surge forward all workers will have to make greater sacrifices. We seem to be forgetting the basic values of the movement. We preach bread labour but do not even clean our own rooms and place of work. 2. The Sarvodaya workers are falling from their ideals. We practise inequality among ourselves. We shall have to live the Sarvodaya ideals first, and then only preach them.

One in ten of all respondents made the simple demand for more workers. Suggestions were also made by a smaller proportion to widen the social composition of the movement to include more young people, intellectuals, villagers, women, and the working and urban classes. There were no references to widening recruitment to include more workers from minority religious groups, but the point was made in the 'additional comments' section of the questionnaire, where a Convenor wrote: 'Sarvodai movement should rise among the national level in every sphere and try to embrace Muslim brothers also; up till now they are very less in number in the movement. We must explore the reasons of this seriously.' From a Representative came the comment:

The movement in Kerala has failed to attract good Christians and Mohammedans. The movement at present is misunderstood as largely a Hindu movement which it is not. Except on some minor points, there is a large area of agreement which we have so far failed to exploit. If some allowance in the initial stage is given in community prayer, strict vegetarianism, etc., large numbers of Christians and Mohammedans can be attracted to the Movement. The religious bias should be kept aside.

Next in the ranking of the categories came proposals concerned with the movement's propaganda and publicity, one in five respondents making a proposal of this kind. Some respondents merely proposed more publicity and propaganda in general terms. More support, however, came for proposals to achieve greater contact with the mass of the population. The method proposed, unsophisticated and traditionally Indian, was that of the walking tour, the padayatra, contacting village after village in a quasi-missionary effort. Interestingly enough, this proposal was not linked with Vinoba's name but put forward as a proposal suitable for workers generally. (It is also, it should be noted, a proposal being actively implemented by the movement, at least in certain areas.) A small percentage of respondents proposed that the movement's literature should be improved both quantitatively and qualitatively. Improving language coverage, making literature more readily available, and making the content more appealing were among the points mentioned. Tiny percentages of respondents advocated propaganda in existing educational institutions and by means of seminars—the latter, again, is a proposal being implemented to some extent, particularly by the Gandhian Institute of Studies.

Far fewer respondents (12 per cent) made proposals relating to the leadership of the movement. Calls for more effective leadership and for leaders to engage in field work were made by only a few respondents. Improvements in leader–worker relations, however, were mentioned by 5 per cent.

Of the remaining categories, only the one concerned with relations with the Government included proposals made by more than 10 per cent of the respondents. The complex relationship of the movement with the Government is expressed in somewhat bitter detail by a Convenor, not in his answer to this question but in 'additional comments' at the end of the questionnaire:

There are many M.L.A.s (Members of the Legislative Assembly), M.P.s, ministers and party leaders who are big capitalists themselves. They hold hundreds of acres of land and huge amounts of money either in their names or in the names of their family members and relatives. They are directly or indirectly owners or partners in some of the centralized capitalistic industries. They own textile mills, rice mills, sugar mills, etc., which are detrimental to the existence of village industries and Khadi. So long as this state of affairs exists there can be no salvation to the millions of down trodden people in India. Because of the financial assistance that is given to most of the Sarvodaya institutions, I think, our leaders and workers dare not to say anything against such injustices of the people in the government. The Sarvodaya workers cannot tolerate this. They must boldly come out and appeal to the M.L.A.s, M.P.s, ministers and party leaders to change their ways of life to suit this poor country of ours. If they don't heed to our appeal we must launch Satyagraha against such people. Then only, and not before that, our Movement will become a revolutionary movement and a real people's movement.

The ambivalence of the relationship between the movement and the Government, noted in answers to the question on obstacles, is echoed in the proposals to improve effectiveness. It should perhaps be emphasized that only a small number of respondents made explicit reference to this relationship. A tiny proportion proposed closer co-operation with the Government, while an equally tiny proportion suggested opposition to any integration of the movement's with the Government's policies. The least important category, the one including proposals to abolish the large landlord system and private ownership, may be relevant at this point, since what is being suggested here is a change of economic system to be initiated by an agency other than the movement, presumably the Government. An answer which makes its point clearly came from a Representative: 'If the Government can reduce the disparity in size of land holdings and the land is so redistributed that there is no landless family.'

A similar ambivalence is apparent in proposals, made by 7 per cent of all respondents, concerned with the movement's relationship with the political parties. The numbers involved are too small to make analysis by level of leadership strictly feasible, but the figures suggest that Representatives and Convenors are more likely than Samiti members to propose a redefinition of the movement's 'neutral' relationship with the political parties.

'Changes in the social climate' (the final category) were proposed by 5 per cent of the respondents. Such proposals, including suggestions to ban 'obscene films', probably conceal a demand for government initiative, although we do not know this from the data.

From this analysis of the leaders' proposals to improve the effectiveness of the movement perhaps little or nothing novel emerges which could be put to practical use by those responsible for the direction of the movement. Many of the proposals are familiar enough, and represent desirable objects without specifying how the desirable is to be achieved: providing adequate maintenance for the workers is a case in point. Some of the proposals are already being implemented, although no doubt not universally throughout the movement. A few tentative conclusions do, however, emerge which contribute to our knowledge and understanding of the movement.

The ambivalence in attitudes among the leaders concerning the movement's relations with the Government and political parties, and its possible implications for the future of the movement, have been discussed earlier in this chapter. Here it may be added that the ambivalence may be but one reflection of more general tensions present at a critical stage in the development of the movement. Tensions other than those directly concerned with the movement's political stance are apparent: for example, the tensions between the 'revolutionary Gandhians' and the 'inert', employee-oriented, Khadi workers.

One interesting suggestion, noted above, advocated the further development of the movement by 'cells'. A member of the Prabandh Samiti made this proposal in the following words:

I think the most promising way forward is through a network of simple self-supporting, self-propagating local cells. One method would be for two to three families or five to six individuals to pool resources of time and labour so that they can both support themselves and offer service of time and labour to the community. Even one family can do a lot in this way. But local self-support is essential.

The idea of spreading an ideology or a belief by the formation of 'cells' is by no means new. The method of using groups of committed people, each of whom activates a further group of adherents in a continuing process, has been utilized by a wide range of movements from early Protestant sects to Communist parties of the present day. As a method of extending a movement like Sarvodaya, by strengthening the local element and counteracting tendencies to centralization, it would seem to be relevant and appropriate. But, despite this suggestion of cells at the local level and some demand for greater initiative from lower levels, the trend of the answers, considered in terms of organization, seems to be towards a more highly organized structure with a greater degree of formalization. Similarly, in terms of the movement's economic basis and the stress on the adequate training of the workers, the trend seems to be towards professionalism. Some of these proposals, if fully implemented, would certainly involve a move towards professional staffing, a more rigidly structured organization, clearer definition of areas of competence and responsibility, and regularized sources of finance. In other words, a move *towards* professionalism, institutionalization, and bureaucratization and a move *away from* the characteristics of a charismatic movement, as formulated by Weber.

It is possible that Weber was mistaken in suggesting the inevitability of the routinization of charisma and its transmutation into either traditional authority or the rational-legal authority of bureaucratic structures. There is some evidence that charismatic leadership of a high order is sometimes found associated with a typically bureaucratic organization: Billy Graham's crusade might be cited as an example.[1] But there is little doubt that the combina-

[1] cf. A. Etzioni, *A Comparative Analysis of Complex Organizations*, 1961, p. 207: 'A structure might be purely bureaucratic, or have some charismatic positions, or have a large number of such positions, or be almost completely staffed by charismatics and governed by the patterns of behavior typical to charismatic movements.' However, it should be noted that Etzioni uses a broader concept of charisma than Weber: 'the ability of an actor to exercise diffuse and intense influences over the normative orientations of other actors'— ibid., p. 203.

tion is relatively rare and that the eclipse of charisma is more common. And, if we are prepared to allow the distinction between 'genuine' and 'pseudo-' charisma,[1] it would be hard to find an example of 'genuine' charismatic leadership associated with a bureaucratic organization. Sarvodaya might turn out to be the exceptional case, but the odds are that it would not. Yet without the continuous creation of 'genuine' charismatic leadership, without a succession of Gandhis and Vinobas, it is hard to see how the goals of the movement, as presently defined, could ever be realized. It is much easier to see how the movement might cease to be charismatic, become bureaucratized, redefine its goals, and settle down to the routine of a rurally-oriented social-work agency.

An alternative course that the movement might follow is to develop in the direction of becoming a passive 'sect' or 'order'.[2] This possibility seems much less likely. The universalistic orientation of the movement clearly illuminates the answers of most of our respondents. There is no evidence in them of any intention to form a model society in isolation from the sinful world. The idea of cells, for example, is linked to the idea of propagation of the movement in the sense of a yeast which ferments and activates the whole mass. There is no suggestion of the encapsulation of a Sarvodaya society within the larger society: even those who want to build model Gramdan villages want them to be models for all other villages, and eventually the whole world, to follow. There is no element in Sarvodaya of *verzuiling*, the forming of columns or blocks and parallel organizations within a society. If we can accept the Banks' explanation of this concept, it would seem clear that the Sarvodaya movement is not conceived by its members in terms of *verzuiling*.

People of the same faith, people with the same dream of a better world order, can through this proliferation of organizations prepare themselves regularly for it and in the meantime more easily sustain the period of waiting. *Verzuiling* is thus to be seen as a form of isolation within an existing society, the consequence of techniques employed to build up

---

[1] See Chapter Four, p. 149 above.

[2] For a discussion of these concepts see D. A. Martin, *Pacifism*, 1965, Ch. 9. Sects may be active or passive, displaying aggression towards or withdrawal from the world. 'The conceptual distinction between the sect and the order turns principally on the way in which the latter recognizes that its standards are not capable of being realized universally'—ibid., p. 191.

solidarity among the committed by concentrating upon the ideological similarity and emphasizing their lack of genuine dependence upon the 'enemy'.[1]

For a universalistic movement like Sarvodaya, looking forward to, and working toward, a world-wide stateless society, based on truth, love, and compassion, there is and can be no enemy. All men, saints and sinners alike, are one: all men are brothers, participating in the eternal unity which some men call God.

[1] J. A. Banks and O. Banks, 'Feminism and social change', in G. K. Zollschan and W. Hirsch (eds.), *Explorations in Social Change*, 1964, p. 551. The concept of *verzuiling* was originally applied to factors in contemporary Dutch life.

CHAPTER EIGHT

DIVERSITIES AMONG THE SARVODAYA LEADERS

IN discussing the characteristics of the Sarvodaya leaders, we have treated them so far mainly as a single group. The focus of attention, either explicitly or implicitly, has been on 'external' comparisons: comparisons between the leaders as a whole and other groups, such as the Indian population or leaders of comparable movements. In the previous chapter, however, the analysis was extended by introducing the variable of level of leadership, and attention was occasionally drawn to certain differences of perception found between three categories of leaders classified according to the level of office which they held in Sarva Seva Sangh. In this chapter we shall be wholly concerned with 'internal' comparisons: attention will be focused not on how Sarvodaya leaders compare with other groups but on how they differ among themselves.

From data already presented, we know that the leaders do not constitute a homogeneous group: the leaders are individuals of various ages, of different caste origins, with varying standards of formal education, and so on. Given this heterogeneity, the question then arises whether the characteristics observed in our 'population' of leaders are associated with one another. For example, is the characteristic of being a top-level leader associated with the characteristics of being more elderly, more highly educated, or less militant on tactical issues? Information about the presence or absence of such associations is essential for a complete description of the population being studied, and a prerequisite of any attempt to explain diversities in behaviour and attitudes.

The information to be presented in this chapter may be interpreted as providing material relevant to an enquiry into the nature and sources of diversity among the Sarvodaya leaders. As in any other collectivity, the potential sources of diversity are many. But, of the variables used in our analysis, several may be deemed of special importance. Among these would be included the variables of social and organizational status, age, regional origin, and religion, all of which previous research has shown to be important sources of political diversity. Each of these variables will be considered in turn and attention drawn to statistically significant associations between them and other variables. In the presentation, however, special attention will be paid to organizational status (level of leadership), which analysis shows to be the most important in the sense that it is the one most frequently associated with other variables. With regard to this variable, its relationships with all the other variables used will be shown, whether or not there is any significant association. In this way the reader may be reminded of the full range of variables employed in the preceding analysis, and of the distributions relating to all leaders which constitute the bases of comparisons between different categories of leaders.

Two further points should be made about the mode of analysis adopted in this chapter, one related to the question of the 'significance' of any observed association, and the other to the meaning of the term 'association' itself. In studying a particular group or population, the simplest procedure for determining whether or not an association exists between characteristics found in it is to categorize the population in terms of two sets of characteristics. A cross-classification then produces a two-way contingency table from which it may be calculated whether a subgroup differs proportionately from the whole group in its possession of any particular characteristic. For example, with respect to our population of 228 Sarvodaya leaders, a cross-classification of level of leadership characteristics with educational characteristics would enable us to determine whether being a top-level leader is associated with being a graduate. If the proportion of top leaders who are graduates differs from the proportion of graduates in the whole group, then an association between the two characteristics exists. If the proportion of top leaders who are graduates is greater, the association is said to be 'positive'; if the proportion is smaller, the association is said to be 'negative'.

If our purpose were simply to describe our *particular group* of 228 leaders, the adoption of this procedure would be adequate to determine the existence of associations, and the question of their statistical significance would not arise. Our particular group, however, is assumed to be a representative sample of all the office-holders from which the group is drawn. Our purpose is to generalize about *all* the office-holders, not a particular group of them. Given this purpose, a proportionate difference between one sub-group and the whole group with respect to their possession of a characteristic is not in itself indicative of an association. The difference may be due simply to chance: an equally representative sample of all the office-holders might reveal another difference or no difference at all. To determine whether the observed difference in the sample being studied is not due to chance, a test of statistical significance must be made. The one used, where appropriate, in the tables below is the chi-square test. Briefly, this tests the significance of the difference between the observed frequency distribution and the frequency distribution expected if there is no association ('the null hypothesis'). From the computation of the chi-square for any given distribution it is possible to express the result in the form of a probability value indicating a level of statistical significance. Thus, the value 0·05 means that deviations from expected frequencies caused by chance variations of sampling would be so large as to produce a chi-square of the order computed for the distribution under consideration only five in one hundred times. In the analysis which follows the value of 0·05 will be accepted as the highest value indicative of a significant association. However, since acceptance of this value is a *convention* that may lead to acceptance of the null hypothesis, when in fact an association does exist, the attention of the reader will on occasions be drawn to possible associations which are not statistically significant at the 0·05 level.

With regard to the meaning of the term 'association', it must be emphasized that the assertion that a significant association exists between two characteristics does *not* necessarily imply there is any *causal* connection: it implies only that the characteristics are found together. The causal determinant of any observed association may be related to one of the two characteristics, or it may be related to some other unspecified characteristic. In some instances an association may be 'apparent' rather than 'real' in the sense that it is a product of other associations. By further analysis of 'partial' associations, holding one variable constant, it is possible to determine whether 'total' associations are apparent or real. Such analysis has been made on appropriate occasions, but the limited size of our sample precludes extensive analysis along these lines.

What is presented, then, in this chapter is the evidence of association or lack of association between selected characteristics found among the Sarvodaya leaders. The associated characteristics may or may not be causally connected. In themselves, of course, the observed associations do not explain anything: they provide merely the stimulus to search for an explanation. In some instances the associations may be explained by reference to a general hypothesis which is posited as holding true of all social movements: for example, the hypothesis that leaders of social movements tend to be drawn disproportionately from the higher social-status groups of the society in which the movement operates. The associations may then be interpreted as additional case-study evidence for the validation (or invalidation) of a general hypothesis about social movements. In other instances an *ad hoc* explanation may appear plausible. For example, if Southern leaders differ significantly from Northern leaders in their attitudes to Congress, this might be explained as consistent with a known general disposition of Southerners towards Congress, the reasons for the disposition being a particular set of historical circumstances. In yet other instances, no explanation may be readily forthcoming: the associations remain brute but puzzling facts requiring further analysis or research.

I. DIVERSITIES ASSOCIATED WITH LEVEL OF LEADERSHIP

Our classification of the Sarvodaya leaders into three categories according to the highest office held at the time of the enquiry is not a classification recognized in the movement, although it has some basis in organizational fact. The hierarchical distinctions between top-, middle-, and lower-level leaders are imputed by us. As we shall see, there is some justification for imputing a hierarchy, even though the distinction between middle- and lower-level leaders is less clear than that between top-level leaders and the rest. Ideologically, it will be recalled, Sarvodaya is strongly committed to the value of equality, one of its major objectives being a society of social, political, and economic equals. The movement's organization, Sarva Seva Sangh, reflects this value commitment, particularly in its decision-making procedure (based on the principle of unanimity or consensus) and in its lack of a clearly articulated organizational hierarchy. The egalitarianism of Sarvodaya is also manifested in the view, often expressed by those engaged in the movement, that the persons we have designated 'leaders', i.e. the office-holders, are also 'workers'. The assumption is that, ideally at least, there is no place in the movement for the distinction between 'them', the leaders, and 'us', the rank-and-file members.

In many social movements which are democratic in their organizational structure, and egalitarian in their ideology, the distinction between leaders and the rank and file is more clear-cut than in the Sarvodaya movement. Since Michels first drew attention to it,[1] one of the best substantiated conclusions of research on social movements is that, on many dimensions, leaders tend *not* to be representative, in a statistical sense, of their memberships. In particular, leaders of movements tend to be drawn disproportionately from the higher social strata, and, further, partly because of their leadership roles, to develop views and attitudes different from those of other members. It seems likely that this is also true of the Sarvodaya movement, although, in the absence of adequate data on the rank-and-file members, the Lok Sevaks, it is not possible to substantiate it. However, differences between leaders and ordinary members of social movements tend to be paralleled by differences *within* the leadership group. That is to say, top-level leaders tend to differ from lower-level leaders in a way similar to that in which leaders as a whole and ordinary members do, the latter constituting simply the lowest level in the leadership scale. Thus, in the British Labour Party, for example, M.P.s tend to be more middle-class than the officers of the local parties, and the latter more middle-class than the ordinary members. On the assumption that Sarvodaya leaders differ in certain respects from non-leaders, we might expect, therefore, to find differences between the leadership levels. What significant differences do we in fact find, and what explanations might account for them?

Demographic characteristics by leadership level

We begin our analysis by examining the distributions of certain demographic characteristics as set out in Table 8:1. As far as the sex distribution is concerned, it will be seen that women tend to be concentrated at the top (Samiti) level of leadership. This suggests that, although women are heavily under-represented in the Sarvodaya leadership, once they are in the movement there may be a bias *in favour* of women in the process of selection of top leaders.

---

[1] R. Michels, *Political Parties*, 1915.

TABLE 8:1

Demographic characteristics of Sarvodaya leaders by leadership level

Level of Leadership	Sex			Marital status			Region of birth*			Age in 1965 (years)					Date of joining movement		
	Men %	Women %	N	Single %	Married, Widowed or Divorced %	N	North %	South %	N	20-39 %	40-49 %	50-59 %	60 and over %	N	Before 1951 %	1951 or after %	N
I Samiti	84	16	(45)	16	84	(45)	78	22	(40)	10	27	19	44	(41)	86	14	(43)
II Representative	98	2	(111)	11	89	(111)	75	25	(110)	27	29	23	21	(102)	62	38	(97)
III Convener	99	1	(72)	10	90	(72)	89	11	(71)	35	29	15	20	(65)	65	35	(57)
All respondents	96	4	(228)	11	89	(228)	80	20	(221)	26	29	20	25	(208)	67	33	(197)
x^2	N.A.**			1·01			4·98			14·73					8·37		
d.f.				2			2			6					2		
$p \leqslant$				0·70			0·10			0·05					0·02		

Note. *Excluding leaders born in present State of Pakistan and those born in the West. Two Samii members, one Representative and one Convenor, were born in Pakistan; two Samii members were born in the West.
**Not submitted to chi-square testing.

The number of women in our sample, however, is too small to permit a test of statistical significance. With regard to both marital status and regional origin the tests show that there is no significant association between the various characteristics and leadership level. Just as the leaders as a whole are broadly representative of the Indian adult population in respect of their marital status and regional origin, so are the leaders at each level of leadership.

The age distribution, however, does reveal significant differences: broadly, the higher the leadership level, the older the leaders tend to be. Thus 63 per cent of those at the Samiti level, compared with 44 per cent at the Representative and 35 per cent at the Convenor levels, were aged 50 years or over. That age is a factor in the selection of leaders is not surprising, and might readily be accounted for by the hypothesis that, normally, leaders of social movements have to serve in them for a period, during which they demonstrate their loyalty and aptitude, before they are selected for the higher offices. That this factor operates in the Sarvodaya movement is further suggested by the distribution relating to date of joining. Top-level leaders were distinctly more likely than other leaders to have joined before 1951, the year in which the Bhoodan campaign was launched.

Caste, class, and status characteristics by leadership level

The nature and extent of the associations between caste, class, and status characteristics among the Sarvodaya leaders have already been discussed in Chapter Three. Our general conclusion was that, as a group, the Sarvodaya leaders were not 'classless' in the sense of being a group in which these characteristics were randomly distributed. With certain notable exceptions, there was a tendency for the pyramids of caste, class, and status to overlap, so that, for example, leaders possessing a 'high' characteristic in one status dimension tended to possess 'high' characteristics in other dimensions. The data to which we now turn may be seen as related to this previous discussion. Our division of the leaders into three categories according to the level of office held may be interpreted as dividing them into *organizational* status groups. From this perspective, the question then arises whether there is any association between organizational status and the various kinds of social status previously considered. For example, are leaders who are high in

TA

Caste, class, and status characteristi

Level of Leadership	Father's Caste					Father's occupational class			Respondent's occupational class		Percenta owning property any typ
	Brahmin %	Kshatriya %	Vaishya %	Other %	N	Middle %	Agriculturalist %	N	Middle %	N	%
I Samiti	39	9	39	13	(44)	95	39	(44)	100	(18)	43
II Representative	37	26	27	9	(110)	92	59	(110)	87	(63)	71
III Convenor	38	37	17	8	(72)	88	55	(69)	85	(40)	77
All respondents	38	26	26	10	(226)ˈ	91	54	(223)	88	(121)	68
χ^2	14·36					1·74	5·35		2·89		12·39
d.f.	6					2	2		2		2
$p \leqslant$	0·05					0·50	0·10		0·20		0·01

Note. *The percentages do not add up to 100 since the categories are not mutually exclusive, some resp

the organizational hierarchy of Sarva Seva Sangh also high in the caste hierarchy, the income-class hierarchy, the educational-class hierarchy, and so on? An affirmative answer to this question would support the general hypothesis, suggested in many studies of social and political movements, that social status is positively associated with organizational status. Even in avowed democratic and egalitarian movements social status appears to be a hidden factor in the selection of individuals for leadership positions.

Inspection of the data presented in Table 8:2 suggests that the general hypothesis holds true of Sarva Seva Sangh, but only with certain interesting qualifications. The distribution relating to the *per capita* monthly income shows a highly significant association

...daya leaders by leadership level

...entage h per pita nthly me of 30/- or ore N	Educational attainment					Self-rated class*					Status consistency	
	Primary School only %	High School and Intermediate %	Graduate %	Postgraduate %	N	Middle %	Lower Middle %	Working %	Peasant %	N	Consistent %	N
(31)	13	22	20	44	(45)	48	31	10	12	(42)	64	(36)
(99)	26	49	15	10	(109)	34	29	11	36	(105)	39	(98)
(60)	28	44	13	15	(72)	27	34	14	34	(71)	43	(65)
(190)	24	42	15	19	(226)	34	31	12	31	(218)	45	(199)
	30·15					5·09	0·55	0·57	8·78		6·82	
	6					2	2	2	2		2	
	0·001					0·10	0·80	0·80	0·02		0·05	

...nselves as both Peasant and some other class.

between level and income: the higher the level, the greater is the proportion of leaders with an income of at least Rs. 30/– per month—a figure approximating to the *per capita* income of the Indian population as a whole. The difference is such that top-level leaders are almost twice as likely as the lower-level leaders to report a *per capita* monthly income of Rs. 30/– or more. The distributions relating to father's occupational class, the respondent's occupational class before joining the movement, and the respondent's rating of himself as middle-class, while not statistically significant, suggest a similar pattern of association. There is also a significant association between level and the respondent's rating of himself as belonging to the peasant class; but in this instance the association exists at the top level only. Samiti members were less likely than Representatives or Convenors to identify with the peasants. This finding is probably related to the fact that Samiti members were less likely than others to be the children of fathers who were agriculturalists. A connection with agriculture, as previously noted, appeared to be a large but not exclusive element in a leader's rating of himself as a peasant.

The distribution relating to educational attainment is also one which distinguishes top-level leaders from the other two levels. Representatives and Convenors were composed of approximately the same proportions of the four educational categories, the median leader at each of these levels being an individual educated up to High School or Intermediate standard. The median top-level leader, in contrast, was a graduate; and no less than 64 per cent of Samiti members were either graduates or postgraduates. A Samiti member, in fact, was more than twice as likely to be a graduate or postgraduate than was a Representative or a Convenor.

It is the distributions relating to caste and property ownership which provide data running clearly contrary to expectations derived from acceptance of the general hypothesis that organizational and social status are positively associated. On the assumption that the caste (varna) hierarchy places Brahmins at the top, followed by Kshatriyas, Vaishyas, and 'Others' (not twice-born), in that order, we find no significant association between caste and leadership level in respect of the highest and lowest caste groups. Brahmins and 'Others' were found in approximately equal proportions at each of the three levels. The distributions of the two intermediate caste groups do show a significant association, but in the direction *opposite* to expectation. That is to say, the higher the level of leadership, the *smaller* is the proportion of Kshatriyas and the *greater* is the proportion of Vaishyas. Both castes are equally represented in the leadership as a whole, but Kshatriyas are under-represented and Vaishyas over-represented at the higher levels of leadership. The pattern is as if, for these two groups, their order in the caste hierarchy were inverted. While no explanation is readily apparent for this finding, it will be recalled from the discussion in Chapter Three that Kshatriya Sarvodaya leaders appeared to be a distinctive group. Compared with other twice-born leaders, they enjoyed a lower income, were less likely to be of middle-class origin, less likely to be graduates, and less likely to rate themselves as middle-class. On the other hand, they were more likely to identify with the peasants and to own property.

The apparently odd association between being a property owner and being of *low* income and educational status that we found earlier to obtain among the Sarvodaya leaders prepares us for the further finding that property ownership is inversely associated with organizational status: the higher the level of leadership, the *smaller* the proportion owning property. 'Property' in this context refers to all kinds of immovable property, landed, residential, and other kinds. When property in land only is considered, the association is even stronger than the one shown in Table 8:2. Thus while 33 per cent of the Samiti reported owning land, 66 per cent of the Representatives and 71 per cent of the Convenors did so. The explanation of these associations should probably be sought in the varying commitment of the leaders to the movement's ideology. In a movement which subscribes to the belief that 'land belongs to God', to own property is not to display a valued characteristic: quite the reverse. To own no property or to have divested oneself of the property once owned thus becomes a sign of adherence to the movement's values, and, as such, a factor involved in selection for office. In evaluating the association, however, it should be noted that Samiti members were less likely than Representatives or Convenors to be the children of fathers who owned land, and therefore probably less likely to have owned land themselves. But the difference between the leadership levels in this respect is not in itself sufficient to account for the observed association. And, as we shall see, there is other evidence that top-levels leaders were more committed than lower-level leaders to the values of the movement.

The remaining distribution presented in Table 8:2 relates to the non-vertical dimension of status: status consistency. In the leadership as a whole, 45 per cent were classified as consistents on five dimensions of status: caste, father's occupational class, educational attainment, household income, and self-rated class. All save one of these leaders were *high* status consistents. The distribution shows that neither Representatives nor Convenors differed greatly from the average for all leaders, but that nearly two out of three of the Samiti were consistents.[1] The finding that top-level leadership is

[1] The association between top-level leadership and status consistency is maintained when educational status (graduate or non-graduate) is held constant.

significantly associated with status consistency strengthens the conclusion that social status is probably a factor in the selection of top Sarvodaya leaders. We may fairly assume that the (high) status consistents are those who can be seen most clearly to be of high status. This is not to say, however, that high status is a *conscious* factor in the selection. It probably operates in a completely unconscious way; and it may well be the case that, in the Sarvodaya as in other social movements, high status is associated with the possession of the kinds of skill required of a top leader.

The associations between leadership level and age, and leadership level and social status, reconsidered

The fact that leadership level is positively associated with age and also tends to be positively associated with several dimensions of social status presents us with a problem of analysis. Are both kinds of association real, or is one kind merely apparent in the sense of being a product of the other? To answer this question we must probe more deeply into the associations, considering the three variables, or kinds of variable, together.

In Table 8:3 level is related to age, with four dimensions of status held constant. The table presents a set of partial associations which are contained, so to speak, in the total association noted above: the higher the level, the greater the proportion of more elderly leaders. With four exceptions, the broad pattern of association is maintained in each of the status groups. And in all groups, save the Kshatriyas, the highest level of leadership has the greatest proportion of leaders aged 50 years or over. The main exception is the Kshatriya group in which the *lowest* level has the greatest proportion of such leaders. Noting this exception, we may draw the broad conclusion that, independently of social status, level of leadership is positively associated with age.

The relationship between leadership level and caste, it will be recalled, was complex. There was no association between leadership level and being a Brahmin or being once-born ('other'). But the higher the level, the less likely were leaders to be Kshatriyas and the more likely were they to be Vaishyas. Table 8:4 presents the partial associations which enable us to determine whether the relationships between level and caste are maintained when age, education, income, and self-rated status are in turn held constant. Though the small numbers on which some of the percentage

TABLE 8:3

Level of leadership and age among Sarvodaya leaders

(Percentages aged 50 years or more in **bold type**)

Level of Leadership	Total in each category (a)	No. aged 50 yrs. or more (b)	(b)/(a)%	Total in each category (a)	No. aged 50 yrs. or more (b)	(b)/(a)%	Total in each category (a)	No. aged 50 yrs. or more (b)	(b)/(a)%	Total in each category (a)	No. aged 50 yrs. or more (b)	(b)/(a)%
(i) according to caste	Brahmins			Kshatriyas			Vaishyas			Others		
I	17	11	**65**	3	1	**33**	15	10	**67**	3	2	**66**
II	38	18	**47**	28	9	**32**	25	15	**60**	10	2	**20**
III	25	9	**36**	24	10	**42**	10	2	**20**	6	2	**33**
(ii) according to education	Graduates			Non-graduates								
I	27	15	**56**	14	11	**79**						
II	24	9	**38**	75	34	**45**						
III	19	6	**32**	46	17	**37**						
(iii) according to per capita monthly income	More than Rs. 30/–			Rs. 30/– or less								
I	29	17	**59**	2	2	**100**						
II	52	21	**40**	40	17	**43**						
III	26	12	**46**	29	7	**24**						
(iv) according to self-rated status	Middle Class			Lower Middle and Working Class			Peasant					
I	18	13	**72**	15	9	**60**	5	2	**40**			
II	34	18	**53**	39	16	**41**	23	5	**22**			
III	16	7	**44**	32	10	**31**	16	5	**31**			

TABLE 8:4
Level of leadership and caste among Sarvodaya leaders
(Percentages of Brahmins, Kshatriyas, Vaishyas, or Others in **bold type**)

Level of Leadership	Total in each category (a)	No. of Brahmins (b)	(b)/(a) %	No. of Kshatriyas (c)	(c)/(a) %	No. of Vaishyas (d)	(d)/(a) %	No. of others (e)	(e)/(a) %
(i) according to age									
				Aged 50 years or more					
I	24	11	**46**	1	**4**	10	**42**	2	**8**
II	44	18	**41**	9	**20**	15	**34**	2	**5**
III	23	9	**39**	10	**34**	2	**9**	2	**9**
				Aged under 50 years					
I	14	6	**43**	2	**14**	5	**36**	1	**7**
II	57	20	**35**	19	**33**	10	**18**	8	**14**
III	42	16	**38**	14	**33**	8	**19**	4	**10**
(ii) according to education									
				Graduates					
I	29	11	**38**	3	**10**	12	**42**	3	**10**
II	27	13	**48**	5	**19**	5	**18**	4	**15**
III	19	8	**42**	7	**37**	3	**16**	1	**5**
				Non-graduates					
I	15	6	**40**	1	**7**	5	**33**	3	**20**
II	81	28	**35**	23	**28**	24	**30**	6	**7**
III	51	17	**33**	20	**39**	9	**18**	5	**10**
(iii) according to per capita monthly income									
				More than Rs. 30/-					
I	28	11	**39**	3	**11**	11	**39**	3	**11**
II	55	21	**41**	13	**22**	17	**29**	4	**7**
III	29	14	**48**	7	**18**	5	**13**	3	**7**
				Rs. 30/- or less					
I	2	1	**50**	0	**0**	0	**0**	1	**50**
II	39	14	**36**	13	**33**	7	**18**	5	**13**
III	30	10	**33**	13	**44**	4	**13**	3	**10**
(iv) according to self-rated status									
				Middle Class					
I	20	10	**50**	1	**5**	9	**45**	0	**0**
II	36	14	**39**	5	**14**	16	**43**	1	**2**
III	19	9	**47**	7	**37**	2	**11**	1	**5**
				Lower Middle and Working Class					
I	16	4	**25**	2	**25**	5	**31**	5	**31**
II	40	17	**43**	15	**38**	5	**12**	3	**7**
III	34	9	**26**	13	**38**	8	**24**	4	**12**
				Peasants					
I	5	2	**40**	1	**20**	1	**20**	1	**20**
II	26	7	**27**	9	**35**	5	**19**	5	**19**
III	18	9	**50**	6	**33**	2	**11**	1	**6**

figures are based must be noted, it will be seen that, with minor variations, the broad pattern of relationships is in fact maintained. The possible exception relates to Brahmins when income is held constant. Among leaders with a *per capita* monthly income of more than R. 30/-, the higher the level, the smaller the proportion of Brahmins, while among leaders with less than this income, the higher the level, the greater the proportion of Brahmins.

In discussing the relation between leadership level and educational attainment we noted that there was no association between being a Representative or Convenor and educational attainment, but that the association was strong between being a top-level leader and being a graduate or postgraduate. The data presented in Table 8:5 enable us to state whether this pattern of association is maintained when age, caste, income, and self-rated status are in turn held constant.

It will be seen that in all the groups listed the proportion of graduates is greatest at the top level, while there are only relatively small differences between the two lower levels. We may fairly conclude, therefore, that, independently of age, caste, income, and self-rated status, being a top-level leader is positively associated with being a graduate.

The association between leadership level and income was strong: the higher the level, the more likely was a leader to enjoy a *per capita* monthly income of Rs. 30/- or more. Again, we may ask whether the association holds good independently of other factors: age, caste, education, and self-rated status. Table 8:6 shows that the direction of the association is not maintained in all the groups listed. Among older leaders, the once-born ('others'), and graduates, the proportion with incomes of Rs. 30/- or more is greater at the lower level than at the middle level. But in all groups the proportion is greatest at the top level of leadership. We may conclude, therefore, that even when age and the other dimensions of status are held constant, there is a positive association between being a top-level leader and enjoying a relatively higher income.

Finally, to complete the analysis in this part, we may reconsider the association between leadership level and self-rated status. It will be recalled that the association was not statistically significant at the 0·05 level, but that the distribution in Table 8:2 suggested a possible association: the higher the level, the more likely were

TABLE 8:5

Level of leadership and educational attainment among Sarvodaya leaders

(Percentages who were graduates in **bold type**)

Level of Leadership	Total in each category (a)	No. of Graduates (b)	(b)/(a) %	Total in each category (a)	No. of Graduates (b)	(b)/(a) %	Total in each category (a)	No. of Graduates (b)	(b)/(a) %	Total in each category (a)	No. of Graduates (b)	(b)/(a) %
(i) according to age												
	Aged 50 years or more			*Aged less than 50 years*								
I	26	15	**58**	15	12	**80**						
II	43	9	**21**	56	15	**27**						
III	23	6	**26**	42	13	**31**						
(ii) according to caste												
	Brahmins			*Kshatriyas*			*Vaishyas*			*Others*		
I	17	11	**65**	4	3	**75**	17	12	**71**	6	3	**50**
II	41	13	**32**	28	5	**18**	29	5	**17**	10	4	**40**
III	25	8	**32**	27	7	**26**	12	3	**25**	6	1	**17**
(iii) according to per capita *monthly income*												
	More than Rs. 30/-			*Rs. 30/- or less*								
I	29	21	**72**	2	1	**50**						
II	55	17	**31**	41	9	**22**						
III	29	13	**45**	31	4	**13**						
(iv) according to self-rated status												
	Middle Class			*Lower Middle and Working Class*			*Peasant*					
I	20	15	**75**	17	8	**47**	5	5	**100**			
II	35	10	**29**	40	12	**30**	26	5	**19**			
III	19	7	**37**	34	10	**29**	18	3	**17**			

TABLE 8:6

Level of leadership and income among Sarvodaya leaders

(Percentages with *per capita* monthly income of more than Rs. 30/– in **bold type**)

(i) *according to age*

Level of Leadership	Aged 50 years or more			Aged less than 50 years		
	Total in each category (a)	No. with > Rs. 30/- (b)	$\frac{(b)}{(a)}\%$	Total in each category (a)	No. with > Rs. 30/- (b)	$\frac{(b)}{(a)}\%$
I	19	17	**89**	12	12	**100**
II	38	21	**55**	54	31	**57**
III	19	12	**63**	36	14	**39**

(ii) *according to caste*

Level of Leadership	Brahmins			Kshatriyas			Vaishyas			Others		
	(a)	(b)	%	(a)	(b)	%	(a)	(b)	%	(a)	(b)	%
I	12	11	**92**	3	3	**100**	11	11	**100**	4	3	**75**
II	35	21	**60**	26	13	**50**	24	17	**71**	9	4	**44**
III	24	14	**58**	20	7	**35**	9	5	**56**	6	3	**50**

(iii) *according to education*

Level of Leadership	Graduates			Non-Graduates		
	(a)	(b)	%	(a)	(b)	%
I	22	21	**95**	9	8	**89**
II	26	17	**65**	71	39	**55**
III	17	13	**76**	43	16	**37**

(iv) *according to self-rated status*

Level of Leadership	Middle Class			Lower Middle and Working Class			Peasant		
	(a)	(b)	%	(a)	(b)	%	(a)	(b)	%
I	15	15	**100**	13	11	**85**	2	2	**100**
II	32	22	**69**	39	23	**59**	23	10	**43**
III	16	10	**62**	30	13	**43**	14	6	**43**

TABLE 8:7

Level of leadership and self-rated status among Sarvodaya leaders

(Percentages who rated themselves Middle Class in **bold type**)

Level of Leadership	Total in each category (a)	No. of Middle Class (b)	$\frac{(b)}{(a)}$%	Total in each category (a)	No. of Middle Class (b)	$\frac{(b)}{(a)}$%	Total in each category (a)	No. of Middle Class (b)	$\frac{(b)}{(a)}$%	Total in each category (a)	No. of Middle Class (b)	$\frac{(b)}{(a)}$%
(i) *according to age*	*Aged 50 years or more*			*Aged less than 50 years*								
I	24	13	**54**	14	5	**36**						
II	39	18	**46**	57	16	**28**						
III	22	7	**32**	42	9	**21**						
(ii) *according to caste*	*Brahmins*			*Kshatriyas*			*Vaishyas*			*Others*		
I	16	10	**62**	4	1	**25**	15	9	**60**	6	0	**0**
II	37	14	**38**	29	5	**17**	26	16	**62**	10	1	**10**
III	27	9	**33**	26	7	**27**	12	2	**17**	6	1	**17**
(iii) *according to per capita monthly income*	*More than Rs. 30/-*			*Less than Rs. 30/-*								
I	28	15	**54**	2	0	**0**						
II	55	22	**40**	39	10	**26**						
III	29	10	**34**	31	6	**19**						
(iv) *according to education*	*Graduates*			*Non-graduates*								
I	28	15	**54**	14	5	**36**						
II	28	10	**36**	74	25	**34**						
III	20	7	**35**	51	12	**24**						

TABLE 8:8

Religious characteristics of Sarvodaya leaders by leadership level

Level of Leadership	Religion of parents:						Religious views of respondent:						Religious upbringing perceived as:	
	Hindu %	Muslim %	Sikh %	Jain %	Christian %	N	Orthodox %	Liberal %	Humanist %	Scientific Spiritualist %	Non-religious %	N	Orthodox %	N
I Samiti	89	0	0	7	4	(45)	3	33	40	52	5	(40)	21	(39)
II Representative	94	1	1	4	0	(109)	1	47	61	44	3	(109)	35	(107)
III Convenor	97	1	1	0	0	(72)	1	37	62	46	7	(72)	24	(70)
All respondents	94	1	1	3	1	(226)	1	41	58	46	5	(221)	29	(216)
χ^2	N.A.**						N.A.	3·06	6·45	0·85	N.A.		3·75	
d.f.								2	2	2			2	
$p \leqslant$								0·30	**0·05**	0·70			0·20	

**Not submitted to chi-square testing.

leaders to rate themselves middle-class. If there is an association of this kind, does it hold good independently of age and the other dimensions of social status? Table 8:7 suggests that it does in the following groups: leaders aged under 50 years, those aged 50 years or more, Brahmins, those with a *per capita* monthly income in excess of Rs. 30/–, graduates, and non-graduates. Most notably, the association is not maintained when caste is held constant. Among Brahmin leaders, the highest proportion who rate themselves middle-class is found at the top level; among Kshatriyas and the once-born ('others'), it is found at the lowest level; and among Vaishyas it is found at the middle level.

The general conclusion we may draw from the analysis of partial associations is that it modifies, but does not substantially change, the picture derived from the earlier analysis of total associations. The associations between leadership level and age, caste, income, education, and possibly self-rated status are real rather than apparent.

Religious characteristics by leadership level

Analysis of the distributions of religious characteristics among Sarvodaya leaders by level of leadership (Table 8:8) may be dealt with briefly. Since the overwhelming majority were children of Hindus, we should not expect large proportionate differences between levels. The distribution suggests a possible negative association between level of leadership and being a child of Hindu parents; but the differences are too small to permit a test of statistical significance. There are also proportionate differences between the levels in respect of perceived orthodox religious upbringing; but there is no significant association. With regard to the various religious views held by the leaders, only Humanism is significantly associated with leadership level: top-level leaders are less likely than others to describe themselves as Humanist.

Political characteristics by leadership level

The first part of Table 8:9 shows the distributions of two kinds of political characteristic: participation through voting in the first three General Elections; and voting for a Congress candidate. In each of the three elections the differences between Representatives and Convenors in voting behaviour are small. The contrast is again between these two levels and the top level. Top-level leaders were less likely than others to vote, but, when they did vote, it is possible that they were more likely to vote for a Congress candidate. Abstention from voting could be interpreted as indicating commitment to the movement's value objective of non-partisan politics. If so, top leaders would seem to be more committed to this value than other leaders. That top leaders who did vote showed a possible greater preference for Congress might be explained by the fact that, being older, they were more likely to express allegiance to the party which in their formative years led the struggle for independence under Gandhi. When we examine the distributions concerned with the leaders' perceptions of which parties were most sympathetic, and which most opposed, to Sarvodaya ideals, it is evident that leadership level is not significantly associated with any party or with the view that no party or all parties are sympathetic or opposed.

Social psychological characteristics by leadership level

Table 8:10 presents the distributions of a variety of social psychological characteristics. The first distribution relates to the kind of environment in which the leaders spent their childhood, and reveals a strong negative association between being a top-level leader and being brought up in a village. While two out of three of all leaders were brought up in a village, the proportion falls to almost one in three at the top level. This finding almost certainly reflects the fact that the occupations of the fathers of top-level leaders were of urban rather than rural based, proportionately fewer of them being agriculturalists. There is little substance in the view that Sarvodaya, like most of India's political movements, is led by urban intellectuals, but it could be held to apply to the top-level leaders.

Given the predominantly urban upbringing of the top-level leaders, we might expect that fewer of them would have been brought up in a joint family, since there is evidence that such families are more common in rural than in urban areas. The relevant distribution suggests that this is the case, although the difference between top and other leaders in this respect is not statistically significant.[1]

When we turn to consider whether or not other members of a

[1] Among Kshatriya and Vaishya leaders the difference between the levels is more pronounced than it is among Brahmins.

leader's family are involved with the movement, we do find a significant association between such involvement and being a top-level leader. Samiti members were almost twice as likely as Representatives or Convenors to have at least one other member of their family involved with the movement. This fact, however, does not appear to have influenced to any marked extent the attitude of a leader's family to his own act of joining the movement. Leaders at all levels reported about the same proportions opposing, not objecting to, and favouring their joining.

Since we know that age is associated with leadership level, we might expect that level would be associated with activity in the Independence movement, the higher-level and also older leaders having had more opportunities to be active. To allow for the age factor, the relevant distribution in Table 8:10 excludes those deemed too young to have been active in the Independence movement. The distribution suggests the possibility that top- and middle-level leaders were more likely to have been active than the lowest-level leaders; but the difference is not large enough to be statistically significant.

We interpreted the reasons given for joining the Sarvodaya movement as providing indirect evidence of the distribution of types of motivation among the leaders, which, in turn, is related to the social psychological texture of the movement.[1] When considering the leaders as a single group, we concluded that emotional-affectual motivations were probably the most important in the Sarvodaya movement, followed fairly closely by value-rational motivations, and that both traditional and purposive-rational motivations were of much less importance. Having been influenced to join by parents was taken to be indicative of traditional motivation; having been influenced by reading the movement's literature, value-rational motivation; and having been influenced by contact with Gandhians (and possibly friends), emotional-affectual motivation. In so far as the relevant distribution in Table 8:10 bears on the question, it suggests that traditional and emotional-affectual motivations were fairly evenly distributed between all three levels. However, it also suggests that top-level leaders were, despite their higher standard of education, less moved than other leaders by value-rational motivations. But it should be recalled that top leaders were older than others and, possibly for this reason, less

[1] Chapter Four, Sections I & II.

likely to remember clearly their reasons for joining. The question provided only a crude probe into motivations and, however suggestive the answers, too much weight should not be placed on them. In the light of answers to other questions, it would certainly be unwarranted to infer that top leaders were more moved than others by the remaining type of purposive-rational motivation—the type which actuates individuals to join social movements in expectation of personal advantages, such as the achievement of material rewards and position.

The relatively high frequency of answers indicative of emotional-affectual motivation was previously explained as related to the charismatic character of the movement. In such movements charisma is not the exclusive possession of one person: other leaders share his charisma or possess charismatic qualities of their own. That charisma is involved in the process of recruitment to the movement is further suggested by the finding that four out of five leaders reported that a particular person or persons, other than Gandhiji, especially influenced their decision to join. Among the persons named, Vinoba, as might be expected, figured prominently, with Jayaprakash Narayan as the second most prominent, but a long way behind. Relating the responses of those who named these two persons to level of leadership suggests that the appeal of both was strongest at the middle level. The differences between the levels in the case of Vinoba are not large enough to be significant. In the case of Jayaprakash Narayan the relatively low frequency of his 'appeal' to top-level leaders may be readily accounted for by the fact that he joined the movement only in 1952, i.e. *after* the great majority of top-level leaders had already joined.

Data on the extent to which leaders held positions in organizations other than Sarva Seva Sangh were used earlier as an indicator of what, following Etzioni, we called the movement's 'embrace'. The finding that 58 per cent of all leaders held a position (usually an office rather than mere membership) in at least one other organization was, we suggested, evidence that Sarvodaya conforms more to the paradigm of a 'liberal' than of a 'totalitarian' movement. Analysis by level of the distribution of absence of membership in other organizations, set out in Table 8:10, shows a significant difference between levels, the middle level on this occasion being distinctive. While one in two of the Samiti and Convenors reported no membership, the proportion of Representatives who did so was

TABLE 8:11

Pledges and dan contributions of Sarvodaya leaders by leadership level

Level of Leadership	Pledges* Percentage of leaders reporting having taken:				Dan contributions Percentage reporting having given:				
	All three %	One or two %	None** %	N	None*** %	Bhoodan %	Other dan only %	Bhoodan & other dan %	N
I Samiti	38	41	21	(42)	44	38	7	11	(45)
II Representative	30	66	4	(109)	48	34	10	8	(111)
III Convenor	29	67	4	(72)	50	33	8	8	(72)
All respondents	31	61	7	(223)	48	35	9	9	(228)
x^2			19·13					1·068	
d.f.			4					6	
$p \leqslant$			0·001					0·99	

Notes.   * Pledges of the Lok Sevak, Shanti Sena, and Jeevandan.
           ** Including those opposed to pledges.
           *** Including non-respondents.

only one in three. Analysis of the types of organization in which memberships were held suggests that the distinctive position of the middle-level leaders was a result of their membership in non-Gandhian and non-political organizations. With regard to both 'institutional' and 'official' Gandhian organizations frequency of membership varied with level of leadership: the higher the level, the greater the proportion of memberships. This kind of association is not surprising: one would expect organizational status to be associated with membership of organizations whose functions are related to those of Sarva Seva Sangh. What is not readily explicable is that middle-level leaders should hold relatively more memberships in non-Gandhian and non-political organizations.

Pledges and dan contributions made by Sarvodaya leaders by leadership level

Our survey data provided us with two kinds of measure of the extent of the leaders' practical commitment to the value-goals of the movement. The first relates to the three pledges frequently taken by active participants: the Lok Sevak, the Shanti Sena, and the Jeevandan pledges. One might expect that higher-level leaders would show relatively more commitment than lower-level leaders. This appears, indeed, to be the case if we take as our measure the frequency of having taken *all* three pledges (Table 8:11). However, if we take as our measure the frequency of having taken *none* of these pledges, top leaders are shown to be less committed than other leaders. This ambiguous finding means that, on these two measures, the group of top leaders contain relatively both more committed and less committed individuals. Those who had taken no pledge included some who, in Quaker fashion, were opposed in principle to taking pledges. Such leaders were found at the top level, but they were few in number and not sufficient to account for the observed difference.[1]

The other measure of commitment relates to the dan contributions made by the leaders. We expected that the distribution would suggest the association: the higher the level, the more likely was a leader to have made a contribution in one form or another. But, although the percentage figures point in this direction, the differ-

---

[1] When educational status is held constant, the pattern of association remains essentially the same: top-level leaders, whether graduates or non-graduates, were more likely both to have taken all three pledges and to have taken none.

TABLE 8:12
Perceptions of the movement's goals and programme by leadership level

Level of Leadership	Percentage referring to each type of goal							Percentage referring to items in The Triple Programme				
	Political %	Economic %	Social %	Moral %	Non-Violence %	Universal %	N	Gramdan %	Khadi %	Shanti Sena %	All three items %	N
I Samiti	27	24	62	29	47	24	(45)	86	54	77	48	(44)
II Representative	37	41	59	31	30	21	(111)	88	70	75	55	(104)
III Convenor	31	47	64	39	28	21	(72)	83	69	70	53	(70)
All respondents	33	39	61	33	32	21	(228)	86	67	74	53	(218)
χ^2	1·79	6·12	0·38	1·76	5·24	0·29		0·75	3·59	0·87	0·62	
d.f.	2	2	2	2	2	2		2	2	2	2	
$p \leqslant$	0·50	0·50	0·90	0·50	0·10	0·90		0·70	0·20	0·70	0·80	

ences are not large enough to be statistically significant.[1] Of course, the possibility of making a Bhoodan contribution (as distinct from, say, sampattidan) depends on whether or not one owns land. If this were taken into account, it is possible that the association would be significant, for there is evidence that top-level leaders were less likely than others to come from landowning families. 40 per cent of the Samiti, compared with 37 per cent of the Representatives and 27 per cent of the Convenors, reported that their fathers owned no land.[2]

Perceptions of the movement's goals and programme by leadership level

In analysing the answers to the open-ended question asking for a brief description of the goals of the movement the leaders' replies were classified in six categories, depending on whether or not an answer referred to political, economic, and social goals, the moral or religious development of man, the movement's commitment to Non-violence, and, finally, the universalistic aspirations of the movement. Analysis of the answers by leadership level reveals one statistically significant association: top leaders were less likely than others to mention economic goals, such as the development of village industries and the provision to all of basic economic needs

[1] Among leaders aged 50 years and over (but not those aged under 50 years) the possibility of an association between top-level leadership and having made a dan contribution is more pronounced. In the older age group 62% of top-level leaders had made a contribution, compared with 52% of Representatives and Convenors.

[2] Leadership level   Father's ownership of land

	None %	5 acres or less %	6–20 acres %	Over 20 acres %	N
I Samiti	40	7	20	33	(45)
II Representative	37	14	34	15	(111)
III Convenor	27	24	25	24	(72)
All respondents	35	15	29	21	(228)

$\bar{x}^2 = 14.96$; d.f. 6; $p \leqslant 0.05$

The table shows, however, that, while top leaders were less likely to have fathers who owned land, when their fathers did so, they were more likely to own larger holdings. Among leaders who were property owners there appears to be a positive association between leadership level and having made a dan contribution. The proportions were: Samiti 87% (15); Representative 68% (66); Convenor 60% (47).

(Table 8:12). Only one of the remaining five distributions showed a variation of frequency between levels suggesting a possible association: the one relating to Non-violence. With regard to this kind of answer, in contrast to the one relating to economic goals, the higher the level, the more likely were leaders to mention Non-violence. The clear absence of association with regard to other types of goal is not, however, without interest. For example, despite their significantly lower standard of education the two lower levels were about as likely as the top level to refer to the universalistic aspirations of the movement.

The lower frequency of top leaders' references to economic goals may be reflected in their answers to the question: 'To which three aspects of the Movement's programme do you attach greatest importance today?' Top leaders were about as likely as others to mention all three items of The Triple Programme. Perhaps, surprisingly, in view of their position, they were not *more* likely to do so. But, when the three items are considered separately, top leaders were rather less likely to mention Khadi. 54 per cent of them did so, compared with 70 per cent of the Representatives and 69 per cent of the Convenors. The difference is not large enough to be statistically significant, but suggests a possible association. The possibility is worth pointing out, since it might be expected that top level leaders, being older and having served longer in the movement, most of them having joined before 1951, would be *more* likely than others to mention Khadi—'the livery of independence'. That they were probably less likely to do so suggests a surprising degree of doubt concerning Khadi among the top-level leaders. This conclusion, it should be noted, is consistent with another finding reported in the previous chapter: top leaders were less likely to perceive the promotion of Khadi and village industries as one of the achievements of the movement.

Views of the Sarvodaya leaders on the problem of succession by leadership level

In highly charismatic movements the major source of leadership and authority derives from the exceptional qualities which his followers discern in the leader. The death of the leader consequently poses in a critical form the problem of succession. In the Sarvodaya movement, we have argued, there are reasons for believing that the problem of Vinoba's successor might be solved

without too much difficulty. The consensus of opinion among the
leaders points to one man, Jayaprakash Narayan, as the most likely
successor. Analysis by leadership level of answers to the question
about the succession reveals, however, significant variations in
responses between the three levels. As Table 8:13 shows, support
for Narayan is strongest at the lowest level, 67 per cent of Convenors, compared with 55 per cent of Representatives and Samiti

TABLE 8:13

Views of Sarvodaya leaders on Vinoba's successor by leadership level

Level of Leadership	No individual named* %	Jayaprakash Narayan %	Other individuals %	N
I Samit	38	55	7	(45)
II Representative	25	55	20	(111)
II Convenor	11	67	22	(72)
All respondents	23	59	18	(228)
χ^2		14·09		
d.f.		4		
$p \leqslant$		0·01		

Note *Includes non-respondents, those favouring collective leadership, and those
stating that a leader would emerge.

members, mentioned him first. However, this difference is not due
to the two higher levels favouring another leader. In fact, only
7 per cent of the Samiti, compared with 22 per cent of the Convenors, mentioned some other individual first. The difference is
largely the result of the higher leaders being less likely to answer
the question, or to answer it in a way which avoided references to
any individual. Included among answers of the latter kind were
those which suggested that a new leader would somehow 'emerge',

and those which favoured the idea of 'collective leadership'. There were ten respondents who favoured the latter, nine of whom were top-level leaders. If we group together non-respondents and those not naming an individual successor, there is a significant positive association between leadership level and such responses.

Responses to opinion statements by leadership level

In this part we propose to analyse the responses of the leaders to a set of sixteen opinion statements concerned with ideological (mainly tactical and organizational) issues facing the movement. Respondents were asked to indicate whether they agreed or disagreed with the statements. Table 8:14 presents the proportions at each leadership level expressing agreement.

The first six statements refer to issues involving the movement's relation with government, Congress and conventional politics. Two of the six distributions reveal significant associations between leadership level and agreement. One is the statement that good candidates should be supported in elections even if they hold a party ticket—a view contrary to the movement's official position, which favours non-partisanship as a step towards partyless democracy. The higher the level, the less likely were leaders to agree.[1] The other statement expressed the view that Kashmir's accession to the Indian Union was not final and irrevocable—an opinion which, while not officially that of the movement, was identifiable with Jayaprakash Narayan's view of the problem in 1965. Proportions agreeing with this statement did not vary directly with level, the Representatives being those least likely to agree. But the top-level leaders were those most likely to agree. Of the four remaining statements in this broad category, the distributions concerning which are not significant at the 0·05 level, the one where differences of response were smallest expressed the view that the movement should make a greater effort to rouse the masses by taking up urgent current problems. On this issue top-level leaders were the least likely to agree. They were also the group least likely to agree: (a) that the movement was too identified with Congress; (b) that the movement should pay more attention to

[1] The association appears to be independent of the leaders' attitudes to the political parties. Among those who saw Congress as the party most sympathetic to the movement, those who saw some other (mainly Socialist) party as most sympathetic, and those who saw no party as sympathetic, proportionately fewer top-level leaders agreed with the statement.

| | 12 | | 13 | | 14 | | 15 | | 16 | |
	Puritanism %	N	Decisions %	N	Central organization %	N	Training %	N	Future surge forward %	N
)	41	(37)	51	(41)	41	(41)	91	(44)	76	(45)
)	33	(105)	81	(103)	68	(108)	91	(107)	93	(111)
)	39	(70)	80	(66)	76	(66)	90	(69)	89	(72)
)	36	(212)	75	(210)	65	(215)	90	(220)	88	(228)
	0·84		14·97		13·68		0·04		9·17	
	2		2		2		2		2	
	0·70		0·001		0·01		0·98		0·02	

Panchayati Raj as a means of achieving the Sarvodaya society; and (c) that, until there was a real non-violent alternative to offer, people should not be asked to non-co-operate with the Government's military efforts.

What general conclusion might be drawn from the pattern of responses to these six statements? With the exception of the statement concerning non-co-operation, on which they tended to be rather *more* militant than others, top-level leaders' opinions were closer to the official policy of the movement, and probably to the views of Vinoba himself.

Four further statements raised issues about items in The Triple Programme. There were only small differences between the levels with regard to the statement that Khadi would eventually give way to mill-made cloth, although top leaders were slightly less likely than others to agree. On the issue of whether, in the event of further aggression, the Shanti Sena should be asked to go to the battle areas to offer non-violent resistance top-level leaders were much less likely than others to agree. On this issue they were *less* militant than other leaders. But, it should be noted, the distributions relating to both these statements are not statistically significant. On the two statements concerned with the Gramdan the differences between top-level and other leaders are significant. Convenors and Representatives were more than twice as likely as Samiti members to agree that more attention should be paid to developing existing Gramdan villages.[1] And top-level leaders were least likely to agree that Sulabh Gramdan made too many concessions to the principles of private property.[2] On the four issues involving the items in the programme we may again conclude that top-level leaders tended to hold views closer to the official line of the movement.

The same conclusion may be drawn from analysis of responses to the issue of the use of 'negative' satyagraha to achieve the movement's objectives. Middle-level leaders proved the most militant on this issue, 74 per cent expressing agreement. Top-level leaders

[1] The association between being a top-level leader and not agreeing that more emphasis should be placed on developing existing gramdans is maintained when educational status (graduate or non-graduate) is held constant.

[2] The association between being a top-level leader and not agreeing that Sulabh Gramdan makes too many concessions is maintained when age (under 50 years or 50+ years) is held constant; and also when naming Jayaprakash Narayan as first choice as Vinoba's successor is held constant. In other words, the tendency of top leaders not to agree with the statement is not related to their age or choice of Narayan as successor.

were the least militant, only 49 per cent agreeing. In this instance, the difference between the levels is statistically significant.

One statement raised the issue of the movement's 'puritanical' attitude to matters such as smoking, drinking alcohol, and birth control. On this issue the differences between the levels were small, the Representatives being least likely to agree that the traditional 'puritanical' attitude of the movement should be changed.

Three further statements expressed opinions on organizational matters. With regard to one of them—the view that the movement's workers lacked adequate training—there was nearly unanimous agreement, with negligible differences between levels. Responses to the other two statements revealed highly significant differences. While four out of five Representatives and Convenors agreed that in practice the movement's policy decisions were made by a few leaders, only one in two of the Samiti expressed the same view.[1] With regard to the statement that the movement needs a stronger central organization than it has at present the responses varied with leadership level: the higher the level, the less likely were the leaders to agree.

Since top-level leaders might be held to be more responsible than other leaders for existing organizational arrangements, we might expect them to be less likely than lower-level leaders to agree with opinions critical of the movement's organization. But, if this hypothesis explains the two significant associations noted above, it also underlines the significance (in the non-statistical sense) of the nearly unanimous opinion of the leaders that workers lacked adequate training. Perhaps, however, training in the Sarvodaya movement is not felt to be a matter for which top leaders are specially responsible.

The final statement expressed the opinion (in 1965) that the movement would take a new surge forward in the next few years. Agreement with it might be interpreted as indicating high morale and confidence in the movement's future. The great majority of leaders did agree with the statement. Perhaps surprisingly, however, top-level leaders were least likely to agree, only three out of four doing so, compared with nine out of ten of other leaders. The significant difference in the response of the top leaders to this

[1] The association appears to be independent of the caste of the leaders. Among Brahmins, Kshatriyas, and Vaishyas, top-level leaders were least likely to agree.

statement might suggest that they were being more 'realistic' than other leaders. If so, this show of greater 'realism' may be thought to have been proved wrong by subsequent events. The new surge forward did in fact come with the launching, a few months after the administration of our questionnaire, of the whirlwind campaign for Sulabh Gramdan.

Militancy and leadership level

The responses to several of the opinion statements, as well as certain answers to some of the open-ended questions, suggest the commonsense proposition that some leaders are more militant than others in their general attitude to policy issues. In order to test this proposition systematically, we constructed a simple index of militancy which enables us to place most of the leaders on a four-point scale, ranging from 'non-militancy' to 'extreme militancy'.[1] Using this measure, seven in ten of all leaders were classified as 'moderate militants', just over one in ten as 'extreme militants', and just under one in five as 'non-militants'.

Cross-classification by leadership level shows that there is a

TABLE 8:15

Militancy and level of leadership

Level of Leadership	Militancy Score					
	0 'Non-militants'	1 'Moderate militants'	2	3 'Extreme militants'	%	N
I Samiti	41	28	22	9	100	(32)
II Representative	11	35	39	15	100	(93)
III Convenor	17	31	44	8	100	(64)
All respondents	18	33	38	12	100	(189)

$\chi^2 = 16 \cdot 97$; d.f. 6; $p \leqslant 0 \cdot 02$

[1] The index was constructed from answers to the three opinion statements, responses to which might fairly be held to indicate a militant or non-militant attitude. Agreement with the statement that satyagraha should be used scored one point, disagreement nil; agreement with the opinion that Shanti Sena should be sent to the battle areas scored one point, disagreement nil; *dis*agreement with the statement that the movement should not ask people to non-co-operate with the Government's military efforts scored one point, agreement nil. The range of possible scores runs, therefore, from zero to three. The analysis includes only those respondents who answered all three questions.

significant association between top-level leadership and 'non-militancy'. 'Extreme militants' were found in roughly the same proportion at all three levels, but top-level leaders were more than twice as likely as others leaders to be 'non-militant'. Table 8:15 shows the distribution in detail.

II. DIVERSITIES ASSOCIATED WITH SOCIAL STATUS

In the preceding section we have already examined one aspect of the diversities among Sarvodaya leaders associated with social status: the aspect concerned with leadership level. In this section, taking several measures of social status as our main variable, we pursue the analysis further by reporting on those variables, other than leadership level, which are significantly associated with social status. We begin by considering whether social status in the form of caste (varna) is an important source of diversity.

Caste

Our data suggest that it is not a very important source. Thus, when responses to the sixteen opinion statements were analysed in terms of caste, it was found that in respect of only one was there a significant association. This was the statement suggesting that in practice the policy decisions of the movement are made by a few leaders. While three out of four of all leaders agreed with the statement, Brahmin leaders were more likely, and Vaishya leaders less likely, to agree. More precisely, 82 per cent of Brahmin leaders and 63 per cent of Vaishya leaders agreed.[1] The direction of the association is maintained when level of leadership and level of income are in turn held constant. However, we are unable to offer any explanation of why Brahmin and Vaishya leaders responded so differently from other leaders to this statement.

Two other variables were significantly associated with caste: joint-family upbringing, and perception of the movement's programme. As noted earlier, 82 per cent of all leaders reported that they had been brought up in a joint family. However, the incidence of such an upbringing was 93 per cent in the case of Kshatriya leaders and only 68 per cent in the case of those leaders who were

---

[1] Proportions agreeing: Brahmins 82% (77); Kshatriyas 77% (57); Vaishyas 63% (54). $\chi^2 = 6\cdot23$; d.f. 2; $p \leqslant$ **0·05**. In this and subsequent footnotes the figures in brackets are the figures for N on which the percentages are based.

not twice-born.[1] The higher incidence of joint-family upbringing among Kshatriya leaders may be partly explained by the fact that they were rather more likely than other leaders to be the sons of agriculturalists and to have been brought up in a village, joint families being more common in rural than in urban areas. Kshatriya leaders were also more likely than others to mention all three items of The Triple Programme—Gramdan, Khadi, and Shanti Sena—when asked to list the three most important aspects of the movement's programme. No more than 53 per cent of all leaders responded to the question in this way, but 70 per cent of Kshatriya leaders did so.[2] The explanation of this association may be that Kshatriya leaders were more likely to perceive Khadi as an important aspect of the movement's programme because this is an item which appeals more than the other items to those with a strong agriculturalist background or connection.

Educational status: graduates versus non-graduates

The standard of formal education attained by a leader proved to be a more important source of diversity than his caste origin. Several characteristics (in addition to those already noted) were significantly associated with graduate status. Graduates were more likely than non-graduates to have been brought up in a town, rather than a village;[3] to be high status consistents;[4] and to describe their current religious view as Scientific Spiritualist.[5] In their perception of the goals of the movement they were more likely than non-graduates to mention specifically social goals and Non-violence.[6]

---

[1] Brought up in joint family: Brahmins 74% (77); Kshatriyas 93% (57); Vaishyas 81% (54); Others 68% (22). $\chi^2 = 7.95$; d.f. 2; p ⩽ **0·02**.

[2] Proportions listing all items of The Triple Programme: Brahmins 53% (76); Kshatriyas 70% (56); Vaishyas 43% (51); Others 55% (22). $\chi^2 = 7.93$; d.f. 3; $p ⩽$ **0·05**. Leaders whose religious upbringing was perceived as liberal were more likely than those with an orthodox upbringing to list all items. But, among both religious groups, Kshatriyas were more likely than Brahmins and Vaishyas to list all three. However, the distinctive position of Kshatriyas is much reduced among those with an orthodox upbringing.

[3] Brought up in a village: graduates 53% (73); non-graduates 75% (146). $\chi^2 = 11.78$; d.f. 2; $p ⩽$ **0·01**.

[4] Status consistents: graduates 64% (64); non-graduates 36% (134). $\chi^2 = 13.96$; d.f. 1; $p ⩽$ **0·001**.

[5] Scientific Spiritualist only: graduates 35% (72); non-graduates 16% (147). $\chi^2 = 9.42$, d.f. 1; $p ⩽$ **0·01**.

[6] Mentioning social goals: graduates 71% (76); non-graduates 57% (150). $\chi^2 = 4.03$; d.f. 1; $p ⩽$ **0·05**. Mentioning Non-violence: graduates 43% (76);

However, on the assumption that the number of pledges taken is an indicator of commitment to the norms and values of the movement, graduates showed themselves to be *less* committed than non-graduates. Proportionately, fewer graduates had taken all three pledges: 23 per cent, as against 36 per cent for non-graduates.[1]

In respect of their responses to the opinion statements graduates differed significantly from non-graduates on four of the sixteen issues. Graduates were less likely to agree: (a) that, in the event of further Chinese aggression, Shanti Sena should be sent to the battle areas to offer non-violent resistance;[2] (b) that Sulabh Gramdan made too many concessions to the principles of private property;[3] (c) that more attention should be paid to developing existing Gramdan villages;[4] and (d) that the movement would surge forward in the near future.[5] On each of these four issues the responses of graduates were in line with those of top-level leaders. Since most top-level leaders are graduates, the possibility arises that the associations are not independent. However, further analysis reveals that the direction of the first three associations is maintained when leadership level is held constant.[6] The fourth association—between being a graduate and being less likely to agree that the movement would surge forward—holds good only for leaders *below* the Samiti level: among top-level leaders there is no such association.

According to our index of militancy, graduate status, like top-

---

non-graduates 27% (150). $\chi^2 = 5\cdot93$; d.f. 1; $p \leqslant$ **0·02**. As noted earlier, top-level leaders, most of whom are graduates, were also more likely than lower-level leaders to mention Non-violence. But the direction of the association is maintained when leadership level is held constant.

[1] All three pledges taken: graduates 23% (74); non-graduates 36% (147). $\chi^2 = 6\cdot64$; d.f. 2; $p \leqslant$ **0·05**. Since top-level leaders were more likely than lower-level leaders to have taken all three pledges, the association is not a reflection of the association between graduate status and top-level leadership.

[2] Agreeing: graduates 31% (72); non-graduates 63% (132). $\chi^2 = 19\cdot49$; d.f. 1; $p \leqslant$ **0·001**.

[3] Agreeing: graduates 53% (73); non-graduates 70% (142). $\chi^2 = 5\cdot57$; d.f. 1; $p \leqslant$ **0·02**.

[4] Agreeing: graduates 29% (73); non-graduates 60% (141). $\chi^2 = 20\cdot56$; d.f. 2; $p \leqslant$ **0·001**.

[5] Agreeing: graduates 80% (76); non-graduates 93% (150). $\chi^2 = 7\cdot62$; d.f. 1; $p \leqslant$ **0·01**.

[6] The association in respect of the Shanti Sena statement is also maintained when peasant status and property ownership are in turn held constant.

level leadership, is also associated with 'non-militancy'.[1] However, this association holds good only for leaders at the lower levels. At the Samiti level the association disappears.[2]

Income status

For the purposes of analysis we divided the leaders into two income-status groups, the line of division being whether or not a leader reported a *per capita* income of Rs. 30/- or more per month. It will be recalled that 41 per cent of the leaders who reported their income were placed in the low-income group and that there was a strong negative association between low income and leadership level. There is also a strong association between low income and a rural upbringing. Thus, while 56 per cent of high-income leaders were brought up in a village, the proportion rises to 83 per cent of low-income leaders.[3]

In their responses to five of the sixteen opinion statements low-income leaders differed significantly from high-income leaders. Low-income leaders were *more* likely to agree: (a) that policy decisions were made by a few leaders;[4] (b) that negative satyagraha should be used to promote the movement's objectives;[5] (c) that Sulabh Gramdan made too many concessions to the principles of private property;[6] and (d) that greater attention should be paid to

[1]
	Militancy score					
	0	1	2	3	Total	N
Graduates	27	37	23	13	100%	(62)
Non-graduates	13	31	44	11	100%	(126)

$\chi^2 = 10.38$; d.f. 3; $p \leqslant 0.02$

It will be seen that the association between graduate status and 'non-militancy' is achieved at the expense of 'moderate militancy': graduates are as likely as non-graduates to be 'extreme militants' (score 3).

[2] At the Samiti level 41% of 22 graduates were non-militant, compared with 40% of 10 non-graduates. Below the Samiti level 20% of 40 graduates, and 10% of 116 non-graduates, were non-militants.

[3] For low-income leaders N = 77; for high-income leaders N = 110. $\chi^2 = 15.28$; d.f. 2; $p \leqslant 0.001$. The direction of the association is maintained when level of leadership is held constant.

[4] Agreeing: low-income 87% (71); high-income 66% (107). $\chi^2 = 9.93$; d.f. 1; $p \leqslant 0.01$.

[5] Agreeing: low-income 77% (70); high-income 63% (107). $\chi^2 = 4.13$; d.f. 1; $p \leqslant 0.05$.

[6] Agreeing: low-income 81% (73); high-income 55% (109). $\chi^2 = 12.83$; d.f. 1; $p \leqslant 0.001$.

developing existing Gramdans.[1] They were *less* likely to agree that
the accession of Kashmir was not final and irrevocable.[2] On each
of these five issues the response of low-income leaders was contrary to that of top-level leaders. It is possible, therefore, that these
associations are not independent of the previously-noted associations between leadership level and responses to the five issues.
However, further analysis shows that the direction of the associations is maintained when leadership level is held constant. We may
conclude therefore that income and leadership level are independent factors in the responses.

Low-income leaders also differed from high-income leaders in
respect of their militancy, proportionately fewer of the low-income
leaders being classified as 'non-militants'.[3] Again, this association
is independent of leadership level.

Property ownership

The division of the leaders into those who did and those who did
not own immovable property was not an important source of
diversity. Among Sarvodaya leaders, it will be recalled, ownership
of property is associated with attributes of low rather than of high
status: property owners are less likely than the propertyless to be
top leaders, to enjoy a high income, and to be graduates. But, as
might be expected, they were more likely to have contributed to
dans, 69 per cent having done so, compared with 33 per cent of the
propertyless.[4]

[1] Agreeing: low-income 67% (72); high-income 44% (110). $\chi^2 = 9.31$; d.f. 2; $p \leqslant$ **0·01**.

[2] Agreeing: low-income 38% (77); high-income 57% (113). $\chi^2 = 6.92$; d.f. 2; $p \leqslant$ **0.05**.

[3]

| | | Militancy score | | | | |
Per capita income	0	1	2	3	Total	N
< Rs.30/- p.m.	4	31	57	7	100%	(67)
> Rs. 30/- p.m.	24	36	24	16	100%	(97)

$\chi^2 = 23.64$; d.f. 3; $p \leqslant$ **0·001**

It will be noted, however, that proportionately more high-income than low-
income leaders are 'extreme militants'.

[4] For property owners N = 128; for propertyless N = 61. $\chi^2 = 21.82$, d.f. 1; $p \leqslant$ **0·001**. Although the association might be expected, it should be noted
that a dan contribution may take the form of a gift of income as well as of prop-
erty.

On only one of their responses to the sixteen opinion statements did the two groups differ significantly. While 63 per cent of those who owned land agreed that Shanti Sena should be sent to the battle areas, 46 per cent of the propertyless were of the same opinion.[1] On this issue, therefore, property owners, like low-income leaders and non-graduates, tended to be the more militant. The association, however, is not independent of leadership level. The direction of the association is maintained only among leaders below the top level: at the Samiti level the direction is reversed and property owners were *less* likely than the propertyless to agree with the statement. Further, in terms of our militancy index, we found no association between property ownership and militancy.

Self-rated status

The division of the leaders into the three self-rated status groups, middle class, lower middle class, and working class, did not prove to be a source of diversity on issues within the movement. The responses of these groups to the sixteen opinion statements did not differ in a statistically significant way.

However, those leaders who rated themselves as peasants[2] responded differently from non-peasants to two of the statements. Peasants were more likely to agree that Shanti Sena should be sent to the battle areas,[3] and that in practice policy decisions tended to be made by a few leaders.[4] On both of these issues the response of the peasant leaders was contrary to that of top-level leaders, a group which contains relatively few who identified themselves as peasants. We must consider, therefore, whether the associations are independent of leadership level. Further analysis shows that only one of the associations is maintained when leadership level is held constant: both at the top and lower levels of leadership peasants were more likely than non-peasants to agree that policy decisions were made by a few leaders. Among Samiti members,

---

[1] For landed property owners N = 78; for propertyless N = 57. χ^2 = 3·94; d.f. 1; $p \leqslant$ **0.05**.

[2] This group (31% of the sample) includes 18 respondents who also identified with one of the other three classes.

[3] Agreeing: peasants 66% (53); non-peasants 44% (137). χ^2 = 7·07; d.f. 1; $p \leqslant$ **0·01**.

[4] Agreeing: peasants 85% (65), non-peasants 72% (139). χ^2 = 3·90; d.f. 1; $p \leqslant$ **0·05**.

peasants were *less* likely than non-peasants to agree with the statement about Shanti Sena.

Comparing peasants with non-peasants according to their militancy score, we find that, like top-level leadership, non-peasant status is associated with 'non-militancy'.[1] But this is another association which holds good only at the two lower levels of leadership. At the top level there were only two leaders identifying with the peasants who could be included in our militancy rating. Both of these were 'non-militants', while one in three of the non-peasant top leaders fell into this category.

Status consistency

The final variable to be considered in this section is status consistency. It will be recalled that this variable is associated with leadership level and educational status—top-level leaders and graduates being more likely than other leaders to be (high-) status consistents. Three further variables were found to be associated with high-status consistency. Self-rated middle-class leaders were more likely than lower-middle- and working-class leaders to be status consistents.[2] The second variable relates to voting behaviour in the General Election of 1952. Status consistents were *less* likely than inconsistents to have voted in that election.[3] Top-level leaders, it will be noted, were also less likely to have voted; but the direction of the association is maintained even when level of leadership is held constant. Status consistency appears therefore to be an independent factor in the behaviour. In this instance it may be that the status-consistent Sarvodaya leaders felt assured of their high status and, as a consequence, were psychologically better equipped to challenge the societal norm by deliberately abstaining from voting. In this context it should be recalled that in 1952 the movement's

[1]

	Militancy score					
	0	1	2	3	Total	N
Peasant	9	27	52	12	100%	(58)
Non-peasant	22	35	31	11	100%	(125)

$\chi^2 = 9.32$, d.f. 3; $p \leqslant$ **0·05**

[2] Status consistents: middle-class 68% (63); lower-middle- and working-class combined 33% (89). $\chi^2 = 18.82$; d.f. 1; $p \leqslant$ **0·001**.

[3] Voting in 1952: consistents 57% (76); inconsistents 72% (95). $\chi^2 = 4.17$; d.f. 1; $p \leqslant$ **0·05**.

concept of partyless democracy had not yet been developed and that two-thirds of the Sarvodaya leaders voted in the election. It should also be added that, when voters alone are considered, status consistents were less likely than inconsistents to vote for the Congress candidate.[1]

On one opinion statement the response of status consistents differed significantly from that of inconsistents. This was the controversial statement that the accession of Kashmir to the Indian Union was not final and irrevocable. Consistents were more likely than inconsistents to agree, the proportions being 59 per cent and 40 per cent, respectively.[2] Again, on this issue the response of consistents was in line with that of top-level leaders. But further analysis shows that at each level of leadership the direction of the association is maintained. Independently of leadership level, status consistency appears therefore to be a factor in determining a leader's response to the statement about Kashmir. This finding reinforces the point that high-status consistency may be an important condition of a leader's taking up an unpopular stance.

When status consistency is related to militancy score, we find that proportionately more consistents than inconsistents are 'non-militant'. But the difference is not large enough to be statistically significant at the level we have adopted.[3]

---

[1] Voted for Congress in 1952: consistents 61% (38); inconsistents 84% (62). $\chi^2 = 6.85$; d.f. 1; $p \leqslant 0.01$.

[2] For consistents $N = 89$; for inconsistents $N = 110$. $\chi^2 = 8.44$; d.f. 2; $p \leqslant 0.02$.

[3]

	Militancy score					
	0	1	2	3	Total	N
Consistents	21	38	28	12	100%	(81)
Inconsistents	13	28	48	11	100%	(92)

$\chi^2 = 7.21$; d.f. 3; $p \leqslant 0.10$

If there is an association between status consistency and militancy among the Sarvodaya leaders, it would seem to be in the same direction as found by those researchers who link status inconsistency with political extremism. But it will be noted that, proportionately, consistents are as likely as inconsistents to be 'extreme militants'.

III. DIVERSITIES ASSOCIATED WITH AGE

Empirical research on voting behaviour has confirmed the popular belief that age is an important source of political diversity.[1] Age differences often manifest themselves in differences of political allegiance, but they are also found *within* political parties and movements, the younger age groups being frequently more radical in their attitudes than the older age groups. However, there is no direct link between age and political allegiance or attitude: the young are not 'naturally' more radical than the old. The mediating and explanatory factor involved is social experience. This experience is related to age in at least two ways. Different age groups are associated with differences in typical life patterns: for example, younger adult groups tend to have larger family responsibilities than either adolescent or more elderly age groups. Social experience may also take the form of being a participant in, or a witness to, some crucial collective event, such as a major war or a revolution. This kind of experience gives rise to the phenomena of political generations which may not be closely linked with biological age groups. Conflict between political generations is not so much between the young and the old as such, as between those who have shared a collective experience and those who have not. Consequently, the dividing line between political generations is not an arbitrary matter, and the conventional age intervals used by the statistician to distinguish the young from the old may cut across different generational groups.

We have already noted that among the Sarvodaya leaders age is associated with leadership level, and we suggested an obvious explanation of this finding in terms of the first kind of social experience. We might also expect 'biological' as distinct from 'political' age to be related to a number of other variables; for example, income, which tends to vary with age. In fact, age is significantly associated with monthly household income, leaders aged 50 years and over tending to report a higher income than those aged under 50 years.[2] Age is also associated with having

---

[1] 'All surveys of voting choice report major differences in the political allegiances of different age groups within specific strata, educational, religious, or ethnic groups.'—S. M. Lipset, *Political Man*, 1959, p. 264.

[2] Since income is also associated with self-rated status, we might expect age to be associated with self-rated status. There is, indeed, a tendency for leaders

made a dan contribution, leaders under 40 years being less likely than older leaders to have made such a contribution.[1]

More interesting is the finding that in respect of only one of the sixteen opinion statements is there a significant association between age and response. The statement concerned was the one relating to Kashmir. Leaders over 50 years of age were less likely than younger leaders to agree that Kashmir's accession was not final and irrevocable.[2] If we may interpret agreement with the statement as indicative of the more radical view, then on this issue—but on this issue alone—the younger leaders were more radical than their elders. On other issues, they were no more radical; and in terms of our militancy index, the younger leaders were not significantly more militant.[3]

'Biological' age, we may conclude, is not a very important source of diversity among the Sarvodaya leaders. Neither, it would appear, is 'political' age. In considering the latter, we distinguished two 'political generations': those who had, and those who had not,

---

aged under 40 years to be less inclined than older leaders to rate themselves middle-class; but the difference is not statistically significant.

Age group (years)	Monthly household income			N
	Rs. 0–100/– %	Rs. 101–300/– %	Rs. 301/– + %	
20–39	22	54	24	(50)
40–9	20	65	15	(54)
50–9	24	45	31	(38)
60+	26	29	45	(38)

$\chi^2 = 14.27$; d.f. 6; $p \leqslant$ **0.05**

[1] Age, however, is not related in a linear fashion with having made a dan contribution. Made at least one contribution: 20–39 yrs. 38% (55); 40–9 yrs. 62% (60); 50–9 yrs. 49% (41); 60+ yrs. 60% (52). $\chi^2 = 7.82$; d.f. 3; $p \leqslant$ **0.05**. It should be added that, while property ownership is associated with having made a contribution, there is no significant association between age and property ownership.

[2] Agreeing: 20–39 yrs. 46% (55); 40–9 yrs. 58% (60); 50–9 yrs. 32% (41); 60 + yrs. 38% (52). $\chi^2 = 16.28$; d.f. 6; $p \leqslant$ **0.02**. The direction of the association is maintained when level of leadership is held constant.

[3] At the lower end of the militancy scale 13% of 100 leaders under 50 years were 'non-militant', compared with 21% of 72 leaders aged 50 years or more; at the higher end of the scale the proportions of 'extreme militants' were 16% and 7%, respectively. These differences are not statistically significant. However, when leadership level is held constant, any suggestion of an association practically disappears at the two lower levels, while at the Samiti level older leaders are twice as likely as younger leaders to be 'non-militants' (41% of 17 older leaders, as against 18% of 11 younger leaders).

joined the movement before 1951, the year in which the Gandhian constructive movement was revitalized by Vinoba's launching of the Bhoodan campaign. It will be recalled that two-thirds of our sample of leaders belonged to the older generation, the remaining third having joined after Vinoba had emerged as Gandhi's 'spiritual heir'. Again, in respect of only one of the opinion statements is there a significant association between 'political' age and response. In this instance the statement was the one which suggested that, while Khadi production would remain important for some time to come, it would eventually give way to mill-made cloth. Since Khadi is very much identified with Gandhi's leadership, we might expect that, if there were any difference between the generations, the pre-1951 would be less likely than the post-1951 generation to agree with the statement. This expectation is in fact fulfilled, the older generation being only half as likely to agree.[1] More surprising, perhaps, is the absence of significant associations between 'political' age and response to any other of the opinion statements. To emphasize the relative lack of generational conflict among the leaders, we may note that 'political' age is also not associated with views on which parties are most opposed and most sympathetic to the movement, with the way in which leaders voted in the three General Elections, and with their first choice of a successor to Vinoba.

IV. DIVERSITIES ASSOCIATED WITH REGIONAL ORIGIN

In our discussion of the social foundations of the movement we observed that, although Gramdan villages are unevenly distributed throughout the country, the leadership as a whole is broadly representative of both the northern and the southern states of the Indian Union.[2] It will also be recalled that each level of leadership is broadly representative of these two regions.[3] In this section we pursue further this line of analysis, in order to determine whether or not regional origin is an important source of diversity among the leaders. Since we are employing only two regional categories, the analysis is perforce very gross, but there are grounds for believing

---

[1] Agreeing: pre-1951 generation 19% (126); post-1951 generation 38% (58). $\chi^2 = 5.56$; d.f. $1; p < 0.02$. The direction of the association is maintained when level of leadership is held constant.

[2] Chapter Three, Section 1.   [3] Section 1 above.

that the simple North–South division is more important in Indian politics than any other dichotomy we could make. While our North region is essentially a residual category comprising states which differ considerably among themselves, our South region is much more of a unity. The four southern states of Andhra Pradesh, Mysore, Madras, and Kerala constitute the heartland of the indigenous Dravidian peoples, and in recent years they have been the strongest opponents of the policy of making Hindi the sole 'official language' for all-India purposes.[1]

In the expectation that the difference of regional origin would be reflected in the Sarvodaya leadership in a variety of ways, we compared Northern with Southern leaders in terms of most of the variables used in the present study. On only four variables did Southern leaders differ significantly from Northern leaders. Three of these were variables of social status. The Southern group contained exactly its proportionate share of Brahmins (38 per cent), proportionately fewer Kshatriyas and Vaishyas, but significantly more of the 'once-born'. It will be recalled that 10 per cent of all leaders were 'once-born', but of Northern leaders 5 per cent fell into this category, while no less than 26 per cent of Southern leaders did so.[2] This finding was contrary to our expectation. In recent decades anti-Brahmin feeling has been a notable feature of Southern politics. We expected that this feeling would manifest itself in the Sarvodaya movement in the form of 'under-representation' of Brahmins in the group of Southern leaders. In fact, there is no such 'under-representation', and the 'over-representation' of low-caste Hindus and Harijans in the Southern group (relative to the leadership as a whole) appears to have been achieved at the expense of the other two twice-born castes.

The 'over-representation' of 'once-born' among the Southern leaders may be related to the further finding that proportionately fewer of them were sons of fathers whose occupational status was

[1] Commenting on the differences between North and South, a recent observer writes: 'The northern peasant and the southern are different in size, in shape, and in colour, as well as in diet, costume, speech and tradition. To the visitor, the long-limbed, heavy-featured, light-brown Bihari, with his Aryan ancestry, seems to belong to a different country altogether from the shorter, delicately featured, almost blue-black Tamil from Madras, with his Dravidian past.'—R. Segal, *The Crisis of India*, 1965, p. 20.

[2] Northern leaders (N = 177): Brahmins 38%; Kshatriyas 29%; Vaishyas 27%; Others 5%. Southern leaders (N = 42): Brahmins 38%; Kshatriyas 17%; Vaishyas 19%; Others 26%. $\chi^2 = 19.46$; d.f. 3; $p \leqslant 0.001$.

358 DIVERSITIES AMONG SARVODAYA LEADERS

middle-class. While 94 per cent of Northern leaders fell into this category, only 82 per cent of Southern leaders did so.[1] Exactly the same proportion (54 per cent) of both groups were sons of agriculturalists, but the Northern group contained more sons of absentee landlords, while the Southern group contained more sons of tenant cultivators.[2] Proportionately more of the Southern leaders of agriculturalist origin tended, therefore, to come from the lower rural classes. This, however, does not explain the third difference in social status between the two groups: the fact that Southern leaders were much less likely to rate themselves as peasants.[3]

On our other measures of social status, Southern leaders did not differ significantly from Northern leaders. Approximately the same proportions of both groups were graduates, owned property, enjoyed a relatively high income, rated themselves as middle-class, and were status consistents.

Further, the two groups were drawn in about equal proportions from the various age groups; they were equally likely to have been brought up in a village and as a member of a joint family; similar proportions perceived their religious upbringing as orthodox; and in both groups the religious views which the leaders currently held were represented in approximately equal proportions. Southern leaders were influenced to join the movement by the various factors we investigated to the same degree as Northern leaders; and, once in the movement, their commitment, as measured by pledges taken and by dan contributions, was similar. In their perception of the movement's programme, in their views on 'the problem of succession', in their voting behaviour, in their militancy, and in their opinion of which parties were most sympathetic and which most opposed to Sarvodaya, they were also not significantly different from Northern leaders.

The remaining fourth variable on which the two regional groups

[1] For Northern leaders N = 173; for Southern leaders N = 44. $\chi^2 = 6.14$; d.f. 1; $p \leqslant 0.02$.

[2] Absentee landlords: North 7%; South 2%; Owner Cultivators: N. 44%; S. 43%; Tenant Cultivators: N. 1%; S. 9%; Landless Labourers: N. 2%; S. Nil; Business: N. 17%; S. 11%; Government Service: N. 13%; S. 11%; Private Service: N. 3%; S. 2%; Artisan: N. 1%; S. 7%; Professional: N. 12%; S. 9%; Priest: N. 1%; S. 5%. For Northern leaders N = 173; for Southern leaders N = 44.

[3] Rated themselves as peasants: Northern 36% (167); Southern 7% (43), $\chi^2 = 13.65$; d.f. 1; $p \leqslant 0.001$.

did reveal a significant difference was response to the opinion statement that the movement was too identified in the public mind with Congress. Slightly over half of all leaders agreed with this statement, but 70 per cent of the Southern, compared with 49 per cent of the Northern, leaders did so.[1] This difference probably reflects the fact that, among the Indian electorate, hostility towards the Congress is rather more evident in the South than in the North. At the time of writing two of the Southern states, Kerala and Madras, are governed by other parties or by coalitions from which the Congress party is excluded.

In sum, we may conclude that, like age, regional origin does not appear to be an important source of diversity among the Sarvodaya leaders.

V. DIVERSITIES ASSOCIATED WITH POLITICAL ATTITUDES, RELIGIOUS UPBRINGING, AND PERSONALITIES

Political attitudes

Although the Sarvodaya movement espouses the doctrine of party-less democracy, is not linked with any party, and its Lok Sevaks pledge themselves not to take an active role in party politics, we have seen that the leaders vary in their attitudes to India's political parties. We also noted that most of the leaders have a background of association with Congress, and that a small minority was formerly associated with one of the Socialist parties or with the Indian Communist Party.[2] From answers to the question 'Which political party, in your opinion, is most sympathetic to Sarvodaya ideals?' it is possible to classify most of the leaders into three political groups: those who thought no party was sympathetic ('neutrals'); those who thought that only Congress was most sympathetic ('pro-Congress'); and those who mentioned one of the Socialist (including Communist) parties ('pro-Socialist'). Using these categories, we may now consider whether political attitude constitutes a source of diversity among the leaders.

We have already established that level of leadership is not significantly associated with our three political categories.[3] How-

---

[1] For Northern leaders $N = 167$; for Southern leaders $N = 40$. $\chi^2 = 5\cdot66$; d.f. 1; $p \leqslant 0\cdot02$.

[2] Chapter Three, Section V. [3] Section I above.

ever, we might reasonably expect to find an association between the political groups and voting behaviour. This expectation is fulfilled in respect of reported voting behaviour in the General Elections of 1952 and 1962.[1] In both elections pro-Congress leaders were more likely than either the pro-Socialists or neutrals to vote; and in 1952, when they did vote, to vote for a Congress candidate.[2]

In their responses to three of the sixteen opinion statements significant differences were revealed between the political groups. Pro-Congress leaders were more likely than others to agree that, until the movement had a real non-violent alternative to offer, people should not be asked to non-co-operate with the Government's efforts to make India strong militarily. 80 per cent of pro-Congress leaders agreed with this statement, compared with 62 per cent each of pro-Socialists and neutrals.[3] Pro-Congress leaders were also more likely to agree that good candidates, even if they had a party ticket, should be supported by Sarvodaya workers. The proportions agreeing with this statement, which runs contrary to the doctrine of partyless democracy, were: pro-Congress 58 per cent; pro-Socialist 49 per cent; neutrals 29 per cent.[4] The third statement expressed the view that the movement should pay more attention to the Government's programme of Panchayati Raj as a means of achieving the Sarvodaya society. Again, the 'bias' of the pro-Congress leaders was in the direction of the response which minimized the movement's opposition to the Congress Government. But, in this case, their 'bias' was rather less pronounced than that of the pro-Socialists. The proportions agreeing with the

---

[1] The data on the 1957 General Election suggest a similar pattern of association, but the differences are not large enough to be statistically significant at the 0·05 level.

[2] Voted in the 1952 General Election: pro-Congress 81% (111); pro-Socialist 53% (40); neutrals 48% (27). $\chi^2 = 18·34$; d.f. 2; $p \leqslant 0·001$. Voted Congress in the 1952 election: pro-Congress 85% (81); pro-Socialist 47% (19); neutrals 58% (12). $\chi^2 = 14·29$; d.f. 2; $p \leqslant 0·001$. Voted in the 1962 General Election: pro-Congress 44% (128); pro-Socialist 25% (44); neutrals 22% (32). $\chi^2 = 8·38$; d.f. 2; $p \leqslant 0·02$. The number voting in 1962 was too small to determine whether choice of party by political group was statistically significant. However, of those whose voting choice was reported, 42 out of 48 pro-Congress, 2 out of 4 pro-Socialist, and 3 out of 7 neutrals voted for Congress.

[3] For pro-Congress $N = 119$; for pro-Socialist $N = 42$; for neutrals $N = 29$. $\chi^2 = 7·22$; d.f. 2; $p \leqslant 0·05$.

[4] For pro-Congress $N = 132$; for pro-Socialist $N = 39$; for neutrals $N = 28$. $\chi^2 = 7·96$; d.f. 2; $p \leqslant 0·02$.

statement were: pro-Congress 75 per cent; pro-Socialist 82 per cent; neutrals 47 per cent.[1] Perhaps more surprising than any of these findings is the fact that pro-Congress leaders did not differ significantly from the other political groups in their response to the statement that the movement was too identified in the public mind with Congress.[2] It is possible, however, that the explicit reference to Congress alerted the pro-Congress leaders and led them to guard against expressing their 'bias'.

Religious upbringing

Turning from diversities associated with political attitudes to those associated with religious upbringing, it will be recalled that we classified the leaders into two groups according to whether or not they perceived their religious upbringing as orthodox. Rather more than one in four (28 per cent) of all leaders fell into the orthodox category, the remainder being classified as 'liberals'.

As noted above, type of religious upbringing was not significantly associated with level of leadership. Nor was it associated with age, caste, regional origin, being brought up in a village, being brought up in a joint family, or with level of commitment as measured either by pledges taken or dan contributions. It was, however, associated with perception of the movement's programme. The orthodox were less likely than the liberals to mention all three items of The Triple Programme.[3] Further analysis suggests that this finding may be related to the fact that the orthodox were less likely to perceive Khadi as an important aspect of the movement's programme; but the reason why they should do so is not readily apparent.[4]

Another significant association proved to be in a direction contrary to our expectation. On the assumption that an orthodox

---

[1] For pro-Congress N = 131; for pro-Socialist N = 39; for neutrals N = 32. $\chi^2 = 12.42$; d.f. 2; $p \leqslant 0.01$.

[2] Agreeing that the movement is too identified in the public mind with Congress: pro-Congress 57% (129), pro-Socialist 54% (35); neutrals 46% (28).

[3] Listed all items of The Triple Programme: orthodox 40% (57); liberal 62% (143). $\chi^2 = 7.41$; d.f. 1; $p \leqslant 0.01$.

[4] Kshatriyas, it may be recalled, were also more likely than other castes to list all three items. Kshatriyas appear rather more likely than Brahmins or Vaishyas to have had a liberal upbringing, but the difference in this respect is not statistically significant. The associations between liberal upbringing and perception of the programme and between being a Kshatriya and perception of the programme would thus appear to be independent of each other.

religious upbringing would be likely to make a person more concerned about moral and religious matters, we hypothesized that the orthodox would refer more frequently than liberals to the moral and religious goals of the movement. In fact, while 38 per cent of the liberals referred to these goals, only 21 per cent of the orthodox did so.[1] Again, the explanation of this finding is not apparent.

Perhaps more explicable is the response of the two groups to the one opinion statement over which they differed significantly. This was the statement expressing the view that the movement needed a stronger central organization. Of the liberals 61 per cent agreed with the statement, compared with 77 per cent of the orthodox.[2] The explanation of the difference may lie in the hypothesis that an orthodox religious upbringing is more likely than a liberal one to engender an 'authoritarian' as opposed to a 'libertarian' attitude to discipline, including organizational discipline. It will be recalled that top-level leaders were less likely than lower-level leaders to agree with the statement. If we hold level of leadership constant, the association between orthodox religious upbringing and agreement on the need for stronger central organization is still maintained. At the top level of leadership the orthodox were more than twice as likely as the liberal to believe in stronger central organization.[3]

Personalities: Jayaprakash Narayan

Finally, to complete our exploration of sources of diversity among the leaders, we may examine briefly diversities associated with preference for particular leaders. This kind of source is complex, since it involves the concept of personality and the image that a leader has in the minds of his followers. Our data do not permit us to examine fruitfully more than one of the Sarvodaya leaders in this connection. However, the leader in question—Jayaprakash Narayan—is the one who clearly ranks second only to Vinoba in the movement at the present time. Our analysis proceeds on the basis of distinguishing 'pro-J.P.'[4] leaders from others, according to whether or not Narayan was listed first as the best 'successor' to Vinoba. It will be recalled that 59 per cent of our respondents

---

[1] For orthodox N = 62; for liberals N = 158. $\chi^2 = 5\cdot81$; d.f. 1; $p \leqslant$ **0·02**.
[2] For orthodox N = 61; for liberals N = 147. $\chi^2 = 5\cdot19$; d.f. 1; $p \leqslant$ **0·05**.
[3] At the Samiti level, 5 out of 7 orthodox agreed, compared with 10 out of 29 liberals.
[4] In the movement Narayan is often affectionately referred to as 'J.P.'.

listed Narayan first, 17 per cent declining to answer the question, and the remainder either naming someone else, opting for 'collective leadership', or stating that an unspecified individual would 'emerge' at the appropriate time.

Cross-tabulation of this variable with other major variables suggests that 'pro-J.P.' leaders are not significantly different from other leaders in respect of their age, regional origin, caste, income, ownership of property, educational status, self-rated status, religious upbringing, current religious position, and views on which party is most sympathetic to Sarvodaya ideals. Further, 'pro-J.P.' leaders are not significantly more likely to belong to the 'political generation' which joined the movement after 1951. The absence of significant association in these respects underlines the wide measure of support for Narayan among the leaders. However, as noted above,[1] Convenors were more likely to be 'pro-J.P.' than Representatives or members of the Samiti.

In view of Narayan's political background as a Socialist leader before he renounced party politics and joined the movement, we hypothesized that 'pro-J.P.' leaders would be more radical or militant than other leaders. Our data provide little to support this hypothesis. Indeed, in their responses to the open-ended question about the goals of the movement, 'pro-J.P.' leaders were significantly *less* likely to mention both social and economic goals— goals which one might expect to be emphasized by those strongly committed to the socialist content of Sarvodaya ideology.[2]

However, in their responses to the opinion statement which refers obliquely to the socialist content of the movement's current programme 'pro-J.P.' leaders were significantly different from others. 70 per cent of 'pro-J.P.' leaders, compared with 53 per cent of others, agreed that Sulabh Gramdan made too many concessions to the principles of private property.[3] The direction of this association is maintained when level of leadership is held constant; and at the Samiti level 'pro-J.P.' leaders were over three times more likely than other leaders to agree with the statement.[4] But

[1] Section I above.
[2] Mentioned social goals: 'pro-J.P.' 60% (134); others 78% (55). $\chi^2 = 5.86$; d.f. 1; $p \leqslant$ **0·02**. Mentioned economic goals 'pro-J.P.' 37% (134); others 56% (55). $\chi^2 = 6.26$; d.f. 1; $p \leqslant$ **0·02**.
[3] For 'pro-J.P.' N = 129; for others N = 52. $\chi^2 = 4.14$; d.f. 1; $p \leqslant$ **0·05**.
[4] At the top level of leadership 14 out of 24 'pro-J.P.' leaders agreed, compared with 2 out of 11 leaders who were not 'pro-J.P.'.

this is the only opinion statement which 'pro-J.P.' leaders responded to in a significantly different way from other leaders. They were not more likely to agree, for example, that 'negative' satyagraha should be used, that Shanti Sena should be sent to the battle areas, and that the movement should advocate immediate non-co-operation with the Government's military efforts—the three statements used in constructing our index of militancy. Perhaps even more interesting is the finding that 'pro-J.P.' leaders were not more likely than others to agree with the two opinion statements that could be most closely identified with policies advocated personally by Narayan: the statements on Panchayati Raj and on Kashmir.

VI. CONCLUSIONS ON DIVERSITIES

In this chapter we have attempted by simple statistical analysis to explore systematically the possible sources of diversity among the Sarvodaya leaders. What general conclusions may be drawn from the analysis?

Fourteen major variables were employed in the analysis, six of them measures of social status, and two related to age. Since only one major variable—level of leadership—was cross-classified with all other variables used in our study, we cannot assess the relative importance of the fourteen variables as sources of diversity simply by noting the number of statistically significant associations found with each major variable. However, the fourteen variables were all cross-classified with the sixteen opinion-statement variables. We may, therefore, use the number of significant associations between major variables and opinion-statement variables as a measure of the relative importance of each major variable as a source of *ideological* diversity.

Using this measure, it is clear that level of leadership proved to be the most important variable in this context. In the course of this part of the analysis 224 cross-tabulations were produced, of which 29 showed significant associations at the 0·05 level. Of these 29, 8 involved level of leadership, 4 educational status, 4 income status, 3 political preference (pro-Congress, pro-Socialist, and neutral), and 2 Peasant self-rated status; 8 of the remaining variables were each significantly associated with 1 opinion-statement variable; and 1 major variable (self-rated middle-, lower-middle-, and working-class) produced no significant association.

Although level of leadership or organizational status may be judged the most important source of ideological diversity, two features of this variable should be noted. First, its significance lies in the distinction between top-level leaders, on the one hand, and the two lower levels, on the other. Our data provide some support for imputing a three-level organizational hierarchy of leadership in Sarva Seva Sangh, but perhaps more support, at least in ideo-logical matters, for a two-level hierarchy. This dichotomy cor-responds roughly to the familiar distinction between those who are 'all-India leaders' and those who are simply 'local leaders'. Com-pared with lower-level leaders, top-level leaders in the Sarvodaya movement are older and of a higher educational and income status; they are more urban in origin; their family association with the movement is greater; they tend to be more committed to the value objectives of the movement; and their views on ideological issues tend to correspond with the generally accepted 'official' policy of the movement. None of these characteristics will surprise students of social movements. However, they have an added significance in a movement such as Sarvodaya, which espouses an egalitarian doctrine and which minimizes, if it does not quite totally reject, hierarchical distinctions. It would seem that even a radical grass-roots democratic movement cannot at this juncture wholly escape the pervasive influences making for hierarchy. Granting that, it remains probably true that Sarvodaya approaches more nearly than any other social movement of comparable size and importance the ideal that it sets itself in this respect.

The second feature to be noted about the level-of-leadership variable is that it is related to the variables of social status. Top-level leadership is positively associated with high educational status, high income status, and high-status consistency. It is negatively associated with property ownership and self-rated peasant status; but, in the society of Sarvodaya leaders these two attributes are associated with low income and low educational status. On ideological issues leaders of high educational and in-come status tended to be in accord with top-level leaders. Thus, for example, graduates, high income leaders, and top-level leaders all tended to disagree that Sulabh Gramdan made too many concessions to the principles of private property and that more attention should be paid to developing existing Gramdan villages. The associations of the three major variables with a particular kind of response, it will be noted, were independent of one another. In other words, each was an independent factor in the response. However, all three factors pointed in the same direction. This suggests that the congruent tendencies of high organizational and high social status might provide the structural basis of important ideological cleavages among the leaders. If such a cleavage exists or were to develop—say, a cleavage between militant and non-militant behaviour—it would tend to be along the divide between those who are, and those who are not, of high organizational and social status.

However, focusing attention on the significant associations between variables may easily give a very misleading impression of the extent of diversities among the Sarvodaya leaders. In the non-statistical sense, it is significant how relatively unimportant as sources of diversity were the variables of age, regional origin, political preference, religious upbringing, and personality preference. On *a priori* grounds each of these variables might have been an important source of diversity. If we had found much evidence of generational conflict, of differences between Northern and Southern leaders, between pro-Congress and pro-Socialist leaders, between those with an orthodox and those with a liberal religious upbringing, and between 'pro-J.P.' and other leaders, we should not have been greatly surprised. We should not, therefore, ignore the negative evidence. Although we cannot substantiate it—since ours is a case study and many of our variables are peculiar to the Sarvodaya context—the overwhelming impression left by the data assembled in this chapter is the high degree of consensus existing among the leaders. By 'consensus' here we do not mean simply the absence of differences on ideological matters, for, as we have seen, on all but two of the sixteen opinion statements, responses were not nearly unanimous. Rather, we mean 'consensus' in the sense of absence of differences associated with structural factors. Organizational and social status, we repeat, were the only structural factors found to be of more than minimal importance.

Perhaps, however, this general conclusion is not so surprising when we recall that we are dealing with a value-oriented charismatic social movement. In Etzioni's terminology, Sarva Seva

Sangh is an organization of the normative rather than of the utilitarian type; and its predominant compliance pattern is one in which normative power is the main means of control and the commitment of the participants is high. We may expect consensus, in the sense defined, to be higher in such organizations than in organizations of the utilitarian type.[1] Sarvodaya is essentially a movement for the revaluation of values. Its charismatic leader, Vinoba, defines the new values and the ways to achieve them. Acceptance of the leader who expresses and embodies the new values is the real bond which unites the followers who engage in the collective enterprise of re-making the world. This bond tends to over-ride most of the mundane considerations of such men as have never felt the impulse to respond to such a calling.

[1] cf. A. Etzioni, *A Comparative Analysis of Complex Organizations*, 1961, p. 131.

CHAPTER NINE

A SUMMARY PROFILE
OF THE SARVODAYA LEADER

WE began this study by asking the simple but large question: Who are the leaders of the Sarvodaya movement for non-violent revolution in India? We posed the question because we knew relatively little about those disciples of Gandhi who have taken his message seriously and who are seeking to realize swaraj in the profound sense that he gave to the term. In the preceding chapters, in an attempt to provide a systematic answer, we have broken down the question into a series of smaller questions. In the process we have shown the complexity of the apparently simple original question, and also, no doubt, raised a number of other questions. The reader who has followed us thus far will not have answers to all the questions that might be asked about the Sarvodaya movement, but he will have answers of varying degrees of validity to at least some of the more important questions that social scientists ask about any social movement.

The truthfulness of answers to large questions lies in the details of answers to smaller questions. Summary generalizations inevitably tell less than the whole truth. Nevertheless, provided this limitation is recognized, generalizations have a function and a place. In this concluding chapter, therefore, we shall attempt to summarize our findings. This attempt takes the form of a profile sketch of that non-existent person, 'the average Sarvodaya leader'.

The subject of our sketch is one of the 9,000 or so Lok Sevaks who, in April 1965, belonged to the organization known as Sarva Seva Sangh, which had its headquarters in 'the holy city' of Benares on the banks of the Ganges. In taking the title of Lok Sevak he has identified himself as one of those Servants of the People whom Gandhiji referred to in his Last Will and Testament. If Gandhi's wish had been carried out, our Lok Sevak would be a member of that Lok Sevak Sangh which Gandhi had hoped would flower in place of a dissolved Indian National Congress. Since Congress did not dissolve but continued as India's ruling party, our Lok Sevak is content to belong to Sarva Seva Sangh, the body which brought under one roof several of the constructive work associations that Gandhi himself had founded. Although he has friendly relations with other constructive work associations which remain outside Sarva Seva Sangh, he believes he belongs to that Gandhian organization which is most firmly committed to the idea of non-violent revolution. In this organization he is one of the 479 main office-holders. His actual office is District Representative, a position to which he has been unanimously elected by the Lok Sevaks of the district in which he works. If we enquire further, this district is probably one of those in the populous Northern state, Uttar Pradesh, where the movement is particularly strong.

Although our leader shares Gandhi's belief in the equality of the sexes, he is aware that, like himself, the vast majority of his colleagues are males. However, most of them are not single men and have not taken the vow of brahmacharya in its strictest sense which Vinoba took at an early age. In this respect he and his colleagues are indistinguishable from other Indian adult males: most of them are married and have children. At the same time, their children, like his, are now probably grown-up or well on the way to becoming so, since most of his colleagues are approaching middle age. He himself is in his forties. This means that he can now look back on some two decades of service in the movement: he joined it in his twenties, soon after leaving school or college, when Gandhi was still alive and before Vinoba launched the Bhoodan campaign.

Casting his mind back to his childhood, he recalls the village in which he was born and brought up—one of the 550,000 villages in which eight out of ten of his countrymen still live. In reality it was far removed from the ideal village which Gandhi conceived as the basic unit of a free and reborn India, but he can understand why Gandhi dreamed his dream of a commonwealth of village republics. In fact the village was divided into the few rich and the many poor, the high and the low caste; factions were rife. But, he believes, it still had the potential of genuine community, if only the villagers could be persuaded to think of themselves as belonging to a single joint family. He himself was brought up in a joint family and, therefore, appreciates the values of such a natural co-operative group. Why, he asks, should not the obligations we recognize to our kin be extended to all who live in the village, and, wider still, to all men and women throughout the world?

But in order for that to happen, many changes would be necessary—changes in the hearts and minds of individuals and changes in the social structure. Genuine community can be built only on the basis of social, economic, and political equality; and that means that the old ideas of caste and class and property must be given up. Our leader is very conscious of the implications of such a condition, because he himself belonged to the class of the privileged. If he was not born a Brahmin, he was at least born a Kshatriya or a Vaishya, entitled to wear the sacred thread of the twice-born. His father was an agriculturalist, but not one of the poor peasants or landless labourers; he belonged to the upper rural class of owner cultivators, owning up to twenty acres of cultivable land. In broad terms, his father could be described as a middle-class peasant. This middle-class status the father passed on to the son, but our leader did not follow his father into agriculture. He probably received a better formal education than his father and went as far as High School, though not to university as did many of his colleagues in the movement. Perhaps for this reason, or perhaps because there were few opportunities in agriculture, he began his working life in one of the middle-class professions, such as teaching. However, he did not stay long in this job before deciding to devote himself full-time to service in the movement.

Our leader no longer attaches importance himself to caste or class distinctions: he subscribes to the ideal of a casteless, classless society. But he is aware that others would describe him as middle-class. He owns or is a joint owner of immovable property—probably his house and a small plot of land, some of which he has donated in Bhoodan. His monthly household income is less than Rs. 200/-, a figure which puts him in the lower-middle-class income group. And if he is asked to state which class he belongs to, he will reply 'Middle' or 'Lower middle class'. He does not feel, therefore, that, compared with his father, he has 'come down in the world'. He probably feels quite assured of his own social status, and if he should occasionally think that, in some respects, he has a lower status than normal for someone of his class, he probably reminds himself that it is largely because he has voluntarily chosen a life of comparative poverty.

In religion he was brought up and remains, like most of his countrymen, a Hindu. But, recalling the religious environment of his childhood, he would not describe it as orthodox. It was a liberal or 'modern' version of Hinduism that his parents believed in and practised; and, perhaps because of this, he experienced no difficulty in adjusting his religious ideas to the non-sectarian ones professed by Gandhi, who saw all religions, and even sincere atheism, as different, but in some sense equally valid, ways of approaching God, Truth, the Ultimate Reality. He accepts Gandhi's belief that God is revealed in service to one's fellowmen, particularly in service to 'the low, the lost, the last, and the least'. He would, therefore, now describe his religion as Humanism, although he might also add that he agrees with Vinoba that the days of religion in the old sense are over, that what is needed is a synthesis of the truths of Science and those of Spirituality—a blending of knowledge of the outer and of the inner worlds. In any case, our leader sees his participation in the Sarvodaya movement as an expression of his most deeply felt beliefs about the nature of reality, as following in the footsteps of the man who sublimely equated swaraj with Ram Raj, the Kingdom of God.

If we then ask what induced him to follow the path trod by the Mahatma, he would reply that he was influenced by his reading about Gandhi and his ideas, but more especially by personal contact with Gandhians, above all by Gandhi's 'spiritual heir', Vinoba. Unlike many of his colleagues who have a relative working in the movement, our leader had none of his family associated with the movement, but his parents or close relatives looked with favour on his participation.

On joining the movement our leader found that it expected of him practical signs of commitment to its ideals. He was called upon to follow Gandhi's example and to practise what he preached. When Sarva Seva Sangh introduced the pledge of the Lok Sevak, he took it readily; and when, in 1957, Vinoba announced the formation of the Shanti Sena, he enrolled in it and took the Shanti Sainik pledge. Like others of his colleagues, he was gratified when the eminent Socialist leader Jayaprakash Narayan decided to quit party politics and join the movement; and he was deeply moved when at the Bodh-Gaya conference of 1954 Jayaprakash offered to dedicate his life for the cause of the non-violent revolution. However, our leader did not himself take the new pledge of Jeevandan, although many of his colleagues did. Perhaps he felt that the steps he had already taken, including a contribution in Bhoodan or some other dan, were proof enough of his dedication, and that he could leave God to decide, when the time came, whether in life he had been a true Jeevandani.

As a member of the movement our leader feels he is one of a fellowship of believers and doers in the righteous cause of promoting truth, love, and compassion. The work is hard and the pay poor and uncertain; but it is no ordinary work that he does, and the spirit of comradeship and sense of service more than compensate for the hardships. Above all, there is the joy of being in the company of India's new saint. That Vinoba *is* a saint, a man of exceptional qualities, the true heir of Gandhi, our leader has no doubt: how else could one explain his power to move men's hearts, to persuade millions of land-hungry peasants to take the first steps towards creating a Kingdom of Kindness? Guided by the inspiration of Vinoba, our leader feels himself to be in the vanguard of a total revolution which will eventually lead to the reconstruction not only of India but of the whole world. The revolution will be total, but not totalitarian. The means chosen to effect it will be consistent with the ends. And in so far as the movement itself is part of the means, it too avoids the defects of totalitarianism. The movement demands much of our leader, but it does not seek to embrace every inch of his life. It remains a movement of free men, and our leader uses his freedom to participate in the activities of other organizations.

'Other organizations', but not any kind of organization. In taking the pledge of the Lok Sevak, our leader has pledged himself not to take part in party and power politics. When Gandhi was alive, our leader was naturally a member of the Congress. But since Gandhi's death he has revised his ideas about politics and resigned from Congress. He voted for Congress in the 1952 General Election, but he has not voted in any election since. He now subscribes to the new doctrine of partyless democracy that Vinoba and Jayaprakash have elaborated, which is seen as a step towards the stateless society. However, despite its faults, he still feels some allegiance to Congress. It remains the party most sympathetic to Sarvodaya ideals. The parties most opposed to these ideals are the Communists, with their ideas of class war and violent revolution, and Hindu communal parties, such as Jan Sangh.

Although our leader subscribes to the doctrine of partyless democracy, he is not quite certain what the doctrine implies. He thinks, but is only half-sure, that it would be right for Sarvodaya workers to help good candidates at election times, even if they are standing with a party ticket. Perhaps our leader's uncertainty is a product of his ambivalent feelings towards Congress. On the one hand, he is half-inclined to agree that the Sarvodaya movement is too identified in the public mind with Congress—perhaps it would be better if the movement could fashion for itself a more distinctive image. On the other hand, Congress remains the ruling party and it is still promoting, even if rather half-heartedly, some of Gandhi's ideas. The movement needs the co-operation of ruling Congress state governments in order to secure Gramdan legislation and funds for village development. Further, our leader is convinced that the movement would make greater progress towards the Sarvo-daya society if it paid more attention to the Government's pro-gramme of Panchayati Raj. Of course, the Government is also taking steps to build up the country's armed forces. This, our leader recognizes, is contrary to the Gandhian ideal; and some of his colleagues feel so strongly about it that they would be prepared to conduct a non-co-operation campaign against the Government over this issue. However, he is sure that this would be a false move until the movement can offer a real non-violent alternative to military defence. Such an attitude is liable to be misinterpreted by pacifist friends from the West, who may suspect that our leader is swayed too much by nationalist sentiment. But he would rebut the charge if voiced. He does not see any conflict between restrained nationalism and regard for men of all nations. And on the trouble-some issue of Kashmir, over which India's national interests are alleged to conflict with those of Pakistan, he is inclined to take the very unpopular line that Kashmir's accession to the Indian Union is not final and irrevocable.

When he is asked to describe the goals of the Sarvodaya move-ment, our leader is most likely to emphasize its social goals. He is less likely to mention its economic goals, its political goals, includ-ing the anarchist idea of a stateless society, its spiritual objectives, its commitment to Non-violence, and its universalistic aspirations. All these he sees as important, but what moves him most is the vision of a social order in which caste and class differences are abolished, social equality obtains, and there is no exploitation of man by man. This vision he knows he shares with Socialists of various kinds, but he believes that the Sarvodaya way is the only sure way of making it come true.

The Sarvodaya way, he explains, is not the way of power politics: it is the way of love, of friendly persuasion, of conversion of individuals on a mass scale to new values. It is not an easy way, but the movement, he believes, has developed a programme of action which shows that it is feasible. The core of this programme is the promotion of Gramdan, the development of Khadi and other village industries, and the building up of the Shanti Sena. Our leader agrees with Vinoba that these three items are the ones to concentrate on. However, if he had to rank them in order of importance, he would give priority to Gramdan, with Shanti Sena and Khadi following in that order.

Our leader is probably aware that, even in the movement, there is some scepticism about the viability in the long run of the Khadi industry. However, he himself is convinced that it will not give way to mill-cloth production in the industrial cities. Perhaps the Khadi industry will be transformed in the future by the establishment of small modern workshops in the villages.

Shanti Sena he sees as a non-violent police rather than as a national defence force. But he is half-inclined to agree with those who urge that, if China renews her aggression on the Northern borders, the Shanti Sena should be sent there to offer non-violent resistance.

On Gramdan our leader is also somewhat uncertain. He has accepted the new, revised version, Sulabh Gramdan, but he must admit that it does make too many concessions to the principles of private property. Sulabh Gramdan, of course, should make it easier to spread the Gramdan idea, and for that reason is to be welcomed. But he is rather inclined to agree that the movement should concentrate on the development of existing Gramdan villages rather than on getting more declarations of Gramdan. It would be nice if the movement could do both. . . .

Vinoba himself, our leader is probably aware, tends to favour the propagation of the Gramdan idea, leaving the main burden of development work to the Government's Community Development agencies and to the villagers themselves. Vinoba may well be right on this issue, but our leader wonders whether single-minded emphasis on the propagation of Gramdan is altogether wise from a tactical point of view. The villagers are beset by many problems, such as high prices and evictions. Our leader is firmly convinced that the movement should take up such urgent current problems as a way of rousing the masses.

Asked about the achievements of the movement so far, our leader is probably conscious of scepticism among the public at large—at least the public in the cities—and among the intellectuals. He knows that the movement has not achieved all that it promised in the early enthusiastic years of Bhoodan. The problem of the land-less labourers is still with us. However, he is convinced that the movement does have practical achievements to its credit, that the Bhoodan and Gramdan statistics are evidence of this, and that, in addition to providing a stimulus to land reform, the movement has played a not insignificant role in changing the social climate in India and in promoting the peaceful solution of social and political problems.

That there are many obstacles to the further progress of the movement our leader would readily admit. Being a self-critical person, he is more likely to draw attention to 'internal' than to 'external' obstacles. Among the 'external' obstacles he identifies are the social and economic context in which the movement operates—casteism, communalism, mass apathy, and illiteracy, for example—and the ambivalent institutions of government and the political parties. High on the list of 'internal' obstacles comes his regret that the movement's workers are too few in number, and also sometimes lacking in dedication and idealism. This criticism of the moral calibre of the workers he might also apply to some of the top-level leaders. At the same time, he might add—without any sense of inconsistency—that the policy of the movement is *too* idealistic, demanding too much of ordinary people. More im-portant than this obstacle, however, are defects in the organiza-tion of the movement: poor co-ordination, lack of finance to maintain workers and their families, and inadequate training of workers.

When his views on organization are probed further, our leader reveals that there is near-unanimity among his colleagues that, although the workers are generally dedicated people, they often lack the training to carry out their jobs effectively. There is less agreement among his colleagues about the efficiency of Sarva Seva Sangh, but a clear majority agree with him that the movement needs a stronger central organization than it has at present. When the distinctive decision-making procedure used in the movement—the procedure of reaching decisions by unanimity or consensus—is referred to, our leader agrees that all workers can indeed join in making decisions about policy, but he adds that, in practice, decisions are made by only a few leaders.

Asked what he would do to make the movement more effective in the future, our leader does not provide many practical suggestions that are either not already being implemented or would not be readily implemented if the movement had the wherewithal to do so. Provision of adequate maintenance for workers is an example of the latter. He refers rather vaguely to ways of improving the policy and programme of the movement: raising finance, modifying the organization, and making more effective use of propaganda techniques.

Asked whether the movement should change some of its traditional attitudes to things like smoking, drinking, and birth control, in order to attract to it today's young people, he answers with a clear No. He does not think that relaxation of the movement's 'puritanism' would serve any good purpose. Obviously, he regards self-discipline and self-restraint as essential virtues which everybody must seek to cultivate.

He does not volunteer the suggestion that the movement should adopt a sharp change of present tactics and launch 'negative' satyagraha campaigns against the Government and the landlords. But when this point is put to him, he remembers the success of Gandhi's campaigns against the British Raj, and agrees that 'negative' satyagraha might well be used, if not immediately then at some time in the future. He is not altogether convinced by Vinoba's concept of 'positive' satyagraha with its 'gentle, gentler, gentlest' approach.

Asked about the future of the movement as he sees it, our leader displays considerable optimism. He mentions Vinoba's speech at the Raipur Sammelan 1963, in which it was pointed out that, like individuals and nations, movements have their ups and downs. He agrees with Vinoba that the period of the movement's downward tendency is over, and that the period of its onward march is coming. He confidently expects a new surge forward in the near future—perhaps a spectacular campaign designed to lay the foundations of gramswarajya by the date of Gandhiji's birth centenary, 2 October 1969. (He does not know that Vinoba is about to launch just such a campaign.)

But—conscious of how much the movement seems to centre and depend on the charismatic figure of Vinoba—we put to our leader one last question: What will happen to the movement when Vinoba passes on? He is prepared for this question: it is similar to the question Western observers used to ask before Nehru's death. 'After Vinoba, who?' The answer is clear: Jayaprakash Narayan, the first Jeevandani; he is the man best qualified to carry on the work of Vinoba, just as Vinoba has carried on the work of Gandhi.

Our profile is finished and we lay down our pen. Sketchy though it is, it is the best we can do. Is it a fair sketch? Have we captured even the main contours of the Sarvodaya leader's face? Will he recognize himself when we show him our work? Or will he gently suggest that we have distorted him by looking at him through Western spectacles, by drawing with a Western pen?

And what will this gentle anarchist say if, sympathetic as he knows us to be, we voice the suspicion that he is engaged on an impossible enterprise, and that he and his movement may be destined to founder on the shoals of institutionalization? Will he remind us of Gandhi's belief that our task is to make the impossible possible, to transcend the limitations that nature seems to have imposed on us? And will he add, with that air of non-attachment which Westerners often find so mysterious and puzzling, the words of the *Gita*, 'No one who does the good ever comes to grief'?

THE QUESTIONNAIRE

CONFIDENTIAL   Prof. G. N. Ostergaard,
Osmania University,
Hyderabad 7, A.P.

SARVODAYA MOVEMENT SURVEY

(*Instructions for completing questionnaire:* Where alternative answers are suggested, please tick ($\sqrt{}$) the correct one. If there is not enough space for other answers, use space at end *or* separate sheet. If any question is not applicable to you, please write: N/A. If you would prefer to remain anonymous, you need not give your name.)

1. Name.................... 2. Sex: Male...... Female......
3. Address................. 4. Date of birth...............
5. Marital status: Unmarried......Married......; Widowed......;
   Divorced......
6. Place of birth:.......... District.......... State............
7. Up till the age of fifteen years, did you live most of your life in a village......; or small town (up to 25,000 population)......; large town/city......?
8. *Education*
   (a) Please tick each of the stages of education you have completed:
   Primary........ High School........ Intermediate........
   Graduation...... Postgraduation......
   Professional/technical/other (specify) ....
   (b) If graduate, name of college/university & main subjects studied:
   ....
   (c) At what age did you complete your full-time education?......
   years
9. *Family data*
   (a) What was your father's occupation? (Please be specific: e.g. if business, what *kind* of business; if teacher, what *kind* of school; if agriculture, whether owner-cultivator, tenant-cultivator, etc.)
   ....
   (b) Did/does your father own land? Yes.... No.... If 'yes', approximately how many acres?
   Cultivable...... acres   Uncultivable...... acres.

(c) Were you brought up in a joint family? Yes.... No....
(d) What was the religion of your parents?......................
(e) What was your father's caste? Brahmin......;Kshatriya......;
     Vaishya......; Scheduled Caste/Tribe...... Other (specify)
     ....
(f) If any of your family are/were actively associated with the
     Movement before or after Independence, please give brief details.

Their relation to you, e.g. uncle	Their position & work in the Movement	Remarks

(g) What was the attitude of your parents &/or close relatives to
     your active participation in the Movement? On the whole, did
     they:
     Oppose...... Raise no objection...... Favour...... Other
     (specify)......

10. *Personal data*
(a) Were you active in the Independence Movement? Yes......
     No......
     If 'yes', in what capacity?...............................
(b) Please list the jobs you have done since leaving school/college

Period (e.g. 1940–45)	Job held	Nature of the work	Salary/honorarium drawn Rs. per mth.

(i) *Before joining the Movement*

(ii) *After joining the Movement*

(c) Please list any official positions, not mentioned above, which you have held or now hold in the Movement's organisations or other Gandhian institutions (e.g. Distt. Rep. Assam Sarvodaya Mandal, Secretary, Gujrat Nai Talim Sangh)

Period	Position held	Name of institution

(d) Please list memberships & official positions you have held or now hold in any other social & political institutions, such as educational societies, co-operatives, religious associations, political parties, legislatures, councils etc. (e.g. 1945–7, Member Rajasthan Provincial Congress Committee).

Period	Position held (whether member/Sec. etc.)	Name of Institution

11. Have you taken the pledge of (a) the Lok Sevak? Yes......
    No......When? Year......
    (b) the Shanti Sena? Yes......
    No...... When? Year......
    (c) Jeevandan? Yes......No......
    When? Year......

12. What is the approximate present monthly income of your household *from all sources*, including wife's and dependants' earnings, if any, rent, investments, etc.

Rs. ...... per month

13. Number of persons, including yourself, dependent on this income. Adults (over 18 years)...... Children......

14. Do you own or share in the ownership of any immovable property? Yes......No......
If 'yes', what is the present approximate value of your own property or your own share of the property?
Residential: Rs. ......Landed: Rs. ......Other: Rs. ......

15. If you have given any land or property in *Bhoodan* or other *dans*, please give brief details of nature, extent & approximate value of the property.
....

16. If you *had* to place yourself in one of the following social classes which one would you say you belonged to?
Upper...... Middle...... Lower Middle...... Working Class ...... Peasant......

17. Would you describe your own religious upbringing as a child as: Orthodox...... or liberal...... or modern/Western......?

18. Would you describe the religious views you hold *today* as: Orthodox...... liberal...... modern/Western...... Scientific Spiritualism...... humanist...... non-religious...... other (specify)......

19. Which of the following reasons influenced you most to join the Movement? Reading Sarvodaya literature...... Personal contact with Gandhians...... Parents...... Friends...... Other (specify) ....

20. If there were any particular leaders, other than Gandhiji, who especially influenced your decision to join the Movement, who were they?
....

21. Did you vote in any of the General Elections? Yes...... No......
If 'yes', which party/parties did you vote for?
1952 .... 1957 .... 1962 ....

22. Which political party, in your opinion, is *most sympathetic* to Sarvodaya ideals?
....

23. Which political party, in your opinion, is *most opposed* to Sarvodaya ideals?
....

Views on the Movement since Independence

24. How would you describe briefly the goal or purpose of the Sarvodaya Movement?

25. Which in your opinion are the most important achievements of this Movement since Independence?

26. To which three aspects of the Movement's programme do you attach greatest importance today?
    1. .... 2. .... 3. ....

27. Vinobaji has been the principal leader and guide of the Movement since Gandhiji's death. When Vinobaji himself eventually passes on, which three persons, in your opinion, would be able to give the best general guidance to the Movement?
    1. .... 2. .... 3. ....

28. What in your opinion are the most serious obstacles to the further progress of the Movement?

29. What proposals would you make to ensure that the Movement becomes more effective in its work in the future?

30. Below are some statements sometimes made about the Movement. Please tick whether you agree or disagree with each statement. If you feel that you cannot simply agree or disagree, please explain briefly your reaction to that particular statement.

	Agree	Disagree
a. The Movement should pay more attention to the Government's programme of Panchayati Raj as a means of achieving the Sarvodaya Society.		
b. The Movement should now concentrate on the development of existing Gramdan villages rather than on getting more declarations of Gramdan.		

	Agree	Disagree

c. The Movement has become too closely identified in the public mind with the Congress Party.

d. The Movement should make more effort than it has so far done to take up urgent current problems such as high prices and evictions, as a way of rousing the masses.

e. While persuasion should be used as much as possible, the Movement should also be prepared to organize satyagraha campaigns as a means of abolishing landlessness.

f. The Movement will have to change some of its traditional attitudes to things like smoking, drinking and birth control if it hopes to attract young people today.

g. While partyless democracy is the ideal to be aimed at, the Movement cannot ignore that parties now exist. Sarvodaya workers, therefore, should help good candidates at election times, even if they have been given a party ticket.

h. All the workers in the Movement can join in making decisions on policy but in practice the decisions are made by only a few leaders.

i. The Movement needs a stronger central organization than it has at present.

j. While the Movements workers are generally dedicated people they often lack the training to carry out their jobs effectively.

k. *Sulabh Gramdan* involves too many concessions to the principles of private ownership of property.

l. The production of khadi will be important for some time to come but we must expect that it will eventually give way to mill-made cloth.

m. It is not true to say that the people of Kashmir have already decided to integrate

	Agree	Disagree

themselves with India. The accession of Kashmir to India is not final and irrevocable.

n. If China renews her aggression, the Shanti Sena should be asked to go to the battle areas to offer non-violent resistance.

o. Until we have a real non-violent alternative to offer, we should not ask people to non-co-operate with the Government's efforts to make India strong militarily.

p. The Movement has had its ups and downs but we may confidently expect that it will make a new surge forwards in the next few years.

Additional Comments

If there are any other comments that you would like to make about the Movement and yourself (e.g. reasons for joining, belief in its creative potentialities, the problems of building up a non-violent organization), please do so. You may also wish to add to some of your replies above.

Thank you for your valuable help in completing the questionnaire.

APPENDIX TWO

RESPONSE TO THE QUESTIONNAIRE

THE Secretary of Sarva Seva Sangh supplied the names and addresses of the 479 persons holding office in the organization in March 1965. With a covering letter from the Secretary, a copy of the questionnaire was posted to each office-holder on 1st April 1965. A verbal reminder was made at a meeting of the Sangh in May 1965, which also provided an opportunity for the office-holders present to contact the senior

Response to the Sarvodaya Movement Survey, 1965

Group	Number of office holders	Number who completed the questionnaire	z
By level of office:			
I Prabandh Samiti: members	25 ⎫	20 ⎫	
Prabandh Samiti: permanent invitees	25 ⎬ 75	12 ⎬ 45	1·69
Nominated members of the Sangh	25 ⎭	13 ⎭	
II Secretaries of State Sarvodaya Mandals	13 ⎫	7 ⎫	
District Representatives	217 ⎬ 230	104 ⎬ 111	0·20
III District Convenors	174	72	1·49
By sex:			
Men	463	221	0·23
Women	16	7	
By region:*			
Southern	79	46	1·49
Northern	400	182	

Note *Office-holders located in the states of Andhra, Kerala, Mysore, and Madras were classified as 'Southern'; all others, 'Northern'. The classification is not identical with the classification of 'regional origin' used in the text, since a few leaders worked in a region (and state) other than the one in which they were born.

author personally to answer any queries about the survey. In addition, a letter of reminder was subsequently sent to non-responding members of the Samiti. A few questionnaires were returned by persons other than those to whom they were addressed. Eliminating these from the 'sample', the number of completed questionnaires was 228, i.e. 47·6 per cent of all office-holders. Four explicit refusals to complete the questionnaire were received.

From the lists supplied by the Secretary we were able to determine the highest office held by each office-holder, their sex, and their regional location. The table above presents the distributions of these character-istics among all office-holders and among those who completed the questionnaire. A comparison of the respondents with the population studied indicates that, within 95 per cent confidence limits, the respon-dents are representative of all office-holders in respect of level of office held, sex, and region. The test employed to determine the representa-tiveness of the 'sample' was that using the normal approximation to the binomial distribution, the critical value for z being 1·96.

GLOSSARY

Adivasis: tribal peoples
Ahimsa: non-injury; non-violence
Akhil Bharat: All India
Ambar charkha: a four-spindle hand operated spinning wheel
Antaryami: inner guide, God
Aparigraha: non-possession
Arthashastra: the ancient Hindu text on the polity, ascribed to Kautilya
Ashram: a religious retreat; place of study and communal life
Asteya: non-stealing, including in its Gandhian connotation refraining
   from possessing things for which there is no real need
Aswad: tastelessness, i.e. taking food only as required to maintain
   physical health
Ati-toofan: super whirlwind or typhoon

Bhagavad Gita: literally, 'The Song of the Lord'; the Hindu religious
   and philosophical poem which sets out the basic paths to self-
   realization
Bhoodan: land-gift; voluntary donation of land for redistribution to the
   landless
Blockdan: extension of the principle of Gramdan to a 'block', an admin-
   istrative unit in the Community Development Programme
Brahmacharya: celibacy; sexual chastity or continence; the first of the
   four stages of life, that of the student
Brahman: Truth, God, the World Spirit
Brahmin: the priestly class, the first order of the varna system
Bread labour: the concept, originally Tolstoyan, that every man should
   perform manual work sufficient to supply his basic necessities
Buddhidan: gift of mental abilities in the achievement of Sarvodaya

Charkha: the traditional spinning-wheel
Crore: ten millions

Dama: subjugation of the senses; self-restraint
Dan: gift, donation
Danadhara: the gift movement
Darshan: contact with or sight of, usually in respect of a venerated
   person
Datoon: twig used for cleaning teeth

Dharma: duty; divinely prescribed code of conduct, appropriate to a class or the various life stages of an individual

Districtdan: extension of the principle of Gramdan to a district, a major administrative unit in India

Gandhi Smarak Nidhi: Gandhi National Memorial Trust

Gramdan: literally, 'gift of the village'; the concept of surrendering individual property rights in land to the village community

Gram panchayat: village council; village level local authority

Gram Sabha: village assembly

Gramswarajya: the system of village self-government envisaged by Gandhi

Guru: inspired or venerated teacher

Harijans: literally, 'Children of God'; term used by Gandhi to re-name the untouchables of Hindu society

Harijan Sevak Sangh: Association for the Service of Harijans

Hartal: a technique of non-violent action involving mass withdrawal of labour and the closing of shops and businesses

Huzoor: a master, in contrast to a servant

Jai Hind!: Victory to India!

Jai Jagat!: Victory to the World!

Jati: endogamous social group, usually translated as 'sub-caste'

Jeevandan: dedication of one's life to the cause of Sarvodaya

Karma: the doctrine that existence is conditioned by the sum of good and evil actions; at the individual level, the doctrine that performance of an individual's dharma is the determinant of his position in his next (re-incarnated) life

Karma Yoga: the doctrine of self-realization through action, particularly service to others

Karmayogi: one who practises the doctrine of Karma Yoga

Khadi: hand spun, hand woven cloth

Kisan: peasant

Kshatriya: the warrior class, the second order of the varna system

Lakh: one hundred thousand

Lok-niti: politics of the people, in contrast to Raj-niti, politics of the state

Lok Sabha: House of the People, the Lower House of the Indian Parliament

Lok Sevak: literally, 'servant of the people'; an adherent of the Sarvodaya movement who has taken the Lok Sevak pledge
Lok-shakti: self-reliant power of the people

Mahabharata: the classical Hindu epic
Mahatma: great soul
Mandal: circle of people, small association
Mantra: religious formula or incantation
Mazdoor: servant or manual worker
Mela: a fair
Mistri: literally, 'mason'; skilled worker or expert
Moksha: self-realization, enlightenment

Nai Talim: Basic Education; the new craft-centred kind of education developed by Gandhi as part of his Constructive Programme
Nirman: construction, development; the third and final stage of Gramdan, in which the Gram Sabha undertakes its programme of reconstruction and development

Padayatra: pilgrimage on foot
Paisa: term for the Indian cent
Panchayat: council; originally, a council of five members
Panchayati Raj: term used to designate the system of rural local self-government in India
Panchayat Samiti: block-level local authority
Para: hamlet
Paramardha: dedication to the Almighty through living for others
Parardha: helpfulness to others
Patra: pot
Prabandh Samiti: executive committee
Prapti: the first stage of Gramdan, in which the villagers agree to accept the conditions of Gramdan
Purdah: veil; traditional seclusion of women
Pushti: the second stage of Gramdan, in which the gift is verified, titles to land legally transferred, and a portion of the village land distributed to the landless for cultivation by them

Raj: rule
Raj-niti: politics of the state, in contrast to Lok-niti, politics of the people
Ram Raj: the Kingdom of God

Samaj: brotherhood, fellowship
Sammelan: annual conference

Sampattidan: gift of money or proportion of one's income

Sangh: association

Santi Parva: 'The Book of Peace', part of the Hindu epic, the Mahabharata

Sarva Seva Sangh: Association for the Service of All

Sarvodaya: the welfare of all; the raising up of one and all

Sarvodaya Samaj: Sarvodaya Brotherhood, consisting of those who have taken the Lok Sevak pledge

Satya: truth

Satyagraha: literally, 'holding fast to truth'; the Gandhian philosophy of Non-violence; (loosely) non-violent resistance

Satyagrahi: one who practises satyagraha

Scheduled Castes and Tribes: publicly designated backward classes and tribes for whom special provisions have been made to protect their interests and to bring them up to the level of other communities in the Indian Union

Shanti Sainik: member of the Shanti Sena

Shanti Sena: Peace Army or Brigade

Shramdan: gift of labour

Statedan: extension of the principle of Gramdan to the level of one of the states of the Indian Union

Sudra: servant class, the fourth order of the varna system

Sulabh Gramdan: simplified Gramdan, the version of Gramdan developed since 1963, which involves a distinction between ownership and possession

Sutranjali: donations of Khadi yarn

Swadeshi: of local or indigenous origin; principle of using locally-made goods; in the extended Gandhian connotation, service to one's immediate neighbours

Swaraj: self-rule, self-government, political independence

Swardha: selfishness

Takli: a simple tool used in hand spinning

Tapas: fervour generated by the practice of austerities

Tola: hamlet

Toofan: whirlwind, typhoon

Upanishads: speculative treatises forming the latter part of the Vedas

Vaishya: the merchant class, the third order of the varna system

Varna: a class in the four-fold division of traditional Hindu society; literally, 'colour'; loosely, 'caste'

Varnasramdharma: code of right conduct related to the four varnas and the four stages of life

Vedas: general term for the collection of ancient texts, hymns and treatises, believed to have been written between 1200 and 900 B.C., and regarded as embodying the essential truths and traditions of Hinduism

Vijana: science

Zamindar: landlord in the zamindari system of land tenure in India, under which the landlord was regarded as proprietor on condition of payment of a stipulated revenue to the state

Zilla Parishad: district-level local authority in the Panchayati Raj system of local government

SELECT BIBLIOGRAPHY

Note: Varanasi = Benares = Kashi.

AKHIL BHARAT SHANTI SENA MANDAL, *The Indian Shanti Sena*, The Shanti Sena Mandal, Varanasi, n.d.

All-India Consumer Expenditure Survey, Volume II: *Pattern of Income and Expenditure*, National Council of Applied Economic Research, New Delhi, 1967.

All-India Rural Household Survey, 1962, Occasional Paper No. 13, National Council of Applied Economic Research, New Delhi, 1965.

All-India Rural Household Survey, Volume II: *Income Investment and Saving*; Volume III: *Basic Tables, with Notes*; National Council of Applied Economic Research, New Delhi, 1965.

ANON. 'Among practical idealists: a Sarvodaya Meet', *Economic Weekly*, 22 May 1965, 843–4.

ANON. 'Satyagraha in Andhra' (Letter from the South), *Economic Weekly*, 14 Mar. 1964, 507–8.

ASHE, G., 'Can non-violence change society?', *Gandhi Marg*, 12, 4 (1968), 345–54.

ASHE, G., *Gandhi: a study in revolution*, Heinemann, London, 1968.

Association of Universities of the British Commonwealth, *Year Book of the Universities of the Commonwealth*, The Association, London, 1955.

Association of Voluntary Agencies for Rural Development, *Panchayati Raj as the basis of Indian polity*, The Association, New Delhi, 1962.

Association of Voluntary Agencies for Rural Development, *Report of a study team on democratic decentralisation in Rajasthan*, The Association, New Delhi, 1961.

BAILEY, F. G., 'Decisions by consensus in councils and committees: with special reference to village and local government in India', in *Political systems and the distribution of power*, Association of Social Anthropologists of the Commonwealth, Monograph 2, Tavistock Publications, London, 1965, 1–20.

BANG, T., & RAM, S., *Samoohik Pad-yatra (its significance and technique)*, Sarva Seva Sangh Prakashan, Wardha, 1956.

BANKER, S., 'Reorientation of khadi in retrospect', *Sarvodaya*, XVII, 10 & 11 (April, May 1968).

BANKS, J. A., & BANKS, O., 'Feminism and social change', in G. K. Zollschan & W. Hirsch (eds.), *Explorations in social change*, Routledge & Kegan Paul, London, 1964, 547–69.

BARY, T. de, *et al.*, *Sources of Indian tradition*, Columbia University Press, New York, 1958.

BASHAN, A. L., 'Indian society and the legacy of the past', *Australian Journal of Politics and History*, 12 (1966), 131–45.

BENDIX, R., *Max Weber*, Anchor Books, Doubleday, New York, 1962.

BENDIX, R., 'Reflections on charismatic leadership', *Asian Survey*, 7, 6 (June 1967), 341–52.

BENDIX, R., *Nation-building and citizenship*, Wiley, New York, 1964.

BHATTA, S. D., *And they gave up dacoity*, Sarva Seva Sangh, Varanasi, 1962.

BHAVE, VINOBA, *Bhoodan and Congress*, Sarva Seva Sangh, Wardha, 1955.

BHAVE, VINOBA, *Bhoodan Yajna; land-gift mission*, Navajivan, Ahmedabad, 1957. First pub. 1953.

BHAVE, VINOBA, *From Bhoodan to Gramdan*, Sarvodaya Prachuralaya, Tanjore, 1957.

BHAVE, VINOBA, *Christ: the love incarnate*, Sarva Seva Sangh Prakashan, Varanasi, 1964.

BHAVE, VINOBA, *Democratic values*, Sarva Seva Sangh Prakashan, Kashi, 1962.

BHAVE, VINOBA, *et al.*, *Election and democracy*, Sarva Seva Sangh Prakashan, Varanasi, 1967.

BHAVE, VINOBA, *The essence of Quran*, Akhil Bharatiya Sarva Seva Sangh, Varanasi, 1962.

BHAVE, VINOBA, *Gramdan: villagisation of land*, 2nd edn., Sarvodaya Prachuralaya, Thanjavur, 1967.

BHAVE, VINOBA, *The present crisis in India*, Sarvodaya Prachuralaya, Tanjore, 1962.

BHAVE, VINOBA, *Revolutionary Sarvodaya*, Bharatiya Vidya Bhavan, Bombay, 1964.

BHAVE, VINOBA, *Sampatti dan*, Sarvodaya Prachuralaya, Tanjore, 1957.

BHAVE, VINOBA, *Sarvodaya and the business community* (compiled by D. Groom), Sarvodaya Prachuralaya, Tanjore, 1958.

BHAVE, VINOBA, *Sarvodaya and Communism*, Sarvodaya Prachuralaya, Tanjore, 1957.

BHAVE, VINOBA, *Science and self-knowledge*, 2nd edn., Sarva Seva Sangh Prakashan, Kashi, 1961.

BHAVE, VINOBA, *Science and spirituality*, Sri Aurobindo Ashram Press, Pondicherry, n.d.

BHAVE, VINOBA, *Shanti Sena*, Sarva Seva Sangh Prakashan, Kashi, 1961.

BHAVE, VINOBA, 'The Sino-Indian conflict', *Gandhi Marg*, 7, 1 (1963), 1–4.

BHAVE, VINOBA, *The steadfast intelligence* (synopsis translated by N. Bilpodiwala), Sarvodaya Prachuralaya, Tanjore, 1962.

BHAVE, VINOBA, *The steadfast wisdom*, Sarva Seva Sangh Prakashan, Varanasi, 1966.

BHAVE, VINOBA, *Swaraj Sastra: the principles of a non-violent political order* (translated by B. Kumarappa), Sarva Seva Sangh Prakashan, Kashi, 1959.

BHAVE, VINOBA, *Talks on the Gita*, Sarva Seva Sangh Prakashan, Kashi, 1958.

BHAVE, VINOBA, *Thoughts on education*, Sarva Seva Sangh Prakashan, Kashi, 1959.

BHAVE, VINOBA, *On World Peace*, Sarvodaya Prachuralayam, Tanjore, n.d.

BHAVE, VINOBA, & NARAYAN, JAYAPRAKASH, *Gramdan for Gram-swaraj*, Sarva Seva Sangh Prakashan, Varanasi, 1967.

BIERSTEDT, R., 'The problem of authority', in M. Berger, *et al.*, *Freedom and control in modern society*, Van Nostrand, New York, 1954, 67–81.

BILPODIWALA, N., *The social order and Sarvodaya*, Sarva Seva Sangh Prakashan, Rajghat, 1963.

BODANI, V., *Bhoodan: the religion of democracy*, Rashmi Prakashan Mandir, Rajket (Saurashtra), 1956.

BODANI, V., *Some evils of party system*, Rashmi Prakashan Mandir, Bombay, 1962.

Bombay, University of, 'An evaluation of the working of the Bhoodan movement', unpublished report by the Agricultural Economics Section, Department of Economics, The University, Bombay, n.d. [*c.* 1957].

BONDURANT, J. V., & FISHER, M. W., 'The concept of change in Hindu, socialist and neo-Gandhian thought', in D. E. Smith (ed.), *South Asian politics and religion*, Princeton University Press, Princeton, N.J., 1966, 235–48.

BONDURANT, J. V., *Conquest of violence: the Gandhian philosophy of conflict*, Princeton University Press, Princeton, N.J., 1958; rev. edn., University of California Press, Berkeley, 1965.

BONDURANT, J. V., & FISHER, M. W., 'Ethics in action: contrasting approaches to social and political problems in modern India', *Australian Journal of Politics and History*, 12, 2 (Aug. 1966), 177–93.

BONDURANT, J. V., 'Force, violence and the innocent dilemma', *Gandhi Marg*, 9, 3 (July 1965), 181–6.

BONDURANT, J. V., & FISHER, M. W., *Indian approaches to a socialist society*, Institute of International Studies, University of California, Berkeley, 1956.

BONDURANT, J. V., 'The nonconventional political leader in India', in R. L. Park & I. Tinker, *Leadership and political institutions in India*, Oxford University Press, London, 1959, 279–98.

BONDURANT, J. V., 'Satyagraha versus duragraha: the limits of symbolic violence', in G. Ramachandran and T. K. Mahadevan (eds.), *Gandhi —his relevance for our times*, Bharatiya Vidhya Bhavan, Bombay, 1964, 67–81.

BONDURANT, J. V., 'Traditional polity and the dynamics of change in India', *Human Organization*, 22, 1 (Spring 1963), 5–10.

BOSE, N. K. (ed.), *Selections from Gandhi*, 2nd edn., Navajivan Ahmedabad, 1957. First pub. 1948.

BOSE, N. K., *Studies in Gandhism*, Bose, Calcutta, 1940; 3rd rev. edn., Merit Publishers, Calcutta, 1962.

BRAIBANTI, R. & SPENGLER, J. J. (eds.), *Administration and economic development in India*, Duke University Press, Durham, N.C., 1963.

BROWN, D. M., *Indian political thought from Ranade to Bhave*, University of California Press, Berkeley, 1961.

BROWN, D. M., *The white umbrella: Indian political thought from Manu to Gandhi*, University of California Press, Berkeley, 1953.

CARTER, A., et al., *Non-violent action theory and practice: a selected bibliography*, Housmans, London, 1966; rev. edn., 1970.

CHATTERJEE, B. B., et al., *Gramdan and people*, Sarva Seva Sangh Prakashan, Varanasi, 1969.

CHATTERJEE, B. B., et al., 'People's perception of Gramdan and Prakhanddan', *Khadigramodyog* (Jan. 1968), 313–27.

CHATTERJEE, B. B., et al., *Riots in Rourkela*, Gandhian Institute of Studies, Varanasi, 1967.

CH'ÊN, J., *Mao and the Chinese revolution*, Oxford University Press, London, 1965.

CHOUDHARY, MANMOHAN, *Freedom for the masses*, Sarva Seva Sangh Prakashan, Varanasi, 1968.

CHOWDHARI, C., *Vinoba in Pakistan*, Sarva Seva Sangh Prakashan, Rajghat, Kashi, 1964.

CRESPIGNY, A. DE, 'Power and its forms', *Political Studies*, 16, 2 (June 1968), 192–205.

CROUCH, H., *Trade Unions and politics in India*, Manaktalas, Bombay, 1966.

DALTON, D., 'Experiments with tradition: an interpretation of Indian ideas on the nature of social and political change', *Journal of Development Studies*, 1, 2 (1964–5), 195–216.

DALTON, D., 'Mahatma Gandhi: the shaping of satyagraha', *Asian Review*, 2, 2 (Jan. 1969), 105–14.

DANTWALA, M. L., 'Prospects and problems of land reforms in India', *Economic Development and Cultural Change*, 6, 1 (1957), 3–15.

DASGUPTA, S., *A great society of small communities*, Sarva Seva Sangh Prakashan, Varanasi, 1968.

DASGUPTA, S. (ed.), *Towards a philosophy of social work in India*, Gandhian Institute of Studies, Varanasi, 1967.

DAVIS, K., *The population of India and Pakistan*, Princeton University Press, Princeton, N. J., 1951.

DEO, SHANKARRAO, 'Congress and constructive workers', *Harijan*, 20 & 27 Feb. 1949.

DEO, SHANKARRAO, *Gramdan movement; onward march: a turning point*, Mouj Printing Bureau, Bombay. Pamphlet circulated at 18th Sarvodaya Sammelan, Oct. 1969.

DEO, SHANKARRAO, *The voter's dilemma and Sarvodaya approach*, Sarvodaya Prachuralaya, Tanjore, 1962.

DESAI, A. R. (ed.), *Rural sociology in India*, 3rd edn., The Indian Society of Agricultural Economics, Bombay, 1961.

DESAI, M., 'Whither Bhudan?', *Gandhi Marg*, 2, 1 (1958), 81–4.

DESAI, N., *Hand Book for Shanti Sainiks*, Sarva Seva Sangh Prakashan, Varanasi, 1963.

DESAI, N., *Shanti Sena in India*, Sarva Seva Sangh Prakashan, Varanasi, 1962.

DHADDA, S., *Gramdan: the latest phase of Bhoodan*, Sarva Seva Sangh Prakashan, Rajghat, Kashi, 1958.

DHAWAN, G., *The political philosophy of Mahatma Gandhi*, 3rd edn., Navajivan, Ahmedabad, 1957.

DICKSON, M., 'Community development and the Gramdan movement in India', *Community Development Journal*, 3, 1 (1968), 33–7.

DIWAKAR, R. R., *Satyagraha: its technique and history*, Hind Kitabs, Bombay, 1946.

DOCTOR, A. H., *Anarchist thought in India*, Asia Publishing House, Bombay, 1964.

DOCTOR, A. H., *Sarvodaya: a political and economic study*, Asia Publishing House, Bombay, 1967.

DOUGLASS, J. W., 'Is there a politics without violence?', *Gandhi Marg*, 12, 4 (1968), 325–44.

DUTTA, R., 'The party representative in Fourth Lok Sabha', *Economic and Political Weekly*, Annual Number, Jan. 1969, 179–89.

EBERT, T., 'Non-violence: doctrine or technique?', *Gandhi Marg*, 11, 3 (1967), 251–60.

ELTZBACHER, P., *Anarchism*, Freedom Press, London, 1960. First pub. 1908.

ELWIN, V., *Religious and cultural aspects of Khadi*, Sarvodaya Prachuralaya, Thanjavur, 1964.

ERDMAN, H. L., *The Swatantra Party and Indian Conservatism*, Cambridge University Press, London, 1967.

ETZIONI, A., *A comparative analysis of complex organizations*, The Free Press, New York, 1961.

FRIEDRICH, C. J., 'Political leadership and the problem of charismatic power', *Journal of Politics*, 23 (Feb. 1961), 3–24.

FUCHS, S., *Rebellious prophets*, Asia Publishing House, London, 1965.

GANDHI, M. K., *Ashram observances in action*, Navajivan, Ahmedabad, 1955.

GANDHI, M. K., *The constructive programme: its meaning and place*, rev. edn., Navajivan, Ahmedabad, 1945. First pub. 1941.

GANDHI, M. K., *My experiments with truth*, Navajivan, Ahmedabad, 1927–9.

GANDHI, M. K., *Sarvodaya*, Navajivan, Ahmedabad, 1954.

GANDHI, M. K., *Satyagraha*, Navajivan, Ahmedabad, 1951.

GANDHI, M. K., *Socialism of my conception*, Bharatiya Vidya Bhavan, Bombay, 1957.

GANDHI, M. K., *Village Swaraj*, Navajivan, Ahmedabad, 1963.

GANDHI, M. K., *From Yeravda Mandir: Ashram observances*, Navajivan, Ahmedabad, 1957.

Gandhian Institute of Studies, *Report, 1961–1963*, The Institute, Varanasi, n.d.

GERARD, G., 'The saints in session', *Anarchy*, 42 (Aug. 1962), 240–5.

GESCHWENDER, J. A., 'Continuities in theories of status consistency and cognitive dissonance', *Social Forces*, 46, 2 (Dec. 1967), 160–71.

GLOCK, C. Y., & STARK, R., *Religion and society in tension*, Rand McNally, Chicago, 1965.

GOFFMAN, E., *Asylums*, Doubleday, New York, 1961.

GOULDNER, A. W. (ed.), *Studies in leadership*, Harper, New York, 1950.

GOYAL, N., *Cultural Revolution in a tribal tract*, Sarva Seva Sangh, Varanasi, 1968. Story of Anand Niketan's efforts to develop Rangpur area in Baroda district.

GROOM, D., *One man's journey*, War on Want, London, n.d.

GROOM, D., *War on Want programme: tour of Lokabandhu—Donald Groom in Cuddapah District Gramdan villages, December 1963*, Cuddapah District Nava Nirman Samiti, Andhra Pradesh, 1964.

GROOM, D., *'War on Want' projects in India*, Report for Dec. 1963–Jan. 1964, War on Want, London, 1964.

GROOM, D., *With Vinoba*, Sarva Seva Sangh Prakashan, Benares, 1961.

GUSFIELD, J. R., 'The study of social movements', *International Encyclopaedia of the Social Sciences*, 14 (1968), 445–50.

HALAPPA, G. S. (ed.), *Dilemmas of democratic politics in India*, Manaktalas, Bombay, 1966.

HALMOS, P., *The faith of the counsellors*, Constable, London, 1965.

HANSON, A. H., 'Grass roots', Chapter XI in his *The process of planning:*

a study of India's five-year plans, 1950–1964, Royal Institute of International Affairs, Oxford University Press, London, 1966, 394–443.

HARRISON, J. F. C., *Robert Owen and the Owenites in Britain and America,* Routledge & Kegan Paul, London, 1969.

HART, L., *Strategy: the indirect approach,* Faber, London, 1955.

HEBERLE, R., 'Social movements', *International Encyclopaedia of the Social Sciences,* 14 (1968), 438–45.

HEBERLE, R., *Social movements,* Appleton-Century-Crofts, New York, 1951.

HENNACY, A., *The autobiography of a Catholic anarchist,* Catholic Worker Books, New York, 1954.

HOFFMAN, D. P., *India's social miracle,* Naturegraph, Healdsburg (U.S.A.), 1961.

HUME, R. E. (trans.), *The thirteen principal Upanishads,* Oxford University Press, London, 1951.

Hyderabad, Government of, *Bhoodan, or land through love,* Department of Information and Public Relations, Hyderabad, 1954.

India, Government of, *Educated persons in India,* Manpower Studies, Planning Commission, New Delhi, 1955.

India, Government of, *Census of India 1961,* Final Population Totals, Paper No. 1, Registrar General, New Delhi, 1962.

India, Government of, *Census of India 1961,* Volume I, Part 2-A(i): General Population Tables; Registrar General, New Delhi, 1964.

India, Government of, *The Gazeteer of India,* Vol. 1, Ministry of Information, New Delhi, 1965.

India, Government of, *Gramdan Movement,* Planning Commission, New Delhi, 1964.

India, Government of, *India 1964,* Ministry of Information, New Delhi, 1964.

India, Government of, *The Khadi industry,* Ministry of Information, New Delhi, 1962.

India, Government of, *Progress of Land Reform,* Planning Commission, Government of India Press, New Delhi, 1963.

India, Government of, *Report of the team for the study of community projects and national Extension Service,* the Balvantray–Mehta Report, Vol. II, Planning Commission, New Delhi, 1957.

Indian Institute of Public Opinion, *A first all-India survey of rural incomes, assets, and expenditure,* Monthly Public Opinion Survey, V (1959).

IONESCU, G. & GELLNER, E. (eds.), *Populism,* Weidenfeld & Nicolson, London, 1969.

IYER, R. N., 'Means and ends in politics', in G. Ramachandran, &

T. K. Mahadevan, *Gandhi: his relevance for our times*, Bharatiya Vidya Bhavan, Bombay, 1964, 174–87.

IYER, S. C., *et al.*, *Gramdan and Development*, Gandhian Institute of Studies, Varanasi (forthcoming).

JAJU, S., *The philosophy of Sampattidan*, trans. S. Ram, Sarvodaya Prachuralaya, Thanjavur, 1965.

JOHNSON, H. M., 'Ideology and the social system', *International Encyclopaedia of the Social Sciences*, 7 (1968), 76–85.

JOHNSON, R. C., *Scientific approach to spirituality*, Grambhawna Prakashan, Patti Kalyana, 1965.

KARVE, I., 'The family in India', in B. N. Varma (ed.), *Contemporary India*, Asia Publishing House, Bombay, 1964, 47–58.

KOCHANEK, S. A., *The Congress party of India: the dynamics of one-party democracy*, Princeton University Press, Princeton, N.J., 1968.

KOCHANEK, S. A., 'The relation between social background and attitudes of Indian legislators', *Journal of Commonwealth Political Studies*, 6, 1 (Mar. 1968), 34–53.

KOESTLER, A., 'Four contemporary saints: I Acharya Vinoba Bhave', in his *The Lotus and the Robot*, Hutchinson, London, 1960, 15–36.

KORNHAUSER, W., *The politics of mass society*, Routledge & Kegan Paul, London, 1960.

KRIMERMAN, L. I., & PERRY, L. (eds.), *Patterns of anarchy*, Anchor Books, New York, 1966.

KRIPALANI, J. B., *Gandhian thought*, Orient Longmans, Bombay, 1961.

KRIPALANI, J. B., *Planning and Sarvodaya*, Sarva Seva Sangh Prakashan, Rajghat, Kashi, 1957.

KRIPALANI, J. B., *Toward Sarvodaya*, Kisan Mazdoor Praja Party, New Delhi, 1951.

KRIPALANI, J. B., *Where are we going?* Vigil, Calcutta, 1954.

KRISHNA, R., *Human values and technological change*, Sarva Seva Sangh Prakashan, Kashi, 1958.

KUMAR, S., *Non-violence or non-existence*, Christian Action, London, 1969.

KUMARAPPA, B., *Capitalism, socialism, or villagism?* Sarva Seva Sangh Prakashan, Varanasi, 1965.

KUMARAPPA, J. C., *The non-violent economy and world peace*, Sarva Seva Sangh Prakashan, Rajghat, Kashi, 1958.

KUMARAPPA, J. C., *An over-all plan for rural development*, Sarva Seva Sangh Prakashan, Rajghat, Kashi, 1958.

LACY, C., 'The Gandhians and Sarvodaya', Ch. 12 in his *The conscience of India: moral traditions in the modern world*, Holt Rinehart & Winston, New York, 1965, 208–25.

LANTERNARI, V., *The religion of the oppressed*, MacGibbon & Kee, London, 1963.

LANZA DEL VASTO, J. J., *Gandhi to Vinoba*, trans. from the French by P. Leon, Rider, London, 1956.

LENSKI, G. E., 'Status crystallization: a non-vertical dimension of social status', *American Sociological Review*, 19 (Aug. 1954), 405–13.

LEWIS, J. P., *Quiet crisis in India*, Asia Publishing House, Bombay, 1963.

LIPSET, S. M., *Political man*, Heinemann, London, 1960.

McROBIE, G., 'Intermediate technology: 1. The village', *Community Development Journal*, 3 (Oct. 1968), 186–90.

Madras State Bhoodan Yagna Board, *Bhoodan and Gramdan in Tamilnad*, The Board, Madurai, 1964.

MAHADEVAN, T. K., *Gandhi National Memorial Trust: an introduction*, The Trust, New Delhi, 1965.

MARTIN, D. A., *Pacifism*, Routledge & Kegan Paul, London, 1965.

MASANI, R. P., *The five gifts*, Collins, London, 1957.

MASANI, M. R., 'Land through love', *Encounter*, 3, 6 (Dec. 1954), 8–13.

MASHRUWALA, K. G., *Gandhi and Marx*, Navajivan, Ahmedabad, 1956. First pub. 1951.

MEHTA, U., *Social and political thought of Sarvodaya*, Laski Institute, Ahmedabad, 1963.

MERKER, B., 'Gandhians or Gandhi?', *Peace News*, 16 & 23 Apr. 1965.

MERKER, B., 'Vinoba's vision', *Peace News*, 9 July 1965.

MERTON, R., *Social theory and social structure*, Free Press, Glencoe, Ill., 1947.

MICHELS, R., *Political parties*, Free Press, Glencoe, Ill., 1949. First pub. 1915.

MILLER, W. R., 'Notes on the theory of non-violence', *Gandhi Marg*, 5, 4 (1961), 321–31.

MILLER, W. R., *Nonviolence: a Christian interpretation*, Allen & Unwin, London, 1964.

MISRA, B. R., *V. for Vinoba: the economics of Bhoodan movement*, Orient Longmans, Calcutta, 1956.

MOHANTY, J. N., 'Sarvodaya and Aurobindo: a rapprochement', *Gandhi Marg*, 4, 3 (1960), 203–11.

MOOKERJI, S. B., 'Ahimsa through the ages: Gandhi's contribution', *Gandhi Marg*, 4, 3 (1960), 220–8.

MOORE B., *Social origins of dictatorship and democracy*, Beacon Press, Boston, 1966.

MORAES, F., 'Gandhi ten years after', *Foreign Affairs*, 36, 2 (Jan. 1958), 253–66.

MORRIS-JONES, W. H., *The government and politics of India*, 2nd edn., Hutchinson, London, 1967. First pub. 1964.

MORRIS-JONES, W. H., 'India's political idioms', in C. H. Philips, *Politics and society in India*, Allen & Unwin, London, 1963, 133–54.

MORRIS-JONES, W. H., 'India's political miracle', *Australian Journal of Politics and History*, 12, 2 (Aug. 1966), 213–20.

MORRIS-JONES, W. H., 'Mahatma Gandhi—political philosopher?', *Political Studies*, 8 (Feb. 1960), 16–36.

MORRIS-JONES, W. H., *Parliament in India*, Longmans, Green, London, 1957.

MORRIS-JONES, W. H., 'Political recruitment and political development', in C. Leys (ed.), *Politics and change in developing countries*, Cambridge University Press, London, 1969, 113–34.

MORRIS-JONES, W. H., 'The unhappy Utopia—J. P. in wonderland', *Economic Weekly*, 25 June 1960, 1027–31.

MUKERJI, B., *Community development in India*, Orient Longmans, Bombay, 1961.

MUKHERJI, P., 'Gramdan in village Berain', *Human Organization*, 25 (Spring 1966), 33–41.

MUKHERJI, P. N., 'Report on Gramdans in Bihar', unpublished, Gandhian Institute of Studies, Varanasi, 1964.

MURTHI, V. V. R., *Commonsense about defence*, Laski Institute, Ahmedabad, 1959.

MURTHI, V. V. R., *Non-violence in politics: a study of Gandhian techniques and thinking*, Frank Brothers, New Delhi, 1958.

MUZUMDAR, H. T., *Mahatma Gandhi: peaceful revolutionary*, Charles Scribner's Sons, New York, 1952.

MYRDAL, G., *Asian Drama*, Pantheon, New York, 1968.

NAMBOODIRIPAD, E. M. S., *The Mahatma and the Ism*, People's Publishing House, New Delhi, 1959.

NANAVATI, M. B., & ANJARIA, J. J., *India's rural problems*, Indian Society of Agricultural Economics, Bombay, 1960.

NANEKAR, S. R., 'Some aspects of grass-roots democracy in India', in G. S. Halappa (ed.), *Dilemmas of democratic politics in India*, Manaktalas, Bombay, 1966, 104–13.

NARAYAN, JAYAPRAKASH, *The challenges after Nehru*, Sarvodaya Prachuralaya, Thanjavur, 1964.

NARAYAN, JAYAPRAKASH, 'Decentralized democracy: theory and practice', *The Indian Journal of Public Administration*, 8, 3 (July-Sept. 1961), 271–86.

NARAYAN, JAYAPRAKASH, *The dual revolution*, Sarvodaya Prachuralaya, Tanjore, 1959.

NARAYAN, JAYAPRAKASH, *Educational ideals and the problem of peace*, Convocation Address, University of Mysore, 1965, Sarva Seva Sangh Prakashan, Rajghat, Kashi, 1966.

NARAYAN, JAYAPRAKASH, *The evolution towards Sarvodaya*, Sarvodaya
Prachuralaya, Tanjore, 1957.

NARAYAN, JAYAPRAKASH, 'Gandhi, Vinoba and the Bhudan movement',
Gandhi Marg, 4, 1 (1960), 23–38.

NARAYAN, JAYAPRAKASH, *Jeevandan*, Sarvodaya Prachuralaya, Tanjore,
1956.

NARAYAN, JAYAPRAKASH, *A picture of Sarvodaya social order*, 5th edn.,
Sarvodaya Prachuralaya, Tanjore, 1961.

NARAYAN, JAYAPRAKASH, *A plea for reconstruction of Indian polity*,
privately circulated, Sarva Seva Sangh, Kashi, 1959.

NARAYAN, JAYAPRAKASH, *Sarvodaya answer to Chinese aggression*,
Sarvodaya Prachuralaya, Thanjavur, 1963.

NARAYAN, JAYAPRAKASH, *Seminar on fundamental problems of panchayati
raj*, All-India Panchayat Parishad, New Delhi, 1964.

NARAYAN, JAYAPRAKASH, *From socialism to Sarvodaya*, Sarva Seva Sangh
Prakashan, Benares, 1959.

NARAYAN, JAYAPRAKASH, *Socialism, Sarvodaya and democracy*, Asia
Publishing House, Bombay, 1964.

NARAYAN, JAYAPRAKASH, *Swaraj for the people*, Sarva Seva Sangh,
Varanasi, 1961.

NARAYAN, JAYAPRAKASH, *Three basic problems of free India*, Asia Publishing House, Bombay, 1964.

NARAYAN, JAYAPRAKASH, 'Whither India?', *Gandhi Marg*, 3, 1 (1961),
198–205.

NARGOLKAR, K., *In the wake of the Chinese thrust*, Adiwasi Gramsarva
Sangh, Kainad, 1965.

NARGOLKAR, V., *The creed of Saint Vinoba*, Bharatiya Vidya Bhavan,
Bombay, 1963.

NARGOLKAR, V., 'Himalayan War', *Seminar*, 46 (June 1963).

NIMBARK, A., 'Gandhism re-examined', *Social Research*, 31, 1 (Spring
1964), 94–125.

NORTH, R. C., 'The Indian Council of Ministers: a study of origins', in
R. L. Park, & I. Tinker (eds.), *Leadership and political institutions in
India*, Oxford University Press, London, 1959, 103–14.

OOMMEN, T. K., 'Charisma, social structure and social change',
Comparative Studies in Society and History, X, 1 (Oct. 1967), 85–99.

OOMMEN, T. K., 'Charismatic movements and social change: an
analysis of Bhoodan-Gramdan Movement in India', Ph.D. thesis,
University of Poona, 1967.

OOMMEN, T. K., 'Myth and reality in India's communitarian villages',
Journal of Commonwealth Political Studies, 4, 2 (July 1966), 94–116.

OOMMEN, T. K., 'Non-violent approach to land reforms', *Zeitschrift
für Ausländische Landwirtschaft* (Heidelberg, Jan. 1970).

OOMMEN, T. K., 'Problems of Gramdan: a study in Rajasthan', *Economic Weekly*, 26 June 1965, 1035–40.

OSTERGAARD, G. N., 'Democracy in India', in G. S. Halappa (ed.), *Dilemmas of democratic politics in India*, Manaktalas, Bombay, 1966, 211–22.

OSTERGAARD, G. N., 'Indian anarchism', *Anarchy*, 42 (Aug. 1964), 225–236.

OSTERGAARD, G. N., & HALSEY, A. H., *Power in co-operatives*, Blackwell, Oxford, 1965.

OSTERGAARD, G. N., 'Sarvodaya, the politics of love', *Bharat* (Birmingham University India Society), 2 (Jan. 1967), 1–7.

OVERSTREET, G. D., & WINDMILLER, N., *Communism in India*, University of California Press, Berkeley and Los Angeles, Calif., 1959.

PALMER, N. D., & TINKER, I., 'Decision making in the Indian Parliament', in R. L. Park, & I. Tinker (eds.), *Leadership and political institutions in India* (see below), pp. 115–36.

PANTER-BRICK, S., *Gandhi against Machiavellism*, Asia Publishing House, London, 1966.

PARK, R. L., & TINKER, I. (eds.), *Leadership and political institutions in India*, Princeton, N.J., 1959.

PATIL, R. K., 'Pattern for rural development', *Gandhi Marg*, 4, 3 (1960), 212–19.

PATWARDHAN, A., *A plea for shrinking currency*, Sarvodaya Prachuralaya, Thanjavur, 1963.

PATWARDHAN, A., *Towards a new society*, Sarva Seva Sangh Prakashan, Rajghat, Kashi, 1959.

PARKIN, F., *Middle-class radicalism*, Manchester University Press, Manchester, 1968.

PHILIPS, C. H., *Politics and society in India*, Allen & Unwin, London, 1963.

POLAK, H. S. L., *et al.*, 'Symposium on bhudan', *Gandhi Marg*, 2, 1 (1958), 25–98.

POSTON, R. W., *Democracy speaks many tongues*, Harper & Row, New York, 1962.

PRASAD, D. (ed.), *Gramdan: the land revolution of India*, War Resisters' International, London, 1969.

PYARELAL, *Gandhian techniques in the modern world*, Navajivan, Ahmedabad, 1953.

PYARELAL, *Mahatma Gandhi: the last phase*, 2 vols., Navajivan, Ahmedabad, 1956 & 1958.

RAM, SURESH, *Progress of a pilgrimage*, Sarva Seva Sangh Prakashan, Rajghat, 1956.

RAM, SURESH, *Towards a total revolution*, Sarvodaya Prachuralayam, Thanjavur, 1968.

RAM, SURESH, *Vinoba—man and message*, Sarva Sangh Prakashan, Varanasi, 1961.

RAM, SURESH, *Vinoba and his mission*, 3rd edn., Sarva Seva Sangh Prakashan, Kashi, 1962. First pub. 1954.

RAMACHANDRAN, G., & MAHADEVAN, T. K., *Gandhi—his relevance for our times*, Bharatiya Vidya Bhavan, Bombay, 1964.

RANADIVE, B. T., *Sarvodaya and Communism*, Communist Party of India, New Delhi, 1958.

RAO, G. R. (Gora), *An atheist with Gandhi*, Navajivan, Ahmedabad, 1951.

RAO, G. R. (Gora), *Partyless democracy—its need and form*, Satyagraha Samaj, Raipur, 1961.

RAO, G. R. (Gora), *Why Gramraj?*, Sarva Seva Sangh Prakashan, Kashi, 1958.

RAO, M. B. (ed.), *The Mahatma: a Marxist symposium*, People's Publishing House, Bombay, 1969.

RAO, P. N., 'Gandhi and the Hindu concept of ahimsa', *Gandhi Marg*, 11, 1 (Jan. 1967), 64–7.

REDDY, V. N. K., *Sarvodaya ideology and Acharya Vinoba Bhave*, Andhra Pradesh Sarvodaya Mandal, Gandhibhavan, Hyderabad, 1963.

REDDY, V. N. K., *Thoreau, Gandhi, Vinoba*, Sahitilata, Hyderabad, 1962.

REISSMAN, L., 'Social stratification', in N. Smelser, *Sociology*, Wiley, New York, 1967, 203–68.

ROBERTS, A., 'The Gandhi experiment', *New Society*, 2 Oct. 1969, 509–12.

ROLNICK, P. J., 'Charity, trusteeship and social change in India', *World Politics*, 14, 3 (Apr. 1962), 439–60.

ROLNICK, P. J., 'Political ideology: reality and myth in India', *Asian Survey*, 2, 9 (Nov. 1962), 19–32.

ROSSI, A., *A Communist party in action*, Yale University Press, New Haven, 1949.

ROTHERMUND, I., *The philosophy of restraint*, Popular Prakashan, Bombay, 1963.

ROY, M. N., *Politics, power and parties*, Renaissance, Calcutta, 1960.

RUDOLPH, L. I., & RUDOLPH, S. H., *The modernity of tradition: political development in India*, University of Chicago Press, Chicago, 1967.

RUSH, G., 'Status consistency and right-wing extremism', *American Sociological Review*, 32 (Feb. 1967), 86–92.

RUSKIN, J., *Unto this last*, Smith, Elder, London, 1962.

SACHIDANAND, *Sarvodaya in a Communist state* (Kerala), Popular Book Depot, Bombay, 1961.

SAHASRABUDHE, A. W., *Report on Koraput Gramdans*, Sarva Seva Sangh Prakashan, Wardha, 1960.

Sarva Seva Sangh, *Bhoodan as seen by the West*, Sarvodaya Prachuralayam, Tanjore, 1958.

Sarva Seva Sangh, *The call of Puri Sarvodaya Sammelan* (including speeches by Vinoba and Jayaprakash Narayan), Sarvodaya Prachuralaya, Tanjore, 1955.

Sarva Seva Sangh, *Constitution* (in Hindi), Varanasi, 1964.

Sarva Seva Sangh, *Decentralized economic order*, Sarva Seva Sangh Prakashan, Rajghat, Kashi, 1961.

Sarva Seva Sangh, *Gramdan in Koraput*, Sarva Seva Sangh, Jeypore (Koraput), n.d.

Sarva Seva Sangh, *The message of Kancheepuram Sarvodaya Sammelan*, Sarvodaya Prachuralaya, Tanjore, 1956.

Sarva Seva Sangh, *Notes on Agenda for the meeting of the National Advisory Committee for collaboration with Akhil Bharat Sarva Seva Sangh to be held at New Delhi, 22 January 1965*.

Sarva Seva Sangh, *Planning for Sarvodaya*, Sarva Seva Sangh Prakashan, Rajghat, Kashi, 1958.

Sarva Seva Sangh & World Union, *Science and spirituality: an exploration*, Report of the Patna Seminar, Aurobindo Ashram Press, Pondicherry 2, n.d.

Sarva Seva Sangh, *Ten years of our publications (1955–1965)*, Sarva Seva Sangh, Varanasi, 1965.

SCALAPINO, R. A., & MASUMI, J., *Parties and politics in contemporary Japan*, University of California Press, Berkeley, 1962.

SCHUMACHER, E. F., *Roots of economic growth*, Gandhian Institute of Studies, Varanasi, 1962.

SEGAL, R., *The crisis of India*, Penguin Books, Harmondsworth, 1965.

SEN, M. (ed.), *The economic aspects of Sarvodaya: proceedings of the Calcutta seminar*, Sarva Seva Sangh Prakashan, Rajghat, Kashi, 1959.

SEN, M., *Gandhian way and the Bhoodan movement*, Sarva Seva Sangh Prakashan, Rajghat, 1964.

SHANTI SENA MANDAL, *The Indian Shanti Sena* (brochure), Shanti Sena Mandal, Varanasi, n.d.

SHAPOSHNIKOVA, L., 'Bhave and land reforms', *The Current Digest of the Soviet Press*, 13, 19 (1961), 3–4.

SHARMA, B. S., 'The philosophical basis of Sarvodaya', *Gandhi Marg*, 4, 3 (1960), 258–62.

SHARMA, B. S., 'The philosophy of Sarvodaya', in J. S. Bains (ed.),

Studies in Political Science, Asia Publishing House, Bombay, 1961, 282–8.

SHARMA, J. S., *Vinoba and Bhoodan: a selected descriptive bibliography of Bhoodan*, Indian National Congress, New Delhi, 1956.

SHARP, G., 'The politics of non-violent action', unpublished D. Phil. thesis, Oxford, 1968.

SHARP, G., *The politics of nonviolent action*, Pilgrim Press, Philadelphia & Boston, 1970.

SHARP, G., *Gandhi wields the weapon of moral power*, Navajivan, Ahmedabad, 1960.

SHIVIAH, 'Grass-roots democracy in India', in G. S. Halappa (ed.), *Dilemmas of democratic politics in India*, Manaktalas, Bombay, 1966, 87–103.

SHUKLA, C., *Gandhi's view of life*, Bharatiya Vidya Bhavan, Bombay, 1951.

SIRSIKAR, V. M., *Political behaviour in India*, Manaktalas, Bombay, 1965.

SKIPPER, K. K., *et al.*, 'The sacredness of ·05; a note concerning the uses of statistical levels of significance in social science', *The American Sociologist*, 2, 1 (Feb. 1967), 16–18.

SMELSER, N., *Theory of collective behaviour*, Routledge & Kegan Paul, London, 1962.

SOROKIN, P. A., *The ways and power of love*, Beacon Press, Boston, 1954.

SOROKIN, P. A. (ed.), *Explorations in altruistic love and behavior*, Beacon Press, Boston, 1950.

TANDON, V., *The social and political philosophy of Sarvodaya after Gandhiji*, Sarva Seva Sangh Prakashan, Varanasi, 1965.

TENDULKAR, D. G., *Mahatma: life of Mohandas Karamchand Gandhi*, 8 vols., Publications Division, Ministry of Information and Broadcasting, Government of India, New Delhi, 1962.

TENNYSON, H., 'Land through love: a dynasty of saints', *Encounter*, 3, 6 (Dec. 1954), 3–8.

TENNYSON, H., *Saint on the march*, Gollancz, London, 1956.

THAKAR, V., *The philosophy of land-gift mission*, Sarvodaya Prachuralayam, Tanjore, 1962.

THORNER, D., *The agrarian prospect in India*, Delhi University Press, New Delhi, 1956.

THORNER, D., & THORNER, A., *Land and labour in India*, Asia Publishing House, New York, 1962.

TINKER, H., 'Local government and politics, and political and social theory in India', in M. J. Swartz (ed.), *Local-level politics: social and cultural perspectives*, University of London Press, London, 1969, 217–26.

TINKER, H., 'Magnificent failure? The Gandhian ideal in India', in his *Reorientations*, Pall Mall Press, London, 1965, 136–54.

TÖNNIES, F., *Community and association*, Routledge & Kegan Paul, London, 1955.

TURNER, R. H., & KILLIAN, L. N., *Collective behavior*, Prentice-Hall, New Jersey, 1957.

UNESCO, *Basic facts and figures, 1960*, Unesco, Paris, 1961.

UNESCO, *Statistical yearbook, 1964*, Unesco, Paris, 1965.

UNNITHAN, T. K. N., *Gandhi in free India*, Wolters, Groningen (Netherlands), 1965.

VARMA, B. N. (ed.), *Contemporary India*, Asia Publishing House, Bombay, 1964.

VARMA, V. P., *The political philosophy of Mahatma Gandhi and Sarvodaya*, Lakshmi Narain Agarwal, Agra, 1959.

VEERABRAMHAM, V., *Progress report on Gramdan villages in Cuddapah district* (March 1964), Anthyodaya Mandal, Cuddapah district, Andhra Pradesh, 1964.

VENTURI, F., *Roots of revolution*, trans. from the Italian by F. Haskell, Weidenfeld & Nicholson, London, 1960.

WALZER, M., *The revolution of the saints*, Weidenfeld & Nicholson, London, 1966.

WEBER, M., *On charisma and institution building*, selected papers edited and with an Introduction by S. N. Eisenstadt, University of Chicago Press, Chicago & London, 1968.

WEBER, M., *The theory of social and economic organization*, Hodge, London, 1947.

WEINER, M., *Party building in a new nation: the Indian National Congress*, Chicago University Press, Chicago, 1967.

WEINER, M., *Party politics in India: the development of a multi-party system*, Princeton University Press, Princeton, N.J., 1957.

WEINER, M., *The politics of scarcity: public pressure and political response in India*, Chicago University Press, Chicago, 1962.

WEINER, M., 'Some hypotheses on the politics of modernization in India', in R. L. Park, & I. Tinker (see above), 18–38.

WEINER, M., 'Struggle against power: notes on Indian political behavior', *World Politics*, 8 (Apr. 1956), 392–403.

WILKEN, F., *New forms of ownership in industry*, Sarva Seva Sangh Prakashan, Varanasi, 1962.

WINDMILLER, M. L., 'Gandhian socialism in India', *Far Eastern Survey*, 23 (1954), 40–5.

WOLFERT, J. F., 'Towards a sociology of authority', in A. W. Gouldner (ed.), *Studies in Leadership*, Harper, New York, 1950.

WOODCOCK, G., *Anarchism*, Penguin Books, Harmondsworth, 1963.

TGA—DD

JOURNALS

Young India, 1919–32	Ahmedabad
Harijan, 1932–51	Ahmedabad
Bhoodan, 1956–66	Calcutta
Gandhi Marg	Quarterly, New Delhi
People's Action, formerly	
Sarva Seva Sangh Monthly	
News Letter	Monthly, New Delhi
Sarvodaya	Monthly, Tanjore

INDEX

property-owning, of leaders, 85–6, 95–102, 320, 322–3, 350–1, 355n., 370

of leaders' fathers, 81–2, 339n., 370

self-rated, of leaders, 94–5, 99–104, 106n., 107, 133–4, 321, 325–31, 351–2, 354n., 364, 370

classless society, 46, 48, 94, 97, 98, 227, 319, 370

class struggle, 44

Clausewitz, K. von, 222, 222n.

Cohn-Bendit, D., 218n.

Cole, G. D. H., 221

commitment of leaders, 159–68, 337–339, 348, 358, 371–2

Committee of 100, v

Communal parties, 134, 372. See also Hindu Mahasabha, Jan Sangh

Communism, 15, 21, 51, 113, 125, 154–5, 180, 228, 278, 285, 290, 297, 372

Communist Party of India, 65, 69, 72, 77, 80, 92, 130, 132, 133, 359

Community Development Programme, 6, 12, 197, 245–6, 260, 261, 374

Congress, Governments, 4, 8n., 18, 240, 241, 243, 244, 245, 246

relations with Sarvodaya movement, 231–50, 290, 302–3, 308, 373

See also Yelwal Conference

Congress, Indian National

composition of A.I.C.C., 68–9, 83, 115–16

composition of M.P.s, 68–70, 78, 80, 83, 84n., 86n., 92, 92n., 110n.

and Gandhi, 5, 28, 368

and Gramdan, 10

and Khadi, 57

opinion of Sarvodaya leaders on relations with, 231–4, 342, 359, 361, 373

and partyless democracy, 50

Sarvodaya leaders' membership of, 127, 157–8, 372

Sarvodaya leaders' perceptions of, 130–5, 290, 296, 303, 316, 359, 360, 360n., 361, 364, 372

Sarvodaya leaders voting for, 128–130, 331–3, 353, 360, 372

consensus, 35, 198, 199, 204, 205n., 231, 267, 270, 366–7, 375. See also decision-making, and Council for National Consensus

Constructive Programme, movement, work, 3–6, 7, 8, 8n., 9, 28, 42, 51, 57, 61, 64, 226, 230, 237, 301, 306, 369. See also Bhoodan, Gramdan, Khadi, social worker, village industries

contraception, 170, 170n.

Convenors, District. See Sarva Seva Sangh

Co-operative movement

British, 32, 44, 67, 139, 205, 250, 264

Indian, 157

Council for National Consensus, 235n

Crespigny, A. de, 178n.

Crouch, H., 78n.

current problems, opinion of leaders on taking up, 236–9, 342, 374

Dalton, Dennis, vi

dama, 168

dan, 278, 283. See also Bhoodan Gramdan, Sampattidan, Jeevandan, etc.

Danadhara, 286

Dasgupta, S., vi, 1n., 160n.

Davies, Miss Marjorie, vi

Davis, Kingsley, 73n.

decentralization, 34, 140, 180, 193, 231, 234, 247, 248, 253, 280. See also Panchayati Raj

decision-making. See Sarva Seva Sangh, decision-making in

Delhi, 11, 88

Delhi–Peking Friendship March, 256

democracy, 35, 205. See also decision-making, Lok-niti, Panchayati Raj, partyless democracy

Deo, Shankarrao, 5n., 23, 256

Desai, Maganbhai, 29n.

Desai, Mahadev, 214n.

Desai, Narayan, 59n., 195n., 217

Dhadda, Siddharaj, 254n.

dharma, 1, 76

Dharmadhikari, Dada, 23, 141, 142n., 219

Dhawan, G., 27n., 28n., 33n., 43n., 115n.

Diggers, the, 37n., 125

direct action, 36, 227. See also non-violent action and satyagraha

Districtdan, 12, 56, 264

diversities among leaders, associated with age, 354–6

Gentiles, 202
Gerard, G., 190n., 208n., 273n.
Geschwender, J. A., 105n.
Gita, 27n., 30, 203, 203n., 377
Glock, C. Y., 113n., 114n.
Go Seva Sangh, 6n.
goals, leaders' perceptions of, 45–51, 339–40
God, 2, 37, 115, 119, 164n., 165, 169n., 170n., 295, 312, 371, 372
Godwin, W., 30, 32n., 38, 39, 44n.
Goffman, E., 157n.
Gokhale, G. K., 1
Gora. See Rao, G. Ramachandra
gradualism, 39, 126, 232
graduates, among Sarvodaya leaders. See class, educational
Graham, Billy, 310
Gram Sabha, 53, 54, 55, 56, 57, 262
Gramdan
    and Bhoodan, 10, 13n.
    campaign for, 12, 56, 71, 131, 216, 237, 248, 261, 262, 263, 264, 271, 273, 345
    case studies of, 22, 22n., 23
    defined, 52–6
    development of, opinion of leaders on, 258–63, 296, 299, 300, 343, 348, 349–50, 374
    legislation, 54, 126, 187
    objectives of, 15, 33, 46, 48, 173, 229, 231, 255, 280, 284, 285
    stages of, 57, 262
    statistics of, 10, 11, 13–14, 71–2, 277
    sulabh, 10, 55–6, 270, 272
    opinion of leaders on, 263–5, 343, 348, 349, 363, 374
    in Triple Programme, 12, 13, 51, 61, 230, 237, 248, 289, 295, 305
    villagers, 24n., 117, 142, 186n., 236
    See also Bhoodan
Gramswarajya, 46, 262, 273, 277, 280, 376. See also Gandhi: on village
Groom, Donald, vi
Guenther, A. L., 98n.
guerrillas, non-violent, 229
Gujarat, 11, 54n.
Gusfield, J. R., 154n., 174n.

Halappa, G. S., 246n.
Halmos, P., 160n.
Halsey, A. H., 67n., 139n.
Hanson, A. H., 246n.
Harbury, Colin, v

Harijan, 5n., 8n., 9n., 30n., 59n., 115n.
Harijan Sevak Sangh, 5, 6, 214
Harijans, 5, 25, 60, 72n., 76, 77, 78n., 117, 139, 215, 357
Harrison, J. F. C., 32n.
Hart, Liddell, 223, 223n., 224, 224n., 225, 225n.
Heberle, R., 27n., 74n., 136n., 137, 137n., 142, 144n., 145, 145n., 154n., 176n., 222n.
Hennacy, A., 43n.
Himachal Pradesh, 11, 60
Hindu(s), Hinduism, 1, 3, 18, 27, 29, 37, 115, 117, 118, 119, 120, 239, 357, 370, 371. See also religious character
Hindu Mahasabha, 132n.
Hindu-Muslim communal unity, 3, 4, 117, 375
Hindustani, 4
Hindustani Talimi Sangh (Basic Education Association), 5, 6n.
Hinings, C. R., vi
Hirsch, W., 312n.
Hobbes, T., 29
Humanism, 31, 119, 122, 123, 371
Hume, R. E., 169n.
Hyderabad, v, 278

ideology, defined, 27, 27n.
    propagated by 'cells', 310
    related to strategy and tactics, 222
    of Sarvodaya movement, 27–61
income. See class, income
Independence Movement
    leaders' service in, 70, 333, 334
India, 1964, 65n., 91n., 116, 245
India, Gazeteer of, 108n.
Indian National Congress. See Congress, Indian National
Indian Renaissance, 1
Indo-Pakistan Conciliation Group, 240
institutionalization, 67–8, 174, 174n., 175, 298, 310, 377
interests, harmony of, 44n.
intermediate technology, 252
Ionescu, G., 32n.
Ishavasya-Vritti, 203
Islam, 118. See also Muslims
Iyer, S. S., vi, 23, 41n.

Jagannathan, 200, 256, 266, 266n.

Jaina literature, 29
Jains, 115, 116, 116n.
James, William, 173
Jammu, 11, 241
Jan Sangh, 132n., 134, 134n., 372
jati, 75n., 79
Jayaprakash. See Narayan, J. P.
jeevandan, 12, 163, 377
  terms, 164–5
  leaders taking pledge, 166, 337, 371, 372
Jehovah's Witnesses, 125
Johnson, H. M., 27n.
joint family. See family, joint
Juyal, B. N., vi

Kanbur, M. G., v
Karanbhai, A. K., 23
Karman, 169
karmayoga, 27n., 30n., 210
Kashi. See Varanasi
Kashmir, 11
  opinion of leaders on issue of, 239–243, 342, 350, 353, 355, 364, 373
Kasturba Memorial Trust, 6, 188, 194
Kautilya, 29
Keithahn, Reverend Ralph, 266n.
Kerala, 11, 15, 22n., 71, 202, 357
Khadi, 3, 4, 18, 45, 48, 57, 58, 58n., 61, 94, 163, 164, 167, 187, 190, 191, 206n., 230, 232, 233, 237, 283, 305, 340, 347, 361
  opinion of leaders on future of, 251–253, 343, 356, 374
  in Triple Programme, 13, 57–9, 60, 61
  workers, 143, 263, 286, 309
Khadi and Village Industries Commission, 6, 57, 58, 156, 188, 190, 194, 259
Khan, Khan Abdul Ghaffar, 117, 118
Khudai Khidmatgers, 117
Kibbutz, 14
Killian, L. M., 19n., 21n., 51n., 150, 150n.
King, Martin Luther, 266
Kisan Mazdoor Praja Party, 126, 129, 129n.
Kisans. See peasants
Kochanek, S. A., 65n., 68n., 70n., 77, 78, 80n., 83n., 84n., 86n., 92n., 110n., 116n.
Koraput, 10, 22n., 52, 258, 261
Kornhauser, W., 153n., 158

Krimerman, L. I., 39
Kripalani, A., 126
Kropotkin, P., 34, 35, 38, 44, 249n.
Kshatriyas, 29n., 75, 75n., 76, 77, 78n., 80, 96, 99, 100, 102, 103, 104, 320, 322, 324, 325, 326, 328, 329, 330, 331, 333n., 344n., 346, 346n., 347, 347n., 357, 357n., 361n., 370
Kumar, Satish, 229n.
Kumarappa, B., 112, 112n.
Kyasthas, 77n., 78n., 106n.

Labour Party (British), 317
Ladakh, 254
land reform, 18, 45, 237, 277, 282, 289, 303. See also Bhoodan, Gramdan
landless labourers, 13, 19, 22, 80, 80n., 81, 81n., 228, 237, 278. See also agriculturalists
landowners, landownership, 9, 10, 13, 13n., 22, 48, 82, 82n., 278, 308. See also agriculturalists, class, property-owning
languages, provincial, 4
Lanternari, V., 150n.
Lanza del Vasto, J. J., 22n.
leadership. See charisma; Bhave as leader; Gandhi, as leader
Lenski, G. E., 105n.
lepers, 4
Lewis, J. P., 252n.
Lipset, S. M., 155n., 354n.
Lohia, Ram Manohar, 129n.
Lohia Socialist Party, 129, 267
Lok-niti, 36, 46, 127, 162, 179, 202, 279. See also partyless democracy
Lok Sabha, 68, 92, 129, 134n.
Lok Sevak pledge, 13, 126–7, 128, 162, 166, 235, 337, 371
Lok Sevak Sangh, 5, 368
Lok Sevaks, 5, 11, 72, 162, 183, 185, 188, 196, 200, 201, 204, 207, 208, 317, 368
Long March, the, 229, 230
love, 2, 8, 20, 32, 265, 300, 372, 373
  politics of, 180, 180n., 269, 374
lower middle class. See class, self-rated

Machiavelli, N., 272
Macmahon line, 254
Madge, Charles, v
Madhya Pradesh, 11
Madras (city), 78, 88